AMBIENT SUFISM

CHICAGO STUDIES IN ETHNOMUSICOLOGY
A series edited by Philip V. Bohlman and Timothy Rommen

AMBIENT SUFISM

Ritual Niches and the Social Work of Musical Form

Richard C. Jankowsky

THE UNIVERSITY OF CHICAGO PRESS
CHICAGO AND LONDON

The University of Chicago Press, Chicago 60637
The University of Chicago Press, Ltd., London

Published 2021

29 28 27 26 25 24 23 22 21 20   1 2 3 4 5

ISBN-13: 978-0-226-72333-4 (cloth)
ISBN-13: 978-0-226-72347-1 (paper)
ISBN-13: 978-0-226-72350-1 (e-book)
DOI: https://doi.org/10.7208/chicago/9780226723501.001.0001

Library of Congress Cataloging-in-Publication Data

Names: Jankowsky, Richard C., author.
Title: Ambient Sufism : ritual niches and the social work of musical form / Richard C. Jankowsky.
Other titles: Chicago studies in ethnomusicology.
Description: Chicago ; Illinois : The University of Chicago Press, 2021. | Series: Chicago studies in ethnomusicology | Audio, video, and musical examples may be accessed on the accompanying website, https:///sites.tufts.edu/ambientsufism. | Includes bibliographical references and index.
Identifiers: LCCN 2020028198 | ISBN 9780226723334 (cloth) | ISBN 9780226723471 (paperback) | ISBN 9780226723501 (e-book)
Subjects: LCSH: Sufi music—Tunisia—History and criticism. | Sufi music—Social aspects—Tunisia. | Music—Tunisia—Religious aspects. | Sufism—Tunisia—Rituals. | Islamic music—Tunisia—History and criticism. | Islamic music—Social aspects—Tunisia.
Classification: LCC ML3197.J363 2020 | DDC 781.7/7009611—dc23
LC record available at https://lccn.loc.gov/2020028198

Contents

List of Illustrations vii
List of Website Figures and Audio, Video, and Musical Examples ix
Notes on Transliteration, Musical Notation, and Accompanying Website xiii
Acknowledgments xvii

1 Introduction: Ambient Sufism 1

2 Ritual Reflexivity: Musicality, Sufi Pedigrees, and the Masters of "Intoxication" 27

3 Ritual Hospitality: Women Sufis and the Musical Ethics of Accommodation 69

4 Ritual Alterity: The Musical Management of Sub-Saharan Otherness 105

5 Ritual Remnants: Legacies of Jewish-Muslim Ritual Musical Convergences 135

6 Ritual as Resource: Set-List Modularity and the Cultural Politics of Staging Sufi Music 173

7 Conclusion: Ritual Niches and the Social Work of Musical Form 201

Glossary 219
Bibliography 223
Index 235

MUSICAL EXAMPLES

2.1 The fātiḥa of the ḥizb 39
2.2 Call and response 1 of the ḥizb 41
2.3 Call and response 2 of the ḥizb 41
2.4 Discrete intensification (rise in tempo and pitch of the dhikr) 42
2.5 Opening line of "Qaṣdī Anẓur Ilīk" (My Goal is to See You) 50
2.6 Rhythmic sequence of the shishtrī section 52
2.7 Opening line of "Yā 'Āshiqīn" (O Lovers) 52
2.8 "Al-Kās Ydūr" (The Cup Goes Round) 57
2.9 Sequential intensification (rhythmic sequence of the brāwil section) 61
3.1 Sequential intensification through rhythmic pairing 81
3.2 Nested temporalities in "'Arī al-Mannūbiyya" (Shame on Mannūbiyya) 86
3.3 Short-long pattern of Shādhuliyya dhikr at its slowest 100
3.4 Short-long pattern of Shādhuliyya dhikr at its fastest 100
3.5 Slow beginning of Shādhuliyya dhikr 101
3.6 Fast ending of Shādhuliyya dhikr compared with fazzānī rhythm 101
4.1 Melody of "Jerma" 121
4.2 Three representations of the sūdānī rhythm 121
5.1 Sequential intensification in the rebaybiyya silsila 147
5.2 Main melody of "Jītak Shākī" / "Mā Sabā 'Aqlī" (I Came to You Complaining / Nothing Enchants My Mind) 151
5.3 Rebaybiyya version of "Ra'is al-Abḥār" (Captain of the Seas) 153

Illustrations

FIGURES

2.1 An ʿĪsāwiyya ḥaḍra 30
2.2 Tempo graph of the ḥizb 43
2.3 Tempo graph of the mjarred section 58
2.4 Schematic of layers of intensification 62
3.1 A Mannūbiyya performance 70
4.1 A sṭambēlī ritual 109
4.2 Graph of rhythmic transformation in sṭambēlī 120
4.3 Alternative representation of rhythmic transformation 122
4.4 A café sṭambēlī performance 127

TABLES

2.1 Songs of the mjarred section 57
3.1 Mannūbiyya silsila 79
4.1 Sṭambēlī silsila (white section) 109
4.2 Sṭambēlī silsila (black section) 110
4.3 Café sṭambēlī silsila 128
5.1 Rebaybiyya silsila 1 146
5.2 Rebaybiyya silsila 2 146
5.3 Comparison of rebaybiyya and sṭambēlī lyrics 155
6.1 Set list of *el-Hadhra* spectacle 185
7.1 Ritual musical potencies: A summary 213

Website Figures and Audio, Video, and Musical Examples

All examples may be accessed on the accompanying website, https://sites.tufts.edu/ambientsufism.

CHAPTER 1

FIGURE 1.1W · Soccer team of saints (internet meme from the 2018 World Cup)

CHAPTER 2

Audio example 2.1 · Fātiḥa and isti'ādha sections of the 'Īsāwiyya ḥizb
Audio example 2.2 · Call-and-response accelerando at 12:50–14:02 of the 'Īsāwiyya ḥizb
Audio example 2.3 · Call-and-response further accelerando, highest pitch, and widest ambitus at 16:02–19:13 of the 'Īsāwiyya ḥizb
Audio example 2.4 · Deceleration and pitch drop preceding maximum tempo at 21:33–22:28 of the 'Īsāwiyya ḥizb
Audio example 2.5 · Call and response at maximum tempo at 26:22–28:32 of the 'Īsāwiyya ḥizb
Audio example 2.6 · Accelerando, pitch elevation, and temporal contraction in the dhikr of the 'Īsāwiyya ḥizb
Audio example 2.7 · "Qaṣdī Anẓur Ilīk," excerpt of solo performance by Walid Mennai of the 'Īsāwiyya
Musical example 2.1w · Deceleration and pitch drop preceding intensification
Musical example 2.2w · Call and response at highest speed

Video example 2.1 · ʿĪsāwiyya ḥizb
Video example 2.2 · Shishtrī (Andalusī song) section of the ʿĪsāwiyya ḥaḍra, beginning with the song "Qaṣdī Anẓur Ilīk"
Video example 2.3 · Wird al-qudūm ("arrival liturgy") of the ʿĪsāwiyya ḥaḍra
Video example 2.4 · "Al-Kās Ydūr" (The Cup Goes Round) of the mjarred section of the ʿĪsāwiyya ḥaḍra
Video example 2.5 · The dramatic handclap marking the beginning of the trance section of the ʿĪsāwiyya ḥaḍra
Video example 2.6 · Trancers during the brāwil section of the ʿĪsāwiyya ḥaḍra

CHAPTER 3

Audio example 3.1 · Shādhuliyya dhikr performed by the Ḥaṭṭābiyya Sufi order
Audio example 3.2 · Shādhuliyya dhikr at slow tempo
Audio example 3.3 · Shādhuliyya dhikr at fast tempo, approximating fazzānī rhythm
Figure 3.1w · Map of shrines invoked in the Mannūbiyya silsila
Video example 3.1 · "ʿĀrī ʿal-Mannūbiyya," performed by Fatima's Mannūbiyya troupe
Video example 3.2 · End of the nūba "Yā Belḥassen," performed by Fatima's Mannūbiyya troupe and featuring the appropriation of the Shādhuliyya dhikr
Video example 3.3 · Ṭabla played by the women's Tījāniyya

CHAPTER 4

Audio example 4.1 · Opening three nūbas in sṭambēlī (for the Prophet, Jerma, and Bū Ḥijba)
Video example 4.1 · Nūba for a baḥriyya spirit, featuring the four-stroke muthallith rhythm giving way to the three-stroke sūdānī rhythm
Video example 4.2 · Nūba for Bū Saʿdiyya, with costumed dancer, at Café el-ʿAlī
Video example 4.3 · "Al-Shaykh al-Kāmal," sṭambēlī version, at Café el-ʿAlī

CHAPTER 5

Audio example 5.1 · Mustapha Ben Romdhane performing "Jītak Shākī" / "Mā Sabā ʿAqlī" and "Ra'is al-Abḥār" in 2004
Audio example 5.2 · Mustapha Ben Romdhane performing "Yā ʿArīfa" (a nūba referencing sṭambēlī) in 2007
Audio example 5.3 · Hedi Doniya's studio version of "Ra'is al-Abḥār"
Video example 5.1 · Nūba for Bābā Jallūl at a mizwid party in 2014
Video example 5.2 · Hedi Doniya performing "Ra'is al-Abḥār" at el-Hadhra

CHAPTER 6

Figure 6.1w · Photo of dancers and mizwid player from *el-Hadhra* 2010
Figure 6.2w · Photo of electric guitarist from *el-Hadhra* 2010
Video example 6.1 · Television feature on *el-Hadhra* by the Carthage International Festival
Video example 6.2 · "Lawlā al-Luṭf" (Without the Grace of God) excerpt from *el-Hadhra*, featuring jazz arrangement

Notes on Transliteration, Musical Notation, and Accompanying Website

TRANSLITERATION

The act of transliterating foreign terms is not only a technical undertaking; it is also an act of hospitality to readers. To me, that means considering the wide-ranging preferences of this book's audience. I think of the reader who reverse-engineers a transliteration into standard written Arabic in order to search Arabic-language resources as much as I think of one who may find themselves conversing with North Africans or in North Africa, where knowledge of local spellings and pronunciation may be more useful. Others may simply wish to be provided enough information to compare instances of similar terms they have encountered elsewhere or to accurately pronounce terms in the classroom, while others still may not want to be unnecessarily distracted by alternate spellings, excessive diacritics, or the need to familiarize themselves with two versions of nouns just because the plural of the language in question may be substantially different from the singular. In this book I have put in place a compromise that maintains systematicity while considering, to the best extent possible, each of those positions (all of which, in different contexts, I identify with).

The material in this book covers different registers of Arabic, from diverse eras and with varying levels of social prestige. Local pronunciation often differs from expectations created by standard orthographies. The context of performance complicates matters further. Religious recitations in classical Arabic share ritual performance space with songs in local dialect, with different styles of pronunciation. Recited and sung phrases often elide syllables, creating a marked distinction between the sounded word and its written representation. In some cases, terms are imported from non-Arabic languages. Local transliteration styles are variable and, owing to Tunisia's history as a former French protectorate, are based on a French system that differs from its English-language counterpart. The idea of representational accuracy, then, quickly reveals itself to be a chimera.

In my attempt to provide as much orthographic information as possible while privileging local pronunciation, I adopt a modified version of the standard *International Journal of Middle East Studies* Arabic transliteration system. Terminology from sub-Saharan languages is transliterated to best approximate local pronunciation rather than technical accuracy in the language of origin. As is standard in the *IJMES*, names of places and living or historical figures are not treated with diacritics but are instead presented in the most common local romanization. This is particularly useful for names of musicians whose recordings carry widely circulating French romanizations (e.g., Louisa Tounsia, not Lwīza Tūnsiyya). However, I give full diacritical treatment to the names of authors published in Arabic, as well as to the names of saints, following standard practice in scholarship on Islam in the region, not only because in these pages many saints have their namesake Sufi orders fully transliterated, but also because their names are also often "words" in songs and recitations, where they are surrounded by other fully transliterated lyrics. Names of ritual practices and institutions follow local pronunciation rather than more widely used romanizations with which specialists may be more familiar. So, Shādhuliyya, following local pronunciation and local scholarship such as Chelbi (1985), Louati (2012), and Centre des Musiques Arabes et Méditerranéennes (2013), instead of Shādhiliyya, which is the standard transliteration more common outside Tunisia, and Tījāniyya (not Tijāniyya), sṭambēlī (not sṭambālī), and so on.

The final exception is plurals. Not only can the plural of an Arabic noun differ substantially from the singular, but several terms used throughout this book have two options for plurals, one of them often associated with ritual settings. Thus, the plural of *nūba* (praise song) is *nwib* in the ritual world but *nūbāt* in the more formal discourse of art music, while the plural of *zāwiya* (saint shrine) is *zwī* in ritual communities but *zwāya* outside those contexts. To simplify matters, I simply add the letter "s" to the end of the singular to indicate plurals. All foreign terms are italicized at their first appearance.

MUSICAL EXAMPLES

Most forms of sonic and musical performance represented in the following pages resist straightforward domestication into staff notation. However, I utilize staff notation to illustrate aspects of the ritual musical experience that, for the most part, have evaded systematic scholarly analysis, such as large-scale processes of transformation, rather than attempting to do justice to the technical details of masterful performances. Thus, examples in staff notation are most productively understood to be snapshots of processes that, taken together, reveal those large-scale transformations. The demand on readers unfamiliar with North African musical systems or staff notation is, I hope, rather modest: the main goal of the transcriptions is to highlight easily recognizable patterns such as increases in tempo (indicated by rising tempo markings), elevations in pitch (indicated by upward movement of notes on the staff), levels of cyclicity (indicated by boxes), and contractions of musical time (indicated by sequential reductions of beats per time unit), to name a few.

In representing rhythmic patterns, I adopt local standards by presenting only the rhythmic skeleton of low and high pitches (without the variations and fills that give the percussion parts their vibrancy). The low pitch (*dumm*, rhymes with "room") is represented by a note with its stem up, while the high pitch (*takk*) is represented by a downward stem. Arab music involves some pitches absent from the musical systems that Western staff notation was designed to represent. The primary example in this book is the half-flat (𝄳), such that B𝄳 falls between B♭ and B♮.

ACCOMPANYING WEBSITE

All audio and video examples, as well as additional photographs, are available on this book's companion website (https://sites.tufts.edu/ambientsufism). The sounds of the ritual musical practices represented in those examples are overwhelming, thoroughly enveloping listeners and saturating the air of the performance space. Therefore, to paraphrase Bernard Lortat-Jacob's directive to listeners of his remarkable 1979 ethnographic recording of Moroccan Berber *aḥwash*, these examples are best heard at a loud volume!

Acknowledgments

Reflecting on the support and guidance I've received over the ten years of research, analysis, and writing that went into this book is a profound exercise in gratitude and humility. Perhaps fitting for a book on ritual journeys, social interconnectedness, and individual transformation, the ritualized act of formally recognizing those who contributed to the musical, intellectual, and physical travels that shaped this project is a poignant and deeply rewarding end to the journey of completing this book.

Matthieu Hagene's and Hamza Tebai's enduring companionship throughout these travels was instrumental not only in facilitating contacts and securing invaluable historical and ethnographic documentation, but also in shaping my understanding both of the largest historical trends and of the minutest musical details. For these edifying extended conversations over the years, I offer my deepest thanks. Adam Jerbi and Sonia Bouzouita offered their friendship, social and cultural insights, network of contacts, and spare bedroom on numerous occasions; I cannot begin to thank them enough for providing a home base during several stays in Tunis. I am also deeply grateful to Belhassen Mihoub and his family at Dār Bārnū, who have continued to welcome me and nurture my field research since my first foray into the world of sṭambēlī twenty years ago.

This book would not have been possible without the support of the musicians and ritualists who generously welcomed me into their performance spaces and spent considerable time with me in interviews and conversations. Walid Mennai facilitated much of my work with the ʿĪsāwiyya Sufi order, which also benefited from the insights of Anis Tounsi, Hatem Meski, and Marouene Meski, while Khāled Ṣāghī of the Tījāniyya, Shaykh Zouheir Jaied of the Ḥaṭṭābiyya, and Shaykh Belhassen and Adnen el-Ghali of the Shādhuliyya Sufi orders generously shared their time, thoughts, and recordings. I thank Fatima Lwelbani and the other members of her troupe, Zahra, Sallouha, and Lamya Hosni, for the education they provided me on women's Sufi practices, and Salah el-Ouergli and Belhassen Mihoub for their continued generosity in showing me the shifting contexts and content of sṭambēlī. Jacob Lellouche kindly shared his knowledge of Jewish cultural practices in Tunis. I am also grateful to Hedi Doniya, Hichem Lékhdiri, Abdulmajid Zarga, Jalal Chaouachi, and Adel Labbasi for sharing their expertise in *mizwid* and *rebaybiyya* performance and history, and to Samir Agrebi, Haythem Hadhiri, Sami Lejmi, and Fethi Zghonda for their insights into the staging of Sufi music.

I have been continuously heartened by the support for this project by my Tunisian colleagues. Hichem Ben Amor's scholarship on Sufi music is a model of meticulousness. Adel Dhouioui kindly shared his voluminous audiovisual documentation of Sufi ritual. Ikbal Hamzaoui assisted with musical transcriptions and, along with Emir Bouzaabiya, facilitated meetings with mizwid musicians, while Amira Hassnaoui and Ridha Moumni provided practical support and intellectual stimulation. I am especially grateful to Anas Ghrab for the many inspiring conversations we had on music scholarship in North Africa, as well as for helping me navigate my archival work at the Center for Mediterranean and Arab Music (CMAM). I also thank Rachid Sellami and Manoubiyya at CMAM for their help in locating source material. For Tunisian Arabic tutoring early in this project, my thanks go to Basma Belhadj and Noura Bellali.

I am indebted to the National Endowment for the Humanities for two Faculty Fellowships to support early fieldwork (2009–2010) and the writing of the book (2017–2018). Financial support for research in the years between these fellowships was generously provided by the Tufts University Faculty Research Award Committee, which provided two short-term research grants, a Senior Semester Leave, and, along with the generous support of the office of Dean Bárbara Brizuela, a book subvention award. I am also grateful to Tufts Libraries for its unwavering support in designing this book's accompanying website, particularly the team of digital scholarship specialists including Anna Kijas, Chelcie Rowell, Andrea Schuler, and Mohammed Emun, all of whom I thank for their expertise, enthusiasm, and patience. I am also grateful to Brad DeMatteo for his assistance with inputting musical transcriptions into music-notation software.

I have been fortunate to receive valuable feedback from several individuals on chapters of this book. I thank Timothy Rommen, Melinda Latour, Sarah Pinto, Tatiana Chudakova, and Emilio Spadola for their constructive responses. Conversations with Taoufiq Ben Amor, Philip Schuyler, and

Edwin Seroussi provided numerous clarifications and inspiring connections. I am also grateful for the expert reports by the two anonymous reviewers, whose constructive suggestions strengthened the book's argument and presentation. Equally encouraging has been Elizabeth Branch Dyson's guidance while shepherding this project from start to finish for the University of Chicago Press. I also thank Barbara Norton for her meticulous copyediting and Mollie McFee for her diligent editorial assistance.

An earlier version of chapter 6 was published in 2017 in the *Journal of North African Studies* under the title "Absence and 'Presence': *El-Hadhra* and the Cultural Politics of Staging Sufi Music in Tunisia." The microrhythmic analysis in chapter 4 first appeared in 2013 in the article "Rhythmic Elasticity and Metric Transformation in Tunisian Stambeli" in the journal *Analytical Approaches to World Music*. Material from several chapters benefited thanks to insightful feedback from audiences at invited talks delivered at Brown University, Columbia University, the Hochschule für Musik und Tanz in Cologne, the New England Conservatory of Music, New York University, the Center for the Humanities at Tufts, the University of California, Berkeley, the Université Cheikh Anta Diop in Dakar (in conjunction with the University of North Carolina at Chapel Hill), the University of Cologne, and the University of Pennsylvania, as well as at conferences of the Middle East Studies Association, the International Council for Traditional Music's Mediterranean Music Study Group, and the Society for Ethnomusicology.

A heartfelt thanks to my mother, Joan; my sister, Deb; and my brother, Mike for always being there. Tola Donna Khin has been a continual source of inspiration and, along with our son Dylan, has been unfailingly understanding and supportive of the long hours and even longer absences put into this book. At ten years old, Dylan has only known a world in which this decade-long project has been in progress. For his ever-inspiring curiosity, humor, and compassion, I dedicate this book to him.

1
INTRODUCTION
Ambient Sufism

During the 2018 World Cup in Russia, a meme circulated among Tunisian Facebook users that imagined the country's national soccer team lineup as made up entirely of local Muslim saints, long-deceased historical figures whose spiritual interventions continue to be sought through offerings and rituals performed during communal and individual visits to their shrines (see fig. 1.1w on accompanying website). It provoked humorous online banter, mainly about why certain saints were on offense and why others did not make the starting lineup. The joke and the thread of comments were not aimed specifically at an audience comprised of people who visit saint shrines or for whom the saints play a role in their devotional lives. Rather, the meme resonated widely because the saints are part of fundamental local knowledge: they are household names, historical personalities familiar to all through a web of associations ranging from experience-near knowledge gleaned from participation at shrine rituals to widely recognized legends about saints, praise songs from popular-music and wedding-band repertoires, and the sheer ubiquity of shrines whose physical locations serve as local landmarks in the urban landscape in and around Tunis. Leading the imaginary soccer team's defensive corps was Sīdī Belḥassen (1196–1258 CE), founder of the widely respected Shādhuliyya order of Sufis, whose shrine stands atop Mount Jellaz, which towers over Tunis's largest cemetery and overlooks the city. Sayyda Mannūbiyya (1197–1267), the renowned female saint who famously cursed the townspeople who criticized her participation in men's Sufi circles, was positioned as a striker; women Sufi healers working at her two shrines in the city continue to attract a steady stream of women visiting to seek healing or marital help. Sīdī Ben ʿArūs (d. 1463), positioned as her partner on offense, is considered a "mad" (*majdhūb*) saint; this founder of the local ʿArūsiyya Sufi order is infamous for his irreverent and nonconformist actions (including nudity and intimacy with women visitors) and miraculous healing powers. The goalkeeper Sīdī Meḥrez (951–1022), whose shrine is a central landmark of the medina, is widely recognized as the guardian and patron saint of Tunis. The list goes on. Beyond the sentiment that the Tunisian soccer team would benefit from divine intervention, this holy roster reinforced the notion that the saints form a constellation of spiritual personalities that continue to be recognized as part of the urban spiritual ecology of Tunis. While their identities are kept alive through collective memory and physical landmarks, the most active societal role played by saints is closely associated with devotional and healing rituals held at their shrines and in private homes. And it is through ritual music and trance that they are called upon to intervene in people's lives.

In Tunisia and across North Africa, such trance rituals animated by recitations and praise songs to Muslim saints are not exclusive to members of formal Sufi orders. Rather, a number of distinct healing and devotional musical traditions coexist, each associated with particular social and ritual communities, which in turn contribute to the widespread diffusion of Sufi ideas throughout society. This book examines several such ritual musical practices in urban Tunisia, including those associated with women, Jews, Tunisians of sub-Saharan descent, and even hard-drinking laborers. It demonstrates how each of their musical practices serves as a musical, social, and devotional-therapeutic niche within a shared larger ecology of Tunisian Sufi musics that extends into the realm of mass-mediated popular music and staged concerts and broadcasts. By proposing the concept of "ambient Sufism," I draw attention to the connections within this constellation of musical evocations of Muslim saints and emphasize their public audibility. In doing so, I chart a path toward two goals. The first, emphasized in the book's title, *Ambient Sufism*, is to demonstrate how musics praising Muslim saints resonate throughout Tunisian society via listening publics associated with numerous genres of music—both ritual and nonritual—that evoke the spiritual and therapeutic power of Muslim saints. It also hints at the centrality of pleasure in these popular styles of devotion while also pointing to the important yet virtually undocumented role of women and minorities in cultivating the aesthetics and values associated with rituals invoking Sufi saints. My second goal, captured in the subtitle, *Ritual Niches and the Social Work of Musical Form*, is to illustrate how musical elements such as ritual musical form have the power not only to support individual trance states, but also to do the social work of simultaneously connecting and differentiating neighboring ritual communities within the landscape of ambient Sufism. Ritualists depend on form, as well as other musical potencies such as timbre and intensification, to achieve their community's ritual goals in producing, for example, efficacious healing and devotional experiences, reflexive participatory stances, and performative records of historical and geocultural movement, as well as in creating welcoming social spaces for alleviating suffering, to name but a few.

Although I inhabited and absorbed this therapeutic and devotional landscape in the course of pursuing a previous project (see Jankowsky 2010), my field research for this book started in earnest in the spring and summer of 2009—the year before the first protests that led to the 2011 Tunisian Revolution[1]—and continued with post-Revolution fieldwork most summers between 2012 and 2018. This book, then, situates the musics of ambient Sufism within a changing postrevolutionary socioreligious climate, one that has been characterized by Islamist threats to the Sufis, ritual practitioners, and musicians whose voices animate this book and who put themselves at risk of physical harm in order to pursue the devotional and healing practices serving the individuals in their ritual communities. Thus, the chapters that follow also contribute to an "ethnomusicology in times of trouble" (Rice 2014), an opportunity to produce a form of scholarship in which the voices and concerns of my field consociates—including the desire to document and give durable scholarly attention to endangered musics and their ethical work—are front and center and shape, in rather direct ways, the theoretical angles I pursue.

A MOMENT OF TRUTH

These times of trouble boiled over in January 2013 as Tunisians responded to Islamist attacks on Sufi shrines in in the two years following the Revolution. A brief excursus into the protests that emerged after arsonists set fire to the shrine of Sīdī Bū Saʿīd illustrates this threat and gives a better idea of the embedded, always within-reach but often just-under-the-radar nature of ambient Sufism. On January 12, 2013, the shrine of the Tunisian Sufi saint Sīdī Bū Saʿīd al-Bājī (d. 1231 CE) was attacked and severely damaged by arsonists emboldened by the release of all accused Islamists from Tunisian prisons and the de facto legalization of Islamist political parties following the overthrow of President Ben Ali in 2011. In those two years more than forty shrines in the country were burned, vandalized, or occupied by mili-

1. Although the media was quick to name the events leading to the overthrow of Ben Ali the "Jasmine Revolution," many Tunisians take offense to this phrase, not only because it could be construed as sanitizing the trauma of the Revolution, but also because it was perceived as perverse in its ignorance of the fact that it was the term used by Ben Ali to designate his own takeover of the presidency from Bourguiba in 1987.

tants for whom the shrines represented a saint-based—and therefore blasphemous and problematically localized[2]—Islamic praxis incompatible with their vision of a globally unified, Wahhabi-inspired Salafism.

The escalation of such attacks led to the cancellation of major Sufi pilgrimages and a substantial reduction in shrine activities. Yet the attacks did not affect only Sufis and those who participate in shrine rituals. They were also considered an affront to a wide swath of the general population for whom these shrines, and the historic figures they represent, are emblems and icons of community and neighborhood identity. For many Tunisians the saints represent a particular kind of Islamic praxis, one that is now often presented in stark contrast to the intolerant and violent Islamist variety that many fear. On the day following the Sīdī Bū Saʿīd attack, a demonstration was held in support of the shrines and against the arsonists, as well as against a government that had done little to protect shrines or to seek justice for similar incidents. News editorials, social-media exchanges, and the messaging of street protests interpreted these acts of arson as attacks on collective heritage and identity. One sign carried by a demonstrator summed up these sentiments (see photo in Seddik 2013), presenting the global and local significance of Sīdī Bū Saʿīd in an intertextual, bilingual manner.

Sidi Bou Saïd blessé	Sidi Bou Saïd is wounded
Sidi Bou Saïd martyrisé	Sidi Bou Saïd is martyred
mais Sidi Bou Saïd patrimoine	but Sidi Bou Saïd is the heritage
de l'Humanité pour l'éternité	of humanity for eternity
رغم الداء والأعداء	Despite the illness and enemies

The French-language lines echo slogans from prior demonstrations that celebrated those who had been killed or injured in the 2011 Revolution. The final line, in Arabic, is from a poem by the famed Tunisian poet Abul Qassim al-Shabbi that continues "I will live upon soaring summits like a proud eagle." Al-Shabbi's lines were chanted regularly during the demonstrations of the Revolution and were now repurposed to the unfinished project of postrevolutionary reform.[3] Indeed, when Tunisian officials—including

2. The anxieties surrounding music and Sufism as undermining the global reformist Islamic project are discussed in detail by Frishkopf (2009).

3. As was the iconic slogan "The People Want to Live" from his 1933 poem "The Will to Live," which was the source of the iconic slogan of the Arab Spring's "The People Want to Topple the Regime" (*al-shaʿb yurīd isqāṭ al-niẓām*). Tunisian educational and Arabization policies led not only to the widespread availability of al-Shabbi's poetry and his phrase "the people want" but also created the conditions for its repurposing in the Revolution (because it was part of the mandatory school curriculum and an early national anthem), as Colla (2012) demonstrates.

President Marzouki, the former Prime Minister Beji Caid Essebsi, and the Ennahda Party leader Rachid Ghannouchi—arrived, they were met with another iconic slogan of the Revolution: *Dégage!* (Get out!), representing protesters' frustration with a postrevolutionary government that seemed unable or unwilling to keep what many perceive as a global Wahhabi movement from threatening those deeply entrenched sociocultural practices surrounding local saint-based institutions (see Omri 2013). The targeting of Sīdī Bū Sa'īd was a moment of truth for many Tunisians, and demonstrations were immediately organized. The otherwise sleepy, idyllic clifftop village overlooking the sea is as popular a day-trip destination for Tunisians as it is for foreign tourists. Members of the economic and political elite have homes there, while Tunisians from all walks of life find solace not only in its breezy outdoor cafés, but also at the shrine of Sīdī Bū Sa'īd itself, where the men's 'Īsāwiyya Sufi order and a women's healing musical troupe regularly perform their ceremonies. The attack thus resonated on cultural, historical, economic, and religious levels.

It was therefore felt acutely by those involved in ritual healing and devotional practices that invoke the spiritual power of Sīdī Bū Sa'īd. This thirteenth-century saint was one of the earliest Tunisian Sufis to embrace music-driven trance rituals, so deeply moved by ritual musical performance that he could not suppress his tears and had trouble controlling his own trance state when attending Sufi ceremonies (Amri 2009).[4] The local 'Īsāwiyya Sufi order calls the shrine of Sīdī Bū Sa'īd its home, its main site of ritual activity and for some their living quarters. It was also in this shrine that the Baron d'Erlanger—the famous colonial-era French scholar of Arab music—learned Tunisian Andalusī music (*mālūf*),[5] as the 'Īsāwiyya are renowned for cultivating this Andalusī musical tradition (Davis 2004). Because Sīdī Bū Sa'īd's power over maritime affairs is believed to extend to the control of sea spirits, his spiritual presence is invoked musically in a number of ritual trance healing traditions across northern Tunisia that treat possession by those spirits. Because the *mizwid* (Tunisian bagpipes) is understood to be particularly efficacious in attracting those spirits, he is also considered a patron saint of mizwid players (Snoussi 1962).

4. While Sīdī Bū Sa'īd's penchant for falling into trance during *dhikr* rituals (recitations of the names of God) and *samā'* ceremonies (music-driven communal devotions) provoked the ire of local religious jurists, interpretations that emphasize the apparent tension between the *'ilm* (acquired knowledge, typically text based) of legalists and the *ma'rifa* (gnosis or knowledge from inspired experience) of Sufis fail to account adequately for the complex, overlapping relationship between Sufis and the religious establishment at the turn of the thirteenth century (Amri 2015).

5. The local pronunciation of *ma'lūf*.

At the outset of the demonstration, the ʿĪsāwiyya Sufi order led the procession from the entrance of the shrine. Marching in two lines facing each other, the men drummed and sang, in call-and-response fashion, pieces from the ʿĪsāwiyya repertoire in praise of Sīdī Bū Saʿīd and Sīdī Ben ʿĪsā, the founder of their order. In many respects, the ʿĪsāwiyya performance resembled the public procession (*kharja*, lit. "departure") they perform every year in honor of the saint: both involved men organized into lines of singers and dancers, surrounded by other members of the order carrying flags representing Sīdī Bū Saʿīd and his shrine, performing ritual pieces that developed according to a logic of intensification featuring an increase in tempo and compression of rhythmic cycles (see chap. 2). Even though the sounds of ʿĪsāwiyya are familiar to nonmembers, the proprietary, ritual nature of the repertoire meant that crowd participation was limited to the semi-anonymous ululations of women and the participation of mostly young men in a line of dancers, with only a few more knowledgeable attendees joining in the singing. Thus, while the musical aesthetics of the ʿĪsāwiyya are easily recognizable through their performance, their musical repertoire is not internalized by nonmembers to the degree that everyone could sing along. This, along with the ʿĪsāwiyya's physical mobility, public-sphere presence, mostly male composition, and ritual specificity of the repertoire, contrasts with the second part of the event, in which a highly recognizable song, spontaneously performed by protesters, has multiple possible ritual sources.

That song was the ritual praise song (*nūba*) of Sīdī Bū Saʿīd called "Ra'is al-Abḥār" (Captain of the Seas). As soon as the ʿĪsāwiyya had ceased playing, the crowd began to sing the refrain:

Ra'is al-abḥār, yā rafīgī, ʿalā allah yā bājī
Fakāk al-muṣāb, yā ṭbīb illī ʿaẓma wājī

O Captain of the Seas, O my companion, O God O Bājī
Liberator of the afflicted, O healer of the weary

Arguably the best-known praise song in northern Tunisia,[6] this song evokes Sīdī Bū Saʿīd's status as protector of the Tunisian coastline and healer of suffering humans. It is a ritual healing song, used to invoke the saint's presence into the dance space of trance rituals of the Mannūbiyya, the women's healing tradition based at the shrine of the female saint Sayyda Mannū-

6. Indeed, in Hishām ʿAbīd's nearly six-hundred-page study of the hagiographies of Tunisian saints, the only praise song mentioned by name is "Ra'īs al-Abḥār" (ʿAbīd 2009: 257).

biyya (chap. 3)—one of the most active shrines in Tunis. There a troupe of women drummers and singers performs a chain (*silsila*) of songs that emphasize women saints, their relationship to male saints, and motherhood. The sea or water spirits (*baḥriyya*) of which Sīdī Bū Saʿīd is understood to be the master are appeased in other trance musics such as sṭambēlī, a healing practice associated with descendants of sub-Saharan migrants in Tunisia whose ritual music, performed on instruments associated with sub-Saharan Africa, evokes a trans-Saharan itinerary of historical movements (chap. 4). The song was also a foundational part of the Jewish trance healing tradition called *rebaybiyya* (chap. 5), performed by mixed Muslim and Jewish troupes featuring the *rebāb* (two-stringed upright fiddle) before that instrument was replaced by the mizwid. Traces of that Jewish Tunisian history of rebaybiyya, which involve trans-Mediterranean movements, remain embedded in the genre that came to be called *mizwid*, the bagpipes-based urban folk genre associated with working-class drinking parties, particularly in the version by the singer Hedi Doniya spread through broadcasts of the staged Sufi spectacle called *el-Hadhra* (chap. 6). *El-Hadhra,* a concert stage event bringing together sounds from numerous Sufi orders, capitalizes on the term "ḥaḍra," which refers to the music-driven rituals of Sufi orders such as the ʿĪsāwiyya, which, in turn, considers Sīdī Bū Saʿīd's shrine one of its ritual centers (chap. 2). The singing of this praise song for Sīdī Bū Saʿīd at the demonstration stems from, and has the power to evoke, any or all of these diverse ritual and musical communities, but because it was performed without musical instruments—and therefore without the most immediately identifiable index of a specific ritual community—its ritual specificity was obscured. As this book demonstrates, each of its respective "home" performance contexts is distinctive in its musical aesthetics, instrumentation, histories, spiritual focus, and communities served. Yet they also overlap by sharing certain spiritual and musical references, such that the figure of Sīdī Bū Saʿīd—like that of a multitude of other saints—constitutes a floating resource in a larger ecology of saint-based practices that is shared, and activated in different ways, by the musical practices of those distinctive ritual niches. The musical sounds associated with this Sufi saint resonate throughout society, in various guises, in social spaces of protest, ritual, and live and broadcast popular music. The mutual availability and interconnectedness of ritual networks, shared resources, adjacent practices, and public audibility surrounding the saints are all captured in the concept of ambient Sufism. I use both words of the phrase advisedly, in ways that are at once more expansive and more specific than those in which they are commonly applied.

WHY "SUFISM"?

The term "Sufism" is a broad, problematic concept, one that tends to obscure more than it reveals. European and North American encounters with practices described as Sufi over the past two centuries have privileged selected literary and musical expressions that support the idea of Sufism as an individual, mystical experience available to all. In such representations, from the knowledge production of Orientalist scholarship to the markets of poetry volumes and world-music recordings, discourse about Sufism for non-Muslim audiences is often "stripped of local practice and the meanings conveyed through the individualized genealogies descended from specific sheikhs" and tends to present Islam as incidental to a Sufism redefined as a global, transcendent spirituality available to all (Bohlman 1997: 62; Ernst 1997). Within the world of Islam, it also serves as a flash point for theological debate, with extremes ranging from arguments that Sufism is antithetical to Islam, on the one hand, to the contention that Sufism is at the heart of Islam (Ernst 1997). In many ways the concept of Sufism, as many insightful studies have shown, is an invention, whether presented as world religion, sect of Islam, or as a genre of world music (Bohlman 1997; Ernst 1997; Frishkopf 2014).

Devotional practices described as Sufi, however, are for the most part social and corporate, deeply grounded in place and time, and they situate ritual activity at the center of an Islamic worldview that sanctions their devotional practices. Each revolves around the actions and teachings of a particular saint, whose shrine (*zāwiya*) is the locus of ritual activity. These shrines, which often house the tomb of the saint, are ubiquitous throughout the North African landscape. Although some are exceedingly modest, consisting of a single, domed room, and others boast magnificent architecture and size, most consist of a marble-floored outdoor courtyard, a room with a domed cupola over the saint's catafalque, and several rooms off the courtyard for lodging, storage, cooking, and other shrine activities. Shrines are located in virtually every neighborhood in North Africa, and many neighborhoods and towns are named after the most prominent saint in their locale; in Tunisia, Sīdī Bū Sa'īd is a well-known example, as is Sīdī Bū Zīd (Sidi Bouzid), the town famous for the protests that started the Tunisian Revolution.

The saints (*āwliyā'*; sing. *walī*) were all once living beings recognized as possessing the spiritual force and divine blessing called *baraka*, derived from their closeness to God. They were exemplary individuals whose posthumous spiritual intervention is often sought to provide a cure for illness, the fulfillment of a supplication or vow, and protection for those who visit the shrine and make offerings. The backgrounds and dispositions of saints varied: some were ascetics, some scholars, some soldiers. Some were considered mad or possessed, in which case their saintliness was often marked by eccentric, even blasphemous behavior that challenged societal and religious norms.[7] Ritual activities and communities developed around the figure of the saint. Individual acts include visits, prayers, and the lighting of candles, all performed in hopes of the fulfillment of a wish. Communal activities typically take the form of ceremonies involving music, trance, and healing. Rituals may happen weekly throughout the year, or weekly through the summer high season, or only occasionally and on demand. Visitors' relationships to saints may be similarly irregular; some are regular visitors to shrines, while others visit more sporadically, their participation refreshed only when searching for healing or support with a life challenge.

Only some of these saints founded formal devotional groups, known in Arabic as *ṭuruq* ("paths"; sing. *ṭarīqa*) and often translated as "Sufi orders."[8] A distinction between social formations surrounding saints who established Sufi orders and those who did not was concretized in French colonial-era scholarship, which distinguished between the *confrérisme* (lit. "brotherhoodism") of the Sufi orders, founded by "serious" saints who taught or modeled devotional methods, on the one hand, and the "cult of saints" or *maraboutisme* of the "popular" or "folk" saints who are venerated locally with no formal ṭarīqa, on the other (see, e.g., Dermenghem 1954). The former category usually includes devotional groups that are male, are formally named after a founding saint with a respected (and often transnational) spiritual genealogy, and boast a collection of hagiographic and ritual texts. The latter is often considered the domain of highly localized practices and identification, involves a higher proportion of women and less educated classes, and is transmitted mainly through oral tradition. Yet in practice the distinction

7. Sīdī Ben 'Arūs is a famous example of a *majdhūb* saint in Tunisia. The presence of such saints in North Africa is one reason I resist translating *walī* as "pious one" as some scholars suggest (and, of course, not all pious ones become saints). Although for some readers the term "saint" may carry with it misleading connotations of a formal process of beatification, as is found in Christianity, I find the term acceptable because it conveys the general idea of a deceased historical figure who is considered especially close to or blessed by God and to whom offerings and prayers are made in hopes of the saint's intervention on the supplicant's behalf.

8. Unlike the term "saint," which I find to be a productive if imperfect translation of *walī*, I avoid the common translation of "ṭarīqa" as "brotherhood." First, as this book illustrates, some ṭarīqas are exclusively female, and women participate—albeit sometimes from the margins—in what are considered men's ṭarīqas. Second, the term "brotherhood" carries with it connotations from Christianity of monastery life, social withdrawal, and asceticism that have been applied to Sufism uncritically and demand correction.

is often blurred, particularly because the saints, as the following chapters reveal, circulate freely throughout both realms, cohabiting ritual space and living side by side in musical repertoires, sharing a capacity to intervene in the lives of humans. My use of the term "Sufism," then, deliberately seeks to avoid the problematic binaries such as *confrérisme/maraboutisme*, serious/folk saints, or formal/informal Sufisms.

It should be noted that, in the Tunis region, the terms "Sufism" (*taṣawwuf*) and "Sufi" (*ṣūfī*) are not the most commonly used in unprompted exchanges among participants to describe themselves or their activities. While "Sufi" is sometimes used as a catchall phrase for musical activities originating at a saint shrine—and at times strategically paralleling the language used by cultural officials for festival themes—it is more likely to define what is *not* "Sufi" in a given ritual. For example, chapter 2 describes a situation in which a member of the ʿĪsāwiyya opines on which aspects of that ṭarīqa's ritual he considers "Sufi" (here understood to be an a cappella recitational style shared with many other ṭarīqas inside and outside of Tunisia) and which elements are more properly considered "ṭuruqī" (lit. "of the ṭarīqas"; that is, localized musical practices specific to a particular ṭarīqa). There is a general sense that the "Sufi" components, such as liturgical recitation, predate the "ṭuruqī" musical developments. Thus, what is and is not Sufi in terms of performance practice is a local matter and dependent on context. The term "Sufi," however, is used quite often to describe the founding saint, always historically distant but brought into the present through ritual. And it is the figures of Sufi saints that are evoked musically to do the work of healing on which I focus. Some of this healing, furthermore, involves a saint's interceding with the world of spirits, thus extending the saints' reach to the domain of possession rituals. In other words, the term "Sufism" in the phrase "ambient Sufism" pulls together all saints and their shrine practices, including those dealing with spirit possession, whether "formal" or "informal" in their ritual social formations, in order to convey the ongoing musical lives of saints that animate the devotional and therapeutic landscape.

WHY "AMBIENT"?

Songs for the saints punctuate social life in numerous ways. They blare onto neighborhood streets on late summer nights when wedding bands perform these popular, catchy tunes, which often generate excitement expressed in ululations, dancing, and singing from the crowd. Through televised broadcasts of staged Sufi spectacles such as *el-Hadhra*, such songs also contribute to the festive and familiar atmosphere of cafés during Ramadan and other holiday evenings. They drift across the areas surrounding shrines as members of Sufi orders perform weekly ceremonies, and they attract listeners to the street when performed in public processions celebrating religious holidays and the anniversary of the death of the saint. Songs for saints are obligatory opening pieces for mizwid concerts, even at drinking parties, and mizwid superstars record these songs on albums that share space with songs about love, betrayal, poverty, and the perils of immigration abroad. Thus, they circulate far beyond the ritual world of shrine activities—and yet even those shrine activities are semi-public, open to all, and are attended not only by those in search of spiritual intervention and healing, but also by the friends and family members accompanying those visitors. Moreover, individuals seeking ritual healing have several choices of shrines and ritual communities from which to choose and often decide which shrine to visit based on which musical troupe creates the "most festive atmosphere" (*plus d'ambiance festive*), as Katia Boissevain (2006: 189) put it. Indeed, many trance healing musicians speak of a good, festive performance using the phrase "'amilnā jaww," meaning "we made [good] ambience," in the sense of creating conditions that enabled attendees to have fun and enjoy themselves, even while healing those afflicted by spirits.

Thus, my use of the term "ambient" refers to two things.[9] First, it evokes the general atmosphere in which songs for saints circulate and are made widely available, even for those who do not deliberately seek them out. The songs, shrines, and saints may enter the foreground through deliberate acts of visitation but are always available in the background, through memories of familial activities or the social rhythm of life, such as the summer wedding season or being out at night during Ramadan. The sheer ubiquity of saint shrines and places named after saints contributes to the sense of saint references as ambience, as background, as continual public presence. The saints are rarely out of reach. While landmarks, architecture, and nomenclature keep the figures of the saints ever nearby, it is mainly through music that the saint's presence and capacity for intervention are actuated. Thus, the term "ambient" pulls together the ideas of sound and background in a productive way. Second, it refers to the sense of ambiance that is associated with ritual, the space of the shrine, and the comfort and alleviation from suffering promised by the saint that is expressed through the music. The sounds of saint songs evoke this sense of hope and desire for intervention; these sentiments are quite often explicitly announced in song lyrics. The ambience is marked by an atmosphere of support and sociability, a "ritual

9. The concept of "ambient Sufism" was partly inspired by Matthew Engelke's study of "ambient faith" in England (Engelke 2012). I express my gratitude to Jeffers Engelhardt for directing me to Engelke's work during his lecture "Music, Mediation, and Post-Secular Religion: Perspectives from Estonia and Greece" (Engelhardt 2014).

warmth" (Turner 2017) that successful devotional and healing rituals are expected to produce. Enjoyment, pleasure, and the serious work of healing and devotion are never mutually exclusive in these contexts. Indeed, they are mutually constitutive.

Two additional points arise from the wide-lens perspective of ambient Sufism. First, the musics of underrepresented communities constitute integral components of the musical ecology of Sufism, even though they are largely absent from dominant narratives of Tunisian history, music, and society. In the chapters that follow, distinctive ritual practices of women, Jews, Tunisians of sub-Saharan descent, and manual laborers drinking after work emerge as central to the development and diffusion of musical invocations of Muslim saints. Second, it is through musical sound that many ideas and feelings related to Sufism circulate so widely throughout Tunisian society. This book is not just a study of music; it is a study of how music contributes to the dissemination of ideas that are increasingly mobilized in debates over religious identity that have arisen in the wake of militant Islamist attacks on Sufi shrines and practices after the Tunisian Revolution in 2011. Each musical genre contributes, in different ways, to the circulation of concepts associated with Sufism, including the centrality of Muslim saints to local and national notions of identity; the importance of relations of reciprocity; the empathy and openness associated with Sufi institutions that provide solace for the suffering; the creation of inclusive social spaces that may cross gender, ethnic, and religious boundaries; the hospitality of ritual; the therapeutic value of trance; and the social work of ritual musical form.

MUSICAL POTENCIES: SUTURING THE SONIC, THE SPIRITUAL, AND THE SOCIAL

This expansive perspective of ambient Sufism, with its landscape of interconnected saints, shrines, and multitude of ritual practices, comes into clearest focus when zooming in on the specifics of musical performance in each of those ritual contexts. Timbre, intensification, and ritual musical form emerge as particularly salient agents in mediating the sonic, spiritual, and social domains of ambient Sufism. I refer to this trio of sonic properties and processes as "potencies" because they are signifying aesthetic forces that act upon subjects. Here I am inspired by anthropologists who gravitate toward the concept of potency, finding that it productively implies a state of gaining power *from* rather than exclusively a state of wielding power *over*. Although mainly used to analyze political power in Southeast Asia, the concept of potency applies to the ritual work of ambient Sufism in that, in the hands of ritual performers, sonic potencies open up access to an "intangible, mysterious, and divine energy" (Anderson 1990: 22) circulating in an invisible realm, the activation of which relies on indexical relationships (i.e., sonic elements signify the distinctive power of each ritual community), is reinforced by witnessing or coparticipating audiences doing interpretive work and involves hearing as a dominant sensory mode (see Errington 1989: 285–286).

The concept of potency also usefully evokes the idea of potential, which serves as a reminder that in the domain of ritual, the possibility always exists that goals are not achieved or that outcomes may be ambiguous. The rituals and physical shrines of ambient Sufism are sites where anticipation runs high, because accessing the spiritual realm is never guaranteed. The capacity to signify, act, or achieve a result is embedded in the concept of musical potencies, and, as the analyses in the following chapters suggest, timbre, intensity, and form are three particularly potent categories of sonic and musical action in the local landscape of trance ritual.

Each ritual and musical community considered in this book has a distinctive soundworld that distinguishes it sonically from the others. The buzzing timbres and bass register of sṭambēlī, with its gumbrī (lute) and metal clappers, are as iconic of sṭambēlī ritual as the piercing, continuous melodies of the mizwid (bagpipes) are of rebaybiyya or the women's voices and shimmering tambourine cymbals are of the Mannūbiyya. Instrumentation in each ritual community is thoroughly fixed and unique to that community. The instruments perform without pause to create an unceasingly reliable cushion of sound. This constancy of sound, its unchanging texture, is an often-overlooked aspect of this kind of ritual music; in Tunis, trance states are supported by such timbral saturation. Musical timbre, as this book shows, is not epiphenomenal but is rather of central importance to ritual efficacy. If music is implicated in social boundary work (Gidal 2016; Stokes 1994), it is primarily through sonic markers of timbre and texture that ritual communities in Tunis are immediately identifiable and distinguished from each other.

Musical form, however, both complements and complicates the boundary work of timbre and texture. The ritual practices analyzed in this book mainly involve two ritual-musical forms: the ḥaḍra of Sufi orders such as the ʿĪsāwiyya; and the silsila, which shapes ceremonies devoted to trance healing, often through spirit possession.[10] In these contexts, musical form does

10. The term "ḥaḍra" is also widely used to refer to *any* ritual or devotional ceremony at a saint shrine that involves communal devotion and healing, typically with vocal or musical performance accompanying physical movements of dance or trance. Thus, the ritual performance of the Mannūbiyya, which is based on the silsila, may nevertheless sometimes be called a ḥaḍra. My use of the terms "silsila" and "ḥaḍra" is, then, fairly specific: in the case

double duty: by emphasizing certain spiritual figures and musical dynamics specific to a specific ritual tradition, it reinforces the distinctive identity of each community. But in doing so, it also relies on the recognition of other niches and the incorporation of musical and spiritual references associated with other domains of ritual (and sometimes nonritual) practice. For example, the silsila musical form that structures the rituals of women Sufis (Mannūbiyya), Tunisians of sub-Saharan descent (ṣtambēlī), and Tunisian Jews (rebaybiyya) is a flexible, loosely hierarchical chain of praise songs (nūbas), with each song named after, and invoking, a specific saint or spirit. The Mannūbiyya silsila emphasizes women saints and others who are important to the community surrounding the saint Sayyda Mannūbiyya; the ṣtambēlī silsila reveals saints and spirits that factor into its trans-Saharan movements; and the rebaybiyya silsila is distinctive for illustrating particular Jewish-Muslim convergences. Yet all of these silsilas overlap: many saints appear in two or all three of them, but with very different musical sounds, instrumentation, and approaches, and often carrying different social meanings layered over similar therapeutic expectations. The silsila thus connects ritually adjacent practices while simultaneously providing the tools for distinguishing them from one another.

The ḥaḍra is a ritual-musical form that operates in a different fashion but nevertheless exhibits some family resemblances and outcomes similar to silsila-based practices. The ḥaḍra is a succession of well-defined ritual sections, each of which features a different sonic or musical approach to the performance of sacred texts and the support of dance or trance. In the case of the ʿĪsāwiyya, the ḥaḍra proceeds from reciting liturgical texts to performing Andalusī songs to singing and drumming accompanying communal dance and individual states of trance. The ḥaḍra has a strong sense of sectionality and global trajectory, realized through particular strategies of sonic and spiritual intensification.

Both the ḥaḍra and the silsila can be considered composite musical forms. Such forms are common in a variety of musics throughout North Africa and the Middle East. The Egyptian *waṣla* form, mainly associated with Arab art music, is a performance scheme comprised of several self-contained, interrelated sections, organized with "a purposeful sense of order and direction" (Racy 1983: 400) that juxtaposes slow and fast tempos, instrumental and vocal pieces, and improvised and solo ensemble textures. Carl Davila (2015) and Scott Marcus (2012) draw attention to the waṣla's capacity to bring together otherwise disparate compositions and poetic texts from different

studies that follow, they both refer to the largest-scale organizational scheme that structures its smaller constituent sonic or musical units.

geographic regions and historic eras, by known and unknown composers. The Maghrebi *nawba* (which, while called "nūba" in local dialects, is not to be confused with the nūba of ritual praise songs considered in this book) is a large-scale song cycle that proceeds through fixed sections. Each section includes a corpus of pieces from which performers pick and choose to make each performance unique. The nawba goes through a fixed progression of different rhythmic patterns, while all the pieces are in the same (or related) melodic mode, providing a unity of pitch material and a diversity of rhythmic material (see Davis 2004). In this, and in the overall progression from slow to fast and instrumental to vocal, it is similar to the waṣla.

Both the waṣla and the nawba are ordered sections of compositional types, with each section having a large corpus of pieces to choose from that concretize a sequential musical form in which certain song types are associated with the beginning of the performance and others with the end. While the waṣla is relatively loose in this regard when compared to the nawba, which is more fixed, they share the capacity to bring together disparate pieces in a uniform way and to adhere to a larger architecture in which each song type has its place, giving a strong sense of order and directionality. In this way, the ḥaḍra and silsila musical-ritual forms share family resemblances with these other composite forms. But the ḥaḍra and silsila can more productively be considered what I call *cumulative musical forms*, that is, large-scale forms in which constituent parts are self-contained but collectively add up to a larger whole that tells a specific story about the ritual community that produced it. As they unfold in ritual musical time, these cumulative musical forms progressively disclose a totality: of their ritual community's history, that community's relationships to available spiritual figures, and socially adjacent ritual communities. The ḥaḍra and silsila adhere to their own logics of development. They also accomplish specific kinds of ritual and social work, so that one way of thinking about this book's organization is to see each chapter as providing additional angles on what musical ritual forms do. Thus, this is not a zero-sum game between musical form and content. Instead, it is a shift of emphasis, not at the expense of content but highlighting the important work of structuring that content and how it is experienced in ritual contexts in real time.

The ḥaḍra and silsila ritual musical forms are modular in that they have smaller units that may be reordered, added, or subtracted. The third type of large-scale musical form, which I call *set-list modularity*, is modular in a different way, according to a different logic with specific implications. This is the formal logic applied to concert-stage presentations, where a plug-and-play organizational scheme underpins a sequencing of songs in a set-list manner, driven by overriding aesthetic criteria such as the juxtaposition of sonic textures, intensities, volume, and instrumentation associated with the production values of concerts and the theater. Moreover, what is modular here is not only songs or pieces, but also ritual traditions from which those pieces were extracted. Set-list modularity prevents audiences from following the idiomatic ritual trajectories of any single tradition from which it draws and therefore, as chapter 6 argues, maximizes the contextual gap between ritual and stage situations.

The musical forms examined in this book, then, provide a large-scale architecture for the entirety of ritual, bringing diverse musical-spiritual units (pieces, songs, recitations) together in meaningful ways and ordering them in a way that provides the ritual with a sense of purposeful direction. Participants expect and anticipate what comes next. A trancer in search of healing will wait for "her" saint's song to be played, with an understanding of where in the silsila it is likely to appear. Sufis completing a recitation in their ḥaḍra know that, while the end of that performance closes one form of expressive devotion, it also signals the beginning of another that proceeds according to different conventions. At a broader level, ritual musical form, in conjunction with timbre, announces each ritual community's distinctive identity. Yet it does so by encouraging connections to be made to adjacent ritual communities, activating sonic resources that reveal both commonality and difference.

RITUAL INTENSIFICATION

Timbre and form intersect with a third sonic element at the heart of the sensory ritual experience: intensification. If ritual is a site where the force of aesthetic processes is put to the test (Hobart and Kapferer 2005), intensification emerges as central to the ritual processes I examine. Sonic intensification maps directly onto increases in physical exertion and experiences of spiritual transformation. Analytical attention to these processes is prevalent throughout this book and is captured in a tripartite model of intensification elaborated in chapter 7. *Discrete intensification* (DI) involves a single phrase repeated in cyclic fashion. DI most commonly involves an increase in intensity through acceleration and a concomitant increase in sonic density and the frequency of beat onsets, although in some cases it involves systematic rise in pitch. *Sequential intensification* (SI), in contrast, is a process whereby one rhythmic pattern modulates to another pattern that exhibits more sonic density. In SI, once a song in one rhythmic pattern ends, a new song begins in a new pattern that features shorter rhythmic cycles, fewer beats per phrase, and faster subdivisions, producing an increase in intensity. Of the three types, *global intensification* (GI) occurs on the longest temporal scale. In the musics I consider here, it takes the form of an increase in sonic density produced by the systematic layering of additional musical instruments, which adds timbral density and volume.

All three forms of intensification, it is crucial to note, rely on the steadiness of cyclic repetition. Cyclicity creates and reinforces baseline sonic experiences and expectations that make possible the gradual shifts in temporality that are at the heart of the rituals analyzed in this book. Constancy and transformation, then, are two sides of the same coin. I propose this model of intensification to gain access, and give a name, to the processes of profound sonic and personal transformation in ritual—in other words, to examine the hyphen in what Jonathan Shannon (2006: 120) calls the "moral-musical conditioning" of Sufi ritual.

How does intensification relate to timbre and ritual-musical form in this analysis? I think of the three as operating interdependently, but at different levels. Timbre maintains an internally unchanging, continuous baseline, intensification provides a sense of internal trajectory, and ritual-musical form creates a large-scale architecture of episodic connections and development. The case studies in this book demonstrate how each of these musical potencies circulate within a shared ecology of ambient Sufism and, as such, articulate meaningful aspects of commonality and difference when they are performed using the conventions of each distinctive ritual community. On a larger scale, these case studies reveal that music does not merely accompany ritual. Rather, ritual itself serves to highlight the power of music to act. It follows that, when ritual music is taken out of its ritual context, it carries with it some of those potencies and expectations, even when adapted to staged concerts or popular-music songs.

In short, this book is about ritual performance. Each chapter presents a different aspect of the social and cultural work of ritual, and collectively they unfold in a succession of themes on ritual possibility, including, in order of appearance, reflexivity, hospitality, memory, alterity, and convergence. The disappearance or disintegration of ritual practices is addressed in the final chapters, which focus on the remnants of ritual in popular music and on ritual as a resource for public spectacle. Although each theme emerges from a specific case study, they (like the cumulative musical forms analyzed within them) may be most productively read in cumulative fashion, with the possibilities illustrated in any single chapter adding layers of interpretive options to the others.

SAINTS, SHRINES, AND SOCIETY

Although the ethnographic context of this book is limited to the city of Tunis and its immediate environs, the saints who are invoked in the region's ritual musics represent a diverse group of geocultural origins and movements. A small sampling of saints is illustrative: Sīdī Bū Saʿīd al-Bājī (1160–1231) had local origins (from the northern Tunisian town of Beja, as his name indicates), but Sīdī Ben ʿĪsā (1467–1526; founder of the ʿĪsāwiyya) simply traveled through Tunisia from Morocco on his way to Mecca. Sīdī Saʿd (d. before 1728) was captured as a slave in central Africa and transported to Tunis via the trans-Saharan trade routes, and Sīdī ʿAbd al-Qādir (1078–1166), who was born in Persia and died in Baghdad, developed a Sufi path that became known as the Qādiriyya, with numerous shrines in Tunisia and circles of followers from Morocco to Indonesia.

Saints also represent different historical eras spanning centuries. Although practices revolving around the spiritual intervention of deceased holy figures presumably have pre-Islamic precursors, in Tunis the appearance, identities, and enduring importance of saints are closely related to the spread and defense of Islam, as well as individual itineraries of pilgrimage, which are built into the pillars of the religion. In Tunis, Sīdī Meḥrez (951–1022), known as Lord of the City (*sulṭān al-madīna*), is held up as an ideal religious figure, a champion of Sunni Islam who defended the city against Zirid incursions (Larguèche 1999: 148). He is credited with intervening to establish a Jewish quarter (*ḥāra*) in the medina at a time when Jews were forbidden to live within the city walls, and centuries after his death his shrine was the main site where slaves of sub-Saharan descent were issued their manumission certificates (see Montana 2013). Sīdī Meḥrez is one of many examples of a saint associated with a particular community but also recognized as an important historical and spiritual figure by a much wider spectrum of the populace. Sayyda Mannūbiyya and Umm al-Zīn are particularly prized by women's ritual communities; Sīdī Bashīr is known as representing Tunisians of Kabyle origin; and Sīdī Saʿd and Sīdī Frej are pillars of the ritual communities formed by Tunisians of sub-Saharan descent. Yet all of these saints are recognized, and invoked in ritual, by other ritual communities. Indeed, it is the norm in all the ritual musical practices discussed in this book to invoke a multitude of saints in ways that signal the specific communities they serve while simultaneously absorbing them into practices beyond those communities.

Thus, as each of these interconnected saints is represented in the physical landscape by a zāwiya serving as a memorial and site of ritual activity, these shrines are places where elements of sameness and difference are constantly intertwined. Sameness because, at a general level, as Carla Bellamy notes, people recognize these shrines as being "of the same fundamental type, and as fundamentally connected with one another" (2011: 4). Shrines are places where a saint's unseen presence and *baraka* (spiritual force, often translated as "blessing") are most immediately available to visitors who come to seek healing or aid. In the aggregate, they form a network within a cartography of similar sites of healing and devotion in which saint-based healing is always available somewhere nearby. Yet each shrine encapsulates the web of historical geocultural migrations and movements that gave rise to their specific ritual communities and the different ethnic, religious, gender, and class backgrounds with which they are associated. The saint's shrine, then, as part of a network of "sames," is also a network of difference. Ritual music, as the chapters of this book suggest, instantiates and activates this duality.

These shrines, however, are more than ritual sites. Historically, they have served as community centers providing aid to the needy, dispute arbitration, lodging for pilgrims, religious education, and recreation. In Tunisia these important social institutions have been entangled with politics up to the present day. During the Husaynid era, saint shrines were frequented by rulers and ruled alike. The beys respected the tradition of shrines operating as asylums for fugitives, and many beys built or renovated shrines for specific communities or for saints they venerated (Brown 1974). They were not necessarily entirely altruistic in their encouragement of shrine activity, as it was also a means for integrating, and thus regulating, minorities and other members of society that were not part of other major social institutions (Montana 2004). Many beys and religious clerics, however, belonged to Sufi ṭarīqas, and Aḥmad Bey, a member of the Shādhuliyya, visited the shrine of Sīdī Belḥassen before and after major journeys, including his monumental state visit to France in 1864 (Brown 1974). Nearly a century and a half later Leila Trabelsi, wife of the now-deposed President Ben Ali (r. 1987–2011), visited the shrine of Sayyda Mannūbiyya regularly, dressed discreetly and accompanied by security guards. These visits were interpreted as acts of supplication in hopes of her giving birth to a boy, a wish that was granted in 2004 (Boissevain 2006: 225).[11] Such continuities of practice, however, took place in a context of recurring threats to them. In the early 1800s Saudi Wahhabist letters to the bey decrying Tunisian shrine practices were refuted by scholars at Tunisia's renowned Zaytouna University. Their rebuttal, entitled *Al-minaḥ al-ilahiyya fī ṭams al-ḍalāla al-wahhābiyya* (God's Gifts in Obliterating the Wahhabi Deviation), defended the legitimacy of Tunisian shrine activities such as visits, sacrifices, and burial rites (Omri 2013). This text reentered Tunisian public discourse as shrines were again under attack in the years following the 2011 Revolution.

11. She also hosted private sṭambēlī trance healing ceremonies at the shrine of Sīdī ʿAlī Ḥaṭṭāb, bringing sṭambēlī musicians discreetly to a room on an upper floor that was off limits to others during the annual group pilgrimage.

Before the postrevolutionary militant offensive against shrines reported above, the strongest and most enduring attack on shrine activities came from within: the postindependence regime of President Habib Bourguiba destroyed, closed, or repurposed a multitude of shrines beginning in the late 1950s. These acts were the culmination of a period of growing suspicion during the French protectorate era (1881–1956) that some Sufi orders were cooperating with the French and encouraging their followers not to support the resistance movement. Moreover, Bourguiba considered shrine practices to be incompatible with his secularist agenda and vision of modern development.[12] Shrine activities and membership in Sufi orders diminished greatly. But, like his failed attempt to convince Tunisians not to observe Ramadan because he had put the country on a "jihad against underdevelopment" (Perkins 2004: 119), this initiative did not eradicate shrine activities. While state suppression in the 1970s led some Sufis to believe a law had been passed prohibiting shrine activities, state-sponsored festivals pulled the music of some Sufi orders into the state's orbit, presenting the music as folklore and professionalizing Sufi performers, who were now required to apply for musicians' cards in order to perform onstage legally (Jones 1977). The establishment of the modern state did mean that the government took over many of the social services provided by shrines, but demand for devotional and healing rituals through trance ceremonies has persisted, even if it is now limited to a smaller number of shrines and ritual troupes fortunate enough to rely on regular schedules of ceremonies. As robust as some of these practices may remain, some chapters of this book reveal disintegrating ritual communities, whose ritual remnants have nonetheless found new life, absorbed into some of the most popular staged and mass-mediated musical genres and thus, perhaps somewhat paradoxically, spreading the sounds of ambient Sufism even further and more broadly across society.

DOCUMENTATION IN TIMES OF TROUBLE

This book attempts to capture the voices, concerns, and priorities of ritual practitioners at a historical moment in which they and their practices have become increasingly at risk. An analytical approach that prioritizes the details of musical form may, at first blush, seem to sideline those concerns in favor of a detached, formalist pursuit. Yet it is precisely in the details of musical performance where many of the ritualists with whom I worked situated

12. This was happening well before independence. In 1934 shopkeepers in Kairouan protested the inclusion of the ʿĪsāwiyya in the program for an international conference for the League of Journalists, claiming it presented a demeaning and backward image of Tunisia to outsiders (Mizouri 1996: 40).

their own ethical interventions, and it is that ethical work that they fear is under threat. Foregrounding their voices, then, means taking seriously the theological and ethical concerns that were highlighted in our conversations and that were part and parcel of discussions of ritual-musical performance: for example, the way that repetition is understood to mold ethical selves, how musical structure facilitates ritual hospitality and the collective memory of minorities, and the tension between music as an aesthetic end and as a spiritual means of transcending and bettering the self. As the sounds of some of the ritual musics discussed in this book are increasingly—albeit very partially—recorded and disseminated by participants, it is an understanding of the ethics of ritual work—accessed, activated, and achieved through music—that remains at greatest risk of fading into obscurity.

There are, of course, disagreements within particular ritual communities, as well as between them, regarding what is proper, right, and acceptable.[13] Yet one point that virtually all of my interlocutors shared, raised again and again in conversations with me, was that they felt the pressures of increasingly conservative religious stances toward music, Sufism, and shrine rituals. Pronouncements against music by Shaykh Houcine Laabidi, imam of the standard-setting Zaytouna Mosque, became common; his 2013 declaration that mālūf music was responsible for the downfall of Islamic rule in al-Andalus made newspaper headlines and was received with incredulity by several Sufis (and non-Sufis) I know. Even more disturbing to them were the widespread acts of arson and vandalism, as well as physical attacks on and threats to shrine visitors by militant Islamists referred to broadly, and not unproblematically, in Tunisia as Salafists.

By prioritizing the voices and concerns of ritualists, this book runs the risk of presenting the kinds of Islamists who attacked the shrines as rather one-dimensional. In our conversations and interviews, ritualists often presented Islamists (generally referred to derogatorily as *bū lḥiy*, or "bearded ones") as influenced by foreign actors and ideologies, particularly Wahhabism (*al-wahhabiyya*) or the Muslim Brothers (*al-khwanjiyya*). The terms "Salafism" (*salafiyya*) and "Salafi" (*salafī*) are used in a general sense in Tunisia to refer to anyone preoccupied with religious "purity" modeled on the first generation of seventh-century Muslim ancestors (*al-salaf*) and therefore rejecting any theological doctrine (or practices such as Sufism) developed since that time. "Salafism" is a term that obscures important differences between nonviolent or quietist, scholarly Salafism (*al-salafiyya al-*

13. Chapters dealing with the Mannūbiyya, Tījāniyya, and ʿĪsāwiyya provide evidence of this, but, as might be expected in an ethnographic work that brings so many adjacent ritual communities into consideration, I broach the issue with due discretion.

'ilmiyya) and militant Salafism (*al-salafiyya al-jihādiyya*), among others, although Salafis tend to reject such labels (Lauzière 2016; see also Wolf 2013). "Islamism" is a broader and more inclusive term referring to movements that seek to infuse political rule with religious doctrine. The terms "Salafi" and "Islamist" are used rather loosely in everyday Tunisian discourse, and doing ethnographic justice means preserving them, for better or for worse, in order to maintain their general discursive imprecision and the specific positionality of the voices of ritualists.

The impact of militant Islamism was palpable in the ritual and musical communities represented in every chapter of this book. Walid, the young 'Īsāwiyya shaykh introduced in chapter 2, described to me how ceremonies and visits came to a complete halt for over a year because everyone involved was "scared of the Salafi trend" (*khūfā min al-tiyār al-salafī*), not only as a physical threat, but also through the powerful verbal attacks accusing visitors of being "unbelievers" (*kāfir*, a highly insulting epithet). When Walid and I traveled together to the western town of Kef to visit the 'Īsāwiyya branch there, we found that the threat was still so palpable that two years after the Revolution, the town's ṭarīqa had still not resumed its ritual activities; moreover, we departed just before a concert was broken up by militant Islamists and a roadside bomb detonated at the town's main traffic circle. Fatima, the leader of the Mannūbiyya troupe introduced in chapter 3, held the ritual performance analyzed in that chapter at her home because, she told us, a threatening group of Salafis had stationed themselves outside the shrine. When the organizers of the staged Sufi spectacle *Ziara* invited me to their performance in the town of Bizerte, they had just hired a large private security firm to protect their performers after learning of increased Islamist attacks on public spaces there. Two months after I conducted an interview on Jewish rebaybiyya with Jacob Lellouche, the unofficial representative of Tunisia's mainland Jewish community, he was forced to close down his restaurant after the Ministry of Interior intercepted credible terrorist threats against it.[14] Specific threats and attacks, while dramatic and traumatic, have been relatively scattered and have become rare outside the southern border regions of the country. Most of the people I worked with seemed rather confident that this was a temporary situation and expressed optimism that a new government would take care of this problem. That confidence was undoubtedly influenced by the country's experience with both of its postindependence regimes, which, if anything, were inarguably successful at sup-

14. The restaurant, perhaps the last venue in the area that brought Jews and Muslims together to socialize with any regularity and intentionality, had to be moved to an undisclosed location, where Lellouche now takes reservations only from known callers.

pressing Islamist dissent and maintaining strict public security before the Revolution.

What has endured, however, is an atmosphere of tension and uncertainty over the future, one that arguably has less to do with security than with the perils of shifting discourse, which was already influenced by an increase in conservative Islamic attitudes against Sufism and shrine practices. Many of the ritualists I spoke with expressed incredulity that they—people who dedicate their time and energy to devotional ceremonies and healing people in the name of God and Muslim saints—were accused of being infidels. The concern is that such actions and discourse will contribute to the spread of negative attitudes toward ritual practices and communities. In danger of being lost are the social interventions made by ritual music, not only as individual healing in the silsila or spiritual transcendence of the ḥaḍra, but also in the social work of activating historical memory, encouraging structures of social support, and creating the conditions for ethnic, gender, and religious boundary crossing. Chapters that examine the adaptation (chap. 4), disappearance (chap. 5), and recontextualization (chap. 6) of ritual music reveal three different processes of loss. In these examples, transformations in musical form signal dramatic shifts in the kinds of social interventions made possible through ritual music. Yet these instances of ritual loss and musical repurposing continue to coexist and overlap with vibrant ritual practices that remain in demand. In the chapters that follow, the study of multiple ritually adjacent practices reveals a synchronic ethnographic approach that nevertheless sheds light on the different diachronic points in which each tradition finds itself. But this is not a situation of unidirectional or teleological loss. As the following chapters show, certain practices facing insurmountable challenges may disappear, leaving only faint and largely unrecognized traces, but they may also be repurposed for new audiences attracted to the ritual credentials of the music. Indeed, these shifts and movements are defining features of ambient Sufism, which above all is about the fluidity, circulation, and transformation of musical instantiations of Muslim saints.

ORGANIZATION OF THE BOOK

This book consists of a series of case studies (chaps. 2–6) bookended by chapters that introduce and contextualize ambient Sufism (chap. 1) and theorize its musical potencies of form, timbre, and intensification (chap. 7). Each case study examines a specific musical-ritual community, provides a different angle on the ritual and social work of musical form, and highlights the voices, preoccupations, and decisions of (at least) one ritual musician to guide the direction of the analysis. Chapter 2 opens this series of case studies with an extended examination of the ḥaḍra ceremony of the ʿĪsāwiyya Sufi order. Highlighting the experience of Walid Mennai, a shaykh of the ʿĪsāwiyya of La Marsa, this chapter approaches the ḥaḍra as a ritual musical form that relies on global and local processes of sonic intensification while also encouraging ritual reflexivity that identifies the virtues and ambiguities of "Sufi" religiosity, Andalusī musical heritage, and ecstatic trance.

The following three chapters shift focus to the silsila form. Chapter 3 is a study of the silsila of the Mannūbiyya women's Sufi healing troupe. Discussion of the ritual decisions of Fatima Lwelbani, the troupe's leader, reveals that the silsila encourages ritual hospitality based on an ethics of inclusivity. This inclusivity, however, stands in tension with the boundary work of timbre and texture that separates ritually adjacent practices. Chapter 4 analyzes the shifting forms of the silsila of sṭambēlī, the trance healing music developed by the sub-Saharan diaspora in Tunisia. The chapter begins by analyzing a sṭambēlī ritual silsila as performed by Salah el-Ouergli, which evokes the trans-Saharan movements of people, spirits, and musical material. Because sṭambēlī ritual work opportunities have been drying up, the chapter then proceeds to an examination of the transformation of the silsila in new presentational contexts of upscale cafés and other cultural spaces, where sṭambēlī musicians such as Belhassen Mihoub adapt the silsila to its new audiences. The theme of recontextualizing ritual music continues in chapter 5, which examines the Jewish trance healing music called rebaybiyya, the remnants of which remain in the sacred repertoire of mizwid, a bagpipes-based music associated with drinking parties of urban manual laborers that became the most commercially successful mass-mediated music in Tunis. The famed singer Hedi Doniya is considered the most iconic performer of this sacred popular repertoire. As he may also be the last living artist who learned the rebaybiyya repertoire from Jewish musicians, his voice is central to the story of rebaybiyya's diffusion into the sphere of popular music. Chapter 6 focuses on the staging of ritual music, particularly in the concert spectacle called *el-Hadhra*, which, since the early 1990s, has been at the center of an industry of staging Sufi music that appears regularly at major festivals and has a mass mediated presence on recordings, television, and the internet. This chapter considers the implications of the modular nature of such stagings, which bring together and juxtapose pieces from different ritual traditions according to a logic of modern concert tastes rather than ritual efficacy. Chapters 4, 5, and 6 thus form a sequence of their own that deals with the transformation and repurposing of ritual music.

Chapter 7 concludes the book by synthesizing the analyses of the social work of ritual musical form and other musical potencies that accumulate throughout the case studies. It offers a music-theoretical perspective that foregrounds the roles of sonic continuity, timbral constancy, gradual transformation, and intensification, while proposing that the sequential, cumulative formal structure of the ḥaḍra and silsila are essential not only to their devotional and therapeutic work, but also to the social work of simultaneously engaging with ritually adjacent practices while carving distinct niches for themselves within the broader shared spiritual and musical ecology of ambient Sufism.

2

RITUAL REFLEXIVITY

Musicality, Sufi Pedigrees, and the Masters of "Intoxication"

The first time I met Walid Mennai, then a twenty-nine-year-old shaykh of the 'Īsāwiyya Sufi order, was in 2009 during a three-day pilgrimage (*ziyāra*) to the shrine of the saint Sīdī 'Alī Ḥaṭṭāb near Tunis. Walid, a call-center worker with an archaeology degree from the University of Culture and Human Sciences in Kairouan, was one of hundreds of pilgrims from a wide array of Sufi orders brought together for the first event of their fourteen-week season (*al-arba'tāsh*, lit. "the fourteen") of heightened ritual activity. He and his fellow 'Īsāwīs were seated in a large oval formation on the ground in the outdoor courtyard of the shrine, reciting the ḥizb, a highly rhythmic liturgical recitation. Walid, who sat across from the *shaykh al-ḥizb*—the leader of the recitation—was, like many of his fellow reciters, chanting loudly in unison with the others while occasionally swaying, nodding his head, or gesturing upward with his hands during certain passages about God and the Prophet.

Thus began the ḥaḍra (lit. "presence"), the three-part devotional trance ritual of the 'Īsāwiyya.[1] The crowd of spectators surrounding the group to hear the ḥizb was considerably smaller than the one that later would attend the second part of the ceremony, called *shishtrī* (after the Andalusī poet 'Abū al-Ḥasan al-Shushtarī) and devoted to singing Andalusī songs, and the

1. Terms such as "al-'aml" (the work), "al-'āda" (the custom), and simply an "'Īsāwiyya" are also sometimes used to refer to the ceremony in its entirety. It is common for writers to use the term "ḥaḍra" to refer specifically to the music and trance section—that is, the third part of the ceremony—without providing a term for the ceremony as a whole. I prefer to use the term "ḥaḍra" for the entire ceremony (as well as the third part, from which it gets its name), not only because it is the most common colloquial designation, but also because it encourages comparison to ḥaḍra ceremonies of other Sufi orders across and beyond the Maghreb.

crowd size was downright negligible in comparison to the one that subsequently would assemble to witness its third and final part (called *ḥaḍra*, from which the ceremony gets its name), which involved dramatic acts of trance such as dancing with fire, rolling on cactus pads, and eating glass and nails. This trance state, grounded by insistent cyclic drumming and called *takhmīr* (roughly, "intoxication"),[2] is what many people think of when they hear the term "'Īsāwiyya."[3] Yet the ḥizb, despite its lack of drumming and outward manifestations of trance, is defined by 'Īsāwīs as foundational to their practice; it sets the stage for an aesthetics of sonic and spiritual transformation that develops throughout the ceremony.

Almost fifteen minutes into the ḥizb, the tempo of the unison recitation had more than doubled through a gradual increase from its initial 68 beats per minute to 166, and the tonal center of the phrase had risen almost an octave as it gradually ascended stepwise through pitch plateaus successively based on (roughly) C, D, E, F, G, G♯, A, A♯, and B. What began as unison chanting of long phrases of drawn-out syllables had gradually given way to short call-and-response phrases comprising rapid volleys of short syllables. The remarkable coordination of so many voices through the increase in tempo, pitch, and volume created a captivating sense of forward motion that had me wondering just how much faster, higher, and louder the group could go. At one point Walid was weeping, his hands wiping tears from his face between shouts of "Glory to the Eternal who always remains!" (*subḥān al-da'im lā yazūl!*), the line from which the ḥizb gets its name (see video ex. 2.1). "I always cry during the ḥizb. I can't control it," he told me a few years later, after we had become friends. "For me, takhmīr [the trance associated with the third and final section] begins with the ḥizb."

This statement emphasizes the holistic individual experience of ritual and reveals that takhmīr, a trance experience involving a heightened sense of spiritual focus and transcendence, is not limited to the final section of the ritual, where it appears most explicitly and dramatically. It also serves as a reminder that, even though 'Īsāwīs themselves (and thus this chapter) emphasize the sectionality of their ritual, that experience is unified through a sense of journey, with ebbs and flows within a robust teleological progres-

2. "Takhmīr," although derived from the word for wine (*khamr*), refers only to spiritual intoxication and is a general word for ritualized trance. The term is not used for alcohol-induced intoxication, which is called *sukrān*.

3. The swelling crowd size suggests that observers' fascination with takhmīr was as strong in the early twenty-first century as it was in the 1950s, when the French anthropologist Émile Dermenghem (1954) bemoaned outsiders' obsession with takhmīr, which he believed came at the expense of understanding the important religious work of the ḥizb, performed seated and a cappella, devoid of musical instruments and trance dancing.

sion. The three shades of meaning of the word "ṭarīqa"—as method, Sufi order, and path—fold together in ritual, and it is ritual musical form that guides participants through and shapes the path of their journey.

Therefore, in the pages that follow I, like most 'Īsāwīs I worked with, approach 'Īsāwiyya ritual by focusing on the intersection of sound and devotion, which entails accounting for the entire ritual process, a physically demanding and spiritually rewarding journey through time that is structured sonically. If the 'Īsāwiyya are perceived—from within and without—as exemplars of religious devotion, musical achievement, and the mysteries of trance, these three elements of 'Īsāwī identity can be loosely yet productively mapped onto its tripartite ritual musical structure that begins with a cappella chanting of the ḥizb, proceeds to Andalusī song in the shishtrī, and ends with the ḥaḍra, featuring the 'Īsāwiyya's highly distinctive music for its equally iconic takhmīr trance state (see fig. 2.4).

This case study suggests that musical form and ritual structure accomplish something, and therefore have agency: that is, they are revealing and constitutive of experience and encourage particular kinds of subjectivities. More specifically, the sonic-ritual form of the 'Īsāwiyya ḥaḍra encourages a particular kind of reflexive stance, one in which participants see themselves in relation to those three fields of Sufi recitation, Andalusī music, and ecstatic trance. This sequencing of ritual episodes relies on and encompasses in-the-moment adjustments and moments of articulation that highlight strong mutual coordination, enabling the group to produce and navigate changing temporalities and episodes of sonic and corporeal intensification. These forms of intensification, I argue, are at the heart of the ritual dispositions encouraged by the structuring of the ḥaḍra, creating a kind of "reverberant" reflexivity, to borrow a particularly apt term from Gobin and Vanhoenacker (2016).

TRANSLOCALITY AND REFLEXIVITY

Across the Maghreb, mention of the 'Īsāwiyya is bound to conjure images of intense drumming and singing, lines of men dancing in white robes, and dramatic trance episodes. It has strong working-class (*sha'bī*) associations and is considered by many to be at the "ecstatic" extreme of a continuum that has the ostensibly more "sober" Sufism of orders such as the Shādhuliyya at the opposite end. 'Īsāwiyya rituals, which often involve dancers testing their physical limits through extreme acts of trance, have a long history of attracting the attention of travelers, journalists, and scholars, many of whom grapple with reconciling what they construe to be a tension between religious devotion and spectacular theatricality (see, e.g., Andé-

FIGURE 2.1. ʿĪsāwiyya ḥaḍra. Individuals who fall into trance break away from the line of dancers (*ṣaff*) on the left and approach the circle (*ḥalqa*) of singers and drummers, where they are under the supervision of shaykhs patrolling the dance space. Photo by the author.

zian 1986; Dermenghem 1954: 303). In Tunis this duality is joined by a third consideration:[4] there the ʿĪsāwiyya also enjoy a reputation for cultivating a high level of musicianship, in part for their preservation and cultivation of *mālūf* the country's Andalusī art-music heritage.

Like most ṭarīqas in the Maghreb, the ʿĪsāwiyya is productively understood as a translocal phenomenon. That is, branches of the ʿĪsāwiyya are found across North Africa and share certain family resemblances,[5] but their methods, priorities, and range of social locations and functions may differ and produce localized meanings and associations. All branches of the ṭarīqa are unified in looking to Sīdī Ben ʿĪsā's life and teachings as a touchstone and inspiration. However, certain practices, ritual forms, musical instruments, melodies, rhythms, texts, and social roles may differ substantially not only

4. There are four main branches of the ʿĪsāwiyya in the greater Tunis area. Two are in coastal towns, Sīdī Bū Saʿīd and La Marsa; one is in the Tunis suburb of Ariana; and another is based at the shrine of Sīdī al-Ḥārī in the Tunis medina. Members of all branches may interact with one another at pilgrimages and ceremonies, particularly during the arbaʿtāsh season, and all four share the same overall ritual structures and textures described in this chapter.

5. The local terms for "branch" are *ḥizb* (pl. *aḥzāb*), not to be confused with the recitation that constitutes the first part of the ritual described in this chapter, and *firqa* (pl. *firāq*), a term that is also used for nonreligious musical troupes and thus reinforces the musical identity of the ʿĪsāwiyya (see Jones 1977: 24).

between, say, Morocco and Tunisia, but also within Tunisia itself.[6] An analytical approach based on ritual reflexivity is particularly useful for shedding light on such translocal phenomena as it reveals what is specific to, and particularly important for, those involved in any single ʿĪsāwiyya order. Reflexivity localizes and specifies. It is meant, I should emphasize, to suggest a range of perspectives and possibilities rather than a mirror that reflects. I am reminded of Victor Turner's evocative imagery as he argues that, in ritual, instead of in front of a single mirror,

> we find ourselves in a hall of mirrors, or rather of magic mirrors, some of which enlarge, others diminish, some distort and some have X-ray properties; each mirror is a cultural field and each after its own fashion receives images from all the others and passes them on transmuted or transmogrified. Within each culture is its own hall of mirrors. . . . But this reflexive potential is actualized most patently in the performative genres, which often quite consciously hold their mirrors not up to nature but to the pre-existing system of mirrors which is humankind-in-culture. Culture is *re*mirrored by one of its own extensions—ritual or art. And this may even result in the *de*-mirroring of the human incumbents of status-roles in the quotidian culture. (2016 [1983]: 340; emphases in original)

Metaphors can be useful starting points, and in this case Turner's mirror metaphor is a step toward overcoming the conceptual divide between ritual thought and ritual action, which has a long and influential legacy in anthropological scholarship. A number of studies challenge that divide by arguing

6. While only vocals and percussion instruments are utilized in the Tunis-based practices analyzed here, in the countryside the *zukra* (oboelike reed instrument) plays a prominent role in leading the musical troupe and shaping the ritual process, the ritual is more strictly organized according to the large-scale nūba form, and similar lyrics are often performed to very different melodies and rhythms (Jones 1977). The ʿĪsāwiyya of Banī Khiyyār, a coastal town on the Cap Bon Peninsula seventy-five kilometers from the capital, feature a clarinet (*karnīṭa*, introduced in the early twentieth when a clarinet player from the bey's military band replaced the troupe's zukra player, who had died) as the lead melodic instrument and a ritual structure notable for its lack of the ḥizb (Ben ʿAmor 2008). Comparison with the Moroccan ʿĪsāwiyya studied by Mehdi Nabti (2010), while illustrating certain spiritual themes, trance states, social contexts, and an overarching logic of sequential structuring comparable to the Tunis context, nevertheless also reveals pronounced differences in instrumentation, rhythmic and melodic modes, nomenclature, and certain ritual priorities. These three studies, coming from different schools of thought and language (English, Arabic, and French, respectively), are remarkable in their application of music-analytical methods to ʿĪsāwiyya ritual musics. What is less evident in these studies, however, is sustained attention to processes of intensification, the role and importance of repetition, virtues of coordination, and teleological transformation, as well as the reflexive aspects of ritual.

that ritual meanings and connotations emerge in their enactment: they are constituted through performance (Bell 1997: 76–83; Hobart and Kapferer 2005; Shannon 2006: 119). Turner reminds us that ritual reflexivity is about perception and possibility, and, in his final line, about individual transformation and the capacity to transcend oneself or even become other, two points that will be elaborated further in this book's considerations of trance.

The work of reflexivity in ritual is further illuminated by Bruce Kapferer's distinction between first-order and second-order reflexivity. First-order reflexivity occurs in the moment of decision making and relies on awareness of self and the needs and perceptions of others. It enables participants "to objectify their action and experience in the context of the rite, and to stand back or distance themselves from their action within the rite so they can reflect upon their own and others' actions and understandings" (Kapferer 1984: 180). This kind of reflexivity is particularly apparent in the healing rituals described in the following chapters, in which ritualists organize the musical repertoire based on a balance between the conventional ritual sequence and the needs of those seeking healing, who require specific songs for their protective saint (or afflicting spirit). In the ʿĪsāwiyya ceremony, it emerges in the concern for mutual coordination between singers and dancers, the caretaking of trancers, and self-referential passages that draw attention to the ritual work of the ceremony.

More immediately relevant to the large-scale structuring of ʿĪsāwiyya ritual is what Kapferer calls "second-level reflexivity," whereby ritual "reflect[s] back on other contexts of meaning in the performance setting or in the social and cultural world out of which ritual emerges" (1984: 181). The sectionality of the ḥaḍra, which follows a succession of distinct sonic-musical approaches, illustrates this clearly and was emphasized in numerous formal and informal conversations with members of the ʿĪsāwiyya. The three sections draw attention to three aspects of the ʿĪsāwiyya's location in Tunisian culture: the ḥizb asserts its "Sufi" credentials, the shishtrī highlights its prominent role in the cultivation of Andalusī music, and the ḥaḍra demonstrates its mastery of the secrets of trance. This sequence of three sections, in turn, produces a cumulative, teleological experience whereby different strategies of intensification are introduced in succession and finally merge as the ritual reaches its culmination. In other words, the ritual musical form of the ḥaḍra not only encourages cultural reflexivity; it also constitutes musical process.[7]

7. The idea of musical form as process has a long history in German Romantic thought on European art music, as Janet Schmalfeldt (2011) demonstrates. Schmalfeldt's own theory presents form in early nineteenth-century art music as a process of "becoming." Since Schmalfeldt (like some of her interlocutors) is mainly concerned with how main and sec-

PART I: THE ḤIZB RECITATION, INCIPIENT MUSICALITY, AND SUFI PEDIGREE

Walid's earliest memories of the 'Īsāwiyya are of hearing the recitation of the ḥizb as a child. In our many conversations, he identified the centrality of the ḥizb to what it means to him to be 'Īsāwī.

> The first time I learned of the 'Īsāwiyya, I was accompanying my father, God rest his soul. He brought me to the 'Īsāwiyya, where I found my uncle, my grandfather, and many of our neighbors reciting the ḥizb. So the first time I learned of the 'Īsāwiyya I learned of their ḥizb. In it there are many teachings, praises, and topics. From it I learned to recite the Qur'an. . . . I grew a bit older and wanted an explanation of the meaning of the ḥizb. I found there was nothing easy; you need training in the Arabic language, training on the level of doctrine, to understand the meaning of divine unity [*tawḥīd*]. (Pers. comm., 2014)

While the 'Īsāwiyya ḥizb is proprietary to the 'Īsāwiyya and is understood to encapsulate their teachings and methods of devotion, the fact that the 'Īsāwiyya cultivate a ḥizb practice is understood from within as evidence of, and a product of, their historical proximity to the Shādhuliyya, widely acknowledged as the earliest and most influential Sufi order in Tunis. Founded by Sīdī Belḥassen al-Shādhulī (1196–1258 CE),[8] the Shādhuliyya boasts a repertoire of eleven ḥizbs of its own that are the focus of its ḥaḍra (the Shādhuliyya do not use musical instruments or engage in music-driven trance rituals; see chap. 3).

On the first and last Thursday of this season, the 'Īsāwiyya visit the shrine of the Shādhuliyya (often simply called Sīdī Belḥassen) to perform their ḥaḍra. These two annual visits on auspicious dates reinforce a social rela-

---

ondary themes, recapitulations, cadences, codas, and other motivic, melodic, and harmonic material shape the compositional choices of individual composers, those concerns may seem far afield from the large-scale musical architecture of ritual I am analyzing here. Yet two aspects of her spirit of inquiry are worth noting for their relevance: first, there is no sense of form without culturally available norms shared by performers and listeners; and, second, conceptions of form rely on a Husserlian sense of protention and retention (i.e., we understand what we hear now based on what we heard earlier and what we expect to hear in the future). In other words, form is less a fixed container or set of partitions than it is an emergent process of revealing.

8. The transliteration of al-Shādhulī and Shādhuliyya reflects local pronunciation and the transliteration choices of Tunisian scholars. The more common transliterations, standard in text-based scholarship in English and French, are Shādhilī and Shādhiliyya.

tionship between the two ṭarīqas that some perceive as mutually opposed or incompatible in their practices and teachings.[9] Yet it is in their cultivation of the ḥizb that the ʿĪsāwiyya most consistently associate their ṭarīqa with the Shādhuliyya. According to Marouene Meski, *shaykh al-ʿaml* (the lead singer; lit. "shaykh of the work") of the ʿĪsāwiyya of the Ariana neighborhood:

> The first part is very, very important . . . you begin with the ḥizb. The first ḥizb is made up of the ayāt of the Qur'an and *awrād* [sing. *wird*; some of the litanies in the ḥizb]. The awrād were not written by Sīdī Ben ʿĪsā but rather by his shaykh, Sīdī Ḥmīd Jazūlī. He was the teacher of Sīdī Ben ʿĪsā. And who was Jazūlī's teacher? Sīdī Belḥassen al-Shādhulī. The ʿĪsāwiyya is a Shādhulī ṭarīqa. Just as the Sulāmiyya, the Qādiriyya, the Ṭaybiyya, and all Tunisian ṭarīqas are from the Shādhuliyya . . . the ʿĪsāwiyya traces its ancestry [*tinsib*] to the Shādhuliyya.[10] (Pers. comm., 2012)

Meski's remarks suggest that the ḥizb carries not only a great deal of spiritual capital, but also social capital that situates the ʿĪsāwiyya squarely within the broader ecology of Sufism and especially close to the Shādhuliyya. Yet the high standard set by the Shādhuliyya also provides a point of self-reflexive critique for some ʿĪsāwis. Walid bemoans the fact that, of the five ʿĪsāwī ḥizbs, only one is currently in use: "Except for a few [ʿĪsāwīs], there is nobody who sits [weekly] reading the litanies (*awrād*), doing the *taṣbīḥ* (recitations counted with prayer beads), or reciting the ḥizbs. Many are just playing around. . . . The opposite example is the Shādhuliyya ṭarīqa, [at] the shrine of Sīdī Belḥassen in Tunis. There, the men are diligent in performing the ḥizbs, diligent in reciting the Qur'an" (pers. comm., 2014).

The text of the ḥizb is inseparable from its sonic enactment in performance.[11] It gains meaning by its communal performance and is shaped by the ebbs and flows, contrasts and continuities, and intensifications and trajectories of its sonic form.[12] While the ḥizb stands as a kind of starting point

9. Geoffroy (1996), for instance, considers the Shādhuliyya to be the "inverse" of the ʿĪsāwiyya, ascribing to the former a philosophy and practice of "instancy" and to the latter one of "ecstasy."

10. Trimingham (1998) provides a more exhaustive catalog of Sufi orders related to the Shādhuliyya and details the influence of al-Jazūlī in North African Sufism.

11. The five ḥizbs of the ʿĪsāwiyya are collected in a 114-page manual that is separate from the *sfīna* (lit. "vessel"), the collection of sung texts. The only ḥizb currently in use is *ḥizb subḥān al-da'im*, although, at the time of writing, Walid informed me he was attempting to revive the study and performance of the other four ḥizbs.

12. In many respects, the performance of the ḥizb is thus similar to the Aleppine dhikr ceremony described by Jonathan Shannon as "moral-musical conditioning," which relies on

of a larger ritual arc, the first ritual episode preceding the others, it also has its own teleology and internal dynamics of repetition, intensification, and development that make it complete unto itself. By commencing the entire ritual, it also announces a particular kind of religiosity, one that firmly situates the ʿĪsāwiyya within a devotional landscape shared with even the most conservative of other Sufi orders in the region. In the ʿĪsāwiyya ḥizb there is no dance, nothing ʿĪsāwis describe as musical pieces, so it is beyond the reproach of any critic who sees the most conservative ṭarīqas, such as the Shādhuliyya, as exemplars of proper, moderate Sufi practice. The formal features and sonic textures of the ʿĪsāwiyya ḥizb share family resemblances with those of the Shādhuliyya, and both involve the communal chanting of praises to God, the Prophet, and numerous saints. For those ʿIsāwīs who separate out "Sufi" from "ṭuruqī" practices (such as Walid, who told me, "After we finish the ḥizb, I see that as the end of the 'Sufi' work"; pers. comm., 2012), the ḥizb is considered the Sufi part (that is, adhering to aesthetic principles of vocal recitation shared with other Sufi orders) of a ritual that then turns to musicality and dance marked as ṭuruqī (that is, performance practices associated with specific historical developments of a given Sufi order).

Sonic-Musical Elements of the Ḥizb

The ḥizb is a composite form that seamlessly incorporates various forms of Islamic language performance.[13] Beginning with the opening verse of the Qur'an, with short Qur'anic passages occasionally worked into the text, it presents not only a long litany of names of saints and Sufis, but also passages of *dhikr*—repeated formulas of *lā ilaha illā allah* (there is no god but God) or *allah* or *huwa* (He). A sonic form full of internal contrasts as well as thoroughgoing strategies of intensification, it is performed as a single event with no pauses, requiring great physical stamina on the part of the reciters (*ḥzāba*), whose performance is also supported by the unceasing progress of the entire group.

In many ways the ḥizb stands apart from the other more explicitly "musical" aspects of the ceremony. Conventional musical terms such as "musi-

---

aesthetic practices that "move participants toward a state (ephemeral, always in need of reenactment) of remembering their higher Self and the divine truths of existence" (2006: 120).

13. See Frishkopf (2013) on the utility of approaching all Islamic ritual as unified within the framework of language performance (LP), which emphasizes the centrality of performed text and is proposed as a basis for comparative analysis according to a ritual's sonic, syntactic, semantic, and pragmatic components.

cal piece" (*qiṭa'a, nūba*), "melodic mode" (*ṭab'* or *maqām*), and "rhythmic mode" (*mīzān* or *īqā'a*) are not used in discourse about the ḥizb. The verb used for performing the ḥizb is "recite" (*yaqrā'*, also "read"). Yet the ḥizb exhibits a marked musicality, with a distinctive temporality, sense of development, and methods of intensification. In terms of pitch and melody, the ḥizb features a strong sense of tonal center with consistent intervallic relationships. Motion tends to be stepwise, in intervals of half, whole, and one and a half steps. Most phrases utilize three pitches, although a few expand to five, while some use only two. Rhythmically there is a strong sense of beat regularity but varying degrees of metric regularity: call-and-response sections tend to be strongly metric, dividing, for example, 32 or 16 beats into equal halves, while some unison sections have a freer metric feel, with irregular phrase lengths (e.g., of 11, 35, 58, 41 beats, among others), albeit with a strong sense of regular pulse.

What I am most interested in here, however, is the total structure of the ḥizb performance, particularly its trajectories of intensification, in order to get at the distinctive rhythmic, temporal, textural, and tonal developments that give the performance its experiential sense of journey and transformation. The main trajectory is one of increasing tempo, pitch, and sonic density. This is marked by (1) gradual, but occasionally abrupt, increases in tempo; (2) tonal modulations that ascend stepwise but are also partially the product of gradual microtonal leanings upward; and (3) a shift from unison singing to the antiphonal call and response of shorter and shorter phrases.[14] These intensifications, however, are not wholly unidirectional. There are occasional delays, decelerations, descents, and returns to unison singing, albeit mainly in preparation for even more extreme intensifications.

Establishing a Sonic and Spiritual Foundation: The Fātiḥa

The *fātiḥa* (lit. "opening") is the first chapter of the Qur'an. This seven-line verse is a foundational text in Islam and an essential part of each of the five daily prayers. Simultaneously a praise of God and a plea for guidance, it is treated by many Muslims as a summary of Islamic worship, and its recitation is considered an index of Islamic piety. It is recited at the beginning of Sufi ceremonies as well as many other rituals, announcing not only the "opening" of the ritual itself, but also that what follows is done in the name of God. Indeed, in the context of 'Īsāwiyya ritual, beginning with the fātiḥa actualizes the assertion made in so many 'Īsāwiyya songs (from later sec-

14. Terms such as "yasra'" (speed up), "yaṭla" (rise), and "tadrīji" (gradually) are commonly applied to such processes.

tions of the ḥaḍra) that begin with the line *nibtadā bismillah* (we begin in the name of God).

bismillah al-raḥmān al-raḥīm	In the name of God, the compassionate and merciful
al-ḥamdu lillahi rabbi al-ʿālamīn	praise be to God, Lord of the worlds
al-raḥmān al-raḥīm	the compassionate, the merciful
māliki yawmi al-dīn	master of the day of judgment
iyyāka naʿbūdu wa-iyyāka nastaʿīn	you we worship and from you we seek help
ihadinā al-ṣirāṭ al-mustaqīm	guide us upon the straight path
ṣirāṭ alladhīna anʿamta ʿalayhim ghayr	the path of those you have blessed, not of those who
al-maghḍūbi ʿalayhim walā al-ḍālīna	incur wrath or who are astray

(based on Nasr 2015)

In many rituals, notably the silsila-based practices discussed in subsequent chapters, the fātiḥa is recited immediately before, and separately from, the performance material that follows it. In the ʿĪsāwiyya ḥaḍra, however, not only is the fātiḥa wholly integrated into the beginning of the ḥizb, but also the development of the rest of the ḥizb depends on incipient references and sonic material that appear in the fātiḥa section. The ʿĪsāwiyya recitation style of the fātiḥa establishes (1) a low tonal center and (2) a slow tempo, both of which make possible the process of intensification through rising pitch and increase in speed. In addition, it (3) creates an association between slow tempo and unison vocal texture, which later will contrast with call-and-response texture at faster tempos. Finally, it (4) sets a precedent for the distinctive strategy of modulating, introducing, or otherwise shifting sonic material in the middle (rather than the beginning) of a passage.

The fātiḥa (audio ex. 2.1)—and thus the ḥizb—begins low and slow: at 66 beats per minute, it establishes a tonal center on D, reaching to the C below at the end of each phrase to lead back up to D. Phrase length is determined by the number and treatment of syllables in the text; the seven lines of the fātiḥa create phrases of 11, 14, 8, 7, 16, 11, and 35 beats.[15] The entire fātiḥa is performed three times; according to Walid, the first is for God, the second is for the Prophet, and the third is for the saints (pers. comm., 2018). The tempo increases gradually, reaching 80 bpm by the end of the third itera-

15. The last phrase is truncated to thirty-three beats in the third repetition as it transitions to the subsequent section.

tion. With each repeat, a stepwise modulation raises the tonal center by a whole step, from C–**D**–E to D–**E**–F♯ to E–**F♯**–G♯ (the pitches in boldface are the tonal centers). How this is achieved is a distinctive feature of ʿĪsāwiyya tonal-formal style: the rising modulations begin not at the beginning of each repeat, but at specific points in the middle of the text (see boxes A and B in musical ex. 2.1). Musical example 2.1 illustrates these stepwise upward modulations, their occurrence in the middle of phrases, the text-driven irregular metric pattern, and the gradual increase in tempo.[16]

Intensification 1: Tempo and Pitch Transformations

Each repetition, then, brings the reciters somewhere: to a faster tempo, to a higher tonal center. Repetition, and thus cyclicity,[17] create the conditions for change. It is not a mere succession of "sames," because each repeat is understood in relation to what came before it while creating expectations for what comes next.[18] Moreover, repetition in the ḥizb—and throughout the ḥaḍra—is associated with temporal and pitch transformations that are inseparable from spiritual transformation.[19] While repetition creates this sense of flow, it also keeps the reciters in place, focused on a single textual passage. According to Walid, threefold repetition—which is common

16. The fātiḥa is followed seamlessly by two short invocations. The first is the *istiʿādha*, a short standard phrase uttered before prayers and supplications, or anytime an individual seeks to ward off malevolent spirits or the devil: "I seek refuge in God from the accursed Satan" (*aʿūdhu billahi min al-shayṭān al-rajīm*). This seventeen-beat phrase is followed by a fifty-eight-beat prayer glorifying the Prophet: "In the name of God, the merciful and compassionate, praise and bless our lord Muhammad and his companions." The first three words reprise the very first phrase of the fātiḥa, with the words "bismillah al-raḥmān al-raḥīm" sung in the same short-short-long rhythm (see musical ex. 2.1), but now a fourth above the original (G instead of D) and at 97 bpm, a parallelism reinforcing the sense of systematic, yet gradual, increases in both tempo and tonal center.

17. "Repetition" here refers to specific iterations of a single musical or lyrical phrase, while "cyclicity" is a large-scale formal principle produced as a result of extended repetition of such phrases. Neither repetition nor cyclicity, it should be emphasized, should be understood as unchanging; rather, they should be seen as constants that carry with them potential for transformation.

18. This supports Don Ihde's argument, drawing on Husserl's philosophy of time, that the listening experience holds traces of the past (retention) and anticipation of future events (protention; Ihde 2007).

19. A point made by Jonathan Shannon in his study of the Aleppine dhikr: "From an aesthetic standpoint . . . transcendence comes about from the perception of temporal transformations in the course of dhikr, specifically from the combined effects of [upward] melodic modulation and rhythmic acceleration" (2004: 387). The widespread distribution of this combination of increases in pitch and tempo in Sufi recitation across the Islamic world is an important reason some ʿĪsāwīs single out the ḥizb as representing their "Sufi" work.

MUSICAL EXAMPLE 2.1. Transcription of the fātiḥa (opening verse of the Qur'an) as performed by the 'Īsāwiyya of La Marsa (audio ex. 2.1). Boxes A and B indicate onsets of upward modulations in pitch levels.

throughout the ʿĪsāwiyya ḥaḍra—encourages the internalization of textual meaning: the first time produces enjoyment, the second reinforces the meaning, and the third results in deeper internalization of the meaning (pers. comm., 2012). Repetition, from this perspective, has the dual capacity to provide stability and the comfort of constancy, on the one hand, while also creating a sense of movement and forward direction, on the other.

By now, the ḥizb has established a baseline set of tendencies and expectations in the domains of tempo (beginning slow and gradually accelerating), register (beginning low and gradually rising), intervals (whole step and half step), texture (unison recitation), repetition (text and melody repeated three times), and modulations (stepwise, *in medias res*). These tendencies continue through the first eight sections of text following the fātiḥa, as the tempo increases from 68 to 131 bpm, and the tonal center rises through D, E, F♯, G, A, B♭, and B♮ (see text, table, and analysis on accompanying website).

Then the rate and style of intensification shift abruptly. The circle of reciters, who had been reciting in unison, splits into two complementary groups, the callers (*qawwāla*) and responders (*raddāda*). The callers intone a litany of attributes of God (beginning with "the Mighty endowed with majesty"), to which the responders reply "there is no god but God" (*lā ilaha illā allah*). Musical examples 2.2 and 2.3 (audio exx. 2.2 and 2.3) illustrate the relentless acceleration of the call-and-response passages from 121 bpm to 280 bpm.

The ḥizb thus undergoes discrete intensification: individual, discrete musical units that are internal to a larger whole are repeated to produce gradual transformations. Here, two systematic processes increase intensity: changes in temporality through acceleration and changes in pitch plateaus through upward tonal movement. Taken together, musical examples 2.1, 2.2, and 2.3 illustrate the simultaneity of acceleration and pitch rise throughout the first half of the ḥizb, revealing the dual process of *discrete temporal and pitch intensification* (DTPI).

A final surge of intensity in the ḥizb maintains the DTPI process while introducing a metric compression that reduces a four-beat phrase to three beats.[20] At this point the reciters all stand up shoulder to shoulder in a circle to begin the dhikr.[21] They recite the name "Allah" in a call-and-response

20. This concluding intensification occurs after a marked deceleration and drop in pitch. See audio exx. 2.4 and 2.5 on the accompanying website.

21. While the term "dhikr" (usually glossed as "remembrance") is often used elsewhere in the Islamic world to refer to a Sufi ceremony, it is used in a general sense by ʿĪsāwīs to refer to extended recitations of the name(s) or attributes of God, and specifically to this concluding section of their ḥizb.

MUSICAL EXAMPLE 2.2. Call-and-response accelerando at 12:50–14:02 of the ḥizb (audio ex. 2.2). Note the high degree of acceleration in the course of twelve iterations of the short sixteen-beat melody.

MUSICAL EXAMPLE 2.3. Call-and-response further accelerando, highest pitch, and widest ambitus at 16:02–19:13 of the ḥizb. Melody and rhythm are general contours; small variations occur throughout the section (audio ex. 2.3).

manner, with every second participant in the circle bending down and reciting the syllable "Al-", followed by the other participants bending down and completing the name by reciting the syllable "-lah" a whole-step higher as the first group bends back up again. The tempo gradually rises, starting at 66 bpm and ending at 308 bpm by the 230th repetition.

Accompanying this massive increase in tempo is a pronounced sense of temporal compression as the number of beats in each iteration decreases from four to three (see m. 7 in musical ex. 2.4). This compression of the rhythmic cycle is a principle of intensification that reappears in various guises throughout the ceremony and, indeed, is a characteristic feature elsewhere in the sonic landscape of ambient Sufism. As the tempo reaches its zenith, the reciters cease bending forward and instead jump slightly in unison, beating their chest with the right hand over their hearts on the first syllable. Throughout this passage the pitch gradually rises, from a low of G♭ to a high of E♭, as the phrase "al-lah" undergoes upward half-step-wise modulations. The dhikr is a full encapsulation of the DTPI model (audio ex. 2.6).

The dhikr's vocal hocket, physical movements, rising pitch, and extremes of tempo require remarkable individual stamina and group coordination. In addition to embodying the tempo and pitch transformations of the ḥizb, the dhikr also encapsulates the ḥizb's participatory demands on vocal stamina, cue recognition, and mutual attunement. Appearing at the end of a forty-minute performance, it serves as the third and final major intensification of

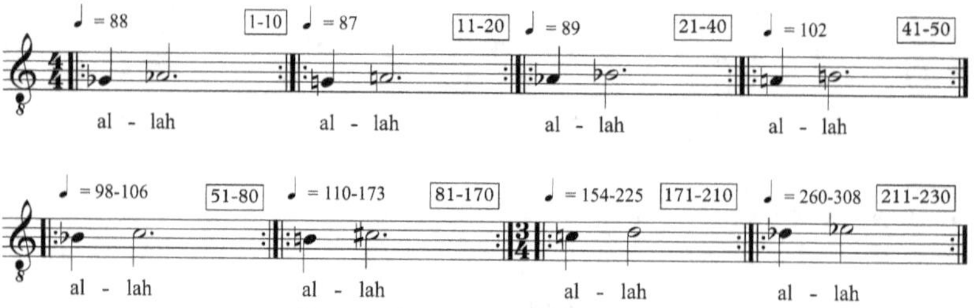

MUSICAL EXAMPLE 2.4. Increase in tempo and rise in pitch of the concluding dhikr of the ḥizb. Tempo ranges indicate starting and ending tempos, respectively, while numbers in boxes account for the 230 repetitions. Pitches represent the most stable tonal plateaus of each section; pitch rises are often gradual upward microtonal movements that produce ambiguities not apparent in staff notation.

tempo (see fig. 2.2).[22] Although it takes great individual stamina to perform the ḥizb at a consistently loud volume and extremes of tempo that reach 280, 395, and 308 beats per minute, the intensity increases systematically until the very end. Walid, in describing the ritual experience as a "journey" (*riḥla*), told me that the excitement and acceleration were akin to a physical journey by foot in which the destination comes into sight and the travelers, excited by the prospect of arrival, increase their speed to make the final surge to reach it (pers. comm., 2018).

Here the ḥizb introduces a physically demanding mode of performance that will culminate in the pushing of the limits of an individual's body later in the trance section of the ceremony. Yet the separation of the ḥizb as introductory is not entirely accurate for all participants. As mentioned at the beginning of this chapter, Walid attests that, for him, trance (takhmīr) begins in the ḥizb. He feels part of something bigger than himself, feels the power of spiritual truths, and cries uncontrollably (pers. comm., 2014): "For me, takhmīr begins as soon as the fātiḥa is recited. There is a spiritual connection [*itiṣāl rūḥī*] to God. We know that in Islam we don't have any intermediaries, no preachers, no priests or other men of God to say 'give me forgiveness.' There is no veil. If I want to call on God, I call on God. [In the ḥizb] I am far from Satan, far from the *jnūn* [spirits]" (pers. comm., 2012).

Group coordination is part of the power of the ḥaḍra. It is a real-time construction of social relationships based on fellow feeling and mutual purpose. According to Walid, one of the distinctive and profound characteristics of the ʿĪsāwiyya is this coordination: "In other music you don't find

22. It remains an open question whether the standardized pattern of three episodes of intensification built into the ʿĪsāwiyya ḥizb performance relate to the ṭarīqa's valuing of threefold repetition described earlier in this section.

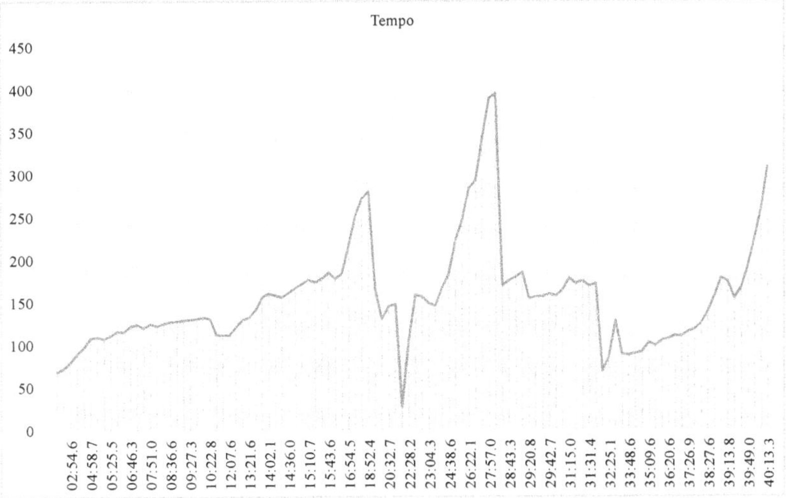

FIGURE 2.2. Tempo graph of ḥizb

the close relationship among singers that enables them to adapt [to each other] and change on the spot" (pers. comm., 2014). For him, this reflects the sense of community within the ṭarīqa, which he recalls with fondness when discussing his earliest memories of attending 'Īsāwiyya ceremonies with his father: "When I was three years old, I heard something beautiful. I saw a group of people gathered together who loved each other [*yuḥibbū ba'duhum*]. And it seemed to me that the reason was because of the 'Īsāwiyya. And any Sufi ṭarīqa that spread across the country, the people love each other. The Prophet (peace and blessings upon him) told us: love your brother as you love yourself" (pers. comm., 2014). Collective performance in the 'Īsāwiyya ḥaḍra enacts, depends upon, and reproduces this community. That community may be at once local, familial, and devotional. Yet it also extends into, and is legitimized by, its location within a much broader geohistorical field of Sufi figures, one that is brought into the here and now through reflexive, textual techniques of memory, to which I now turn.

The Ḥizb and the Art of Memory

The hizb tests not only the limits of individual stamina and group coordination, but also memory: it is performed without written texts. The most rhythmically and textually dense section of the ḥizb (see text below) carries semantic messages that are particularly poignant for the 'Īsāwiyya. The recitation involves a litany of names of holy people, calling forth a field of historical spiritual references into the present.[23] Reaching back to the seventh century with the reference to al-Baṣrī, this litany provides a historical and geographical tour of the landscape of Sufis and other holy figures including widely renowned Sufi figures such as Junayd (d. 911, Baghdad) and al-Ghazālī (d. 1111, Tus, Persia), saints influential in the Moroccan milieu where the ʿĪsāwiyya first emerged (such as Abū Yaʿza, Abū Muḥammad, and al-Jazūlī), and founders of North African Sufi orders with a widespread presence in Tunis, such as the Qādiriyya, Sulāmiyya, and Shādhuliyya. While some of the more obscure names may not be recognized by all participants (see Johnson 1979: 85), they are brought into the present in oral performance, where they contribute to the construction of a wide geohistorical landscape of spiritual figures within which contemporary ʿĪsāwis situate themselves.

bi-ʿabd al-salām / yā ilahī / w-abī salhām / yā ilahī	By ʿAbd al-Salām / O my God / and Abū Salhām / O my God
bil-shādhulī / yā ilahī / wal-ghazālī / yā ilahī	by al-Shādhulī / O my God / and al-Ghazālī / O my God
abī madyan / yā ilahī / w-abī yaʿzī / yā ilahī	Abū Madyan / O my God / and Abū Yaʿzī / O my God
abī shʿaīb / yā ilahī / w-abī mahdī / yā ilahī	Abū Shaʿīb / O my God / and Abū Mahdī / O my God
sīdī mālik / yā ilahī / w-abī muḥammad / yā ilahī	Sīdī Mālik / O my God / and Abū Muḥammad / O my God
abī ibrahīm / yā ilahī / w-abī ilyās / yā ilahī	Abū Ibrahīm / O my God / and Abū Ilyās / O my God
abī al-ʿābās / yā ilahī / bi-sīdī jākīr / yā ilahī	Abū al-ʿĀbās / O my God / by Sīdī Jākīr / O my God
abī zakrī / yā ilahī / w-abī dāwid / yā ilahī	Abū Zakrī / O my God / and Abū Dāwid / O my God
ibn baqā / yā ilahī / w-abī muḥammad / yā ilahī	Ibn Baqā / O my God / and Abū Muḥammad / O my God
bi-sīdī muḥammad / yā ilahī / bi-sīdī aḥmad / yā ilahī	by Sīdī Muḥammad / O my God / and Sīdī Aḥmad / O my God
bi-sīdī muḥammad / yā ilahī / abī mahdī / yā ilahī	by Sīdī Muḥammad / O my God / Abū Mahdī / O my God

23. This genealogical litany of names is called a *silsila*, not to be confused with (although related in terms of the general principles of spiritual relationships to) the silsila ritual musical form examined in subsequent chapters.

abī mahdī / yā ilahī / bi-sīdī muḥammad / yā ilahī	Abū Mahdī / O my God / by Sīdī Muḥammad / O my God
al-jazūlī / shay'in lillah / bi-sīdī muḥammad / yā ilahī	al-Jazūlī / God's follower / by Sīdī Muḥammad / O my God
bi-sīdī ḥanīnī / lā ilahī	by Sīdī Ḥanīnī / O my God
baraka al-sādāt / yā ilahī / m'anā tḥaḍir / yā ilahī . . . [repeated three times]	the blessing of the saints / O my God / be present with us / O my God . . .

(see also Johnson 1979)

The ḥizb sets up an interpretive frame (Bateson 1972 [1955]) through which it and subsequent events in the ritual are understood. It does so by introducing and emphasizing both textual and sonic baselines or precedents for the rest of the ritual that, in turn, lie at the heart of the ritual's reflexivity. Textually, this part of the ḥizb serves more or less explicitly as a means of reifying a kind of continuity between contemporary 'Īsāwī practice and the values and practices associated with Sufi figures from a remarkably expansive historical and geocultural field. Indeed, all these figures, and particularly Sīdī Ben 'Īsā (who is also referred to in this section as Sīdī Ḥanīnī, Sīdī Muḥammad, Ibn 'Īsā, and Sīdī), are called upon to enter the ritual space through the repeated appeal to "be present with us" (*taḥḍir ma'nā*). The verb "taḥḍir" (be present) is a cognate of "maḥḍar" (assembly), a term that also appears in this section, as well as of "ḥaḍra" (presence), the term for the entire ritual ceremony as well as the third and final section featuring trance. The centripetal forces of these calls thus enact Kapferer's second-order reflexivity, whereby ritual encourages a particular kind of self-understanding, one that, in this case, reflects back on a wider social and spiritual historical landscape. These figures are nodes in a constellation of spiritual references for the 'Īsāwiyya, who performatively absorb those figures into their own history and lineage with each recitation.

All these figures also share ritual performative space with the message of oneness and unity (*tawḥīd*) emphasized in other passages and especially in the various approaches to dhikr embedded in the ḥizb, reinforcing the Sufi stance that there is no contradiction between the theology of tawḥīd and the recognition of the spiritual power of Muslim saints. Yet how the oneness of God and the saints in their plurality is evoked is also crucial. Sonically, both oneness and plurality are performed in a recitation style that is the fastest, most energetic, and most reliant on the highest level of intragroup coordination—in other words, where intensification reaches its peak. Just as sonic temporal units compress during this process of DI, so too does the recited text condense in form, narrowing its scope to shorter and shorter phrases intoning the names of God, the Prophet, and saints, as well as the call for them to "be with us," for these most intense culminating passages. The unquestionably "religious" nature of the ḥizb texts and a cappella texture provide it not only with an irreproachable spiritual identity, but also with one that sanctions a particular kind of musicality, one featuring specific approaches to coordination, repetition, and intensification that are found in other parts of the ḥaḍra. Recitation of the ḥizb thus acts reflexively as an internalization of the virtues of repetition, acceleration, intensification, and coordination that are at the heart of its sonic performance and that reappear, in various guises, in subsequent sections of the ritual.

PART II: THE SHISHTRĪ SECTION AND ANDALUSĪ MUSICALITY

Through its vocal recitation of a text comprised of praises to God, prophets, and saints, as well as Qur'anic passages and references to a vast geohistorical landscape of esteemed Sufi figures, the ḥizb asserts a particular kind of religiosity, one that overtly situates the 'Īsāwiyya within a widely respected domain of Sufi ritual practice. The shishtrī section that follows it, in contrast, represents what in many respects is a very different aspect of 'Īsāwī identity: one linked to a history of cultivating the Andalusī music called *mālūf*, Tunisia's art-music tradition. While the text of the ḥizb is overt and explicit in its declarations of religious devotion, the shishtrī often involves the musical setting of poetic texts that may not be explicitly about God or devotion but rather about worldly love, wine, and other themes common in Arabic poetry that are connected to the region's Andalusian heritage and open to metaphorical religious interpretations.

In featuring Andalusī poetry and mālūf musical modes, melodies, and structures, the shishtrī section of 'Īsāwiyya ritual connects to perhaps the most widespread and prestigious of poetic and musical expressions in the region. The role of music here is multifaceted: 'Īsāwīs have told me it serves many functions, from pedagogical tool and freer of the mind to attraction for new initiates and example of finding God everywhere, yet is reducible to none. It also localizes 'Īsāwiyya Sufism. While the recitation of the ḥizb and the drumming and singing of the ḥaḍra are proprietary to Sufi contexts, mālūf is heard in many contexts, from concerts and festival stages to national radio and television broadcasts and private recordings. Its repertoire is performed by media stars as well as schoolchildren and adults taking part in private and state-sponsored cultural institutions such as the "houses of culture" (*diyyār thaqāfa*) that brought mālūf to the furthest reaches of the country (Davis 2004). Mālūf, then, is characterized by a sense of widespread familiarity. This sense of familiarity, of being at home, is a theme that emerges from Walid's take on the role of the 'Īsāwiyya in the town of La Marsa. He suggests that familiarity with the sounds of mālūf can even serve as a surrogate for kin relations connecting people to the 'Īsāwiyya:

> We are now in the year 2014. What is the 'Īsāwiyya ṭarīqa's remaining presence in Tunisian society? In La Marsa [a northern coastal suburb of Tunis], you could say that the 'Īsāwiyya is part of the Marsawī identity. They love the 'Īsāwiyya. Because if it wasn't one's grandfather, it was his maternal uncle. If it wasn't his maternal uncle, it was his paternal uncle. If there wasn't anyone in his family, then it was his neighbor. And if he didn't have anyone at all, it would happen that he would hear the 'Īsāwiyya at people's homes—we still have 'Īsāwiyyas in people's homes—and he'd hear something. Something coming out of the mālūf, out of the music he knows today. (Pers. comm., 2014)

While mālūf localizes, it does so through its geohistorical reach to medieval Andalusia, considered across North Africa to be a "lost paradise" representing a pinnacle of Arab cultural achievement from which mālūf emerged (Glasser 2016a; see also Davis 2004; Shannon 2015). The ritual section called *shishtrī* explicitly activates that link, evoking one of the most influential Andalusī Sufis.

Musical Linkages: Shishtrī and Mālūf

Abū al-Ḥasan al-Shushtarī (1212–1269) is a figure of paramount importance in North African Sufism. A celebrated medieval Andalusī poet-composer, he is credited with being the first to compose mystical verses in the colloquial *zajal* poetic form, which, along with the *muwashshaḥ*, revolutionized Arabic poetry by prioritizing local vernaculars over the "high" register of Arabic represented by the monorhymed *qaṣīda* form. Importantly, the muwashshaḥ and particularly the zajal are poetic forms that are designed to be sung, and together they form the lyrical basis for Andalusī musical practices across North Africa. By presenting mystical ideas and imagery in an attractive, singable, vernacular form, al-Shushtarī played a key role in popularizing Sufism, making it widely accessible and reinforcing the association between musical performance and Sufi practices (Alvarez 2009).[24]

24. Al-Shushtarī lived during a tumultuous time in al-Andalus and North Africa. As the Christians reconquered Cordoba and al-Andalus was beset by drought, plague, and famine,

While the shishtrī section of the ʿĪsāwiyya ceremony involves the singing of poems attributed to al-Shushtarī, it draws on a broader repertoire of Andalusī music that came to be called mālūf. In the late sixteenth and early seventeenth centuries, a Sufi named Sīdī Qashshāsh is credited with introducing Andalusī musical practice into the Sufi shrines of Tunis, utilizing the *ṭār* (tambourine) and *rebāb* (upright fiddle) in his ceremonies. Qashshāsh's contemporaries, such as Sīdī ʿAbd al-Salām (founder of the Sulāmiyya Sufi order; d.1573) and Qashshāsh's disciple Sīdī ʿĀmār (founder of the ʿAwāmriyya Sufi order; d. 1638), also adopted Andalusī musical practices in their ceremonies (Jones 1977: 16; see also Saidani 2006: 22). For the ʿĪsāwiyya today, the shishtrī part of ritual is less about a specific repertoire of poems exclusively by al-Shushtarī (although it does include some of those) and more about the figure of al-Shushtarī as a link to al-Andalus and a forebear in bringing Andalusī musical aesthetics and mystical lyrics full of metaphors of intoxication into Sufi contexts.

ʿĪsāwīs refer to the mālūf they cultivate as "serious mālūf" (*mālūf al-jidd*), in contrast to its so-called secular art-music counterpart, which they refer to as "light" or "nonsense mālūf" (*mālūf al-hals*).[25] Today, the two strains of mālūf could be described in binary terms that offer maximal contrast: while the latter is often performed in concerts on prestigious stages by large orchestras, is taught in public and private conservatories, and enjoys a history of government patronage and a published canon of musical notation, the former is sung by a circle of Sufis in a shrine, accompanying themselves on only small kettledrums (*naqqārāt*) and ṭār, and who learned through oral tradition (although texts are circulated internally) and perform the music as a transition between the ḥizb and the trance section of a Sufi ritual. Such a stark image of difference, however, belies the musical system the so-called sacred and secular approaches share and a history in which the lines between the two often blurred. The musical system is made up of many shared songs in the same melodic and rhythmic modes, often with the same lyrics (which may be reinterpreted as religious in the Sufi context), and is

a religious revival took place that included a strong mystical tendency. Al-Shushtarī traveled across North Africa, with one biographer noting stays in Tunis and Gabès before he settled in Egypt, where he died in 1269. His circle of followers was absorbed into the Shādhuliyya ṭarīqa, which continues to sing his poems in Egypt (Alvarez 2009).

25. Although the term "hals" connotes "nonsense" in this context, this should not be interpreted as a dismissive opinion of non-Sufi mālūf. Indeed, all the Sufis I worked with were proud of their contribution to the wider field of Andalusī music that they share with their so-called secular counterparts. Non-Sufi art-music performers and commentators also use a similar term that connotes joking and fun (*mālūf al-hazl*) to refer to mālūf as an art-music practice, which they contrast with what they call the "raw" or "artless" mālūf (*mālūf al-khām*) of Sufis.

organized into a large-scale form called *nūba* in which a series of individual pieces in one melodic mode progress through a series of different rhythmic modes.[26] The shared history includes Sufi mālūf groups that performed outside the shrine, sometimes with melody instruments, at cafés or family celebrations for the wider community, while some of the most influential Tunisian musicians and scholars learned mālūf inside the Sufi shrine.[27]

The mālūf of the 'Īsāwiyya not only shares a modal system with the mālūf of coffeehouses and conservatories, but also preserves certain elements of that system that have otherwise vanished. The mode *rahāwī*, for example, is understood by many Tunisian musicologists and musicians to have "disappeared" from the mālūf, with the 'Īsāwiyya preserving the last vestiges of the mode (Guettat 1980: 217; Louati 2012: 265). Just as important to the 'Īsāwis with whom I worked was their sense that the 'Īsāwiyya cultivated deep knowledge and performative mastery of the Tunisian modal system. On a broad scale, the shishtrī and ḥaḍra sections (that is, the second and third parts of the ceremony) are conceptually organized musically, like mālūf, into a nūba form based on unity of melodic mode and diversity of rhythmic mode in the form of a prescribed rhythmic sequence.

Performing Shishtrī: Qaṣdī Anẓur Ilīk

"Qaṣdī Anẓur Ilīk" (My Goal Is to See You) is the very first song of the 'Īsāwiyya's printed text collection (*sfīna*, lit. "vessel") and is therefore also referred to as "the opening of the shishtrī" (*istiftāḥ shishtrī*). The shaykh al-'aml takes over from the shaykh al-ḥizb as the lead vocalist and voice of musical ritual authority in the shishtrī (and the ḥaḍra section that follows it). The circle of singers he leads regroups as new singers join the circle while others exit to prepare themselves for the dancing and singing they will perform in the following section.

The soundworld of the shishtrī section overlaps with that of the ḥizb in maintaining a basis in choral vocal performance, lending a sense of continuity between the sections. But other aesthetics mark a dramatic contrast between the two: whereas the ḥizb is not considered singing, but rather

26. This sense of nūba (classical Arabic *nawba*) as a large-scale musical form involving a sequence of songs in different rhythmic modes in Andalusī and 'Īsāwiyya musics is not to be confused with the nūba examined in chaps. 3, 4, and 5, where the term refers to a single song devoted to a saint or spirit.

27. Early twentieth-century Tunisian musical legends Ahmad al-Wafi and Khmaïs Tarnane received spiritual-musical training in 'Īsāwiyya shrines (Jones 1977: 30; Chelbi 2002: 89). Baron Rodolphe d'Erlanger, the colonial-era scholar who dedicated most of his adult life to preserving Tunisian mālūf, learned the repertoire in the shrine of the 'Īsāwiyya in Sīdī Bū Sa'īd (Davis 2004: 50).

MUSICAL EXAMPLE 2.5 (AUDIO EXAMPLE 2.7). Opening line of "Qaṣdī Anẓur Ilīk" (My Goal Is to See You). Note the melismatic text-melody relationship, which contrasts with the highly syllabic approach of the ḥizb.

reciting, the opposite is true of the shishtrī. The ḥizb is overwhelmingly syllabic and performed with no instruments, while the shishtrī is highly melismatic (see musical ex. 2.5), in Andalusī style, and adds two percussion instruments, the naqqārāt (small kettledrums) and ṭār (tambourine), to its texture. Unlike the ḥizb, the shishtrī adheres to the nūba musical form, which, in the context of the ʿĪsāwiyya, means songs follow a succession of three (sometimes four) rhythms, performed without pause, as well as structural application of the system of melodic modes that it shares with Tunisian art music.[28] The opening line of "Qaṣdī Anẓur Ilīk," shown in musical example 2.5, reveals characteristics that distinguish the melodic mode called *ʿirāq*: it begins with a characteristic four-note syncopated anacrusis taking up the last five beats of the eight-beat rhythmic pattern before descending stepwise to low G to produce a tetrachord called *dhīl* (lit. "tail") below the root on G-A-B♭̸-C (see video ex. 2.2 for the ritual performance, and audio ex. 2.7 for a solo excerpt).

The opening line of the lyrics, from which the song gets its title, is:

qaṣdī anẓur ilīk / wa-nshāhad maqāmik / wa-nsalam ʿalīk
my goal is to see you / and see your shrine / and greet you

28. "Qaṣdī Anẓur" begins in the mode *ʿirāq*, with a D-E♭̸-F-G root tetrachord overlapping an upper tetrachord of G-A-B♭̸-C. When reduced to an octave scale, ʿirāq appears indistinguishable from the Tunisian mode *ḥsīn*. However, modes are more than these scales; they are defined largely by additional notes above and below, how certain pitches are treated, and specific melodic and rhythmic motifs.

In capturing the idea of visiting a shrine to experience the divine presence of the Prophet (the identity of "you" is revealed later), these lines not only maintain the spiritual hierarchy by beginning with the Prophet, but also enact a reflexivity whereby the ʿĪsāwiyya narrate their own ritual intentions and actions. This aligns with Kapferer's first-order reflexivity. But with each performance of shishtrī, they also reinforce their connection to, and privileged place in, the wider field of Andalusī art music. This second-order reflexivity, in which participants take a stance on their relationship to wider social fields, is embodied in the performance of music but is also discursive, because the language participants use in conversation shares the same terminology as Andalusī art-music discourse, and directly compare shishtrī to art music: "It is mālūf, but mālūf jidd [serious mālūf]" was a common refrain, and the connection to al-Andalus is reinforced in the very name "shishtrī," whose namesake, I was reminded often, is a town in al-Andalus.

Intensification 2: Sequential Rhythmic Modulation

In addition to the melismatic approach to text-melody relationships, the shishtrī section also introduces to the ritual a new form of rhythmic intensification: sequential intensification. SI involves the modulation from longer to shorter rhythmic modes in a prescribed sequence. The normative sequence of rhythms in the shishtrī section proceeds from *bṭāyḥī* to *dkhūl brāwil* to *brāwil* and concludes with *khatm*, effectively approximating an 8/8-4/4-2/4-3/4 metric progression.[29]

The progression through this sequence of rhythms provides a strong sense of intensification resulting from a consistent decrease in the length of the rhythmic pattern and a concomitant decrease in the number of attacks per cycle. Fewer attacks per cycle allows for maximal increases in tempo and sonic density, producing heightened intensity. The sequence culminates with the khatm, a three-beat rhythm that takes the form of a short-long pattern.[30] Because this rhythm is another example of the short-long three-beat model introduced in the dhikr of the ḥizb analyzed above, a shared logic to culminating intensifications emerges. In other words, the most "religious" section (i.e., the ḥizb) relies on the same concluding intensification principles (that is, culminating in a transition to a three-beat, short-long rhythmic pattern) as the section indexing a wider "secular" field of music (i.e., the

29. Not every shishtrī performance modulates through all four rhythms. This one skipped the brāwil and jumped straight into a piece in the khatm rhythm.

30. Depending on the phrasing of the melody, khatm may approximate 3/4 or 6/8 metric designations.

MUSICAL EXAMPLE 2.6. Sequence of rhythmic modes utilized in the shishtrī section of the ʿĪsāwiyya ḥaḍra. The sequence represents a trajectory to shorter, faster patterns with fewer attacks per cycle (see video ex. 2.2, which transitions from bṭāyḥī to dkhul brāwil to khatm).

MUSICAL EXAMPLE 2.7. First line of "Yā ʿĀshiqīn" (O Lovers) in the dkhūl brāwil rhythmic mode (see 0:55 in video ex. 2.2). Note the maintenance of the melismatic relationship between text and melody and the intensification through a faster, shorter rhythmic mode than the previous bṭayḥī rhythm.

shishtrī) connected to mālūf. Yet another shared feature between the ḥizb and the shishtrī is an abrupt deceleration that precedes a more dramatic intensification: here the bṭāyḥī rhythm is slowed down in the last few cycles before transitioning to the quicker, shorter dkhūl brāwil song "Yā ʿĀshiqīn" (O Lovers) and finally closing with a brief thirty-four-second khatm piece.[31]

"Yā ʿĀshiqīn" corresponds to the mālūf song of the same title, featuring the same rhythm and a very similar melody (see Būdhīna 1992: 65–66 for the mālūf lyrics and Būdhīna 1995: 44 for the mālūf melody). While the ʿĪsāwiyya sfīna includes the same lyrics contained in mālūf anthologies, it also includes additional verses sung by the ʿĪsāwiyya that are not found in printed mālūf collections: *yā muslimīn ṣabrī ʿayyā / wa-ānā nurājā* (O Muslims, my patience is weak / and I am waiting):

This sequence of rhythms also appears in the same order in mālūf, although in mālūf additional rhythmic forms are interspersed.[32] In this cere-

31. The khatm piece is unidentified here. It was evident during the performance that the piece was new to most of the singers, who stopped singing and visibly strained to hear what the shaykh al-ʿaml was singing. As a result, the vocals were overpowered by the drums.

32. A complete mālūf nūba cycle consists of a sequence of musical forms: *istiftāḥ* (instru-

mony, a short (roughly nine-minute) nūba based on "Qaṣdī Anẓur Ilīk" was the only piece performed during the brief shishtrī section. But even within this condensed section, the ʿĪsāwiyya introduced to the ritual a form of familiar musicality—specifically, melodic and rhythmic modality shared with Tunisian art music—that shapes what comes next in the ḥaḍra section. That ḥaḍra section, however, while adhering to these modal expectations, also introduces its own set of distinctive musical trajectories. It does so, additionally, in support of communal dance and individual trance.

PART III: THE ḤAḌRA AND THE DRUMS OF "INTOXICATION"

Part of the cultural work of the ḥizb and the shishtrī is to connect the ʿĪsāwiyya to meaningful geographical and historical others near and far. The ḥizb reinforces the ʿĪsāwiyya's location within a transnational spiritual landscape and centuries-long history of Sufi recitation, while the shishtrī connects to the historical and geographic movements of the field of Andalusī music and situates them centrally within the history of mālūf. In many ways, the ḥaḍra draws on and distills elements from both the ḥizb and shishtrī to produce what for many observers and participants is the most distinctive episode of ʿĪsāwiyya ritual. Its iconic status is illustrated by the fact that the entire ceremony and this section of the ritual share the same name.

Like the ḥizb recitation, the ḥaḍra features responsorial singing and a series of marked DIs characterized by gradual yet extreme increases in tempo. Like the shishtrī, it involves SI through prescribed rhythmic sequences and is made up of musical pieces whose general modal principles are shared with Tunisian mālūf. Yet the ḥaḍra's musical form and content are distinctive. The ḥaḍra proceeds according to a tripartite sequence beginning with the "arrival liturgy" (*wird al-qudūm*), an a cappella series of songs during which the line of dancers enters. This is followed by the *mjarred*, a group of songs in the ʿĪsāwiyya's iconic five-beat handclap pattern, which in turn is followed by the brāwil, when the drums enter and individuals may break away from the line of dancers to enter into states of trance. These three subsections of the ḥaḍra section each have internal conventions for dealing with texture, meter, rhythm, and mode while contributing to the global trajectory of the ritual that culminates in trance. Through its conventions for in-

---

mental introduction, no percussion), *mṣaddar* (instrumental overture in 6/4 meter of the same name), *abyāt* ("verses," in *barwal* and bṭāyḥī rhythms), *bṭayḥī* (songs in the rhythm of the same name), *tūshya* (instrumental interlude), *mshadd* (instrumental interlude in rhythm of the same name), and a sequence of *barwal, draj, khfīf,* and *khatm* (all songs in their respective rhythms). See Louati (2012), Davis (2004), and Guettat (1980).

tensification, the ḥaḍra continues pushing the limits of group coordination and individual stamina, as its musical form provides the architecture of self-transformation and spiritual elevation. With the addition of a line of dancers who also perform as responsorial singers, the importance of transitions and coordination is also elevated.

The Dancers Arrive: Wird al-Qudūm, the "Arrival Liturgy"

The arrival of the line of dancers is a highly anticipated moment of heightened affect. Dressed in flowing white robes, the members of the "line" (ṣaff) of dancers march in single file until they are situated directly in front of the singers, who remain seated in their circle. Ululations by women in the adjacent room resound throughout the courtyard as the slow, majestic twenty-beat phrase pattern of the song "Aẓẓam Aẓẓam b-illah Lā Yanām" (God's Majesty Never Sleeps) announces the arrival of the dancers.[33] At the unhurried starting tempo of 72 bpm, the dancers stand shoulder to shoulder in a single line, hold hands, and perform a four-beat pattern of slowly bowing forward, stepping back, bowing forward, and stepping down, all in time with the twenty-beat phrasing of the melody. They immediately fulfill their role as responsorial singers, singing their twenty-beat response to that of the circle of singers (*hallāla*, which had previously been divided into two antiphonal groups, the qawwāla and raddāda; see video ex. 2.3).

The lyrics begin in praise of God but quickly localize, praising Sīdī Ben ʿĪsā and reflexively drawing attention to the spiritual work of the ḥaḍra and the centrality of trance.

aẓẓam aẓẓam b-illāh lā yanām	God's magnificence never sleeps
wāḥid fī malikihi bāqī	he is unique and eternal in his kingdom
lā tajʿal finā yā allah	protect us, O God,
lā maḥrūm ū-lā shāqī	from deprivation and misery
aẓẓam aẓẓam b-illāh lā yanām	God's magnificence never sleeps
fī qalbī zād niyāra	he increased the light in my heart
yā mawlānā bin ʿīsā al-ḥabīb	O our master Ben ʿĪsā the Beloved
yā sulṭān al-khammāra	O sultan of the "intoxication"

33. The ʿĪsāwiyya distinguish between songs sung in the presence of the line of dancers and those sung without dancers present. Ceremonies without dancers are called *manga*, which involve the same repertoire (particularly from the mjarred section) but sung to different melodies. Prior to the arrival of the dancers in this ceremony, the *hallāla* had been singing a different version of "Aẓẓam Aẓẓam," in a sixteen-beat pattern in the *mazmūm* mode. They switch to a different version of the song, in a twenty-beat rhythm and in the *raṣd dhīl* melodic mode, as soon as the dancers arrive.

aẓẓam aẓẓam b-illāh lā yanām	God's magnificence never sleeps
fī qalbī zād ḥalāwa	he increased the sweetness in my heart
yā mawlānā bin 'īsā al-ḥabīb	O our master Ben 'Īsā the Beloved
yā sulṭān al-'īsāwiyya	O sultan of the 'Īsāwiyya
aẓẓam aẓẓam b-illāh lā yanām	God's magnificence never sleeps
fī qalbī zād muḥibba	he increased the love in my heart

Two additional songs complete the arrival liturgy sequence. Without interruption, the group transitions to "Allah Dā'im Ḥayy" (God Is Always Living) before concluding with "Men Ghā'ib Sirr Allah" (Whoever Wants to Know God's Secret). The latter undergoes a major tempo intensification reminiscent of the ḥizb. Beginning at 64 bpm, it nearly quadruples in speed, ending at 223 bpm. As the tempo reaches its peak, the line of dancers replaces its bow-step movement with short vertical jumps, with each dancer hitting his chest with the right hand in the same manner as the climax of the dhikr in the ḥizb. This episode of DI ends with a pronounced clap of the hands by the shaykh al-ḥaḍra, who has left the line and taken a step toward the seated singers, visually communicating with the singers as he demonstratively spreads his arms outward before clapping his hands to coordinate their transition to the mjarred section.

The Handclaps Begin: Mjarred, the Iconic 'Īsāwiyya Musical Form

With the shaykh's clap, the tempo has been reset to 97 bpm and the mjarred handclap pattern begins, adding a new layer of percussive accompaniment to what had so far been a cappella vocals. The mjarred is a song form based on its sparse, cyclic namesake five-beat pattern of 2 + 3 beats: clap-rest-clap-rest-rest. The mjarred, of which there is a vast repertoire, is almost exclusively associated with the 'Īsāwiyya and serves as an index of the artistry and distinctiveness of their ritual methods. Five-beat rhythmic patterns are exceedingly rare in Tunisian ritual music and entirely absent from art music such as mālūf and popular music such as mizwid.[34] Walid noted with some disdain that the number of mjarreds performed in any given ritual has decreased, a trend he connected to the increasing focus on trance and a decrease in the amount of time 'Īsāwis spend training in the realm of the ḥizb and mjarred.

As the dancers step and bend in time with the mjarred rhythm, they

34. In Tunisian Sufi contexts outside the 'Īsāwiyya, the five-beat rhythm is also found in the repertoire of the Sulāmiyya but in a section of repertoire taken from, and named after, the 'Īsāwiyya.

take on one of three roles. In some passages they sing entire lines of text, alternating with the circle of singers, while in others they repeat a name of God, either *huwa* (He) or Allah, adding a second layer of vocals to the sung melody. At the very end of select mjarred pieces, dancers take over the vocals to sing a dhikr pattern, that is, singing God's name without the accompaniment of clapping, increasing in tempo and energy until reaching a climax that resets the tempo and begins a new mjarred or moves on to the next section.

The mjarred, like the wird al-qudūm and brāwil sections that bookend it, adheres to the logic of the mālūf nūba in that a sequence of pieces remains in the same or related melodic modes. A corollary is that once the performers depart from any given mode, they cannot return to it in the same section. But it differs from the mālūf nūba logic in that there is no sequence of rhythms; each piece in the section is in the same five-beat mjarred rhythm, and thus, only DI factors into the mjarred. In this performance there are six pieces. Four are in the mode *ḥsīn*, one is in *ḥsīn ṣabā*, and one is in *aṣba'īn*.[35] All three modes share the same "tonic" or reference pitch, and modulating between them is not uncommon. The latter piece also serves a structural role that intersects with its modal relationship to prior pieces: it is conventionally the final mjarred performed before the brāwil section.

The song "al-Kās Ydūr" (The Cup Goes Round; video ex. 2.4) illustrates how elements of the ḥizb are carried over into the mjarred. The antiphonal call-and-response format introduced in the ḥizb reappears in the mjarred, where it overlaps with an additional vocal component of the dancers' singing. The singing takes the form of dhikr, which also first appeared in the ḥizb. Here, it layers the repeated name of God over the melody of the seated singers, incorporating dhikr into the antiphonal fabric of the song. Musical example 2.8 illustrates this musical adaption of the dhikr while also revealing the virtues and ambiguities of cyclicity inherent in the mjarred (which, in turn, reveal the limits of staff notation for representing such cyclicity). In this piece, the beginning of the sung text is offset from the clap and the "huwa" response of the dancers. The phrasing of the main melody begins on what is represented in the transcription as beat 1, which is a rest in the handclap pattern, while the "huwa" sung by the dancers—along with the dancers' steps—begins on beat 4 and aligns with the clap. All three sonic components overlap, giving a sense of multiple possible beginning points;

35. *Ḥsīn ṣabā* has the same intervallic material as ḥsīn but focuses on the mode's third step. Reduced to scalar form, ḥsīn uses the pitches D-E𝄳-F-G-A-B𝄳-C-D, while aṣba'īn uses D-E𝄳-F♯-G-A-B𝄳-C-D.

TABLE 2.1 Songs of the mjarred section, with melodic mode, duration, and tempo change

Piece	Melodic mode	Duration	Tempo (beginning / ending), bpm
"Bisma al-Karīm Bdayna" (We Begin in the Name of the Most Generous)	ḥsīn	8:10	97 /136
"Allah Yā Mulānā" (God O Master)	ḥsīn	7:38	133 / 600
Solo tahlīl (while drums are heated)	ḥsīn	1:50	119 / 122
"Ṣalū Yā Khwānī" (Pray, O Brothers)	ḥsīn	6:10	111 / 139
"al-Kās Ydūr" (The Cup Goes Round)	ḥsīn ṣabā	8:52	123 / 551
"Anā Bdayt Bismillah al-Ḥayy al-'Aẓīm" (I Began in the Name of the Magnificent Living One)	aṣba'īn	5:10	120 / 532

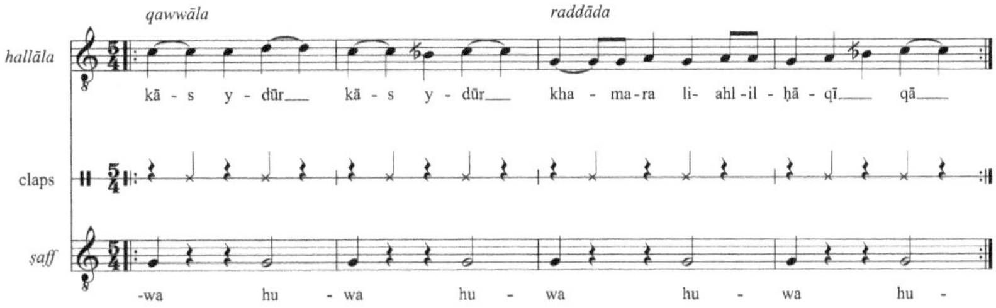

MUSICAL EXAMPLE 2.8. "Al-Kās Ydūr" (The Cup Goes Round), from the mjarred section of the ḥaḍra. Note the staggered relationship between the hallāla, ṣaff, and handclap phrasing.

the transcription could have started on any of those beats and given a different sense of phrasing and onsets.

"Al-Kās Ydūr" begins at a tempo of 123 bpm, but the process of discrete temporal intensification (DTI) brings it to a maximum of 551 bpm when the piece ends nine minutes later (video ex. 2.4). This DTI process via pronounced tempo acceleration is a feature of every mjarred piece, making the temporal shape of the experience of the mjarred section similar to that of the ḥizb. Indeed, the contour of the tempo graph of the entire mjarred section (fig. 2.3) is strikingly similar to that of the ḥizb (see again fig. 2.2).[36]

Also carried over into the mjarred repertoire from the shishtrī section is poetic language full of metaphors of intoxication as well as musical mo-

36. The 'Īsāwiyya further distinguish between slow mjarred sections (called *tathqīla*, "heavy") and faster sections (called *khafīf*, "light").

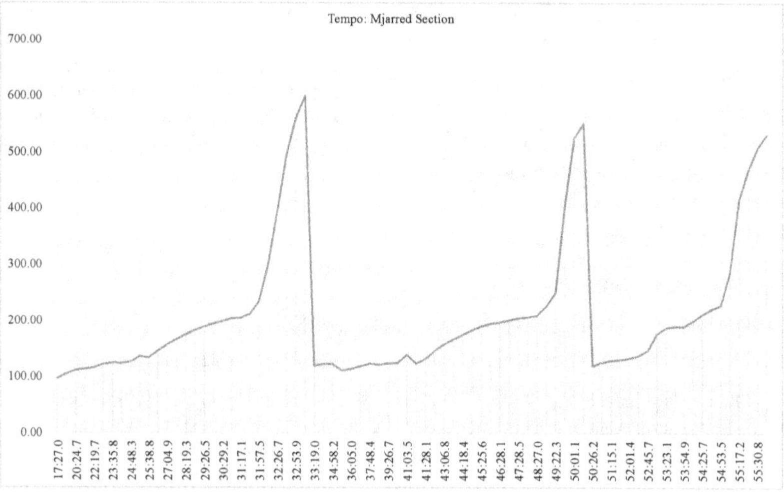

FIGURE 2.3. Tempo graph of the mjarred section

dality, including the logic of performing a sequence of pieces in the same or related modes. Stepping back a bit further, this song's lyrical themes of saintly healing and the narrator's complaint of being left alone and disregarded are held in common with adjacent trance healing practices in the wider ecology of Sufism discussed in the following chapters. That those shared themes are performed in the ʿĪsāwiyya's trademark five-beat mjarred handclap pattern is illustrative of the dual tendencies that pervade the condition of ambient Sufism in Tunis: marking ritual-musical distinctiveness, on the one hand, while sharing space in a wider spiritual commons, on the other.

al-kās ydūr al-kās ydūr	The cup goes round, the cup goes round
al-khamra li-ahl al-ḥaqīqa	the wine of the people of truth
yā khammār ū-yā ʿammār	O cupbearer, O pourer
isqīnā khamra sharīqa	pour us the wine of illumination
yā sattār ū-yā jabbār	O Veiler, O Almighty
ijʿalnā min ahl al-ḥaqīqa	make us the people of truth
bisma al-dāʾim huwa al-dāʾim	in the name of the Eternal, He is the Eternal
rabbi al-karīm ʿālim al-asrār yā wāldī	God the Most Generous, knower of secrets, O father
yighfir dhanbī yustur ʿayibī	forgive my sins, protect me from my faults

huwa al-sattār huwa al-jabbār yā wāldī	he is the Veiler, he is the Almighty, O father
yā bābā al-ḥājj yā bābā al-ḥājj	O father the pilgrim, O father the pilgrim
yā shaykh dāwīnī nabrā yā wāldī	O shaykh heal me, O father
yā bābā al-ḥājj yā bābā al-ḥājj	O father the pilgrim, O father the pilgrim
yā shaykh dāwīnī nabrā yā wāldī	O shaykh heal me, O father
fī yūm al-ʿaīd, fī thānī al-ʿaīd	on the holy day, and the day after
al-shaykh zārūh al-fuqqara yā wāldī	the Sufis [poor ones] visit the shaykh, O father
fī hādhī al-dār fī wusṭ al-dār	in this house, in the middle of the house
fī wasiṭhā ḥusn al-ḥaḍra yā wāldī	in the midst of this beautiful ḥaḍra, O father
hammaltūnī khallaytūnī	they disregarded me, they left me alone,
fī baḥr mā nʿarif lahu ʿaūm	at sea I don't know how to swim
ayn al-rijāl al-ṣūfiyya	where are the Sufis

The Drums Enter and Trance Begins: The Culminating Brāwil Section

The close of the mjarred section brings the ritual to a dramatically new level of experience, one that reaches musical, spiritual, and corporeal extremes not attained in previous sections of the ritual. When the final mjarred song accelerates in tempo and the singers are given their drums, anticipation builds as the nine-drum ensemble waits to kick in. Once the mjarred reaches its peak tempo, with the dancers jumping in place chanting "huwa" to the five-beat handclap pattern, the shaykh al-ḥaḍra again steps out of the line of dancers with outstretched arms, ready to clap to signal the transition to the next section. This time, however, the singers outfitted with drums hold their instruments up in the air and strike them in unison with the clap, creating a thunderous layer of sound as they introduce a new form of sonic texture to the ritual (video ex. 2.5). In addition to two tambourines (ṭār) and one pair of kettledrums (naqqārāt), instruments featured earlier in the shishtrī, the brāwil section introduces the large handheld frame drum called the *bendīr*, eight to twelve of which are typically played. The sonic intervention is not only in the realm of volume. Each bendīr has two to three snares stretched across the inside of the drumhead that generate a buzzing sound with each articulation of the instrument. These snares, in combination with the jangling cymbals of the tambourines, contribute to a density of sonic texture that (1) until now had been absent from the ritual and (2) is a feature shared with other trance musics analyzed in this book. Thick, buzzing, jangling timbral profiles are a constant in the musics of ambient Sufism, particularly those that involve individualized trance dance practices. The bendīr, with its signature buzzy timbre, is iconic in the realm of ambient Sufism as an instrument associated with trance episodes in Sufi contexts, because the mere presence of the bendīr in any context creates expectations (or, outside ritual, an evocation) of trance. While the bendīr is perceived by some as a symbol of the excesses of certain Sufi orders (see chap. 3), some Sufis reference it as a symbol of ritual power; as Marouene Meski (shaykh al-ʿaml) told me, trance (takhmīr) requires the bendīr drum (pers. comm., 2012).

Beyond these indexical and sonic interventions, the introduction of the bendīr also accomplishes significant intensificatory work. The unison strike that begins the brāwil section punctuates the end of the mjarred section's DI, which, in this performance, increased the tempo from 120 bpm to a hurtling 532 bpm. The subsequent reset in tempo, with the arrival of the drums of the brawīl section, however, also marks the beginning of a new process of SI. The SI of the brāwil section takes the form of a series of rhythmic modulations similar to those of the shishtrī, but with a distinctive form often called the ʿĪsāwiyya nūba. This sequence consists of three rhythms: *bṭāyḥī ʿīsāwī*, dkhūl brāwil, and *hrūbī* (musical ex. 2.9). As in the shishtrī sequence, SI is achieved through the progression of rhythmic patterns that decrease in both length and number of attacks while increasing in tempo, in a process of ever-increasing sonic density. The bṭayḥī ʿīsāwī rhythm differs from the bṭāyḥī pattern of the shishtrī section (and of mālūf) by beginning with three onbeat dumms instead of a syncopated dumm-takk-takk pattern (the rhythm begins, however, on beat 4, the takk aligning with the demonstrative clap of the shaykh al-ḥaḍra, which provides another example of modulatory changes commencing in the middle of musical units; see again musical ex. 2.9). This proprietary rhythmic pattern arguably ʿĪsāwicizes the mālūf rhythm, integrating and applying it for its purposes of supporting trance, thus doing double duty of marking sameness and difference at once—another common theme in the musics of ambient Sufism.[37] Dkhūl brāwil is identical to the rhythm of the same name that appears in the shish-

37. To be clear, this is not to suggest that the bṭayḥī pattern of what would become "official" mālūf was a historical precedent of the bṭayḥī of the ʿĪsāwiyya trance section. Indeed, Shaykh ʿAli Darwish's 1932 transcription of a mālūf nūba (in the sīka mode) performed by Shaykh Khmaïs Tarnane shows how Tarnane's approach to the nūba exhibits rhythmic structural tendencies—including a bṭāyḥī rhythm with three dumms—that reveal the "influence

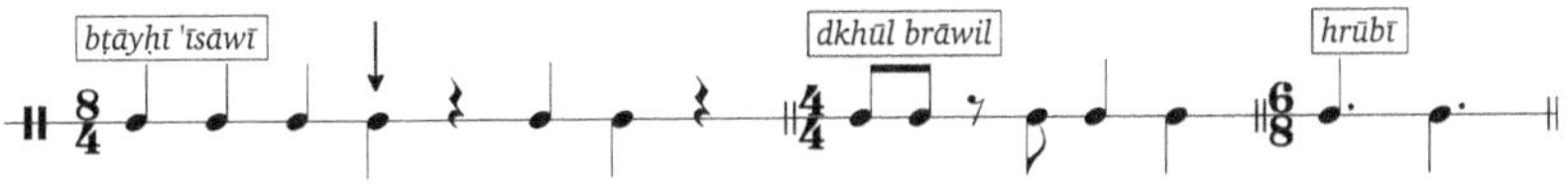

MUSICAL EXAMPLE 2.9. Sequential intensification (SI) illustrated through the progression of rhythmic modes utilized in the brāwil section of the ʿĪsāwiyya ḥaḍra. The sequence represents a trajectory to shorter, faster patterns with fewer attacks per cycle. Downward arrow indicates the metric location of the first attack commencing brāwil section, aligning with the shaykh al-ḥaḍra's clap.

trī, although in the brāwil section it occasionally serves as a culminating rhythm played at an extreme tempo. The hrūbī rhythm is a fast 6/8 pattern with a strong sense of ternary subdivisions created by the emphasis on one (dumm) and four (takk).[38]

Intensification 3: Global Increases in Timbral Density

The dramatic arrival of the drums aligned with the shaykh's dramatic handclap commencing the brāwil section not only marks the end of the DI of the mjarred and the beginning of a new pattern of SI in the form of a succession of rhythmic patterns; it also establishes the final segment of the process of GI that had been building since the beginning of the ḥaḍra section. GI, in this case, takes the form of textural accretion: the unaccompanied singing of the arrival liturgy was followed by the addition of handclaps in the mjarred, which, in turn, ceded to the sonic layers of the nine-piece drum ensemble in the brāwil. Each of these steps represents a new plateau of sonic density through the addition of layers of volume and timbral thickness, culminating in the thunderous drum ensemble of the ḥaḍra section.

This moment of the clap and first strike of the drums is momentous musically, I argue, largely because it articulates the first moment in the ritual when all three types of intensification I have outlined occur together. It punctuates the extreme tempo limit of the DI of the mjarred, confirms the GI of a series of increases in textural density, and brings the ritual to a new plateau of sonic experience by introducing a new pattern of SI that extends and furthers a sense of anticipation for continued intensification. The clap and first strike, then, serve as a kind of intensificatory fulcrum, a point where multiple intensifications coalesce and overlap, giving it considerable affective ritual power (see fig. 2.4).

---

of the mystical Sufi school" on his musical culture (Centre des Musiques Arabes et Méditerranéenes 2013: 12–13).

38. The hrūbī rhythm is sometimes also called *khatm,* perhaps in reference to its role as a culminating rhythm in triple meter. Ben ʿAmor (2008: 188) reports that this rhythm is also called *khatm* by the ʿĪsāwiyya of Banī Khiyyār.

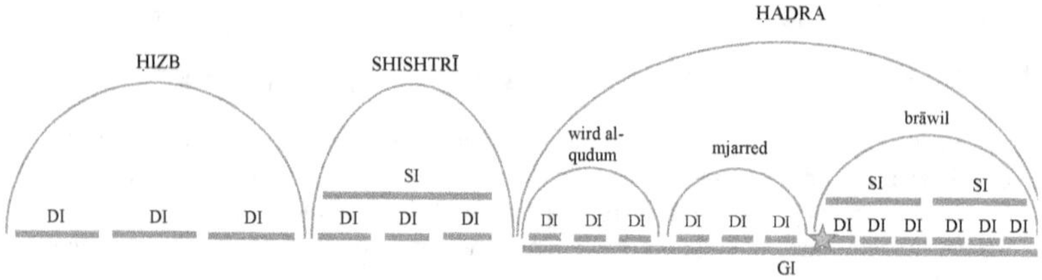

FIGURE 2.4. Schematic of the layers of intensification of the ḥaḍra ceremony. The star indicates the shaykh al-ḥaḍra's final clap and the entrance of the bendīr frame drums, a moment of heightened affect where the layers of intensification overlap most profoundly. DI = discrete intensification; SI = sequential intensification; GI = global intensification

AMBIGUITIES OF MUSIC AND TRANCE

The dramatic clap and first strike of the drums mark a heightened ritual moment not only because of what they accomplish in terms of sonic intensification; they also announce the imminence of dramatic trance episodes, often accompanied by shouts, cries, and other outward indications of strong emotion, as well as acts of self-harm that push the limits of the physical body. As the first bṭāyḥī 'īsāwī song, "Nibtadā Bismillah 'Alim fī Kul Makān" (We Begin in the Name of God, Who Knows Every Place), begins, the first trancer steps out of the line of dancers. While the others continue to dance, holding hands and bending forward and back at the waist, he approaches the drummers and bends at the waist in time with the line of dancers, but more vigorously. With a pained expression on his face, he emits a scream and begins to remove his white robe. The shaykh al-ḥaḍra intervenes, pulling the robe back down. The trancer resists, and the shaykh holds him more forcefully, in a bear hug, as the trancer screams again in frustration, pointing his index finger toward the sky. After the shaykh speaks into his ear, the dancer relents, resuming the up-and-down motion of his dance while the shaykh holds his robe from behind to prevent him from running into the singers. Because they are guests at the shrine of Sīdī Belḥassen, a site defined by the practices of the Shādhuliyya and their insistence on physical comportment, today the 'Īsāwiyya will not engage in the ecstatic feats, such as dancing with fire or rolling on cactus pads, that require trancers to be bare-chested.

At any other shrine, however, the 'Īsāwiyya perform numerous dramatic feats of trance. In the immense outdoor courtyard of the shrine of Sīdī 'Alī Ḥaṭṭāb (where this chapter began), filled with hundreds of spectator-pilgrims, five dancers break away from the line as soon as the brāwil begins. They stand immediately in front of the singers and maintain their forward and back bends, but in a more intense manner. Several have pained expressions on their faces; others cry out. One takes off his robe, leaving him bare-chested, then proceeds to pick up burning stalks of halfa grass handed to him by a fellow ʿĪsāwī. He dances by passing the flames of the burning stalks across his chest and under his arms, walking around the line of dancers, then drops them on the ground, kneels, and extinguishes the fire with his bare hands. As the musicians transition to the faster dkhūl barwal rhythm, a palpable sense of intensification occurs: the rhythms are faster, phrases are denser, trance dance movements become more vigorous, and additional trancers break from the line (see video ex. 2.6 for this transition and various feats of trance). A shaykh holds a carpenter's nail high up in the air as ululations from the women in the audience fill the courtyard; he then dramatically drops it into the throat of a trancer. Others, kneeling with arms outstretched and fingers pointing to the sky, are handed shards of glass that they chew on, while another rolls on cactus pads spread on the ground. These dramatic trance actions are preceded and followed by vigorous forward bends at the waist on every other beat of the music, giving each trance its own standardized developmental arc. Once the culminating hrūbī rhythm begins, the level of intensity increases yet again. As the tempo reaches its peak, the remaining trancers move more and more vigorously until they collapse into the arms of a shaykh, who recites the fātiḥa into the trancer's ear to conclude his trance. There is an interlude of several minutes before the next sequence begins. Trancers who lie prone on the ground recover slowly. Drumheads that have detuned are heated over a brazier, and a cappella songs in praise of Sīdī Ben ʿĪsā are sung until the drums are ready and the next nūba, and thus the next sequence of bṭāyḥī ʿīsāwī-dkhūl brāwil-hrūbī, begins.

The trance episodes elicit a range of opinions and attitudes among the public, commonly in the expression of a sense of awe or wonder, but also revealing what many ʿĪsāwīs consider to be fundamental misunderstandings about them. The ʿĪsāwiyya's taxonomy of trance, in which certain trance activities are associated with names of animals, does not make things clearer. The lion (*sbʿa*) eats broken glass, the cat (*qaṭūs*) eats raw meat, the ostrich (*nʿām*) swallows nails, and the camel (*jmāl*) rolls on cactus pads.[39] All four types of trance are considered unique to the ʿĪsāwiyya. Three additional trances complete the list, two shared with other trance traditions and one distinctive to the ʿĪsāwiyya. The swordsman (*sayyāf*) pierces his flesh with skewers or cuts himself with a sword, a practice that is also considered a specialty of the Qādiriyya in Tunisia and many other countries (Zarcone 1996). A trancer may also dance with fire, passing the flames of bundles of burning

39. There was once a trance state that involved eating scorpions. It has disappeared from practice in Tunis but remains in the southern parts of the country.

halfa grass over his bare-chested body. This is the only unnamed trance of the ʿĪsāwiyya, and it is also practiced in sṭambēlī (see chap. 5), particularly in the trance for Sīdī ʿAbd al-Salām, the founder of the Sulāmiyya Sufi order. The final trance type differs from the others and is also proprietary to the ʿĪsāwiyya. It is a named figure called ʿAkāsha, who dresses in a dark hooded cloak (*kashabiyya*), is bound in chains and runs around the ritual area in an agitated manner, often so near the startled onlookers that they step back. He attempts to break the chains and after three attempts (sometimes successful, sometimes not) is picked up by several men and carried away. The appearance of ʿAkāsha signals the end of the ceremony.

This taxonomy is not explanatory of trance motivations, goals, or experience. Trancers who "trance the lion" (*tkhammar al-sbʿa*) may make movements that evoke the animal, but they thoroughly reject the idea that they are possessed by spirits, animal or otherwise. Instead, their trances take on these forms because of the highly charged symbols of ʿĪsāwī history and legend. The lion evokes the legend of Sīdī Ben ʿĪsā, in which the saint transformed into a lion to protect his followers; it is why the lion is considered the pinnacle of ʿĪsāwī trance experiences. Many non-ʿĪsāwīs assume that these dramatic trance states are the result of possession by spirits (jnūn), while some aver that they are products of the spiritual force and blessing (baraka) of the saint Sīdī Ben ʿĪsā. Every ʿĪsāwī trancer I have spoken with has scoffed at these explanations. The jnūn, they say, are scared away by recitations of the fātiḥa and the ḥizb, as well as other Qur'anic messages embedded in the lyrics of songs. The ritual space is cleansed by sacred words, creating a safe space Walid described as "far from the spirits and far from Satan" (pers. comm., 2015). The point of musical ritual performance is to attract spiritual forces; as Hatem, a trancer who began trancing as a cat and now trances as an ostrich, told me: "It is *wajd* [trance from the overwhelming sense of divine presence]. There are no jnūn. You heard the ʿĪsāwiyya. There is no dhikr for the jnūn. No, there is dhikr for God, for the saints, and for the Prophet. In our work, we scare away the jnūn" (pers. comm., 2012). They also reject the idea of Sīdī Ben ʿĪsā's baraka or *karamāt* (miracles) resulting in trance states. If this were true, I was told several times, there would not be any blood or physical damage from the swords or cactus spines.

How, then, do ʿĪsāwīs understand takhmīr? The term "takhmīr" evokes the concept of divine intoxication, a term for a state of transcendence with a long history in Sufi thought and practice. Hatem and Walid both used it interchangeably with "wajd," which is etymologically related to the notion of finding—a term found throughout the historical and geocultural expanse of Sufism to refer to trance characterized by passion or strong emotion related to experiencing the presence of the divine (see Lewisohn 1997; Rouget 1986). But the specifics of ʿĪsāwiyya trance forms are related to two aspects of ʿĪsāwī identity. The first concerns a legend of Sīdī Ben ʿĪsā, and the second is about transcending the limits of the body. Discussions with ʿĪsāwīs about trance inevitably led to the recounting of the legend of Sīdī Ben ʿĪsā's trek through the desert as he led his followers to Mecca: Traveling by land from Morocco, they had to cross the Sahara Desert. When they ran out of food and water, his followers asked Sīdī Ben ʿĪsā what they should do. He responded, "Whatever you find in front of you, say 'bismillah' [in the name of God] and eat it." According to the legend, all they found was broken glass (*gzāz*), cactus (*hindī*), scorpions (*aqārib*), and pieces of metal, but they said "bismillah" and ate them, and were nourished for the remainder of their journey.

As with all Tunisian saints, the story of Sīdī Ben ʿĪsā's miraculous acts is central to establishing his sainthood, his proximity to God. It was by invoking God that Sīdī Ben ʿĪsā's capacity for miracles was activated. Nobody I spoke with, however, saw the ḥaḍra as a reenacting this legend. Rather, the legend sets historical precedent and narrative continuity connecting contemporary ʿĪsāwīs to Sīdī Ben ʿĪsā's first generation of followers over five centuries ago. As Walid put it, "I am proud of that story. I am practicing what my ancestors did" (pers. comm., 2012). But what does it mean to individuals who fall into trance? What is trance?

> Why do we continue to do takhmīr today? Why dance on cactus and eat it? Why eat glass? Why eat nails? If you're going to take it from a purely spiritual perspective [*min jānib ruḥānī baḥt*], it is acceptable. It tests your patience and your tolerance for suffering [*takhtibur ṣabrik u-takhtibur iḥtimālik*]. . . . [It is] a test of the disciple's [*murīd*'s] patience and endurance. More than a miracle, more than a break from everyday life, it is a direct connection to another life. It is not about other beings like Satan or the jnūn. I still cannot find a definition of takhmīr. Knowledge can only come from practice [*al-tʿarīf yilzim ykūn bil-mumārisa*]. (Pers. comm., 2012)

In the end, takhmīr is not a verbalizable experience, which is partly the point. I was told many times it is a *sirr*, meaning "mystery" or "secret," but not in the sense of a secret that can be articulated but is withheld from others. The secret, once experienced, is not translatable. It is sui generis. What is observable, from within and without, is that takhmīr involves a test of individual endurance and stamina, overcoming the limits of the physical self and becoming other. As Walid put it, it is "a direct connection to another life." That ʿĪsāwīs call their white woolen cloak *bden* (body) and remove it in the course of their trance is suggestive of this sense of transformation, of accessing another aspect of the self available only through ritual.

ʿĪsāwīs associate takhmīr with rhythm, melody, repetition, and transformation. But all of these are explicitly connected to text, which is an object of intense focus and contemplation. The idea of such conscious focus in the context of a trance state that is assumed to be one in which the trancer is devoid of such consciousness is not so much a paradox of trance as it is a structural duality that is at the heart of trance. For Judith Becker, trance is characterized in part by "intense focus," but one accompanied by the "loss of the strong sense of self" (2004: 43). Deborah Kapchan sums up the situation elegantly in her description of trance as the "volitional invocation of the non-volitional" (2007). The inseparability of textual meaning and musical experience emerges in ʿĪsāwī reflections on the role of text in ritual. For Walid,

> the harmoniousness in the Sufi ritual is what attracts the ears. It allows you to concentrate on the meaning of the words. When the sound becomes like this, with continuity, with question and answer, the ears become accustomed to it and you'll find the soul feels comfortable. The first "impact" is the impact of the melody they are singing, a beautiful melody, [which] will directly provide the meaning of the words . . . it gives you religious knowledge in the form of music. What does that mean? It means you don't worry about it [*mā taqlaqsh minū*]. If you're reading forty chapters [of text], after the second, third, or fourth you'll get tired. You'll say leave me alone, let me rest. But if you study through song, you say it and repeat it, say it and repeat it, you understand the meaning. (Pers. comm., 2014)

For Marouene,

> the rhythm is what gives you takhmīr. But the rhythm always goes with the words, and the dancers, the people who trance [*yitkhammir*], always listen to the words. Because the words give you the intoxicated/elated feeling [*nashwa*]; in your mind you will enter takhmīr. And that's the ʿĪsāwiyya. (Pers. comm., 2012)

If music is central to the ʿĪsāwī ritual experience, it is also understood from within to have a certain ambiguity, even a perilous potential. The ʿĪsāwiyya, like most other ṭarīqas in the Tunis area, are both esoteric and exoteric. That is, they cultivate forms of knowledge and experience known only to initiates, but also perform them often for nonmembers to witness in public or semipublic contexts such as pilgrimages, holidays, weddings, and circumcisions. Thus, they are acutely aware of how they are seen by others. Musical aptitude, in which they take pride, provides them with a distinctive and powerful mode of experiencing spiritual awareness and transcendence. It is also understood as attracting new recruits. Yet it can also lead to misunderstandings, or at least narrow understandings, of what the ʿĪsāwiyya is about. When Walid and I talked about the impact of Islamists on the ʿĪsāwiyya after the 2011 Revolution, he acknowledged the threat they posed but used the discussion as an opportunity for self-reflection, concluding that problems with the ʿĪsāwiyya are self-imposed and could only be rectified by the ʿĪsāwiyya themselves:

> And I am sorry, as I told you, because these days, a few ʿĪsāwiyya groups are regrettable [*munadim*]. It hurts me, it causes me great pain. Some have abandoned it in terms of its religion, in terms of its spirituality, to become something folkloric, for dancing, drumming, and trancing. This is something all of us who love the ʿĪsāwiyya feel. Because, if it becomes folklore, it will become just theater. Instead of a way of life . . . there are very few who sit and read the wirds [awrād], who do the taṣbīḥ, or recite the ḥizbs. Reasons, we always want to find reasons.
>
> The [bad] state of affairs in our country may have become, in our times, in the name of the Muslim Brothers, or in the name of the Islamists, or in the name of terrorists, leading to the problems of not being able to go to the shrines. . . . However, this is not the main reason. The principal reason has to do with us. We have not fulfilled our responsibility. . . . If only the elders, God bless them, were still living, [for] they brought us to this ṭarīqa and we need to bring the [new] generation to the Sufi ṭarīqa, not to its musical tinge. Hopefully God will help us. And hopefully we can return it to its high standard. (Pers. comm., 2014)

Ritual reflexivity creates conditions for self-critique. For Walid, the problem of folklorization is not about the ʿĪsāwiyya being on stage. He supports ʿĪsāwiyya stage performances and shares them proudly via social media, acknowledging that the ṭarīqa has an artistic heritage that deserves public recognition. This artistic heritage, though, is inseparable from the spiritual remit of the ṭarīqa. Indeed, ʿĪsāwīs such as Walid view aesthetic performance as indexing proper religious devotion. When initial tempos are too high, the rhythmic breathing of dancers is too throaty, too few mjarreds are sung, or dancers begin takhmīr too early or dance too frenetically, they are considered to be breaches of spiritual decorum, not just aesthetic excesses. And here the ʿĪsāwīs return to the ḥizb: they insist that takhmīr should only be permitted for dancers who have memorized and mastered the ḥizb, for the ḥizb teaches, among other things, an approach to the ḥaḍra that emphasizes patience and discipline. In a February 5, 2018, Facebook announcement, Walid initiated weekly meetings to address this concern: "We are starting ʿĪsāwiyya exercises in the zāwiya every Wednesday after the evening prayer. Before art and musical mastery, rules of conduct for the gathering [*ādab al-majlis*] are the guides. . . . God help us, this concerns everyone and the door is open."

The centrality of language even in the most "musical" aspects of the ʿĪsāwiyya ḥaḍra lends support to Michael Frishkopf's (2013) argument that all aspects of Islamic ritual, whether sung, chanted, or spoken, are unified in, and should be subsumed under the rubric of, "language performance." He rightly suggests avoiding etic conceptual categories that attempt to differentiate between, for example, music, chant, and prayer, not only because they arbitrarily and incompletely distribute scholarly investigations among academic disciplines (i.e., music scholars tend to focus on aspects of ritual with identifiable melodic patterns, while religious scholars focus more on those performance acts closer to speech, such as prayers), but also because in doing so the unity of ritual experience—which often moves seamlessly between the "music" and "speech" ends of the continuum—is obscured. While this chapter has illustrated this blurring of boundaries between "music" and "non-music," it has also revealed how the concept of music and its potencies are also used in an emic way and do important work in how ʿĪsāwīs understand their own practice. They recognize the centrality of music to the ʿĪsāwiyya's legacy and take seriously the responsibility of maintaining a high level of musical mastery. They use music to support the religious text: the music further develops textual themes and sonic performance strategies that are introduced in the ḥizb. The sonic development of the ritual tells its own story, one that emphasizes different aspects of ʿĪsāwī identity, but aspects that are commensurable, combinatorial, and teleological. The sonic-musical ritual form of the ḥaḍra produces, and relies on, a performative reflexivity. The three sections of the ceremony emphasize their closeness to the irreproachable realm of Sufi recitation (ḥizb), demonstrate their mastery of Andalusī music (shishtrī), and show their capacity as keepers of the secrets of takhmīr, where, even as words fail to explain the experience, ʿĪsāwīs demonstrate their privileged access to it.

3
RITUAL HOSPITALITY
Women Sufis and the Musical Ethics of Accommodation

As Fatima Lwelbani and her musical troupe were playing their ritual trance ceremony dedicated to the thirteenth-century female saint Sayyda Mannūbiyya,[1] Fatima's pet turtle walked across the floor and stopped in front of the musicians.[2] It was December 2014 and Fatima, the seventy-four-year-old leader of the group, and her fellow musicians were seated on cushions in the kitchen floor in her small apartment (see fig. 3.1). Sallouha, who was singing and playing frame drum, yelled *khallī yitkhammar!* (let it trance!), provoking laughter from all. This moment of levity belied the disconcerting circumstances of the performance. There were no trancers present because we were not at the shrine where the ritual was scheduled to take place; instead, we were in Fatima's apartment in the Tunis medina after she suspended our plans to meet at a ceremony she had agreed to lead at the shrine of Sīdī ʿAmor. She had cancelled the ceremony after being informed that militant Salafis were once again stationing themselves outside the shrine where, on a previous visit, they had chased and physically threatened Fatima and her troupe.[3] "They had knives and swords with them," she said, describing a harrowing escape; "they came at us from the mountains

1. "Sayyda" (lit. "lady") is an honorific in this context serving as the feminine equivalent of Sīdī, indicating what I am choosing to translate as "saint."

2. Fatima had invited my friend and fellow ethnomusicologist Hamza Tebai and me to learn about her musical approach to ritual. I thank Hamza for introducing me to Fatima and facilitating interviews and this recording session.

3. In the aftermath of the 2011 Revolution, the shrine of Sayyda Mannūbiyya in Manouba had been severely damaged by arsonists as part of a widespread militant Salafi offensive against these sites of ritual activity. Although five of the arsonists were arrested and sentenced to five years in prison, others continued to intimidate and harass shrine visitors there as well.

FIGURE 3.1. Fatima Lwelbani (*left*) and Sallouha Hosni of Fatima's Mannūbiyya troupe. Photo by the author.

and the sea . . . thank God our driver was fast so we could get away." She continued:

> Since the Revolution, everything fell apart [*halkit al-dunyā*]. They [Salafists] closed [the shrine of] Sīdī 'Alī Ḥaṭṭāb and burned Sayyda Mannūbiyya and Sīdī Bū Sa'īd. Since then, whoever goes to those shrines is responsible for their own life; they will be either slaughtered or burned. So we stopped working. But now things are starting to move, but slowly, as they rebuilt Sīdī Bū Sa'īd and [reopened] Sīdī 'Alī Ḥaṭṭāb. Still, it is not the same. They question and stop the people who go there. (Pers. comm., 2014)

Fatima's narrative of the state of affairs of her troupe and the zāwiya shrine system it inhabits revealed an overriding concern with the social services they provide, particularly for the poor.

> If you go to Sīdī 'Alī Ḥaṭṭāb, you see the people and you pity them. They are remembering God and [hear] the dhikr, and there are all sorts of food including goat, lamb, sheep, and couscous. Poor people there feel happy. Poor people and students and those who don't have any money, they can eat their fill there. (Pers. comm., 2014)

That the shrines were closed because of Salafi threats meant that the most vulnerable in society, and those such as Fatima who make a modest living from serving them, are disproportionately affected. The system of shrines is, above all, a network of sites of hospitality. "People come to us suffering," she told me, "and we cure them." The music-driven healing rituals of troupes such as Fatima's are integral components of that hospitality. This chapter shows how the musical form of the silsila—the flexible "chain" or sequence of songs for saints—is an active agent in this ethical work of ritual hospitality. Recognition of and hospitality toward others is a defining feature of ethics, for the silsila is not only music, not only ritual music, but ritual *healing* music. In this book I avoid using the term "saint veneration" to describe such practices, for it obscures the overriding goal of healing, of relieving suffering. If ethics is bound up in the treatment of others, in acts of recognition and inclusion, then the silsila of the Mannūbiyya emerges as a structure encouraging hospitality that is at once musical, ritual, and social.

In the performance of the silsila Mannūbiyya analyzed in this chapter,[4] no fewer than seventeen saints and other figures in this spiritual landscape are named, praised, and implored to descend into the ritual space through their respective songs, giving the saints a sonic materiality activated in ritual and supportive of trance healing. Inspired by Fatima's description of the silsila as a "journey" (*riḥla*), this chapter takes a (much more selective) journey to those ritual sites of practice evoked by the silsila, opening up into a consideration of the "boundary work" (Gidal 2016) of ritual music, drawing attention to acts of reinforcing and bridging boundaries between, for example, the gendered ritual spaces of the silsila and the men's Sufi dhikr. To that end, this chapter traces the points of convergence and divergence between the Mannūbiyya, the women's Tījāniyya, and the men's practices of the Tījāniyya and Shādhuliyya. Beyond analyzing the ethics of plurality revealed through the connections made musically through the silsila, this chapter probes a specific instance in which Fatima adapted her silsila and its timbral norms to accommodate the ritual needs of visitors from an adjacent women's healing tradition called the women's Tījāniyya (*tījāniyya al-nisā'*), a situation that posed ethical challenges that were solved musically. In short, this chapter highlights the overlaps and disjunctures between the silsila and its ritually adjacent practices and illustrates how musics of ambient Sufism work ritually and ethically in the service of hospitality.

4. The Mannūbiyya, like other women's trance troupes, are also referred to as rebaybiyya (Fatima Lwelbani, pers. comm., 2014). Chap. 5 provides further clarification of this term and how women's rebaybiyya is differentiated from (male) Jewish rebaybiyya.

SAYYDA MANNŪBIYYA

Before the troubles following the Revolution, Fatima and her group enjoyed a standing appointment every Sunday leading trance rituals held at the shrine of Sayyda Mannūbiyya. Sayyda ʿAisha Mannūbiyya (1197–1267) is the only female saint in Tunis to have an official hagiography (*manāqib*, a customary record of the virtues and miracles attributed to major saints) and a regular schedule of principally male dhikr rituals in addition to women's trance ceremonies at her shrines (Amri 2008; Boissevain 2006). Like many saints in the Tunisian religious landscape, Sayyda Mannūbiyya is remembered for her piety, commitment to Qur'anic study, and miraculous acts during her lifetime, as well as, after her death, for her continued capacity to heal or otherwise intervene in the lives of visitors to her shrine. Little is known about Sayyda's life beyond the tales from her hagiography and the legends that circulate orally, many of which are concretized in the lyrics of praise songs. Taken together, these sources reveal themes of one woman's independence and strength of personal character and religious conviction, as she is portrayed as transcending the limitations of her expected gender roles and overcoming accusations that she acted immorally and brought shame to her household and community by spending her nights outside the house with a (male) circle of Sufis.

Today, Sayyda Mannūbiyya's shrines continue to attract young women, particularly brides or brides-to-be, looking for blessing and good fortune, although women of all ages and marital statuses take part in visits and ceremonies. The walls of one room in her shrine in the Manouba (Mannūba) neighborhood are covered in names written by visitors seeking her intercession; sometimes these are pairs of names, female and male, representing a marriage wish that came true for the couple. Women who have experienced a crisis involving behavior perceived as morally questionable may attribute the situation to affliction or possession by spirits and may visit the shrine for weekly trance healing rituals to appease those spirits and to partake in a community of support and sociability. Consideration of Sayyda Mannūbiyya's history and legends reveals that her own sexuality and gender emerge as unusual and ambiguous. She challenged gender norms by refusing a life of marriage and family. She left her father's home and eluded marriage to her betrothed cousin (depending on the version of this legend, by either killing him with a poisoned arrow, making him crazy and impotent, or turning him into a woman in order to maintain her own chastity). In each of these versions of the legend, her virginity remains intact and valorized, a theme in the profiles of women saints that Boissevain interprets as analogous to the requisite *voyage initiatique* associated with their male counterparts (2006: 35). Yet Sayyda Mannūbiyya's challenging of gender norms runs up against her depiction as an icon of femininity: she is widely described as a beautiful, even ravishing woman who used her looks and charm to attract male followers, going so far as to visit taverns to find men to bring to her Qur'anic reading circle (Boissevain 2006: 22). Accusations of prostitution are also common in commentary on the saint, who is equally likely to be described as chaste and as a seductress.

In giving up traditional female roles, Sayyda Mannūbiyya also entered into the social and devotional world of men, specifically the circle of Sufis led by Sīdī Belḥassen al-Shādhulī (1196–1258), founder of the Shādhuliyya Sufi order. As indicated in the previous chapter, the Shādhuliyya is the oldest continuously active ṭarīqa in Tunis, widely respected and often considered the "mother" ṭarīqa of the region's other Sufi orders. Although the Shādhuliyya neither use musical instruments nor promote outwardly ecstatic states of trance, they nevertheless support many of their ritually adjacent neighbors that do utilize music in the pursuit of trance states—for example, hosting 'Īsāwiyya ceremonies during the fourteen weeks of heightened ritual activity each summer at their shrine (see chap. 2). This shrine's prestige is embodied in its magnificent location atop the hill emerging from the Jellaz cemetery, offering vistas of the city of Tunis and evoking the legendary role of Sīdī Belḥassen as its spiritual watchman. That Sayyda Mannūbiyya was a spiritual disciple of Sīdī Belḥassen, learning from the master himself, is an important part of her spiritual profile that not only links her to the most prestigious Sufi institution in the city, but also enables both her detractors and followers to insist that Sayyda was a learned, educated Sufi and therefore that contemporary trance practices do—or, for critics of the Mannūbiyya, do not—follow the spirit of devotion approved by the saint and access her continued capacity for intervening in her followers' lives.

Sayyda Mannūbiyya's connection to the Shādhuliyya is reflected in song lyrics, architectural memory, and ritual performances. At the shrine of Sīdī Belḥassen, one room of retreat (*khalwa*) is dedicated to Sayyda Mannūbiyya. Although it is now used as a storage room, women continue to see and hear evidence that Sayyda Mannūbiyya's spirit returns to visit the room (Boissevain 2006: 117). While the overwhelming majority of visitors to Sayyda Mannūbiyya's two shrines are women, many men recognize her as a saint, and men from the Shādhuliyya Sufi order perform their liturgy at Sayyda's shrines weekly, a testament to Sayyda's spiritual filiation to the Shādhuliyya and Sīdī Belḥassen.

The main legend depicting Sayyda Mannūbiyya's demonstration of miraculous acts, and thus her *walāya* (sainthood or closeness to God), is what Boissevain calls the "myth of consecration and separation":

> The people of Manouba spoke poorly of her, telling her father that she was dressing immodestly and wearing makeup to attract attention. Upon returning from her prayers, he told her that her appearance and behavior, including spending her nights outside the home reading [religious texts], had brought him shame (*ʿār*). So she asked him to bring her the family's bull. She gathered the people of Manouba and had the butcher slaughter it. She distributed the meat to all the households and instructed them to return the bones to her when they were finished. When they had done so, she arranged the bones inside the skin of the bull in the courtyard of her home. She extended the hooves of the animal toward Mecca and recited a prayer sequence three times, commanding, "By the grace of God, rise." The bull was reanimated and licked the hand of her father, and Sayyda cursed the people, saying, "People of Manouba, old and young, may God sow discord among you," and concluded with a recitation of the ninety-nine names of God. (Adapted from Boissevain 2006: 27)

The two main themes that emerge from this legend are emphasized in the most widely performed praise songs for Sayyda Mannūbiyya. The first, voiced in the song "ʿĀrī al-Mannūbiyya" (Shame on [Sayyda] Mannūbiyya; see below) is the concept of shame (*ʿār*), more specifically being blamed for disgracing one's family. In addition to being wrongly accused of indecent behavior, Sayyda's refusal to marry her cousin was perceived by her family as shameful. The injustice of being accused of immoral acts and the despair resulting from pressure to marry someone chosen by parents resonate with visitors to the shrine who seek relief from similar situations threatening personal and familial rupture. The second is the trait of defensiveness against injustice, which in the legend takes the form of vengeance against the townspeople. The song "Naghghāra Yā Sayyda" calls on Sayyda to protect her followers and also highlights the relationship of reciprocity between saint and visitor.[5] In everyday Tunisian parlance, the term "naghghāra" may be used critically to refer to someone who is touchy or defensive. In the context of a praise song, however, it takes on positive connotations of empathy, as it implies that the saint herself feels slighted when one of her followers is wronged and will therefore take action to relieve suffering and redress the

5. The sung line continues, "Tell me what you want me to do" (*dabr ʿalayyā bi-dabbāra*, lit. "give me your orders").

injustice. The Moroccan feminist scholar Fatima Mernissi recognizes the power these narratives and sentiments have for women who visit the shrines of women saints:

> The psychic and emotional value of women's experience in sanctuaries is uncontested and evident. Sanctuaries, which are the locus of antiestablishment, antipatriarchal mythical figures, provide women with a space where complaint and vituperations against the system's injustices are allowed and encouraged. They give women the opportunity to develop critical views of their condition, to identify problems, and to try to find their solution. (Mernissi 1977: 111)

Mernissi concludes that, paradoxically, these antiestablishment sentiments and complaints about injustice are "neutralized" in the shrine and therefore have little chance of being carried outside of it to effect change on the dominant power structure. Yet saint shrines decenter and provide alternatives to the state's bureaucratic and market-based logics of care. They pursue social justice through radically open hospitality that not only provides an alternative to, but can also preempt and challenge, dominant bureaucratic, market-based forms of charity (Mittermaier 2014), secular justice systems (Bellamy 2011), and individualized clinical healing (Jankowsky 2010).

Shrines are also sites where women inhabit positions of authority. The two shrines of Sayyda Mannūbiyya host individual visitors who may visit regularly or infrequently to make offerings and pleas to the saint, receive ritual and spiritual guidance from the shrine's caretaker (*ūkīla*), and enjoy the company of other women sympathetic to their struggles. More formal gatherings involve leadership by the *muqaddama* (who may also be the leader of the musical troupe), whose status is equivalent to that of a shaykh. The model of female spiritual authority embodied in the figure of Sayyda Mannūbiyya is suffused throughout the practices that animate both shrines. One is in the neighborhood of Gorjani, where Sayyda relocated after fleeing from her father. The other shrine, and the more active of the two, is located on the presumed site of her father's home in Manouba (Mannūba; Mannūbiyya is the Arabic *nisba* [adjective] meaning "of or from Mannūba"). While it may appear counterintuitive for a shrine to be erected in the neighborhood of Manouba, whose townspeople Sayyda cursed, the relationship between the shrine, the saint, the town, and the shrine's visitors is complex. The current shrine in Manouba was not built until the early nineteenth century, under the auspices of the Husaynid regime. Many of the beys of the regime supported the institution of the zāwiya. Not only were many beys members of Sufi ṭarīqas and visitors to saint shrines, but they also saw the value of the institution for integrating (and surveilling) disparate parts of society. Nineteenth-century beys had a particular devotion to Sayyda Mannūbiyya and frequented her shrine in Gorjani (Boissevain 2006: 84). Mahmoud Bey (r. 1814–1824) built the current Manouba shrine,[6] which was expanded by Aḥmad Bey (r. 1837–1855) at a time when the village was a spring and summer vacation resort for the kingdom's dignitaries (Amri 2008: 32), and the shrines were mainly associated with the elite families of Tunis. A century later, however, the village and the shrine were increasingly associated with rural immigrant families moving to the city during an era of profound urban development and rural-to-urban migration. A women's prison, a psychiatric hospital, and numerous agencies for housing and welfare for the handicapped were established, all within one kilometer of the shrine, turning a previously elite vacation spot into an urban neighborhood synonymous with the needy, psychologically challenged, and incarcerated. Many people today see these developments as evidence of Sayyda's departing curse's coming true (Boissevain 2006: 30–32), which only bolsters her reputation as a saint with the power to intervene in the world of the living.

The figure of Sayyda Mannūbiyya thus straddles multiple dualities such as male and female worlds, values of virginity and accusations of prostitution, compassion and vengeance, established urban bourgeoisie and rural migrant newcomers, and learned, "sober" saint and icon of ecstatic devotional practices. These ambiguities of the saint's social and spiritual profile are activated and reinforced in ritual, where the saint is felt to intervene directly in the lives of individuals. Yet these rituals do not rely on Sayyda Mannūbiyya alone. Rather, they invoke a number of saints and spirits to descend into ritual and heal women through trance, with Sayyda Mannūbiyya and her shrine playing host to streams of visitors, both spiritual and human. It is through the musical form of the silsila that this hospitality is achieved.

THE MANNŪBIYYA SILSILA: PLURALITY, CONSTANCY, TRANSFORMATION

In contrast to the ḥaḍra analyzed in chapter 2, which brings together a diversity of sonic and musical forms, all pieces in the silsila are of the same ilk: each piece of the silsila repertoire is a nūba (pl. *nwib*),[7] meaning a praise

6. It is unknown when the shrine was first constructed. One historical account attests to its existence at the end of the seventeenth century (Boissevain 2006: 45).

7. This is not to be confused with the nūba (pl. nubāt) of mālūf, the Andalusī art music designated as Tunisia's national musical heritage. In mālūf, the term "nūba" refers to an entire cycle of songs in the same melodic mode (*ṭab'* or *maqām*). See Davis (2004) on the nūba of mālūf and Guettat (1980) on the nūba across the Maghreb.

song for a spiritual figure who is summoned into the ritual to heal through trance. In contrast to the nūba of the ʿĪsāwiyya and of mālūf, both of which are sequences of pieces in the same (or related) melodic mode, a nūba in the context of the Mannūbiyya—and of the ritual practices analyzed in chapters 4 and 5—is a single praise song. Yet it maintains the general idea of a musical unit that is followed by another structurally similar unit: nūba (the pronunciation of *nawba* in Tunisian dialect) literally means one's "turn," and to things *bi-nūba* is to do them in succession. The silsila, as a sequence of nūbas, is thus a succession of invocations of individual saints and other spiritual figures who take their "turn" descending into the ritual space where they are understood to provide the spiritual force to engender trance. Understood in this way, the term "nūba" is particularly evocative of the inseparability of sound and spirit, and, indeed, nūbas are often referred to simply by the name of the spiritual figure being summoned, with the name of the nūba (often the first line of sung text, following widespread convention in Arabic song) used especially for clarification when a saint has multiple nūbas.

The trance ritual led by Fatima at the shrine of Sayyda Mannūbiyya invokes a large number of saints and spirits, each of which has its own nūba (or two). The silsila, as a succession of nūbas, embodies and activates a structural pluralism that gives each constituent member of the silsila his or her due praise, time, and focus. While the order of nūbas in the silsila is variable, there are some conventions that are specific to the Mannūbiyya. After reciting the fātiḥa (the opening verse of the Qur'an), the silsila always begins with a nūba for the Prophet. Beginning in this way reinforces theological precepts central to Islam, namely the primacy of the word of God and the spiritual and theological stature of the Prophet. A nūba for Sayyda Mannūbiyya comes next, positioning her closest to the Prophet and above the remainder of saints who will be summoned, marking her spiritual power through sonic and structural proximity. The remainder of the silsila (see table 3.1) includes, among others, another female saint, Umm al-Zīn; Sayyda's spiritual companions and guides Sīdī Bū Saʿīd and Sīdī Belḥassen al-Shādhulī; other founders of Sufi orders such as Sīdī Ben ʿĪsā, Sīdī ʿAlī Ḥaṭṭāb, and Sīdī ʿAbd al-Qādir; the "patron" saint of Tunis Sīdī Meḥrez; and the female spirit Ummī Yenna, who is also part of the spirit-possession practices of sṭambēlī and the women's Tījāniyya.[8] Each saint is also understood to be able to control certain spirits (jnūn, sing. *jinn*), such that trancers may be possessed by a spirit but trance to a song for a saint who intervenes. With few exceptions, each member of the silsila was a historical figure, with particular life

8. The Tunisian pronunciation (and transliteration) is Tījāniyya; the standard transliteration is Tijāniyya.

activities and spiritual achievements, who is memorialized through a physical shrine (often housing the saint's tomb) that is the locus for a number of individual and communal ritual practices of praise, devotion, and healing.

Despite common claims that the various Sufi orders simply follow different paths toward the same goal, it is crucial to underscore that the practices of one ṭarīqa are often criticized by members of others. While, for example, the dramatic trance practices of the 'Īsāwiyya and Qādiriyya are often met with awe, they also elicit condemnation from those who find them excessive and outside the bounds of proper Tunisian Sufism. The separatist doctrine of the Tījāniyya, as well as its claims that one of its prayers is as efficacious as six thousand recitations of the Qur'an, makes it particularly vulnerable to critique (see below). I have heard the multilayered, round-style singing of the Ḥaṭṭābiyya criticized by members of other ṭarīqas for making the words incomprehensible and therefore religiously ineffectual (given the centrality and agency of the recited word), a critique that is at once aesthetic and theological. Certain saints may also be met with disapproval, such as Aḥmed al-Tījānī and his claim to be the final, authoritative saint in Islam (*khatm*, lit. "seal"), Sayyda Mannūbiyya bringing shame on her family and town, and the scandalous behavior of the "mad" saint Sīdī Ben 'Arūs.

Part of the work the silsila structure accomplishes, however, is to enable these multiple histories and traditions of saints to come together and coalesce without contradiction. Each saint of the silsila is legitimized as equally capable of intervening in the spirit world and healing humans through trance. Fatima likens the ritual progression through the silsila to a riḥla, that is, a journey, one that evokes these multiple personages, sites of ritual activity, and diverse practices and histories (see web fig. 3.1w). While the concept of ziyāra (pilgrimage, lit. "visit") connotes an individual or communal visit to a specific saint's shrine and all the sensory, spiritual, and social knowledge and experiences associated with it, riḥla is associated with the Islamic tradition of traveling to acquire new knowledge. A ziyāra is a form of travel to a single, specific destination, while riḥla connotes a journey away and through, with the expectation of accumulating knowledge. The silsila, then, can be construed as a series of way stations through a journey where each nūba provides additional knowledge for, and of, the Mannūbiyya. Table 3.1 lists the seventeen nūbas performed by Fatima's group in the December 2014 performance.

All of these spiritual figures and references are brought into the distinctive soundworld of the Mannūbiyya. This soundworld is remarkably consistent: every song features nonstop cyclic rhythms of one to two *darbūka* drums, three large and heavy tambourines, and unison and antiphonal sing-

TABLE 3.1 Mannūbiyya silsila as performed by Fatima's troupe

Nūba	Spiritual figure	Identity	Melodic mode[a]	Rhythmic mode
"Inzād al-Nabī"	Prophet Muḥammad	Birth and mother of the Prophet	ḥsīn ṣabā	mdawr ḥawzī (6/8)/ sūga (2/4)
"'Arī al-Mannūbiyya"	Sayyda Mannūbiyya	Female saint	dhīl	khatm (6/8)
"Māk Sulṭān"	Sīdī Meḥrez	Patron saint of Tunis	dhīl	khatm (6/8)
"Yā Bābā Tījānī"	Sīdī Aḥmed al-Tījānī	Founder of Tījāniyya	dhīl	fazzānī lībī (4/4)
"Sīdī Ben 'Īsā"	Sīdī Ben 'Īsā	Founder of 'Īsāwiyya	dhīl	mrabba' (4/4)
"'Alā Umm al-Zīn"	Umm al-Zīn al-Sahliyya	Female saint	ḥsīn	fazzānī (4/4)
"Naghghāra Yā Sayyda"	Sayyda Mannūbiyya	Female saint	ḥsīn / mḥayr 'irāq	fazzānī (4/4)
"Bābā Jallūl"	**Sīdī 'Abd al-Qādir al-Jīlānī**	**Founder of Qādiriyya**	**mḥayr sīka / aṣba'īn**	**fazzānī (4/4)**
"Nādūlī Nādūlī"	**Sīdī 'Abd al-Qādir al-Jīlānī**	**Founder of Qādiriyya**	**mḥayr sīka**	**khatm (3/4)**
"Irfa' Ra'sik"	Sīdī 'Alī al-Ḥaṭṭāb	Founder of Ḥaṭṭābiyya	aṣba'īn	mrabba' (4/4)
"'Addālā 'Addāla"	Sīdī 'Amr Bū Khatwa and others	Local saint	ḥsīn ṣabā	mrabba' (4/4)
"Nādīt Rahum Jūnī"	Sīdī 'Abd al-Salām	Founder of Sulāmiyya	mḥayr 'irāq / ḥsīn	khatm (6/8)
"Ra'is al-Abḥār"	**Sīdī Bū Sa'īd**	**Guardian of seas; master of baḥriyya spirits**	**nwā / sīka**	**fazzānī (4/4)**
"Allah Allah Yā Bābā"	**Sīdī Manṣūr**	**From Sfax, also guardian of seas**	**nwā**	**fazzānī (4/4)**
"Bābā Baḥrī"	**Sīdī Manṣūr**	**From Sfax, also guardian of seas**	**nwā**	**khatm (6/8)**

TABLE 3.1 Continued

Nūba	Spiritual figure	Identity	Melodic mode[a]	Rhythmic mode
"Ummī Yenna"	**Ummī Yenna**	**Baḥriyya spirit, also "daughter" of Sīdī Bū Sa'īd**	**nwā**	**khatm (6/8)**
"Yā Belḥassen"	Sīdī Belḥassan al-Shādhulī	Founder of Shādhuliyya	mazmūm	fazzānī (4/4)

Boldface type in the body of the table indicates nūbas that are grouped together and performed in succession to produce episodes of sequential intensification.
[a] The names of melodic modes (*ṭubū'*) and some rhythmic modes (*mwāzīn*) are based on post facto analyses and are not used in musicians' discourse. The melodies are suggestive of these modes. I use the mode names not to fix the identity of the nūbas, but rather to reveal larger patterns of relationships in the silsila.

ing by the drummers. The dominant sound is that of the tambourines (*bnāder*; sing. *bendīr*; in this context, referring to frame drums with cymbals), whose cymbals jingle with every stroke of the drum, producing a shimmering sound and expanding the temporal envelope created by the drum stroke. This particular combination of sounds does the work of differentiating the Mannūbiyya from adjacent ritual musics while also adhering to certain underlying principles shared by those other traditions. More specifically, the instrumentation of several large tambourines, darbūka, and choral women's voices is definitive of the Mannūbiyya (shared only by very similar women's trance practices),[9] while the principle of constancy of timbre and texture is a feature of all silsila-based ritual musics in the region, a point that will become clearer in the following chapters as the case studies accrue.

This constancy is reinforced through the cyclic nature of the musical form. The short rhythmic cycles of the percussion are insistent, regular, and played in unison at a steady tempo. All listeners, but particularly trancers, are therefore able to become absorbed into the comfort of a rhythmic cushion that sustains the similarly regular movements of the body. Occasional ornamentations or cross-rhythms performed by a drummer add excitement (because of the timbral similarity of the drums, these short bursts of syncopation constitute addition without subtraction as the variations blend into the whole while the underlying pattern continues). Owing to the modular nature of the silsila, in which the order of songs is flexible, there is no

9. One performs occasionally at the shrine of Sīdī Bū Sa'īd, and another is based in the town of Sousse. The term "rebaybiyya" is sometimes used to refer to women's silsila-based ritual musics in general, but it took on a specific association with trance healing rituals of the Jewish community of Tunisia (see chap. 5).

overriding sense of modal unity or trajectory in either rhythmic or melodic modes throughout the silsila (in contrast, say, to the ʿĪsāwiyya ceremony analyzed in chap. 2). Because the silsila is made up of mostly interchangeable single units or small clusters of units, nūbas—and the trancing that goes with them—near the beginning of the silsila are no more or less intense than those at any other point. Therefore, the GI model prevalent in the ʿĪsāwiyya ḥaḍra is not replicated in the silsila. Instead, the Mannūbiyya silsila features DI through acceleration of a single rhythm, as well as occasional SI produced by pairs or small clusters of related songs in the same melodic mode performed in a sequence that increases in intensity with modulation from one rhythm to another, particularly from fazzānī to khatm.

For example, in Fatima's performance, outlined in table 3.1, two nūbas for Sīdī ʿAbd al-Qādir are performed in succession. They share melodic modal unity (both are in the mḥayr sīka mode), but the first is in the fazzānī rhythmic mode while the second is in khatm, a rhythm often used to close a sequence (indeed, the term itself means "seal," investing it with the expectation of closure). Another, more extensive example is the set of four songs for spiritual figures associated with spirits and saints of the sea (baḥriyya). Sīdī Bū Saʿīd, Sīdī Manṣūr (in two nūbas), and Ummi Yenna form a sequence of nūbas, all in the same melodic mode, while the rhythmic mode, like the Sīdī ʿAbd al-Qādir example, also progresses from fazzānī to khatm, providing a sense of a cohesive unit with its own trajectory, unity, and closure. These rhythmic sequences illustrate the SI model introduced in chapter 1 and illustrated in chapter 2, where SI is achieved primarily through rhythmic modulations that proceed through a series of shorter and faster patterns. Musical example 3.1 shows the rhythmic modulations and tempo accelerations for these two clusters of nūbas. The faster subdivisions generate more temporal and timbral density, increasing the level of sonic saturation.

Most song texts are in the form of short quatrains. Each quatrain is complete and independent both melodically and textually; the melody is largely the same for each quatrain of a given song, and the text of each quatrain can stand as an independent image or idea while contributing to the larger whole. There is a high degree of flexibility in textual presentation, as qua-

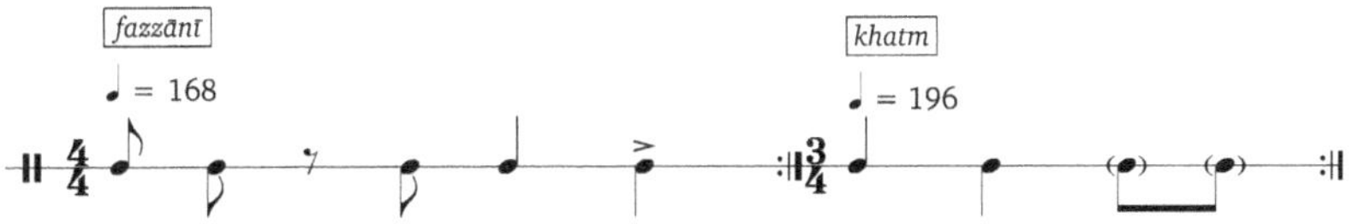

MUSICAL EXAMPLE 3.1. Sequential intensification (SI) via acceleration and rhythmic modulation from fazzānī to khatm rhythms (khatm can also be felt in 6/8, depending on the melodic phrasing)

trains may be inserted, repeated, or omitted, and their constituent parts may be altered or recombined. This flexibility also allows for a good deal of intertextuality, as similar phrases on themes such as the suffering of the visitor, the healing power of the saint, or certain images associated with shrines (their water wells, domes, and landscapes) are sung in many nūbas of the silsila. One of the most striking examples in the Mannūbiyya repertoire is a commonly inserted line of text calling on God to bless the mother of the saint for bringing him into the world, an expansion of the network of personalities praised by the Mannūbiyya that reinforces the role of women in the lives of saints.

Indeed, the Mannūbiyya silsila begins with "Inzād al-Nabī," a praise song to the Prophet that celebrates his birth. It is among the most widely sung devotional songs in Tunisia, where it accompanies holiday and life-cycle celebrations such as weddings and the mawlid. Beginning a ritual with a praise to the Prophet is a widespread and often expected act throughout the Islamic world. It situates the ritual within a wider shared Islamic outlook that celebrates the Prophet as the model of right living. A song that celebrates the Prophet is a performative, in the linguistic sense of a speech act that not only describes something but also acts upon the world, consummating an action (see Austin 1975), in this case making the assertion that music and song are legitimate ways of praising the Prophet.[10] The text of the song reflexively refers to this in the line "bring the bendīrs, O [people of the] ḥaḍra" (*hizzū al-bnāder yā ḥaḍra*), evoking an image that is not only self-referential for the women playing and listening to the bendīrs of the Mannūbiyya troupe, but also evokes other contexts and occasions (particularly the Sufi ḥaḍra described in chap. 2) in which the Prophet is praised musically. That this nūba is specifically about the birth of the Prophet also highlights the role of motherhood, a recurring theme throughout the silsila, as several nūbas include lines of sung text asking God to bless the mother of the saint for bringing him into the world. Beginning with "Inzād al-Nabī" is as fundamental to asserting the identity and values of the Mannūbiyya as is following up that nūba with one for Sayyda Mannūbiyya herself.

"ʿĀrī ʿal-Mannūbiyya"

This nūba for Sayyda Mannūbiyya has pride of place as the first song following the invocation of the Prophet in this journey of the silsila (video ex. 3.1).

10. In fact, this nūba is also sometimes called the *taʿlīla*, a term whose etymology connects it to shades of meaning that include entertainment and explanation or justification.

Like many songs of the silsila, the lyrics reference such themes as the act of visiting the shrine, the visitor's state of suffering, pleas for help, words of praise, and references to specific aspects of the shrine, including the sonic dimension, as well as the saint's legends. In this nūba, the theme of shame is also prominent. As with other songs dedicated to Sayyda Mannūbiyya, in certain lines the singers temporarily speak from the perspective of the townspeople or Sayyda's father, that is, those who claimed she had brought shame on them.[11] In this nūba, it occurs in the boldface text in the printed lyrics below, which is a refrain repeated after each subsequent quatrain.

ʿārī ʿal-mannūbiyya, ʿārī ʿal-mannūbiyya	**Shame on Mannūbiyya, shame on Mannūbiyya**
ʿārī ʿal-mannūbiyya, yā umīma yā sharaʿiyya	**Shame on Mannūbiyya, O my legitimate mother**[12]
w-ʿārī ʿalā al-maḥbūba, lī sākina mannūba	Shame on the beloved, who lives in Manouba
rabbī w-āʿṭāhā al-tūba, yā ū-hiyya millī ṣghīra	God granted her repentance, since she was a child
yā lillā yā maḥlāhā, ṭalbit rabbi w-āʿṭāhā	O sweet Lady,[13] she asked God and he provided
ḥūriyya fil-janna maʿhā, hiyya umīma sharaʿiyya	Virgins are with her in heaven, my legitimate mother
lillā jītak lil-dār, jibt bākū al-nawwār	O Lady I came to your house with a bouquet of roses

11. In two other praise songs to Sayyda Mannūbiyya (presented in French translation in Boissevain 2006: 235–236), there are lines of sung text where the singers take on the role of the townspeople or Sayyda's father accusing her of bringing shame—for example, "You brought shame on us," "I blame you and scold you," and "Your shame is on my face." This concept of shame appears in songs to other women saints. A nūba for Umm al-Zīn in Būdhīna's anthology of Tunisian song (1997: 271, 273) includes a concluding section titled ʿĀrī ʿalā Lillāyā, which also mentions Sayyda Mannūbiyya. This kind of textual reproach, in which the lyrics of the nūba activate a legend associated with the saint or misunderstandings surrounding her behaviors, differs from another textual strategy in which the narrator blames the saint for not delivering the healing or reprieve expected after the narrator made offerings to the saint (as in "Ra'is al-Abḥār," for example).

12. The meaning of *ʿārī* is "my shame," giving the sense that "Mannūbiyya brought shame on me" or "disgraced me."

13. Like the term Sayyda, *lilla* (or *lālla*) is an honorific applied to female saints; it is the equivalent of "Sīdī."

yā sayyda yā umm al-qmār, umīma yā shara'iyya	O Lady O Mother of Moons, my legitimate mother
lillā jītak al-yūm, nibkī u-qalbī mahmūm	O Lady I came to you today, crying and distressed
yā sayyda 'alīk nlūm, yā umīma yā shara'iyya	O Lady I blame you, O my legitimate mother
lillā fī fumm al-bāb, hāy taqrā fil-kitāb	The Lady is at the doorstep, she is reading the Book
ma'hā al-shaykh al-ḥāṭṭāb, yā umīma yā shara'iyya	With her is Shaykh Ḥaṭṭāb, O my legitimate mother
lillā mūlat al-bīr, mūlat al-dīwān al-kbīr	Lady, owner of the well, master of the big ceremony
yā sayyda yā bashīr, yā umīma yā shara'iyya	O Sayyda, O Bashīr, O my legitimate mother
lillā jītak u-njīk, ū-dīmā nādī bīk	Lady I came to you and will again, I always call upon you
yā umīma al-'ār 'alīk, yā umīma yā shara'iyya	O my mother shame is upon you, O my legitimate mother
lillā jītak l-'ashiyya, ṭalbit rabbī bi-'aṭīyya	Lady I came in the evening, I asked God for a gift
sayyda mā tkhallī biyya, yā umīma yā shara'iyya	Sayyda don't leave me, O my legitimate mother
lillā fī bāb swīqa, 'alā ra'shā taqrīṭa	The Lady is in Bāb Swīqa, a bandana on her head
ṭbāl ma'ā al-mūzīqa, ū-sayyda mannūbiyya	Drums and music and Sayyda Mannūbiyya
lillā mā aḥlā al-qurjānī, rīt al-sayyda b-'ayānī	Lady how sweet is Gorjani, I saw Sayyda with my own eyes
ma'āhā aḥmad al-tījānī, umīma rākī shara'iyya	With her is Aḥmed al-Tījānī, you are my legitimate mother

The rhyme scheme of the refrain is thus AAAA, while the rhymes of most verses create the pattern BBBA, CCCA, DDDA; A is the concluding line, "O my legitimate mother," and reinforces in almost every quatrain the idea of the saint protecting those seeking her aid, asserting a new layer of extra-familial affiliation announced in familial terms. Not only does the saint take on a maternal (and, in the case of male saints, paternal) role, but the other regular participants also become symbolic family members, such as aunts and sisters, providing support. In her study of the social conditions of trance dancers at Sayyda Mannūbiyya, Sophie Ferchiou notes that it is often an acute personal crisis having to do with marriage, sexuality, or childbirth that leads women to seek therapy at Sayyda Mannūbiyya. These crises affect the family, not just the individual. According to Ferchiou (1991b: 216–217), "The first possession crisis—perceived as an illness—always occurs at a critical moment: loss of virginity, in a context of traditional control of sexuality; a sentimental deception or forced marriage; a natural abortion; a still-born child or the death of an infant. In Tunisian society . . . these misfortunes are considered as transgressions or serious faults." Such situations are often diagnosed as having been caused by spirit possession. The spirits need to be placated, and they can also be mastered by a saint who holds power over them. Each patient has "her" nūba that either calls the spirit to descend into her body to be appeased through the gift of dance, or calls upon a saint to intervene to chase the spirit away. The process is not one of exorcism. Instead, it involves the management of a potentially lifelong relationship with the spirit and saint that requires, above all, regular trance dance ceremonies. Among the musical conditions that support trance in the Mannūbiyya silsila is the cultivation of continuity, which can be construed as timbral constancy and a cyclicity tethered to nested temporalities.

Repetition and Nested Temporalities

Repetition does two seemingly contradictory things at once. First, it can draw attention to the nuances and details, such as expressive timing, at the micro level (Margulis 2013: 59), encouraging an attunement to small details. But it can also create the comfort of constancy that allows attention to be diverted elsewhere, for instance to changing lyrics. Repetition can be a musical virtue itself, and it can create the conditions for transformation. Because trance is a social act that requires witnessing as part of the therapeutic process, and only a handful of people (and often only one or two) are trancing at any given moment, there is an "audience" of listeners who can listen to the music without engaging in trance dance but whose sensory experience overlaps with that of trancers as both experience the same musical conditions for the trance.

How does the Mannūbiyya aesthetic support trance states? Structurally, the music sets up expectations that are continually, and predictably, met

MUSICAL EXAMPLE 3.2. Nested temporalities in "'Arī 'al-Mannūbiyya" (Shame on Mannūbiyya)

through the layering of multiple units of repetition. All of these nested temporalities are interdependent and operate in slightly different ways. Musical example 3.2 illustrates the simultaneity of the levels. The rhythmic cycle (highlighted in black) is the shortest musical unit, repeated without interruption throughout the entirety of the song. This rhythm, which is not named by Mannūbiyya musicians, approximates the widespread khatm ("closure") rhythm introduced in chapter 2.[14] This rhythm establishes a strong sense of downbeat with a directionality created by a series of offbeat high sounds (takks) leading to the low (dumm) sound that aligns with accentuated articulations of the vocal melody. The rhythm of that vocal melody (dark gray) repeats three times in each quatrain before a slightly different rhythm, starting with three quarter notes, provides a kind of resolution. The lyrics of that resolution (medium gray) reappear in most verses, contributing another layer of expectations that are satisfied regularly and within relatively short time spans. The complete melody of the full quatrain (light gray) is also repeated throughout the entirely of the song, with few small variations. Thus, even when a new element is introduced (a melodic variation or new line of text), there is a strong sense of continuity at numerous levels including rhythm, timbre, and texture, as well as the complete melody. In Richard Middleton's (1983) terms, there are both musematic (short units, such as the rhythmic cycle) and discursive (longer units, such as the whole melody) repetitions. What is particularly important in the context of trance is that the musical instruments never stop; there is never a change in ensemble texture. This continuity, together with the musical form based on nested temporalities, contributes to a specific sense of constancy and met expectations. They all contribute to the potential for flow, in the sense proffered by Csik-

14. It also approximates a rhythm called *dzīrī* (lit. "Algerian"), or *srārī* in some Tunisian folk music contexts.

szentmihalyi (1990), whereby outside distractions are minimized, satisfying regularity is emphasized, and participants enter a zone of balanced concentration whereby they may become one with the activity. This rhythmic and formal constancy, along with timbral saturation, produces a kind of musical hospitality that maximizes the potential for trance, and thus healing, and is characterized by immediacy that is distinct from but complements the large-scale hospitality encouraged by the inclusive and flexible silsila musical structure.

Let me be clear that I am not arguing that these nested temporalities and the virtue of constancy and saturation are unique to the Mannūbiyya, or trance musics, for that matter. Indeed, at some level, they are common in folk, ritual, and popular musics not only in the Arab world but across the globe. What I am doing here is laying the groundwork for subsequent analysis in the next two chapters that will contribute to a larger theory of silsila-based trance musics in Tunis and in which the virtues of constancy and nested temporalities are further amplified, particularly as melody instruments are introduced. One aspect of that theory relates to how repetition creates the conditions for sonic and temporal transformation, particularly intensification. It is typical for a trance dance to increase in intensification as the musicians stop singing close to the end of the song and intensify their drumming in both speed and volume. A particularly illuminating approach to this strategy of DI occurs in the nūba for Sīdī Belḥassen, to which I now turn.

Adapting the Dhikr of the Shādhuliyya

A main source of Sayyda Mannūbiyya's "shame" depicted in the nūba and legend described above was her commitment to spending nights outside her home at predominantly male gatherings of Sufis. It is widely believed that she was a disciple of the Sīdī Belḥassen al-Shādhulī, a relationship that is attested through ritual practice, oral tradition, and Sayyda's hagiography.[15] Sīdī Belḥassen is a major figure in the history of Sufism who inspired the establishment of the Shādhuliyya, a prestigious and widespread ṭarīqa throughout the Maghreb and Egypt, as well as numerous related ṭarīqas started by his disciples, who maintained the Shādhuli spirit while developing new doctrines and practices. Sīdī Belḥassen discouraged asceticism and

15. Because hagiographies take liberties with concepts of historical time and physical space, as Nelly Amri notes, it remains unclear whether Sayyda Mannūbiyya had a relationship with Sīdī Belḥassen himself, or rather followed his teachings after he departed for Egypt (Amri 2008; Boissevain 2006: 116).

withdrawal from society, instead emphasizing a Sufism tied to the community (Geoffroy 1996).[16]

In Tunis, this practice follows an elaborate annual calendar with changing content depending on the month and week, but all ceremonies revolve around recitation of eleven ḥizbs, a series of liturgical recitations attributed to the saint; these are preceded by solo sung qaṣīdas and prescribed verses of Qur'anic recitation and followed by a dhikr ceremony performed standing and increasing in intensity.[17] It is known as a Sufi path that encourages a Sufism of sobriety (*sahw*); yet while it does not allow musical instruments or encourage dramatic acts of trance, it generally tolerates those that do, welcoming other ṭarīqas to perform rituals at their zāwiya, for example, during al-arbaʿtāsh, the fourteen weeks of heightened ritual activity each summer. Other ṭarīqas typically perceive the Shādhuliyya as the "mother" ṭarīqa of Tunisia, factoring into their own Sufi histories despite differences in practice or doctrine. It is associated with the political and economic elite in Tunisia, thus acting as an intermediary between the state and the people during the Husaynid era (Andézian 1996). The relationship between Sayyda Mannūbiyya and Sīdī Belḥassen thus connects Sayyda directly to the most prestigious Sufi figure and institution in Tunis.

yā belḥassen, yā shādhlī / yā belḥassen, yā shādhlī / yā belḥassen, yā shādhlī / yā bābā ḥamlī kādnī	O Belḥassen, O Shādhlī / O Belḥassen, O Shādhlī / O Belḥassen, O Shādhlī / O Bābā my burdens weigh on me
ṭalʿatū ḥafyāna, yā bābā / sākin al-jabāna yā sīdī / ṣāḥib al-mghāra bābā / ḥamlī kādnī	I ascended it [the hill] barefoot, O baba / Who lives at the graveyard, O Sīdī / owner of the cave, baba / my burdens weigh on me
ū-baḥdhā al-bīr yā bābā / dīwān kbīr yā sīdī / ḥājj bashīr bābā / w-anā ḥamlī kādnī	Near the water well there is a big [ritual] gathering / Ḥājj Bashīr, bābā, / my burdens weigh on me

16. The Shādhuliyya are credited by some sources with establishing one of the first cafés in Tunis by formalizing and ritualizing the drinking of coffee—which became a social act par excellence in the region—after all Shādhulī ceremonies at his zāwiya in Tunis (Mustaysir 2014: 25).

17. Each ḥizb is also accompanied by a *waẓīfa*, which, in this context, means a prayer inspired by the ḥizb, recited in a similar manner.

fil-mghāra ū-tjīk / jamī' al-dhakkāra yā bābā / rānī muḍāma / w-anā ḥamlī kādnī	In the cave, the dhikr group comes to you, O bābā / I have been wronged / and my burdens weigh on me
w-'azīz 'alī / yā lābas al-qashābiy ya yā bābā / mā tkhallī bī / w-anā ḥamlī kādnī	You are dear to me, you who wear the qashābiyya robe, O sīdī / don't leave me / my burdens weigh on me
w-'azīz khwātā / yarḥam al-umm illī jābātā / yā bābā mā aḥlā ṣfātih / w-anā ḥamlī kādnī	Dear to his brothers, God bless the mother who brought him / O baba how sweet his qualities / my burdens weigh on me
allah, allah . . . [repeated seventy times]	Allah, Allah . . .

The nūba for Sīdī Belḥassen follows a quatrain textual form similar to that for "'Arī 'al-Mannūbiyya." Its main theme is a description of the ritual activities of the Shādhuliyya at their zāwiya and the act of visiting it, while the recurring line closing each quatrain complains of the narrator's misfortunes, which are the reason for seeking the saint's intercession. The musical timbre and texture are the same as all other parts of the silsila, with the same unison drumming and singing, in addition to discrete intensification as the nūba reaches its end. The rhythmic pattern is fazzānī (see musical ex. 3.1). In short, Sīdī Belḥassen is absorbed into the soundworld of the silsila Mannūbiyya, presented as one nūba among many others dedicated to a saint capable of healing through facilitating trance. The DI strategy in this nūba, however, provides an adaptation of Shādhulī practice, as the Mannūbiyya musicians intensify the drumming while singing the name "Allah" over and over, in an explicit appropriation of the Shādhulī dhikr.

With the lights turned off (as the men also do in their dhikr ceremony), the musicians continue drumming and chant "Allah" repeatedly. The nūba, which began at a tempo of 154 bpm, ends nearly 30 percent faster, at 190 bpm, after seventy repetitions of the name "Allah" (see video ex. 3.2). This is a powerful, intensely affecting moment. At this point in the ritual the women in attendance ululate, filling the air with the high-pitched wails associated with ritual moments of heightened energy and impact. Dancers reach the climax of their trance and begin to faint, their exhausted bodies sinking on the ground. Fatima, in her role as healer, wakes the patients, gives them some water, censes their bodies with incense, and recites a bit of the Qur'an over them until they are ready to "leave all better" (*trawwaḥ lā bās 'alīhā*). Sweets and money are thrown to the musicians in celebration and appreciation.

The Shādhuliyya dhikr this nūba indexes is remarkably similar in form, content, and affect. Fatima reported that she got goosebumps just describing to me the scene of the chanting of "Allah" or "huwa" (He) in the dark, a practice common to men's Sufi orders. She described the Shādhuliyya, Qādiriyya, and 'Īsāwiyya performing the dhikr together at the communal pilgrimage to the shrine of Sīdī 'Alī Ḥaṭṭāb, where they turn off the lights and recite the name of God between midnight and three o'clock in the morning, as lit candles remain in bowls of water without dying out and people fall into trance to the ground (pers. comm., 2014). In the dhikr, as in the Mannūbiyya nūba, sonic and musical potencies create the conditions for participants to be taken over by unseen forces, fall into trance, and emerge transformed. So many other ritual elements distinguish the Mannūbiyya from their male Sufi counterparts, from musical structure, timbre, and lyrical content to the explicit function of trance healing of individuals in succession. Indeed, it is rare for male Sufis to acknowledge any commonality between their practices and those of the Mannūbiyya. Yet the Mannūbiyya's integration of the dhikr into their silsila demonstrates shared spiritual references, sonic strategies, and sensory experiences that reveal their coexistence within the shared ritual ecology.

The Silsila as Journey and Accommodating Diversity

The indexing of the sounds of the Shādhuliyya dhikr provides a powerful example of the personalities, practices, and sounds of the "home" tradition of Sīdī Belḥassen (particularly the dhikr of the Shādhuliyya ṭarīqa) becoming domesticated into the distinctive soundworld of the Mannūbiyya. This act of adoption and adaptation—in both spiritual and musical terms—occurs in virtually every nūba of the silsila. When Fatima's group plays the nūba for Sīdī Ben 'Īsā, for example, it does more than invoke the saint's presence to induce trance. It also evokes a well-known field of practices, sites, and sounds associated with the 'Īsāwiyya Sufi order described in chapter 2. Sīdī 'Abd al-Qādir's nūba calls up images of the Qādiriyya ṭarīqa and its dramatic trance practices, as well as the legend of Sayyda Mannūbiyya in which he confirms Sayyda's sainthood (*walāya*) while she is still in her mother's womb (see Boissevain 2006: 26). When it is Ummī Yenna's turn, the song for this spirit also conjures up the ritual world of spirit possession traditions with which she is most closely associated, such as sṭambēlī (see chap. 4) and the women's Tījāniyya (see below).[18] The nūba for Sīdī ʿAlī al-Ḥaṭṭāb evokes the practices of the Ḥaṭṭābiyya Sufi order, with its distinctive round-style antiphonal singing, as well as the massive group pilgrimage to the shrine of Sīdī ʿAlī al-Ḥaṭṭāb, where ritualists from the traditions referenced in the silsila—including the Mannūbiyya—gather annually, attending each other's performances and kicking off the fourteen-week summer ritual season, during which many will again cross paths with each other (see chap. 7). All of these nūbas reference very different devotional communities with very different sonic and musical practices, but they all are brought into the singular, distinctive soundworld of the Mannūbiyya, where each nūba is a node with layers of associations and connected to the others and beyond.

At the macro level of musical organization, the silsila, taken as a whole, charts a broad historical and geographic itinerary of local Sufism, evoking a landscape of shrines and a history of Sufis and saints in the Tunis area. These shrines, sites of devotion and healing, are local and sometimes regional or even national landmarks—icons of neighborhood identity. They are familiar—through direct or indirect contact—not only to participants in each of the traditions evoked, but also to nonpracticing Tunisians in the area, for whom they are landmarks or sites of familial memory. The performance format of the silsila maps a sacred topography of Tunis, explicitly situating the Mannūbiyya trance ritual within a devotional and therapeutic landscape characterized by a network of kindred practices that depend on the spiritual intervention of saints (see again web fig. 3.1w). Each saint, despite his or her specific role and practices associated with his or her "home" tradition, is confirmed through the silsila as being equally capable of healing individuals through their spiritual intervention in ritual trance.

This is a structural accommodation. Above, I argued that the saints of the silsila are all domesticated and treated equally, their differences flattened out as they are brought into the distinctive soundworld of the Mannūbiyya silsila. While lyrics may reference, either directly or indirectly, the different soundworlds of the different "home" traditions of the saints, only in the case of Sīdī Belḥassen do they performatively enact specific characteristics of the home traditions of different saints, performing a connection to an adjacent Sufi tradition but nevertheless absorbing it into the timbres, textures, and structures of the Mannūbiyya. I now turn to a specific and rather explicit instance of accommodation in which musical and ritual changes were made musically to accommodate another tradition and serve its community. This

18. Ummī Yenna is also considered to be the "daughter" of Sīdī Bū Saʿīd, thus connecting the world of spirits and saints.

speaks to the adaptability of the silsila, but also to the way that timbre and texture index specific ritual communities—to the extent that, if texture and timbre are not maintained, the music loses its therapeutic efficacy.

The Ṭabla Drum and Sifsārī Cloth

The nūba in question is that of Sīdī Aḥmed al-Tījānī (b. 1735, Algeria; d. 1815, Morocco), the founder of the Tījāniyya Sufi order. In Tunisia, the Tījāniyya has developed into two distinct yet related practices: (1) a Sufi order that is made up mostly of men but that, unlike any other ṭarīqa in Tunis, also allows women to attain the status of muqaddama (an official position of authority), and (2) the "women's Tījāniyya" (tījāniyya al-nisā'), a trance healing tradition for and by women, involving a group of three or four women singing, seated around the perimeter of a wide, bowl-shaped drum called the Tījāniyya ṭabla (ṭabla tījāniyya, hereafter ṭabla; see video ex. 3.3), which they play together simultaneously. Fatima's narrative about being invited to lead healing rituals of the women's Tījāniyya provides a productive point of departure that communicates the stakes involved in ritual musical decisions. It focuses on her encounters with two highly charged symbols of the women's Tījāniyya, namely the ṭabla drum and sifsārī cloth:

> This is the story: There were three [Tījāniyya women] who used to play on the big ṭabla, each on a side, but they died, one of them was ninety years old . . . and the story comes back to us. How? When people went to [the shrine of] Sayyda or Belḥassen on Sundays, there were old people and some who trance [*yaṭīḥ 'alīh*, lit. "he (the saint) falls on him"] and they told me, "Please, aunt Fatima, bring us Sīdī Aḥmed [al-Tījānī]" [i.e., through singing and drumming]. But when we played the ṭabla, it did not work [*mā tb'atnāsh*, lit. "it did not follow us"], as Sīdī Aḥmed's ṭabla is not our specialty—he is not in our hands [i.e., we cannot summon him]. And Sayyda doesn't like the ṭabla, she really doesn't like the ṭabla or the ṭār, these she dislikes. We finished making our ṭabla and started working, but the ṭabla broke. We tried a second time and the ṭabla was burned. (Pers. comm., 2014)

That Sayyda Mannūbiyya does not tolerate the ṭabla while Sīdī Aḥmed can *only* be summoned by the ṭabla demonstrates the centrality of musical sound not only to the identities of different devotional and healing communities, but also to the efficacy of healing. It also reveals a concomitant rift between the Mannūbiyya and the women's Tījāniyya, two ritually adjacent traditions that constitute the most active women's trance practices in Tunis.

The women's Tījāniyya hold two weekly gatherings at their shrine in the

Bāb Manāra neighborhood of the Tunis medina. On Fridays they perform the Tījāniyya *waẓīfa* (communal liturgy), including the recitation of the ṭarīqa's iconic prayers Ṣalāt al-Fātiḥ and Jawharat al-Kamāl, in a ceremony similar to that of their male counterparts. On Tuesdays, the trance healing ceremony takes place, attracting a larger number of participants. Like their male counterparts, they avoid the bendīr because they associate the instrument with what they consider the excesses of other music-driven rituals in Tunisian saint shrines. Indeed, the bendīr is the symbol par excellence of what the Tījāniyya consider the decadence of other ṭarīqas; when discussing what is distinctive about the Tījāniyya, Khāled Ṣāghī, a member of the men's Tījāniyya ṭarīqa, referenced the instrument in his argument that the Tījāniyya in Tunis "did not let the ṭarīqa go astray, I mean to get involved in superstition and bendīr. As bendīr is forbidden in the ṭarīqa, there is no bendīr, no incense, no smoke in the air. . . . There is only discipline, dhikr, respect" (pers. comm., 2014).[19] Putting on hold, for the moment, the complex relationship between the men's and women's Tījāniyya practices, one important point of agreement between the two is this prohibition of the bendīr. There are two types of bendīr in use in the practices alluded to in Ṣāghī's comment, both of which feature a distinctive buzzing timbre. One has two or three gut snares pulled taut along the inside of the drumhead, which produce a subtle yet consistent buzz with every drum stroke. These are the drums played by the majority of Sufi ṭarīqas such as the 'Īsāwiyya and other ritual groups in shrine contexts throughout Tunisia. The other is the large tambourine of the Mannūbiyya, distinguished by rows of pairs of small cymbals that shimmer with every articulation.[20] These drums are primarily associated with devotional ritual music contexts, where they are played in unison by numerous musicians and usually for the purpose of creating the conditions for trance dancing. Because of the insistent cyclic nature of the drumming patterns, the musical texture of rituals involving these drums is characterized by a markedly constant buzzing and/or jingling sound that creates a thick sonic fingerprint. Discursive references to the bendīr immediately evoke these powerful sounds and contested ritual contexts. Statements such as "we don't use bendīr" are ethical pronouncements, shorthand for asserting

19. There is at least one exception to this prohibition against the bendīr. One Tījāniyya group in the northern suburb of La Marsa received permission from the shaykh to start a Tījāniyya group that performs outside the zāwiya and uses the bendīr. Conditions were imposed, such as avoiding praising al-Tījānī in public events, but permission was granted, according to Ṣāghī, because of economic opportunity ("some people make a living from such things") and the popularity of Sufi performances on local and national stages (pers. comm., 2014).

20. A third variant of the bendīr is larger, has no cymbals, and is mainly associated with the popular-folk music called mizwid, discussed in chap. 5.

a stance that views devotional and healing rituals involving music and trance at shrines as morally suspect.

The women's Tījāniyya navigated this interdiction by utilizing the ṭabla, which they maintain is not subject to the same prohibition because it was authorized by the Prophet himself in one of his revelations to Sīdī Aḥmed. The ṭabla is a large bowl-shaped drum, big enough to accommodate four musicians playing it while situated equidistant around the drum. The drum's timbre is clear and simple, with none of the complex buzzing and jingling that characterizes bendīr-based musics (see video ex. 3.3). Lilla Shrifa, a muqaddama of the women's Tījāniyya, explained that at first Sīdī Aḥmed reprimanded his followers for using the ṭabla but then encouraged the use of the instrument after being instructed to do so by the Prophet (Melliti 1993: 186–187). This interpretation does not contradict the taken-for-granted prohibition of drums that Tījānīs understand, yet it allows for the possibility that an exception was granted by Sīdī Aḥmed himself, ostensibly for women, an exception that men's Tījāniyya adepts continue to recognize in practice as they tolerate, although rarely explicitly condone, the women's ṭabla-based trance rituals.

While the women's Tījāniyya enact their ban on the bendīr—and the implicit critique it accompanies—with every performance, Fatima's claim that Sayyda's distaste for the ṭabla is so strong that Sayyda intervened to destroy the instrument could be construed as a countercritique. And indeed, there is more to Fatima's reticence about the women's Tījāniyya, as she explains in relation to a well-known women's Tījāniyya shrine:

> At [that one] they "work him" [invoke Sīdī Aḥmed] with bad things, blasphemy [*kufr*]. Sayyda Mannūbiyya is literate and educated, Sīdī Belḥassen taught her, she was his student, and that's why she doesn't like stories such as this. At [that one], what do they do? They bring girls who want to marry but cannot because of a magic spell [*tāba'a*][21] or affliction [*'aks*] and cover them with a [white] sifsārī as if they are dead; it is a stupid thing because there is only God [i.e., it is inappropriate for humans to appropriate these symbols of death]. When I went there, I was frightened and shivering as they covered them and started reciting prayers as if they were dead, and people throw money and sugar and sweets and breadcrumbs [onto the sifsārī]; when I remember it I get scared. I couldn't bear it. Men are not allowed, it is not a shrine, no tomb, no signs, [just] a house. Sayyda doesn't like that. We couldn't stand it, you understand, because only God knows. . . .

21. Boissevain (2006: 41) defines "tāb'a" as an evil spell (*mauvais sort*), while Johnson (1979: 154) notes that "Ta'aba" is also the name of a particular "rapacious female" jinn.

> So we went back to work only at Sayyda and follow the other saints except Sīdī Aḥmed and Sīdī Ibrāhīm al-Riyāḥī [the saint who first established the Tījāniyya ṭarīqa in Tunis]. (Pers. comm., 2014)

Fatima's objection to the practices of the women's Tījāniyya are both affective (she feels scared, shivering from fright) and moral (the shrine is not the kind of sacred building one expects; one should not draw upon imagery of death). The white sifsārī is a highly charged symbol in this ritual context. For Fatima, the white cloth covering a patient lying on the ground too closely resembles a funeral shroud, an image reinforced by the chanted prayers over the body, which resemble those of funeral rites. Yet the sifsārī is an iconic ritual accoutrement for both the men's and women's Tījāniyya practices. In both the men's and women's weekly Tījāniyya waẓīfa, collective recitation of the Jawharat al-Kamāl prayer is understood to summon the Prophet and the four orthodox caliphs, who are believed to arrive in the room at the seventh repetition of the prayer and situate themselves where the sifsārī is laid out to accommodate these five invisible guests. This highly distinctive use of the sifsārī goes back to al-Tījānī's practice of using one to purify any space he chose as a site for performing the waẓīfa, particularly the street in front of his home in Fez where he gathered his followers (Abu-Nasr 1965: 53; Melliti 1993: 259). In women's Tījāniyya rituals, it is used in both their recitational and trance ceremonies. In the waẓīfa recitation, everyone present attempts to have it cover at least part of their feet as the liturgy is chanted. In trance ceremonies, it is used after each trance to cover the dancer; later it is worn over the dancer's shoulders. For attendees in serious need of healing, the sifsārī may be used to cover the patient entirely (Melliti 1993: 257), as Fatima witnessed.

The Mannūbiyya, like other silsila-based trance practices discussed in this book, also use a cloth that is draped over trancers. But these cloths, called *sunjuqs* ("banners"), in contrast to the sifsārī, are bright and colorful and are loosely associated with the color preferences of the saints summoned or the spirits they control. Sunjuqs are also used to decorate and cover the raised rectangular frame of the catafalque situated above, or representing, the tomb of the saint and function as flags paraded in front of the procession of Sufi ṭarīqas and other ritual groups as they perform their public processions (*kharjāt*, lit. "departures"; sing. *kharja*) outside a shrine. They are, in other words, emblematic of ritual practices associated with zāwiyas throughout the devotional landscape of Tunis. While the difference between a white sifsārī and a colorful sunjuq may appear rather subtle at first glance, particularly to those not affiliated with such ritual practices, the distinction conveys a profound message: the colorful sunjuq of the Mannūbiyya connects them to the wider network of ritual practices in Tunis as much as the white sifsārī reinforces the distinctive doctrine of the Tījāniyya that separates it from that network.

While Fatima refuses to "follow" Sīdī Aḥmed and Sīdī Ibrāhīm al-Riyāḥī by performing their specific ceremonies, visiting their sacred sites, or utilizing their ritual accoutrements, she does not question the legitimacy of these saints or the needs of women seeking therapy by trance dancing to the nūbas of these Tījāniyya saints. She chose to accommodate those needs, but with ritual decisions to address what she perceived as the problem of the ṭabla and sifsārī:

> So I told them, those who need Sīdī Aḥmed can come with us, we will play bendīr because it won't bother him. . . . For those who want Sīdī Aḥmed, we use only the bendīr, without the ṭār and darbūka . . . [for him] we play only the bendīr that have no cymbals and no snares [i.e., so it sounds more like the ṭabla] . . . and when they ask us to do the sifsārī, we use the sunjuq instead; I use the large sunjuq to cover the patient. We put the sunjuq over her, make incense, put some olive oil from Sayyda on her, we perform the dhikr for Sayyda first, then we play [the nūba for] Sīdī Aḥmed, that's it. If she gets better, that's good; if not, you take her to the shrine of Sīdī Aḥmed because it is out of our hands. (Pers. comm., 2014)

By making these adjustments, namely replacing the sifsārī with the sunjuq and selecting drums with no snares or cymbals, Fatima recognizes and accepts the distinctive practices of the women's Tījāniyya, even those she finds troubling. However, she does not adopt them, but rather adapts them to the terms of the Mannūbiyya. Success is never a guarantee in ritual work, and Fatima reports that there are instances when the trance will not succeed and the patient needs to go to the site of women's Tījāniyya healing for more treatment. A single nūba for Sīdī Aḥmed cannot treat all cases. Although Sīdī Aḥmed is considered the patients' savior (*ghawth*) and master of the group of spirits called *ruḥāniyyāt*, which in turn can control more malevolent spirits, ritual treatment is a process that often requires the nūbas for the specific spirits involved to be played in order to placate those spirits. For that kind of treatment, sufferers must seek out the women's Tījāniyya directly.

While the ṭabla and sifsārī play highly symbolic roles that are specific to the histories and identities associated with al-Tījānī and reinforce the closed-world exclusivity and separation of the Tījāniyya from other saint-based and Sufi practices in Tunisia, the silsila-based approach of Fatima's ritually adjacent trance practices enables her to accommodate the ritual needs of those healed by Sīdī Aḥmed al-Tījānī and incorporate him into her ritual healing world while rejecting the symbols and practices—specifically the ṭabla and sifsārī—that are defining features of the healing tradition of the women's Tījāniyya.

By performing a nūba for Sīdī Aḥmed in the Mannūbiyya style, preceding it with a portion of the Shādhuliyya dhikr, and using the incense and oil central to the Mannūbiyya healing ritual, Fatima absorbs Sīdī Aḥmed into the ritual fabric of the Mannūbiyya. The silsila form made it easy and intuitive for Fatima to adopt a nūba for Sīdī Aḥmed. In many ways, the nūba for Sīdī Aḥmed resembles other constituent parts of the silsila: it has a sung text in quatrains with a refrain as well as melodic and rhythmic modes shared with other songs in the silsila, all performed by four singers playing drums. What is different, aside from lyrics that praise Sīdī Aḥmed, is the timbre of the drums as the troupe switches out their usual bendīrs for drums that are similar in shape and size but have no cymbals or snares in order better to approximate the musical timbre associated with ṭabla, Sīdī Aḥmed's preferred instrument.

The nūba for Sīdī Aḥmed, then, is and is not fully of the Mannūbiyya soundworld. It is an exception that proves a rule. While the musical adaptation of choosing different (yet similar) instruments makes this nūba a sole exception in the silsila of the Mannūbiyya, the accommodation of the needs of a ritually adjacent group and the incorporation of a nūba for their saint into the silsila illustrates the flexibility and inclusive ethos of the silsila. While the silsila, taken as a whole, surveys the local devotional ritual landscape through its incorporation of so many spiritual figures associated with just as many devotional and healing practices, this chapter has focused on how three nūbas ("'Arī 'al-Mannūbiyya," "Sīdī Belḥassen," and "Sīdī Aḥmed") rely on the musical potencies of timbre, intensification, and form to realize the ethical work at the heart of their ritual performance.

DHIKR AND MEN'S ADJACENT DEVOTIONAL PRACTICES

Sīdī Belḥassen and Sīdī Aḥmed founded Sufi ṭarīqas with men's practices that link, implicitly and explicitly, to Sayyda Mannūbiyya. How do the men's devotional practices relate to the women's? In what ways are they commensurable with, or stand in opposition to, those of their female counterparts? Are the men's practices also productively understood as rituals of hospitality?

The men's devotional ceremonies of the Shādhuliyya and Tījāniyya embody the teachings and practices of their respective Sufi orders and are largely concerned with strengthening the spiritual fortitude of participants.

In putting these ceremonies into conversation with the women's practices, many contrasts emerge, as the men perform chanted, rather than sung, texts; do not use musical instruments; pursue a corporate, unison experience rather than a focus on individual healing; and direct most of their energies toward fewer spiritual personalities but especially God and the Prophet. Yet there are points of convergence with the women's practices and with the wider ecology of devotional practices. The men's liturgies are also used, albeit obliquely, to treat spirit possession, and women of the Mannūbiyya and the women's Tījāniyya, among others, seek this treatment as a supplement to their trance ceremonies, especially for particularly acute spirit afflictions. Moreover, while the recitations of the Shādhuliyya and Tījāniyya liturgies operate according to their own logics of repetition, transformation, and intensification, they also betray a certain musicality, particularly in the use of rhythm, that has a clear if subtle correlation to other trance rituals with more frankly musical identities.

Shādhuliyya Rituals at Sayyda's Shrines

The Shādhuliyya liturgy indexed by Fatima's group at the end of the nūba "Sīdī Belḥassen" is part of a Shādhuliyya devotional ceremony that, in many ways, contrasts with the women's silsila-based ritual in its ritual objectives, logics, and aesthetic priorities. The rigorously monitored communal chanting of the men's liturgy is as highly scripted, quantified, corporate, and restrictive in its devotional subjects (limited mainly to God, the Prophet, Sīdī Belḥassen, and Sayyda Mannūbiyya) as the insistent drumming and praise singing of the silsila are flexible, individualized, and inclusive of dozens of spiritual beings. In the silsila, women take turns dancing and trancing to "their" saint as part of an individualized process of healing based on appeasing numerous saints (or possessing spirits) in succession. The Shādhuliyya ceremony, in contrast, absorbs each participant into the collective, with lengthy meditations repeating the names of God, the profession of faith, and prayers to the Prophet. These contrasts, as well as the dramatic intensity of the silsila ritual contrasting with the serene yet powerful chanting of the dhikr, however, belie certain underlying similarities in how music and sound work in ritual.

At Sayyda's shrine in Manouba, the Shādhuliyya perform their ceremony on Sunday evening, after the women hold the afternoon trance ritual. The men's ceremony begins with two recitations in praise of Sayyda Mannūbiyya before moving on to the Shādhuliyya liturgy. This liturgy (called "wird") is entirely a cappella and centers on the communal chanting of the ḥizbs and additional prayers, and Qur'anic recitations. The ceremony concludes with dhikr. The ḥizbs, prayers, and Qur'anic passages change on a weekly basis and are prescribed in accordance with an elaborate ritual calendar. The dhikr, however, is performed in the same manner each time: with the lights turned off, two lines of men stand facing each other and chant the name "Allah," at first in the low register and at a very slow tempo before speeding up, then repeating the same process with the name "Huwa" (He). As the tempo increases, the lines begin alternating the names to maintain a tempo that would be otherwise impossible to achieve by unison recitation (McGregor 1997: 268). As noted above, it is this form of dhikr that Fatima refers to when she reports that she performs *wird al-shādhulī* in her ceremonies. This dhikr is characterized by repetition and transformation in both rhythm and pitch. The transformation is of two kinds—stepwise and gradual—and the act of transformation is emphasized by performing the dhikr at both extremes of slow and fast tempos. The dhikr begins with the unison chanting of the name "Allah," split into two discrete syllables, short and long, respectively. In the performance available on the companion website (audio ex. 3.1),[22] the first syllable, "Al-," lasts for one and a half seconds, and the second, "-lah," lasts for fifteen. In the final second of the articulation, the voices perform a descending slur that drops about an octave below the G on which it began.[23] The voices then rise back up to their starting pitch and repeat the process until it has been performed seven times.[24]

Then a regular rhythmic pattern begins in which two lines of men standing face each other and chant "Allah." Half the men pronounce the first syllable with a deep guttural breath, and the other half produce a longer sustained note on the second. At 4:47 the pitch rises up about a half-step to G♯. At 5:15 it rises up another half step to A, then A♯ by 5:30, B by 6:00, C by 6:30, C♯ by 7:30, and D by 8:45, ending at 9:35 with another slurred octave descent. At its fastest tempo, the first syllable takes up 40 percent of the phrase, while the second lasts for 60 percent, maintaining but sig-

22. Performed by the Ḥaṭṭābiyya ṭarīqa in 2009 at the shrine of Sīdī ʿAlī al-Ḥaṭṭāb. The Ḥaṭṭābiyya claim descent from the Shādhuliyya and maintain aspects of Shādhulī ritual practice, such as the ḥizbs and dhikr, while adding the Ḥaṭṭābiyya's own distinctive round-style singing to other parts of their ḥaḍra (Shaykh Jaied, pers. comm., 2012).

23. The original pitch is closer to F♯, but I transpose it up to G to conform to local academic practices of transcription.

24. During Shādhuliyya ceremonies dedicated to Sayyda Mannūbiyya, the lights are turned off and the word "Allah" slowly transforms to "Huwa" (He), increasing in speed until only the sound of the letter *h* is audible, what the Shādhuliyya call the *ketta* (whisper) (see Boissevain 2006: 121). It is important to note that such dhikr patterns are not limited to the dhikr per se; they are also often embedded within other aspects of the Shādhuliyya wird. For example, the chanting of prescribed Qur'anic verses every Saturday includes a passage of 129 repetitions of the phrase *yā laṭīf*, and the ḥizb al-tawḥīd has the phrase *lā ilaha illa allah* repeated 550 times, followed by 50 repetitions of a prayer to the Prophet.

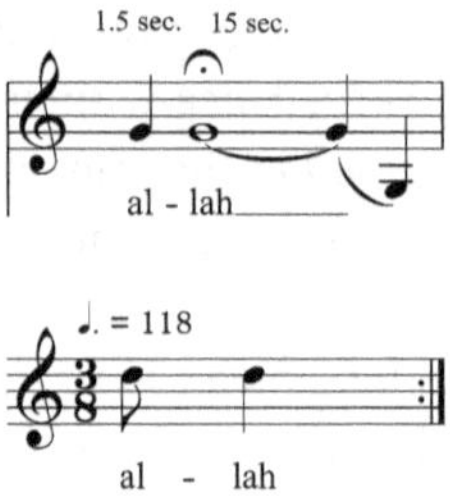

MUSICAL EXAMPLES 3.3 AND 3.4. Short-long pattern of the Shādhuliyya dhikr at its slowest (*above*) and fastest (*below*) tempo

nificantly truncating the short-long temporal relationship established at the beginning. Such a fast concluding rhythm characterized by a short-long durational relationship is immediately recognizable as a principle shared in many domains of Tunisian music, including the acceleration of the five-beat ʿĪsāwiyya mjarred (2 + 3 beats) described in chapter 2, the fast version of the three-beat *mdawr gharbī* rhythm in mizwid (1 + 2 beats), and the three-beat khatm rhythm (1 + 2 beats) serving as the final and fastest rhythmic cycle in ʿĪsāwiyya ritual and in suites of Tunisian art music. Most relevant to this chapter, the Mannūbiyya utilize the same khatm (1 + 2) rhythm in several of its nūbas, particularly in the closing nūba of each episode of SI. The Shādhuliyya dhikr, then, not only approximates a rhythm that is central to the Mannūbiyya silsila but adheres to larger rhythmic principles shared with many other domains of musical practice in Tunisia, namely a short-long 1:2 (sometimes 2:3) temporal ratio that serves as the fastest, concluding piece of a performance or section of a performance. Like portions of the ʿĪsāwiyya ḥizb, this dhikr also shares the principle of DPTI, whereby intensity is developed through tempo acceleration, contraction of the rhythmic pattern, and a rise in pitch.

The rhythmic transformation of Shādhuliyya recitation also reveals unexpected rhythmic similarities to the world of trance and popular music. A recitation recorded at the shrine of Sīdī Belḥassen illustrates its rhythmic transformation through DI.[25] The first choral response of *lā ilaha illā allah* (seven syllables, owing to elision of last two words) is 9.3 seconds long, at 52 beats per minute (audio ex. 3.2). It gradually increases in tempo to 220 bpm, a more than fourfold increase, pushing the reciters toward the maximum tempo capable of being maintained collectively while articulating the syllables. As it reaches this zenith, the rhythm transforms to a denser, quicker pattern, with many of the syllables elided so much that they are hard to dis-

25. The recordings referenced in this section were generously provided by members of the Shādhuliyya, including Adnen el-Ghali, with the permission of their shaykh.

MUSICAL EXAMPLE 3.5. Slow beginning of the Shādhuliyya dhikr passage from their *ḥizb al-tawḥīd*

MUSICAL EXAMPLE 3.6. Shādhuliyya dhikr at its fastest tempo (*above*) and its alignment with the rhythmic contour of the fazzānī rhythm (*below*)

tinguish from their neighbors (audio ex. 3.3). The resulting rhythmic pattern strongly resembles the fazzānī rhythm, an iconic rhythm of mizwid, rebaybiyya, and of course the Mannūbiyya. This rhythm, iconic of the bodily and social extremes of often stigmatized trance-and popular-music contexts, is considered distant from—and often presented as standing in opposition to—the staid, disciplined, and virtually irreproachable devotions of the Shādhuliyya. Yet the rhythm of the dhikr unquestionably follows the rhythmic contours of fazzānī: the accented syllables align squarely with the dumms and accented final takk that define the rhythm. That such radically different contexts rely on such similar rhythmic principles reveal, if only implicitly, shared participation in a spiritual and musical commons.

Repetition in the Shādhuliyya liturgy creates the conditions not only for the participants' internalization of sacred texts and ideas, but also for transformation and intensification. However, it is also based on rhythmic patterns that are not only similar to those in other more explicitly musical settings, but also function similarly as high-energy patterns associated with musical climax and, in ritual, the moment of spiritual healing or transformation. This musical analysis reveals underlying principles of rhythm and intensification that Sufi ritual, even when it avoids "musical" terminology, shares with musical domains, both ritual and secular. Despite certain stark contrasts with the silsila form in terms of melody and text, the Shādhuliyya dhikr illustrates a common grounding in certain principles of rhythmic form and function. Such points of commonality are missing from analyses that insist on the binary opposition of recitation (Sufi dhikr) versus singing (women's trance music).

Another nuance of that binary reinforces this point. In considering who performs, and for whom, it is important to note that the musicians performing a silsila—such as the Mannūbiyya troupe—perform *for* others, namely others who enter into trance, as well as for an audience consisting of those in the gathering who are not dancing at the time or are accompanying the patients. Musicians do not fall into trance; in the rare instance that one does, she would be relieved of her musical duties (which would be impossible for her to fulfill in trance) and resituated in the ritual as a trancer and recipient of other people's music making. In Gilbert Rouget's (1986) terms, there are two categories of participant: the musicians (the makers of music) and the musicated (the recipients of the music).

The dhikr could be construed as standing in stark contrast: there is no distinction between those performing the sound, receiving it, and witnessing it. Participants create the conditions for their own spiritual journey; in Rouget's terms, all participants in the dhikr are musicants, that is, people who perform the music and are simultaneously the ones targeted by the sound. This stance, however, only accounts for the male participants. It must be pointed out that women, who are in an adjacent room at the shrine of Sīdī Belḥassen or the Tījāniyya shrines, seek therapy from experiencing the sound of the men's liturgy: the women are separated visually but not auditorily (see also Ferchiou 1972). Indeed, the sound of the men's recitations has a direct impact on women seeking treatment for spirit possession. And, in turn, the piercing ululations of the women, as they see the therapeutic effects on those falling into trance, are audible to the men, confirm for them the power of their recitation, and heighten the level of excitement. In this case, the men are their own musicants, but they also play the role of musicians for the musicated women.[26]

Dhikr and Silsila: Overlaps and Disjunctures

The women's trance ceremonies of the Mannūbiyya and the men's liturgical recitations of the Shādhuliyya are widely considered to be at opposite ends of the ritual spectrum, with the former stigmatized as folk healing based on superstition and the excesses of women's "play" and the latter representing the apex of learned, respectable Sufi practice. Yet this conceptual separation belies the way they share space in the local ecology of Sufism. The Mannūbiyya and Shādhuliyya not only recognize each other's founding saints but also integrate them into their respective ritual practices. Sīdī Belḥas-

26. Or, to borrow Turino's (2008) terms, the men's fully "participatory" musical experience is nevertheless mainly "presentational" from the stance of women being healed.

sen al-Shādhulī is an important nūba in the Mannūbiyya silsila, one that adapts the men's dhikr into the women's trance ceremony. And the inverse: Sayyda Mannūbiyya is important enough to the Shādhuliyya that they have a weekly appointment at her shrine in Gorjani to perform their ceremony, which, at that site, includes recitations dedicated to Sayyda Mannūbiyya. Both ritual practices involve healing women's spirit possession, the Mannūbiyya doing so explicitly and centrally, the Shādhuliyya in a more concealed, peripheral way with women in an adjacent room. Even though there are no musical instruments in the men's dhikr, there is a familiar if implicit musicality, particularly in the rhythmic patterns of the dhikr. Both the dhikr and the silsila rely on specific approaches to repetition, as well as a foundation of overriding constancy in timbre and texture. But the two practices coexist, sometimes in the same spaces, albeit separately; and as Michael Lambek puts it with regard to Islam, sorcery, and spirit possession in Mayotte, they are "as likely to be talking past each other as to a common purpose" (1993: 396). For Lambek, the distinctions between such practices

> are not resolvable. Invocation of one does not logically entail any of the others, nor does it rule them out. They address overlapping but somewhat different issues; each conceptualizes the world and the sense of problem somewhat differently. If they were fully commensurable, one could be reduced or subordinated to the other; there would be no reason for all of them to remain present . . . [and the] systems exist side by side without an obvious sense of contradiction. (1993: 397)

In Lambek's formulation, the silsila and dhikr are incommensurable, not incompatible; incompatibility presupposes logical contradiction, which is not the case here. The saints are recognized by all, although they hold different, yet overlapping, meanings. The music and trance experience differs in fundamental ways between dhikr and silsila, but some underlying principles are shared, and each is locked into its place as a devotional niche within the wider ecology. Indeed, the mutual recognition of saints and the shared practice of sonic interventions in spiritual lives (as different as those practices may be) connect the silsila and dhikr to each other within the wider shared field of ambient Sufism. Yet, despite some points of convergence, one cannot fully substitute for the other. The journey of the silsila provides a survey of the surrounding devotional landscape, an inventory of saints and spirits available for activation in ritual. The silsila thus absorbs and internalizes the other, just as a trancing body absorbs and internalizes the other (i.e., a possessing spirit); both the silsila and trance healing are based on an ethics of plurality, of inclusion, of accommodation. The silsila has fewer conditions of hospitality than the Shādhuliyya dhikr, which recognizes and tolerates but does not systematically incorporate such a diversity of spiritual figures. Structurally, the dhikr is inflexible, in contrast to the silsila, which provides a structural survey of the devotional landscape and encourages musicians to likewise survey the women gathered and adapt to the needs of those present. Fatima described the musical-ritual approach as *bil-tatbīʿ* (lit. "by following"), by which she implied both following a succession of nūbas and also following the needs of those gathered. Here the ethical work of Mannūbiyya ritual is inseparable from, and made possible by, its musical potencies of timbre, intensification, and form.

4

RITUAL ALTERITY

The Musical Management of Sub-Saharan Otherness

"Sṭambēlī is dead; there is no more sṭambēlī" (*sṭambēlī māt; mā 'aditsh sṭambēlī*). I often heard this refrain from my teacher Baba Majid (1922–2008) in the early 2000s and regularly encountered similar sentiments from his son Belhassen and Baba's former apprentice Salah both before and after the 2011 Revolution. Sṭambēlī, the spirit-possession practice developed by displaced sub-Saharans and their descendants in Tunisia, has a long history of experiencing external and internal pressures that have jeopardized its vitality (see Jankowsky 2010). But when Baba uttered those words to me in the early 2000s, he did so, for example, as he prepared for a three-day pilgrimage that would attract hundreds of attendees; and when Salah (who took over Baba's troupe after his death) made similar statements in 2009, it was as we drove together to one of several private healing ceremonies he was leading for Baba's former clients in a span of two weeks. In contrast to the Mannūbiyya's calendar of weekly standing appointments at the shrine of Sayyda Mannūbiyya, sṭambēlī ritual performances have relied heavily on healing ceremonies in private homes and an annual three-day ceremony held at the shrine of Sīdī Frej. The statement that there was no more sṭambēlī was a shorthand used by musicians to point to many areas of perceived decline: musicians were scarce and had the wrong priorities, clients were coming for the wrong reasons, healers were taking advantage of them, and shared knowledge and "spirit" (*rūḥ*) were disappearing as elders passed away. But the statement was also meant to be taken at face value: opportunities for ritual work were indeed dwindling. The annual pilgrimage was reduced from three days to two and then one and was sometimes skipped altogether in the years following Baba's death, while the number of days and then weeks between domestic ceremonies increased, leaving musicians with an unreliable performance calendar and an equally unreliable income.

Ever since the Tunisian independence movement in the mid-twentieth century, the political messaging of modern development has portrayed healing practices such as sṭambēlī negatively, dismissing them as backward and incompatible with the nation's future. Elders with ritual experience (as healers, musicians, and patients) were dying, and their children were increasingly unlikely to continue to participate. As social institutions that buttressed the black community disappeared—such as the "communal house" system that voluntarily congregated sub-Saharans and their descendants according to their ethnolinguistic origins and served as ritual performance sites—sṭambēlī became further integrated into the fabric of the wider therapeutic landscape while ceasing to serve a black community, since a sense of ritual community based on descent from displaced sub-Saharans had been all but lost. As a result, sṭambēlī lost the specificity of its sub-Saharan ethnolinguistic and geocultural referents as fewer and fewer participants were left who were able to read them; in other words, it became associated with "Africa general" at the expense of "Africa specific."[1]

Many sṭambēlī musicians also pointed to internal shortcomings for the decline in ritual work, particularly before the Revolution. Specifically, they blamed certain sṭambēlī healers for engaging in charlatanism to try to drum up more work. These healers, called *ʿarāyif* (sing. *ʿarīfa*, lit. "she who knows"), work in partnership with master musicians (*yinnawāt*; sing. *yinna*) to diagnose, teach, and heal clients. Baba Majid expressed his frustration with ʿarīfas he worked with who began promising potential clients that holding a sṭambēlī ceremony to appease the spirits would guarantee that their child would pass the baccalaureate exam. This was part of a more widespread phenomenon that Salah drew attention to just before the 2011 Revolution:

> And the sick, where are they? They go and see the doctor or the psychiatrist. They are sent to the psychiatric hospital. [They're told] "He's having a nervous breakdown." But there is something else. They go and see the people who . . . are psychics (*ʿarafāt*), card readers (*katāba*), sorcerers (*ʿazzāma*), in short, crooks. They go and see them, and these people steal their money. . . . They take the money and yet the sickness is never cured. (Quoted in Hagene 2011)

1. See Jankowsky (2010) for more on this point; cf. the Moroccan case in Witulski (2018).

Here Salah bemoaned what he and many others I know consider to be the problematic aspects of the local therapeutic landscape: "healers" operating inside and outside the shrine network who take advantage of the vulnerable. The ethics of certain sṭambēlī healers are sometimes called into question by sṭambēlī musicians, and in general sṭambēlī and its adjacent ritual practices such as the Mannūbiyya are perceived as guilty by association with this threat. In addition, many potential clients are directed toward biomedical therapies reliant on individual psychiatric diagnosis and healing via medication at the expense of the therapeutic systems of ambient Sufism in which a patient enters into a new field of social and spiritual relations, takes charge of embodying her affliction through trance, and seeks comfort in a community of witnessing that ritual healing practices such as sṭambēlī provide.

After the Tunisian Revolution of 2011, the frail sṭambēlī ritual economy was threatened further. Zahra Hosni, one of the Mannūbiyya musicians in Fatima's troupe (see chap. 3), told me that her family stopped holding sṭambēlī ceremonies in their home due to fear of Salafis nearby hearing the music. Moreover, many who attend sṭambēlī rituals are decreasingly familiar with spirit possession and increasingly uncomfortable in the potential presence of spirits, creating an atmosphere of quietness, uncertainty, and passivity among attendees. "Now they are afraid," Walid Mennai (the 'Īsāwiyya shaykh introduced in chap. 2) told me. "Afraid of the spirits. That's why they sit quietly, not like it used to be."

That is patently not the case at presentational performances of sṭambēlī on concert stages, where enthusiastic audiences dance to, and cheer for, songs performed on the festival stage and in upscale cafés as sṭambēlī music experiences a resurgence in the public sphere. Since the Revolution, musicians and audiences have taken renewed interest and pride in sṭambēlī as a distinctively Tunisian musical practice. In these public spaces, trance (in the ritual healing sense) is something to be avoided. Yet participation through dance and physical movement is the norm, meaning that sṭambēlī's movements from ritual to nonritual spaces is accompanied by an increase in participatory experiences—albeit one that is increasingly distant from ritual and experience-near knowledge of the trance healing practice. If sṭambēlī ritual embodies and intervenes in the social and spiritual encounters between sub-Saharan and North Africans, these concert performances take a rather different approach to negotiating the relationship between self and other, the familiar and the alter, that historically has been at the heart of sṭambēlī. The silsila musical form, as this chapter illustrates, is implicated in this boundary work.

GEOCULTURAL WORK OF THE SṬAMBĒLĪ RITUAL SILSILA

Spirit possession rituals are not only about individual cases of healing and support. They also do the grand social work of exercising the historical imagination. Across the African continent, spirit possession is as much about sociopolitical encounters as it is about spiritual interventions. Spirit pantheons are often organized into groups or families of spirits with locally meaningful identities corresponding to neighboring ethnolinguistic groups, immigrant populations, local ancestors, encroaching colonial powers, religious figures, and others connected to heavily freighted sociohistorical encounters (Besmer 1983; Boddy 1989; Échard 1989; Emoff 2003; Kramer 1993; Makris 2000; Stoller 1989). The formal structure and drama of spirit possession rituals typically do not reenact such encounters in narrative or linear fashion but rather evoke "unspecified events" (Feuchtwang 2010: 290), often serving as nondiscursive reminders—"palimpsest memories," to use Rosalind Shaw's (2002: 15) term—of often unspeakable traumas such as war, colonial oppression, and slavery. In cases such as sṭambēlī, in which the spirit-possession practice was developed in diaspora by the community of, and descended from, displaced sub-Saharans, the trans-Saharan movements and subsequent encounters are embodied in the musical sound of every note played. Sṭambēlī ritual work relies on timbres, textures, and other aesthetics that, in the context of Tunisia, index sub-Saharanness: the bass-register pentatonicism and shimmering sound quality of the gumbrī lute; the insistent, metallic pulsations of the *shqāshiq* iron clappers; the distinctive "sub-Saharan" vocal style (which does not emphasize clear diction), delivering lyrics that combine dialectical Arabic with phrases that originated in Hausa, Kanuri, Zarma, and other sub-Saharan languages. In other words, sṭambēlī ritual is not so much a representation as it is a product of the legacy of sub-Saharan and North African encounters. Attention to the sṭambēlī silsila, however, reveals additional contours of a topography of encounter that is at once social and spiritual, historical and geocultural.

Like the Mannūbiyya silsila, the sṭambēlī silsila progressively discloses a local landscape of saints and their respective shrines. Unique to sṭambēlī, however, is its inclusion of dozens of spirits in its silsila, as well as its classificatory scheme, which situates the saints as part of the first, "white" section of the silsila and the spirits as comprising the second, "black" section. The silsila in tables 4.1 and 4.2 captures the structure of a ceremony held in August 2009 at Dār Bārnū (the Bornu House), the home of Baba Majid's family and the last of the "communal houses" at which slaves and other dis-

FIGURE 4.1. Sṭambēlī troupe performing the 2009 ceremony. Salah el-Ouergli plays gumbrī; shqāshiq players are (*left to right*) Belhassen Mihoub, Noureddine Soudani, and Lotfi el-Hamami. Photo by the author.

TABLE 4.1 Saints of the "white" silsila, with nūba durations and tempos from a 2009 performance; duration and tempo markings provided to illuminate patterns of intensification

Nūba	Rhythm	Tempo (beginning / ending), bpm	Duration (min:sec)
"Ṣlat al-Nabī"	sūdānī	96 / 130	4:30
"Jerma"	sūdānī	130 / 134	1:15
"Bū Ḥijba"	sūdānī	134 / 147	2:02
"Sīdī Marzūg"	sūdānī	118 / 142	4:35
"Sīdī Sa'd"	sūdānī	116 / 154	5:22
"Sīdī Frej"	muthallith	110 / 126	4:20
"Sīdī Bū Ra's al-'Ajmī"	muthallith	102 / 119	4:23
"Sīdī 'Abd al-Salām"	muthallith	94 / 118	2:53
"Sīdī Manṣūr"	sūdānī	116 / 148	5:37
"Sīdī 'Amr"	muthallith	110 / 126	4:44
"Sīdī 'Amār"	sūdānī	136 / 170	2:00
"Sīdī 'Amr Bū Khatwa"	muthallith, sūdānī	102 / 138, 150 / 170	11:17
"Sīdī 'Abd al-Qādir"	sa'dāwī, sūdānī	78 / 99, 126 / 136	5:50

TABLE 4.2 Spirits of the "black" silsila, with nūba durations and tempos from a 2009 performance

Spirit family	Nūba	Rhythm	Tempo (beginning/ ending), bpm	Duration (min:sec)
Baḥriyya	"Mulāy Brahīm"	muthallith	88 / 106	6:28
Baḥriyya	"Baḥriyya"	muthallith, sūdānī	106 / 116, 150	3:37
Baḥriyya	"Yā Badam Khayaru"	sūdānī	120 / 136	1:44
Baḥriyya	"Jawayay"	muthallith	95 / 100	3:01
Baḥriyya	"Bābā Mūsā"	muthallith	100 / 104	2:55
Baḥriyya	"Sarkin Gari"	muthallith	104 / 108	3:02
Banū Kūrī	"Istiftāḥ al-Kḥūl"	sa'dāwī	73 / 75	2:51
Banū Kūrī	"Sārkin Kūfa"	sūdānī	96 / 106	1:25
Banū Kūrī	"Dundurūsū" 1	bū sa'diyya	72 / 76	1:17
Banū Kūrī	"Dundurūsū" 2	sūdānī	107 / 113	1:38
Banū Kūrī	"Ḥaddād"	bū sa'diyya	72 / 76	1:21
Banū Kūrī	"Garūjī"	sa'dāwī	86 / 92	1:41
Banū Kūrī	"Kūrī"	sūdānī	136 / 156	9:16
Banū Kūrī	"Migzū"	sūdānī	136 / 152	0:45
Banū Kūrī	"Jamarkay"	muthallith	100 / 100	0:58
Banū Kūrī	"Bābā Magojay"	muthallith	114 / 124	1:36
Banū Kūrī	"Danilya"	sūdānī	134 / 140	0:55
Banū Kūrī	"Ubānā"	sa'dāwī	86 / 91	2:19
Banū Kūrī	"Jīgū" 1	sa'dāwī	91 / 95	3:00
Banū Kūrī	"Jīgū" 2	sūdānī	133 / 136	0:28
Banū Kūrī	"Jato" 1	sūdānī	120 / 130	2:27
Banū Kūrī	"Jato" 2	muthallith	104 / 104	0:27
Bēyāt	"M'allem Sofū"	sa'dāwī	74 / 81	3:15
Bēyāt	"Lawra"	sa'dāwī	81 / 90	1:19
Bēyāt	"Badawrī"	muthallith	105 / 114	1:26
Bēyāt	"May Gājiya"	sūdānī	122 / 136	2:45
Bēyāt	"May Ftīla"	bū sa'diyya	83 / 84	0:46
Bēyāt	"Matango"	sūdānī	114 / 118	0:44
Bēyāt	"Sīdī 'Alī Dīwān"	sūdānī	110 / 122	1:19
Bēyāt	"Irzīqī"	muthallith	104 / 110	2:19
Bēyāt	"Jījī"	sa'dāwī	91 / 91	1:45
Bēyāt (Sghār)	"Miryamū"	muthallith	103 / 109	2:14
Bēyāt (Sghār)	"Nānā 'Aysha"	sūdānī	117 / 122	1:47
Bēyāt (Sghār)	"Sīwā"	sūdānī	122 / 152	2:32
Adjacent saints	"Sīdī Belḥassen"	bū sa'diyya	64 / 71	4:11
Adjacent saints	"Lilla Malīka"	muthallith	94 / 100	3:39

placed sub-Saharans of central African heritage congregated. It is now a domestic space, housing three generations of Baba's surviving family. Yet it maintains a status as a former ritual center and a site of sṭambēlī knowledge, the latter kept alive through the musical activities of Baba's son Belhassen (discussed below), who learned sṭambēlī from his father there. Salah al-Ourgli also learned sṭambēlī at Dār Bārnū, at times living there or across the street during his childhood. When Baba died, Salah took over leadership of the musical troupe that served Baba's former clients, with Belhassen leading the accompanying shqāshiq players and responsorial singers. This troupe performed the 2009 ceremony, which coincided with what the musicians considered the end of an era of reliable ritual work. Although the ceremony included an impressive musical repertoire of forty-eight nūbas, only four attendees danced (each to only one or two nūbas) and no sṭambēlī healer ('arīfa) was present, illustrating a situation in which ritual knowledge of spirits, their attributes, and their ritual ordering and categorization now remain mainly in the hands of musicians and their repertoire rather than being distributed within a community of musicians, healers, and dancers (patients) and their families.

Regardless of the number of dancers participating, sṭambēlī musicians perform a silsila that includes most of its saints and spirits. In any ceremony it is possible, and common, to skip a nūba here and there, repeat one (or more) if necessary, and occasionally insert a nūba in an unconventional place in the order. These choices are mainly made in response to the immediate needs of those present, signaling gestures of ritual hospitality elaborated in the previous chapter. With so few dancers and unexpected needs arising during this 2009 ceremony, the musicians performed a rather complete and conventional silsila. They began, as all sṭambēlī ceremonies do, with the nūba for the Prophet to commence the white section (table 4.1) of saints, which includes spiritual figures that are also part of the Mannūbiyya silsila, such as Sīdī Manṣūr, Sīdī 'Amr Bu Khatwa, Sīdī 'Abd al-Salām, and Sīdī 'Abd al-Qādir. But just as the Mannūbiyya silsila foregrounds saints who factor into its history and identity, so too does the sṭambēlī silsila, which highlights several saints of sub-Saharan origin. Sīdī Frej and Sīdī Sa'd are the most prominent of these. Both were originally from the Bornu region of central Africa and came to Tunis as slaves. Once in Tunis, their miraculous powers and closeness to God were recognized by black and Arab Tunisians alike. By 1728 at the latest, the two saints had shrines built posthumously in their honor that until recently served as neighborhood shrines as well as central sites of sṭambēlī ritual activity.

Jerma/Bilāl: Embodying the Familiar and Alter

The first and second nūbas of a silsila are particularly important in establishing sonic principles, ritual priorities, and cultural imperatives, as the Mannūbiyya example illustrated in the previous chapter. In sṭambēlī, the requisite first nūba for the Prophet is immediately followed by Jerma, the sṭambēlī term for Bilāl ibn Rabāḥ (580–640 CE), a seventh-century East African slave who became one of the Prophet's companions and the first caller-to-prayer in Islam.

The sṭambēlī silsila thus takes a well-known Islamic figure, arguably the most prominent African in the history of Islam, and situates him at the head of the silsila, "tied" and second only to the Prophet. Yet what is particularly important about Bilāl in the context of sṭambēlī is that this familiar figure is hidden: the name of the nūba is not "Bilāl," but rather "Jerma," the Songhay name for Bilāl and one unknown in Tunisia outside the sṭambēlī network. Among the Songhay, Bilāl is the head of the Jerma spirits, who, through their ability to bring or withhold rain, wind, thunder, and lightning, are the most powerful and feared family of spirits (Stoller 1995).[2] In sṭambēlī, Bilāl suffers from none of these dangerous connotations. However, his identity in sṭambēlī is masked not only by the use of the Songhay name Jerma, but also through the lyrics to his nūba, which preserve words from the Jerma (Zarma) language:

wayay wayay jerma	Truly, truly, Jerma
kakabilālā bābā	come, come, Bilāl, father
jadī irḥam	have mercy, grandfather
kakabilālī bābā	come, come, Bilāl, father

Thus, Bilāl's identity is realized only through this performance of his transnational and transhistorical routes, from the Arabian city of Medina at the time of the Prophet, to the Jerma spirit pantheon of the Songhay of Niger, and finally across the Sahara Desert to Tunis and the sṭambēlī pantheon. His presence in sṭambēlī ritual is not sounded directly but is *re*-sounded: while Bilal's Islamic identity is acknowledged, it is only made accessible via his Songhay alias. The nūba for Bilāl thus asserts sameness and

2. In Sudan, Bilal is also the legendary figure who gave Sudanis the first *tumburah*, the stringed instrument played by descendants of slaves in their possession ceremonies (Makris 1996: 169).

difference simultaneously: the widely familiar (Bilāl) is presented prominently, but only in terms of the alter (Jerma). This theme of making the familiar alter and making the alter familiar returns below in my consideration of the staging of sṭambēlī. It is also magnified in the second part of the silsila devoted to spirits.

The Spirits: Integrating Alterity

The integrative capacity of the sṭambēlī silsila, a product of centuries of trans-Saharan movements and encounters, continues in the second, black part of the silsila dedicated to a larger pantheon of spirits. Unlike the saints, who were once living human beings, the spirits were never human. Yet they are understood to have humanlike characteristics and are referred to as "the other people" (*al-nās al-ukhrīn*). They are gendered, have kinship relations, and are characterized by distinct personalities with individualized preferences, behaviors, and tendencies. They are also referred to by two other terms that provide additional layers of definition. The first is the term "blacks" (*al-kḥūl*), which distinguishes them from the white saints of the first part of the silsila. The second is "holy ones" (*ṣalḥīn*), which defines the spirits as distinct from the jnūn of Islam while situating them on the same level of power and respect as the saints (since the term "ṣalḥīn" is often used in the full phrase I translate as "saints": *'awliyā' al-ṣalḥīn* or "holy ones close [to God]"). To be one of the ṣalḥīn is to be considered a spiritual power within the world of Sufism in Tunis.

These spirits are organized into three main families: Banū Kūrī (Kūrī's children or Kūrī's tribe), Baḥriyya (water spirits), and Bēyāt (royalty). There are two other groups, the Brāwna ("from Bornu") and the Sghār (children), which are composed of spirits that are often subsumed under the Banū Kūrī and the Bēyāt, respectively. Elsewhere I have described at length the identities and membership of each of these families and the movements of many of their members from sub-Saharan spirit pantheons to the sṭambēlī context, where they sometimes took on new characteristics and identities (Jankowsky 2010). Here I simply wish to emphasize that, while all the categories of spirits are understood as originating in sub-Saharan Africa, each one represents a different set of relations between sub-Saharan and North Africas. The "blackness" of Banū Kūrī is emphasized in ritual (through dress and food), they are understood to be Christian, and, because they have no parallels in Tunisian cosmology (as do the Baḥriyya) or references to official Tunisian history (as do the Bēyāt), are the most "other" of the groups. The Baḥriyya reveal parallels between the sub-Saharan and North African conceptions of spirits: these water spirits of sub-Saharan Africa required little or no modification to enter into the cosmological framework of North African Islam, which holds similar assumptions about the presence of potentially malevolent spirits in and around water (video ex. 4.1). Finally, the Bēyāt provide a powerful commentary on Tunisian history: the arrival of the Bēyāt spirits corresponds directly to the decline of the Husaynid regime, which ruled Tunis, and the subsequent suppression, after their departure, of sṭambēlī and other popular spiritual practices under nationalist regimes.[3]

In ritual, the families are played in a specific order: Baḥriyya first, followed by Banū Kūrī, and closing with the Bēyāt. The members of each family, and thus their nūbas, are also performed in a relatively fixed order, from oldest/most powerful to youngest/least powerful. Dancers tend to be possessed by a succession of spirits in each family, in contrast to those who dance in the white part of the silsila and are moved to trance by only one, sometimes two, saints. Each spirit has its own distinctive trance movements. A dancer whose afflicting spirit is in the Banū Kūrī family wears a black cloak and may crawl on the ground toward the gumbrī while possessed by Dakākī, rise to her knees, alternate reaching each arm into the air on each beat while possessed by Kūrī, strike her torso and legs with a club while possessed by Migzū, and perhaps continue the process with other spirits in the family. Dancers possessed by certain Baḥriyya spirits make dance movements associated with swimming and water, while several Bēyāt spirits remain seated, calmly surveying their surroundings while dressed in gold, all behaviors befitting their status as royalty.

In Tunis, sṭambēlī practitioners are understood to be specialists in diagnosing and treating spirit affliction. Sṭambēlī boasts the largest and most elaborate spirit pantheon in the local therapeutic landscape, with most spirits considered proprietary to, and affliction only healed by, sṭambēlī ritualists. Adjacent practices specialize in other classes of the spirits. In Tunis, migrants from the southern oasis town of Nefta brought spirit-possession practices associated with that town's patron saint, Sīdī Bū ʿAlī, while the women's Tījāniyya specializes in spirit possession by spirits called the *ruḥā-*

3. While each spirit group has a few core members whose identities are definitive of their group, the categories can be somewhat porous or overlapping. While in some instances this apparent flexibility may simply be the product of uncertainty or variability, generally speaking it highlights the fact that spirits (and some saints, for that matter) may have multiple memberships in different categories. It is the relationships among spirits that are performed in the silsilas, rather than strict adherence to a single rigid order. For example, Ummī Yenna is often described as a member of the Baḥriyya, but Baba Majid usually performs her nūba with those of her husband, Kūrī's, family in the Banū Kūrī, while others situate her along with her daughters in the Bēyāt.

niyyāt that are under the control of Sīdī Aḥmad al-Tījānī (see chap. 3). The vast majority of the spirits in the black part of the silsila are unique to sṭambēlī. Very few exceptions occur, such as Ummī Yenna's (omitted from the 2009 performance) presence in Mannūbiyya silsila, where she is attached to, and considered the "daughter of," the saint Sīdī Bū Sa'īd (see chaps. 1 and 5).

Yet upon the conclusion of this extended performance of otherness in the black silsila, the ritual often yields to one or two additional nūbas for saints to close the ceremony. These saints are not considered part of the white section but instead are performed for attendees who find healing in the trance practices of adjacent ritual niches. In this performance, nūbas for Sīdī Belḥassen and Lilla Malīka were played, a gesture of hospitality toward attendees who either participate in the rituals of the Mannūbiyya or have a spiritual relationship with either of those two saints. These can be considered a second category of saints in the ritual world of sṭambēlī. The first category of saints are *intrinsic* to sṭambēlī and found in the white silsila: they have proprietary sṭambēlī melodies, rhythms, and lyrics and are performed at the beginning of the ceremony. The second category of saints are *adjacent*, "on-demand" nūbas that are performed at the end of the ceremony and share melodic, rhythmic, and lyrical material with the more widely circulating versions. Thus, while both intrinsic and adjacent saints are performed using sṭambēlī's distinctive sounds, the melody and lyrics for the nūbas of adjacent saints are based on the version of the songs that originate outside sṭambēlī. Adjacent saints, then, are recognized and integrated into ritual, but in a way that incorporates a sense of distance by highlighting their lives outside of sṭambēlī. Yet both categories share sṭambēlī's musical potencies of timbre, rhythm, intensification, and form.

These multivalent and potentially ambiguous identities of saints in the sṭambēlī context caught the attention of A. J. N. Tremearne, who over a century ago predicted that Muslim saints eventually become spirits, noting that this was the case of Ma'llem Sofū (one of the Bēyāt in table 4.1), a Muslim saint also part of the Hausa bori pantheon (Tremearne 1968 [1914]: 151). Yet he also noted that, in Tunis, *local* saints had curiously remained distinct from the spirits (421). This is still the case, suggesting that the local spiritual infrastructure, with its associated shrines, rituals, and communities, demands that the identities of local saints remain clearly preserved so that they can remain part of the mutual availability of ritually adjacent niches of ambient Sufism. There are some ambiguities and blurred lines between saint and spirit that are built into ambient Sufism as a whole, for certain saints are understood to have mastery over some spirits, and therefore it is not always clear whether a trancer is possessed by a spirit that the saint controls or is "taken away" into trance by the saint whose nūba is being performed.[4] Yet the separateness of the saints also reveals the robustness of the entrenched identities, sites, and practices associated with local saints. This separateness, which at first blush may seem paradoxical, creates the conditions for recognition and incorporation, both structural features of ambient Sufism, as well as the potential for ritual hospitality that emerges from them. The musical form of the silsila enables the "sub-Saharanness" of the concept of spirit families—featuring successions of spirits played in order—to be seamlessly maintained in North Africa. It also provides room for incorporating and highlighting local saints while adhering to a sequential logic shared by other silsila-based ritual musics.

Timbral Saturation, Sonic Constancy

It is mainly the sectionality of ritual that distinguishes saints from the spirits. The sectionality that separates them, however, can be obscured by the fact that sonically—that is, in terms of timbre, texture, instrumentation, and intensification—the nūbas for the spirits are no different from those of the saints. Like the Mannūbiyya, sṭambēlī relies on general principles of timbral saturation, sonic constancy, and intensification. How it does so, however, sets it apart as a distinctive ritual musical niche. This is similar to how both practices rely on the silsila structure yet use that structure to announce their specific, different identities.

The gumbrī, the three-stringed lute that leads the sṭambēlī ensemble, features a cylindrical body fully transpierced by the neck of the instrument and equipped with a metallic resonating plate (*shaqshaqa*) that buzzes with every articulation of the strings. The instrument has a lineage clearly traceable to the Lake Chad region of central Africa, Tunisia's main source of slaves. In sṭambēlī, the gumbrī is the instrument that "speaks" (*yitkallem*) to the saints and spirits, enticing them (*yijbidhum*, lit. "pulls them") into ritual. The communicatory function is reflected in these terms and technical and morphological terminology: the right hand "speaks," while the left hand "answers"; and the lowest string is the elder (*shayb*) because it speaks in a low voice, the middle string is the youth (*shāb*) because it speaks in a higher voice, and the highest string is called *kulu*, which Baba Majid reported is a sub-Saharan word translated as "the one who replies."

4. In Islam, ancestors or other previously living persons cannot possess or inhabit the body of a living person, although spirits can. Saints, as previously living persons, may appear to possess individuals in trance but are understood to be "taking away" or "falling on," rather than possessing, the dancer.

As a rule, the gumbrī never ceases playing during any nūba. As a vessel for communication, the continuous sound of the gumbrī could be construed as an act of musical hospitality to the saints and spirits. It calls them and sustains their visits. The dancing body is the offering given as the final step in a healing process that, if successful, leaves the dancer protected from spirit affliction for the upcoming year. Dancers inevitably work their way up to a position directly in front of the gumbrī, where they are best situated to experience the timbral complexity of the instrument's acoustics. Dancers are also thus positioned with shqāshiq to both their left and right, creating an immersive surround-sound experience. The shqāshiq, often described as "following" the gumbrī, also do not stop in the midst of any nūba. In the three-nūba opening sequence analyzed in the following section, the three-stroke *sūdānī* rhythmic cycle is performed over 870 times, nonstop, over roughly nine minutes (audio ex. 4.1). This incessant cyclicity of short (three- to five-stroke) rhythmic patterns provides a sonic and temporal cushion that complements the reliable timbral saturation of the dance space; the two work together to produce a hospitable comfort of constancy.[5]

The ritual musical forms of the sṭambēlī nūba and silsila feature similar nested temporalities and trajectories to those of the Mannūbiyya. The smallest unit of the rhythmic cycle played by the shqāshiq provides a constant reference, while at the next level the gumbrī's melodic line is repeated and merged with call-and-response vocals, producing a larger musical phrase that is also repeated. Continuity, predictability, and gradual transformations are the watchwords at the level of the nūba, while the directionality and inclusivity of the silsila structure, again like the Mannūbiyya, orient listeners and participants toward a large-scale structure whose flexibility and tendency toward completeness encourage hospitality toward humans and spirits alike.

Rhythmic Elasticity, Nonisochrony, and Intensification

Thus far this book has emphasized three musical domains in which each ritual musical community demonstrates adherence to widely shared struc-

5. I came to this conclusion after dancing to a nūba in the 2009 ritual performance described in this chapter. My most vivid and enduring memory of the event was the sensation of having my physical movements supported by the short, consistent, and reliable patterns of the shqāshiq surrounding me, which in turn enabled my self-consciousness to fade away. At one point I was tending toward being on "autopilot," for, as I regained my proprioception, I realized I had made my way to the far side of the dance space without knowing it. At that point I made my way back to my original position in front of the gumbrī and bowed to signal the end of my dance.

tural principles of ambient Sufism, on the one hand, while activating those principles in a specific way that asserts the individual character of each ritual niche, on the other. The first domain is ritual musical structure. The previous sections have shown how sṭambēlī's specific silsila structure and content set it apart from those ritually adjacent practices while revealing a shared reliance on the flexibility and hospitality of the silsila. The second domain is constancy of sound and timbre. What is most immediately and obviously apparent when encountering the sounds of sṭambēlī is its distinctive timbres and textures, which set it apart from its ritual musical neighbors while also relying on shared principles of ritual saturation such as sonic continuity and timbral constancy. The buzzing, metallic timbres of the gumbrī and shqāshiq immediately and unambiguously announce sṭambēlī. Like the other traditions discussed in this book, during a nūba the instruments never cease playing, providing a continuity of sound and timbral constancy that is a feature of other ritual musics of ambient Sufism utilizing different instrumentation.

The third domain is intensification. All ritual forms in this book undergo processes of intensification, combining in one way or another discrete, sequential, and/or global models of intensification. Sṭambēlī occasionally uses sequential intensification (SI), particularly when it switches from a four- or five-stroke rhythm to the three-stroke sūdānī rhythm to close a nūba (see video ex. 4.1 of Baḥriyya progressing from the four-stroke *muthallith* rhythm to sūdānī). However, the most common process is discrete temporal intensification (DTI), which involves a single repeated pattern transforming via acceleration. Tables 4.1 and 4.2 show the beginning and ending tempos of each nūba, demonstrating that marked acceleration is a standard aesthetic principle.[6] What most clearly sets sṭambēlī apart from its neighbors is the form this intensification takes rhythmically. When the two most common sṭambēlī rhythms undergo tempo acceleration, the relative spacing between strokes changes. For example, the three-stroke sūdānī rhythm begins at a slow tempo with a long-short-medium (LSM) pattern but gradually shifts to one approximating a short-short-short (SSS) pattern. In contrast, when the five-beat mjarred rhythm of the ʿĪsāwiyya (see chap. 2) increases in speed, the relative spacing does not change: it remains at a ratio of 2:3 (SL) irrespective of tempo, while the relative spacing of the drum pattern strokes of the ʿĪsāwiyya and Mannūbiyya likewise do not change when the tempo increases. The difference is one of underlying metric principles. The rhythms of

6. The five-stroke *bū saʿdiyya* and four-stroke hemiolalike rhythm of *saʿdāwī exhibit,* on average, the smallest amount of acceleration owing to their structural properties (see Jankowsky 2013).

the ʿĪsāwiyya and Mannūbiyya—like almost all musics in the region—rely on a model of isochrony, that is, a system whereby each beat is subdivided into nominally equidistant subpulses (analogous to the Western metric system, which is also based on the potential, for example, of a quarter note to be subdivided into two eighth notes or four sixteenth notes and so on). Sṭambēlī, in contrast, has nonisochronous tendencies. This can be best explained through a brief analysis based on microrhythmic timing. Again, the nūba for Jerma is particularly illustrative of this distinctive aspect of sṭambēlī.

"Jerma" not only emphasizes and preserves the historical geocultural connections described above; it also announces and reveals these distinctive rhythmic principles of sṭambēlī. These principles depend on, and are disclosed by, the normative increase in tempo that occurs in most sṭambēlī nūbas. The overall progression is one of markedly gradual, insistent, acceleration, with only occasional abrupt jumps in tempo. "Jerma," as the second of a sequence of three nūbas "tied together" (*murābiṭ mābīnhum*), has a quantifiable musical in-betweenness that reveals the sṭambēlī principle of rhythmic elasticity (audio ex. 4.1, 4:30–5:15). "Jerma" is preceded by the nūba for the Prophet and followed by a nūba for Bū Ḥijba. All three nūbas are in the same three-stroke rhythm called *sūdānī* and are performed as a single unit with seamless transitions between them.

Sūdānī ("sub-Saharan") is the most widely used rhythmic pattern in sṭambēlī. These rhythms are played on the shqāshiq by the troupe's responsorial singers. Unlike the drums utilized in the rituals of the ʿĪsāwiyya and Mannūbiyya, sṭambēlī rhythmic instruments do not produce low and high (dumm and takk) pitches to create its rhythmic contours. Instead, the shqāshiq produce a single, constant level of pitch, providing an overriding sense of pitch uniformity. This constancy, coupled with the cyclic nature of the rhythmic system, creates the conditions for a distinctive transformation of temporal space.

As the tempo increases, this pattern's intensificatory trajectory takes the form of subtle and gradual, yet drastic, metric transformation. This transformation is one in which each of the three strokes of the pattern—each of different durations—shift from asymmetrical to symmetrical, that is, approaching equidistance at the highest tempos. What begins as a long-short-medium (LSM) pattern (roughly, dotted quarter-eighth-quarter) eventually and gradually becomes a short-short-short (SSS) pattern (roughly, three eighths), a transformation not only in rhythmic pattern but also in metric perception.

At its beginning tempo of 96 rhythmic cycles per minute (cpm), the sūdānī rhythm has an LSM pattern of stroke durations. This pattern, however, does not conform to a temporal grid of nominally equidistant subdivisions

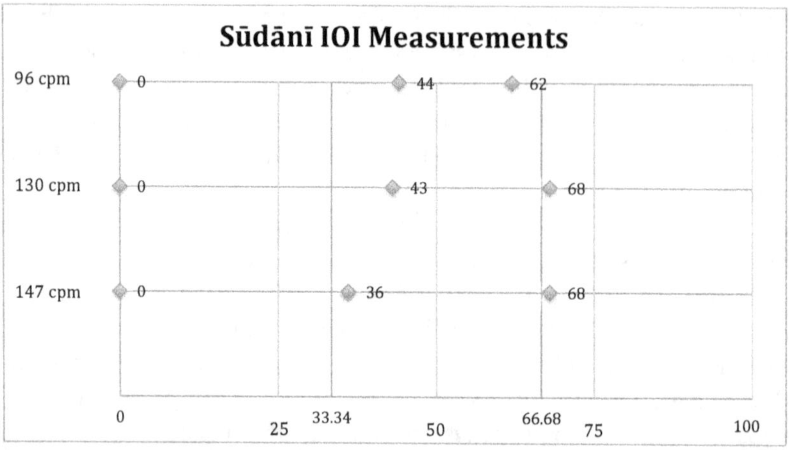

FIGURE 4.2. Transformations in rhythmic timing accompanying tempo increase for the opening sequence of nūbas ("Ṣlāt al-Nabī," "Jerma," "Bū Ḥijba") in the sūdānī rhythm. Graph illustrates how the three strokes of the rhythm becoming increasingly equidistant as the tempo increases (cpm = rhythmic cycles per minute).

(such as eighth, sixteenth, triplet, etc.). Instead, as figure 4.2 shows, the first rhythmic stroke takes up the first 44 percent of the cycle, the space between the second and third attacks takes up 18 percent of the cycle, and the space between the third attack and the first attack of the following cycle is 38 percent. In microrhythmic analysis, these durations are called inter-onset intervals (IOI), and their relationship in this case is expressed in an inter-onset interval ratio of 44:18:38. As "Ṣlāt al-Nabī" ends and the next song, "Jerma," begins, the average tempo has reached 130 cpm and the rhythmic cycle's IOI ratios have transformed from 44:18:38 to 43:25:32. With higher standard deviations than those of the ratios of "Ṣlāt al-Nabī" and "Bū Ḥijba,"[7] the actual measurements at this point are the most prone to variation, as this stage of the song is situated in between the relative stability of both the song's initial rhythmic pattern and the eventual final pattern. When that final pattern occurs (at the end of "Bū Ḥijba"—that is, by the end of this three-nūba chain of songs), the tempo reaches 147 cpm and the average IOI ratio has transformed further to 36:32:32, almost equidistant but maintain-

7. Little biographical information is known about Bū Ḥijba (a shortened version of Sīdī Ṣālah Bū Ḥijba), though he may be Bū Ḥajba, the barber venerated in the interior town of Gabès (Pâques 1964). That so little is remembered about him may appear to belie his prestigious position following the nūbas of the Prophet and Bilāl. That he is "tied" to Bilāl's nūba may explain why a saint who has fallen out of favor (because most of the clients who trance to his nūba have passed away) continues to appear in such a prominent place in the ceremony. Another important factor is that this nūba was one of Baba Majid's favorites on which to improvise.

MUSICAL EXAMPLE 4.1. Main melody of "Jerma" (lead vocals omitted)

ing a slightly elongated first IOI. Taken together, these IOI ratios reveal a rhythmic cycle undergoing a process of temporal compression and a transition from nonisochronous to nearly isochronous timing patterns, from 44:18:38 to 43:25:32 to 36:32:32.

Because the rhythmic cycle is not divided into equidistant underlying pulses, the sūdānī pattern defies unequivocal representation in conventional metric terms that rely on duple or triple subdivisions. Instead, it adheres to a nonisochronous metric framework. The insistent, relentlessly cyclic strokes of the shqāshiq establish these patterns as the norm, not as aberrations from a nominally isochronous metric grid, that follows its own logic of development. They create a strong sense of groove that both relies on and obscures the microtiming complexities of the patterns. "Jerma," however, is the most variable of the three. In terms of microtiming, the nūbas for the Prophet and Bū Ḥijba are more stable as they are at the extremes. The in-betweenness of "Jerma" means that it grows out of the former while tending toward the latter. When approximated in conventional notation, the beginning cycles of "Jerma" can be represented roughly by musical example 4.1.

However, the metric feel of the pattern might approximate musical example 4.2 (eighth-sixteenth-sixteenth) if listeners cognize the second, accented stroke as falling around the 50 percent mark—that is, as falling "on" the offbeat, particularly at slower tempos. Thus, sūdānī could be represented in notation as approximating any of the three rhythms in musical example 4.2, depending on context and tempo:

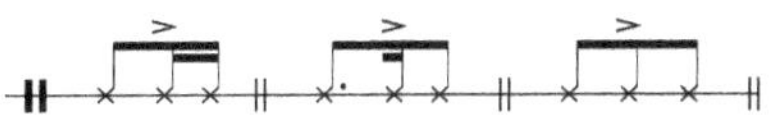

MUSICAL EXAMPLE 4.2. Three possible representations and feels of sūdānī rhythm. Other notational options are possible, since some nūbas emphasize the accented stroke so drastically that it can feel like the "onbeat."

Ambiguities of actual timings notwithstanding, what is most consistent in this rhythm, and most important for my analysis, is its trajectory from non-equidistant to nominally equidistant forms. Figure 4.3 offers an alternative visual representation of the gradual transformation of the rhythmic cell.

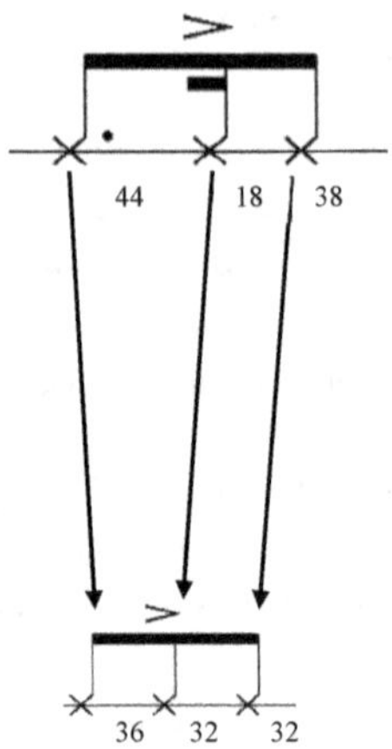

FIGURE 4.3. A visual representation of the rhythmic transformation of the sūdānī rhythmic mode

While the rhythmic patterns at this subpulse level are nonisochronous, it is important to note that timing at the "beat" level (that is, the first attack of each cycle) is nominally isochronous. This means that the regularity of downbeats can provide the constancy and stability that support trance dance movements, despite any ambiguities or transformations at the level of intracycle rhythmic timings.[8]

Crucially, even though the relative temporal spacing between rhythmic attacks changes as the tempo increases, it is still considered the "same" rhythm. Put somewhat differently, the concept of the sūdānī rhythm includes, and is indeed defined by, this transformational potential. Yet these are gradual transitions. They do not just "switch" the feel; for much of the song the rhythm is in between those two ends of the spectrum, hinting at both.[9] This normative transformational process, as well as its nonisochro-

8. This supports Justin London's metric well-formedness constraint, stating that if inter-onset intervals (IOIs) on the subpulse level are nonisochronous, "then the IOIs of the beat cycle must be nominally isochronous (i.e., categorically equivalent, though subject to expressive variation)" (2012: 128).

9. These nonisochronous subdivisions are too uneven and too unstable over time to allow them to be assigned to a single (even nonisochronous) meter. The sūdānī rhythmic cycle cannot be accurately or consistently divided into halves or thirds. Even if we posited

nous timing patterns, illustrates how the sṭambēlī soundworld shares certain principles with other practices in the local ecology of ritual musics while simultaneously carving out a distinctive niche within that shared space. With other silsila-based practices, sṭambēlī shares, among other things, aesthetic principles of temporal transformation, nested temporalities with short rhythmic cycles at their foundation, and constancy of timbre and texture. How those principles materialize is where sṭambēlī sets itself apart from those kindred ritual practices—namely, in its distinctive timbre and texture, proprietary modal system, and unique principle of rhythmic elasticity.

Does this mean that metric ambiguity or tension is related to the establishment of a state of trance? Jean During's work in Baluchistan suggests that ambiguity of rhythmic structure can disorientate the listener, "forc[ing] him to abandon his intellectual and psychomotor references . . . [and] might well allow the listener to 'let go' and permit access to the state of trance" (During 1992: 301).[10] Steven Friedson's account of trance dance in Malawi emphasizes the ambiguities of the "multistable" 3:2 metric simultaneity that he concludes leads to a "loosening up of perceptual boundaries," which may be "a significant factor in the promotion of trance states" (1996: 143). It is tempting to follow this line of thought, and the literature by students of trance, especially by those of us who have danced in trance ceremonies, is replete with accounts of strong experiences of music (and spirit) and the seemingly paradoxical combination of "intense focus" and the "loss of the strong sense of self" (Becker 2004) that seems to characterize such states. The tension between correlation and causation looms large in this literature, and care should be taken not to slip into musical reductionism in which native explication and the numerous other ritual factors that affect the sensorium are downplayed or ignored (see Jankowsky 2007). Rouget reminds us that all trance musics and responses to those musics are first and foremost culturally conditioned. If ritual involves a "radical slowing down . . . of the tempo of ordinary life" (Kapferer 2005: 48) that, through repetition, draws attention to the constituent elements of aesthetic forms such as music, then a more synthetic view of music and ritual becomes possible.

that the initial sūdānī pattern was nominally binary, and that "expressive timing" explained the 44 percent initial IOI, this interpretation no longer holds true by the end of the song. And even if we allowed that, at the end of the song, the meter had shifted to a ternary subdivision, we would still be hard-pressed to account for the middle of the performance, when the feel is between these two extremes. In the context of a continuous tempo increase, it is impossible to locate a specific point at which this supposed metric shift occurs.

10. It is striking that During's example of Baluchi folk music is, like sṭambēlī, based on a rhythmic system that is not shared with other musical styles in the same cultural area.

A more cautious, and perhaps more productive, point of departure, then, might be to hypothesize that music-driven trance states depend upon a more general coordination of localized musical and ritual teleologies; the specific elements that transform to achieve their ends may differ from one tradition to the next, but they share in the cyclicity, continuity, constancy, and large-scale structuring principles of ambient Sufism that guide and reshape the sense of time.[11]

DISINTEGRATION OF THE SILSILA

A complete ritual performance of the sṭambēlī silsila has become increasingly rare. The cumulative experience of the sṭambēlī silsila form is one that encourages a reading of ritual as a mode of historical remembrance. The musical routes through the silsila bring into being the ritual presence of saints and spirits, whose sonic materiality, in turn, provides the geocultural and historical referents that direct participants into fields of meaning. It is only through music that these unseen beings arrive in ritual, and therefore it is only through music that the histories and meanings they evoke are manifested in front of witnesses in a systematic, semipublic way. These histories, it should be emphasized, are not presented in a linear, narrative representational format. Rather, they are partial, abstract, and just below the surface. They are embedded in the music, song lyrics and languages, dance movements and ritual accoutrements, the private knowledge of spirit affliction shared between healer and patient, and informal discourse within the sṭambēlī community. With each passing generation, that knowledge becomes less and less specific. Levels of understanding of song lyric phrases in sub-Saharan languages, for example, have devolved over the decades, with few able to identify the specific language and far fewer, if any, able to translate their meanings. While lexical comprehension diminishes, the sounds of those foreign languages retain—and even increase, through their incomprehensibility[12]—the power to evoke otherness and index sub-Saharan Africa. In other words, the specificity of African referents is replaced by a generalized African otherness.

11. Moreover, although the sūdānī and muthallith rhythms are the most elastic sṭambēlī patterns and account for the majority (74 percent) of sṭambēlī nūbas, the two other rhythms proprietary to sṭambēlī (the four-stroke sa'dāwī and the five-stroke bū sa'diyya) have very low elasticity and are still capable of eliciting trance. See Jankowsky (2013) for systematic microtiming analyses of all four rhythms.

12. This supports Paul Stoller's (1997) assertion that, in Africa, the power of words in ritual practice may be located in the sounds themselves as much as—and often more so than—their lexical meanings.

This shift is particularly apparent in the transition from ritual to performances on the public stage. In ritual, a relatively self-contained yet welcoming and porous community is configured around a population of clients in need of healing from afflictions attributed to spirits. The "audiences" for these rituals typically involve other patients and healers, as well as the friends and family of patients and musicians—that is, people who have relationships with sṭambēlī participants—and thus ritual knowledge is always within reach. Audiences for stage performances, in contrast, have less proximity to ritual knowledge and are not directly invested in immediate therapeutic outcomes. But that healing potential, the general knowledge of sṭambēlī's Africanness and capacity to intervene in the spirit world, is part of the allure of sṭambēlī music for its new audiences. Onstage, sṭambēlī musicians self-represent as the link to that musical-ritual power, but without actually engaging in it. They are entrepreneurs of the self (Comaroff and Comaroff 2009) who self-present as representatives of an ethnic, cultural, and ritual community, more specifically a group with knowledge of and power over the spirit world, and, in turn, and even more specifically, knowledge and power that comes from beyond, from sub-Saharan Africa. It is a step removed from ritual, yet it is not a proxy for it; ritual here serves as a referential resource.

A voluminous literature on heritage industries, the expediency of culture, and self-reflexive marketing of ethnicity has shown the various ways in which cultural expressions of minorities are produced, packaged, and presented to audiences, to serve various sociopolitical and economic ends, and result in ambiguities of representation and commodification (e.g., Comaroff and Comaroff 2009; Kirshenblatt-Gimblett 1998; Yúdice 2003). My aim here is to examine one aspect of sṭambēlī stage performances, namely the transformation of musical logics of presentation and the cultural work of those transformations of form in meeting the expectations of new audiences. Sṭambēlī musicians widely perceive sṭambēlī as being on the brink of extinction. Asserting, celebrating, and marketing cultural *dis*tinction is widely seen as the most efficient way of defending against cultural *ex*tinction (Comaroff and Comaroff 2009: 10). Like Salah, quoted above, Belhassen looks inward to ritual for the source of the problem, identifying the deception of dishonest healers as the main reason for the decline of sṭambēlī: "Let me tell you something! Do you know why sṭambēlī did not evolve and didn't move forward? It's because some people have used it to trick other people and make money off them. I had people come to me and tell me stories [of] how they have been deceived . . . and . . . I have even witnessed such situations in person" (quoted in Hassnaoui 2017: 120).

Belhassen's father often shared similar complaints with me, explaining his refusal to work with a particular healer who promised potential clients that their children would pass their exams or find a suitable spouse by holding sṭambēlī ceremonies. Sṭambēlī's association with ritual situates it in a social space perceived as potentially therapeutic but also susceptible to suspicions of deceptive practices that plague the broader field of traditional healing. The moral positioning of sṭambēlī musicians reveals an important aspect of the decline in demand for sṭambēlī healing. Rather than compete with the few remaining yinnas for ritual work, Belhassen has seized performance opportunities in the circuit of cultural spaces in Tunis, building a reputation and a show format that has brought his troupe increasing success and visibility. He identifies stage performance as having healing potential, although in a different vein: "I decided to start something of my own that is not a healing ritual but healing through entertainment. . . . We need to move forward and think beyond healing and produce more music" (quoted in Hassnaoui 2017: 119, 120).

These performances typically take place at relatively posh cafés, art galleries, and other "cultural spaces" in Tunis (see Hassnaoui 2017). On July 25, 2014, I accompanied Belhassen and his sṭambēlī troupe to their performance at Café el-ʿAlī, a hip spot in the Tunis medina where partial outdoor seating provides views over the city and a contemporary beverage menu featuring fruit blends as well as tea priced three times that sold in street cafés. The members of the troupe were set up, as in ritual, with the gumbrī (played by Belhassen) in the middle, flanked by shqāshiq players who sang responses; owing to the small size of the stage, the shqāshiq player with the least amount of experience (and therefore the one responsible for menial tasks such as carrying the gumbrī to and from the venue) remained in the back. They played in a seated position in front of microphones, with Belhassen sporting a cowrie shell–studded fez, the iconic headwear not of sṭambēlī but rather of the Moroccan *gnāwa*,[13] which Belhassen and other sṭambēlī musicians look to as a model of success in bringing African ritual musics onto the public stage (see fig. 4.4). Putting on hold, for the moment, the nuances of self-presentation, this new form of access to sṭambēlī, and the implications of the social intimacy of the café space, I return to considering musical form and its capacity to be adapted and hospitable to new audiences and contexts.

13. Gnāwa is a ritual musical healing practice developed by Moroccans of sub-Saharan descent. It shares many family resemblances with Tunisian sṭambēlī but has enjoyed much greater success in national and international commercial music markets. See Chlyeh (1999), Kapchan (2007), and Witulski (2018).

FIGURE 4.4. Belhassen Mihoub (*left*) and Noureddine Soudani performing at Café el-ʿAlī in July 2014. Photo by the author.

Ambiguities of the Alter and the Familiar

In terms of the repertoire chosen that night, Belhassen's performance prioritized the familiar over the alter; that is, it stuck mostly to nūbas with references to recognizable local saints and excluded almost all the less familiar spirits of the black portion of the ritual. The nūbas for the saints feature lyrics that are mainly in Arabic and include common religious phrases and praises to God, the Prophet, and saints that are used in a variety of religious contexts (e.g., *lā illaha illā allah*, the Islamic testimony of faith introduced in chap. 2). The silsila touched on the Baḥriyya, the most common form of possessing spirit in all Tunisian trance healing traditions. In doing so, however, it capitalized on ambiguities of identity of some spirits, such as Mulay Brahīm, in ways that prioritize sameness over difference. The performance maintained a semblance of a silsila, in that it began with the nūba for the Prophet ("Ṣlāt al-Nabī") and quickly transitioned to the iconic sṭambēlī saints Sīdī Saʿd, Sīdī Marzūg, and Sīdī Frej, who are of sub-Saharan African origin but have shrines in the Tunis area and are recognized as spiritual figures locally, by Arab and black Tunisians alike (see table 4.3).

The first eight nūbas unquestionably approximate the ritual structure

TABLE 4.3 Silsila performed by Belhassen and his troupe at Café el-ʿAlī in 2014

"Ṣlāt al-Nabī"	Standard sṭambēlī opening nūba
"Sīdī Saʿd"	Former sub-Saharan slave; iconic sṭambēlī nūba
"Sīdī Marzūg"	Former sub-Saharan slave; iconic sṭambēlī nūba
"Sīdī Frej"	Former sub-Saharan slave; iconic sṭambēlī nūba
"Sīdī Bū R'as al-ʿAjmī"	Standard sṭambēlī nūba
"Bābā Baḥri"	Another name for Sīdī Manṣūr (see next nūba); standard sṭambēlī nūba
"Sīdī Manṣūr"	Saint from Sfax; master of Baḥriyya spirits; standard sṭambēlī nūba
"Sīdī ʿAmr"	Standard sṭambēlī nūba
"Al-Shaykh al-Kāmal"	ʿIsāwiyya mjarred adapted to fezzānī by Hedi Doniya, in turn adapted by Belḥassen for sṭambēlī
"Sīdī Ḥammūda"	Standard sṭambēlī nūba
* "Bū Saʿdiyya"	Masked dancer represents this legendary first musician of sṭambēlī
* "Wallah Salām ʿAlaykum"	Traditional Tunisian song, not from sṭambēlī repertoire; but the version by Hedi Doniya was groundbreaking in including a gumbrī
"Sīdī ʿAbd al-Qādir"	Standard sṭambēlī nūba; founder of the Qādiriyya Sufi order
"Sīdī ʿAmr Bū Khatwa"	Standard sṭambēlī nūba; local saint
* "ʿArbiyya"	Sṭambēlī Sghār spirit but also represents Lilla ʿArbiyya, female saint
* "Mulay Brahīm"	Sṭambēlī Baḥriyya spirit but also name of Moroccan saint
* "Zambala"	Fun nūba celebrating a party or feast, not in ritual repertoire

of the sṭambēlī silsila. With the exception of the absence of "Jerma" and "Bū Ḥijba," the two nūbas "tied" to the Prophet, the silsila begins as it does in ritual, following a normative yet flexible succession of saints. The tenth, eleventh, and twelfth nūbas ("Sīdī Ḥammūda," "Sīdī ʿAbd al-Qādir," and "Sīdī ʿAmr Bū Khatwa") are equally at home in this part of the silsila.

Dance, both presentational and participatory, occurs during several of these nūbas. At many points during the performance, an ʿarīfa accompanying the troupe stood in front of the musicians and performed relatively gentle, trancelike movements of bending forward and back at the waist of the type common in ritually adjacent practices such as the Mannūbiyya. She approached audience members and encouraged them to join her. Many resisted, but eventually the small space in front of the musicians was filled with young women and a few young men, with the former disregarding the ʿarīfa's dance style and instead dancing in the conventional Arab style seen at weddings or other functions. The men were more inclined to mimic the trance moves, although they also tried out dance patterns more reminiscent of reggae or ska practices. While these inclusive, recreational dance episodes for noninitiates may at first blush appear to be at a far remove from ritual, they are in fact very similar to ritual episodes that occur in ceremonies, such as the extensive initiation ritual, that include a pre-sunset ceremony. As I have described elsewhere (Jankowsky 2010), in ritual there is a small window of opportunity for noninitiates to "have fun" getting up to dance, often with conventional (secular) Arab dance moves, and even to try out trance moves. Some of these novices do fall into trance, in which case they are then treated by the ʿarīfa, are considered "chosen" by the spirits or saints, and may undergo initiation into the sṭambēlī community. Thus, somewhat paradoxically, the recreational dance of the café performance does reflect ritual practice, albeit a contained, limited, ritual practice that itself is designed be fun, inclusive, nonthreatening, and (in terms of healing) nonritual.

The five nūbas marked with asterisks in table 4.3 are particularly revealing of the musical decisions made in the effort to be hospitable and appealing to the audience by highlighting the familiar. Three do this cultural work in a relatively implicit way, while the other two are more explicit. The nūba "Bū Saʿdiyya" is the most explicit and dramatic example. It is a highly anticipated moment in the show, as it features one of the musicians dressed up in the masked costume representing Bū Saʿdiyya, the legendary first musician of sṭambēlī. Legend has it that Bū Saʿdiyya, a hunter from central Africa, walked the entirety of the trans-Saharan trade routes in a desperate attempt to find his daughter, who had been captured by slave raiders. Once in Tunis, Bū Saʿdiyya would play the shqāshiq in the streets, trying to attract attention and find his child. The legend ends tragically: he never does find her. However, Bū Saʿdiyya became a role played by individuals in the sṭambēlī community. Dressed up in a masked leather costume appointed with cowrie shells, animal skins, and ragged strips of cloth (all representing Bū Saʿdiyya's difficult journey from central to northern Africa), a member of the sṭambēlī community would be assigned to visit local weekly markets to seek out new arrivals from sub-Saharan Africa to guide them to the support network of communal houses. But the most common image of Bū Saʿdiyya is of itinerant black musicians dressed in the costume, who played the shqāshiq, ṭabla drum, or gugāy (one- or two-stringed fiddle) for donations in the street and at public festivals, and would often play up the fearsomely exotic expectations of the role by pretending to chase away onlookers (see Jankowsky 2010). Bū Saʿdiyya is arguably the public face of sṭambēlī, although with divergent or ambiguous meanings for those inside and outside the sṭambēlī network. Bū Sa'diyya is neither a saint nor a spirit and typically does not appear in healing rituals. Playing the nūba "Bū Sa'diyya" for café audiences entails a kind of historical continuity, one in which the alter (the figure of Bū Sa'diyya) is in fact familiar, since it has a long history of representing sṭambēlī and its alterity publicly (video ex. 4.2).

The second nūba that explicitly negotiates the space between the familiar and the alter is the song "Wallah Salām 'Alaykum" (Greetings Upon You), a song in praise of saints. This is a song from the Tunisian *turāth* (cultural heritage) whose provenance has slipped into obscurity. It was popularized by Hedi Doniya, the singer whose name is virtually synonymous with the nūba repertoire of the mizwid genre (see chap. 5). Released in the early 2000s on the Tunisian Foni label as the lead number on a CD of the same name, it was arranged by Zouheir Gouja, an ethnomusicologist at the Institut Supérieur de Musique in Tunis. Gouja, a champion of fusing musical genres, added shqāshiq and the gumbrī playing of the late Hafez Haddad (another former apprentice of Baba Majid) to the piece to serve as a bass line for the higher-register mizwid bagpipes and the percussion section of bendīr and darbūka. It became part of Doniya's regular repertoire, receiving television and radio airplay as well as over half a million views on YouTube. As not just the only mass-mediated song in recent history to feature the sounds of sṭambēlī but also one by a superstar of the most popular music genre in Tunisia, this song brings the familiar and the alter together in a unique way by evoking the familiarity of a popular song that depended on the less familiar sounds of sṭambēlī.

That process is even more complex in "al-Shaykh al-Kamal" (The Perfect Master). The song originates from the 'Īsāwiyya mjarred repertoire (see chap. 2). Hedi Doniya popularized the song by performing it with mizwid instrumentation and transforming the 'Īsāwiyya's iconic five-beat mjarred foundation into mizwid's iconic four-beat fazzānī rhythm. Belhassen's version takes the Hedi Doniya version and adapts it to sṭambēlī instrumentation, rhythm, and aesthetics. The call-and-response format creates room for calling out the names of saints, such as Sīdī Ben 'Īsā, in between the repeated formula *lā ilaha illā allah*, connecting not only important spiritual figures but also three highly distinct genres ('Īsāwiyya, mizwid nūba, and sṭambēlī) of musical and ritual invocations of saints. Aspects of the ecology of Sufism layer upon each other in this performance (video ex. 4.3).

"'Arbiyya" and "Mulay Brahīm" are the only two nūbas for spirits played in the entire performance. Their inclusion speaks to two aspects of the café silsila that nudge the silsila even further toward the familiar. First, these two exceptions prove the rule of excluding virtually all spirits from the performance (two, or only 12 percent of nūbas in this performance are spirits, versus thirty-five, or 70 percent, in the ritual analyzed above). Second, these two spirits have ambiguous identities, serving as spirits in the sṭambēlī pantheon but also construed, in other contexts, as saints. ʿArbiyya is one of the Sghār (Children) spirits in sṭambēlī. But there is also some slippage between this persona and Lilla ʿArbiyya, a female saint whose shrine in the medina of Tunis is a popular destination for women having reproductive difficulties (Boissevain 2006:40; Johnson 1979: 115). The lyrics are equally vague, using only Arabic and mentioning only her name and the kerchief (*maḥrama*) she holds; *ʿarbiyya ʿarbiyya ʿarbiyya ū-maḥrama* is a lyric that could pertain equally to the ritual accoutrements of a possessing spirit or the clothing accessory associated with the female saint. Mulay Brahīm exhibits a similar ambiguity. Although in sṭambēlī he is a powerful Baḥriyya spirit, making the dancers he possesses move in a swimming motion, Mulay Brahīm is also the name of a saint in Morocco, where the honorific "Mulay" is roughly equivalent to "Sīdī"; his sṭambēlī nūba is also in vernacular Arabic, typically performed with no sub-Saharan words or phrases. These two spirits thus exhibit a productive ambiguity in which both identities (saint and spirit) are available and thus boundaries between the familiar and the alter blur without contradiction.

Sṭambēlī café performances thus deal with the familiar and the alter in a manner distinctive from but dependent upon its ritual referents. The musical form of the café performance brings sṭambēlī closer to its audience's prior, experience-near knowledge by prioritizing aspects of ritual that absorb or parallel the practices of ritually adjacent trance traditions: it avoids the large repertoire of nūbas for spirits considered the most "other" and instead limits songs for spirits to those with ambiguous identities that overlap with the domain of saints, and showcases the "familiar alter" public figure of Bū Saʿdiyya and the mass-mediated mizwid collaboration with Hedi Doniya. When I asked Belhassen about his process of choosing repertoire, he did not indicate a conscious preference for the saints, responding that he chooses the nūbas for which he has a musical affinity. He acknowledged, however, that very few of those are from the spirit part of the silsila. Mizwid has always been his favorite music to listen to (indeed, before he developed his sṭambēlī musicianship in his father's troupe, Belhassen dreamed of being a mizwid percussionist), and the mizwid nūbas are all for saints. Furthermore, in the sṭambēlī repertoire most songs for saints are longer and more complex, with more sections than those for the spirits, and therefore Belhassen is more strongly drawn to them. Regardless of intention, while minimizing the otherness of its spirits and sub-Saharan lyrics, Belhassen's approach to café sṭambēlī does so without compromising the defining timbral, textural, melodically pentatonic, and rhythmically elastic and cyclic aspects of its musical aesthetics.[14]

The singing voice, however, gains a primacy and clarity in café sṭambēlī that it does not enjoy in ritual. While call-and-response vocals praising the spirit or saint are a feature of almost every sṭambēlī nūba, the style of singing and attitudes toward vocals in ritual distinguish sṭambēlī from its ritual and musical peers. The gumbrī's role as musical leader and vehicle of communication is so pronounced that, in rituals where there is amplification, only the gumbrī—and not the vocals—is outfitted with a microphone (see again video ex. 4.1). The lyrics, which mostly consist of short praises and messages of welcome, are not as descriptive and narrative as those of the Mannūbiyya. It is in the delivery of the lyrics, however, that sṭambēlī's otherness is most evident: the vocal style and lyrics are referred to as *ʿajmī* (lit. "non-Arabic"), owing to their admixture of sub-Saharan phrases and dialectical Arabic as well as the nasal, understated delivery of the words, which, in contrast to the ideals of enunciation in most Arab musics, is not concerned with the listener's comprehension.

In the café context, however, sṭambēlī vocals are emphasized. Onstage, the call-and-response singers are assigned a microphone, and a sound engineer mixes the inputs to provide projection and clarity. This emphasis on vocals is particularly important for negotiating the familiar: not only does this approach resituate the sṭambēlī soundworld within the landscape of vocalcentric Arab music, but it also allows for immediate and unambiguous recognition of sung text, especially the familiar names of saints such as Sīdī Ben ʿĪsā and Sayyda Mannūbiyya, which often elicit cheers and ululations from listeners (see, e.g., 0:18 and 0:45 in video ex. 4.3). If the selective restructuring of the sṭambēlī silsila in the café context privileges the familiar over the alter, the primacy of vocals in such performances carries and bolsters that messaging, which, in turn, underscores sṭambēlī's location within the shared culture of ambient Sufism.

Social Intimacy and Artistic Appreciation

Sṭambēlī ritual, like other rituals discussed in this book, cannot be reduced to therapeutic outcomes or the perpetuation of historical memory.

14. The most common timbral adjustment made by sṭambēlī musicians on stage is the removal of the resonating plate (*shaqshaqa*) from the gumbrī. While Belhassen keeps the shaqshaqa in place for these café performances, it is removed in most sṭambēlī fusion projects, such as the group Dendri, which features Salah (lead vocals, gumbrī, and *gambara*) and Belhassen (response vocals and shqāshiq) in an ensemble that also includes drum set, electric bass, electric guitar, and keyboards.

Among the many aspects of ritual experience, socializing is one of the most important. Ritual creates a social intimacy between individuals gathered for a common purpose in a shared space. Sṭambēlī in particular provides a space for the mixing of genders, age cohorts, and ethnicities. But elders are the voices of ritual authority, and socializing among the youth is done under their watchful eyes, as well as those of relatives and acquaintances. For young musicians, ritual performance also carries with it the pressures of mastering an extensive repertoire and performing it well enough for successful healing. While members of the ritual gathering may appreciate the artistic value of the musicianship, they do not communicate that appreciation to musicians through applause or acclamations. Cultural spaces of the café, in contrast, offer spaces of sociability for young men and women, particularly students, artists, and musicians, without the supervision of their elders. There is no pressure to succeed therapeutically, there is more latitude for experimenting with repertoire, and audience appreciation is conveyed immediately through clapping and cheers. These new contexts are noteworthy for their intimacy. They are not major venue stages but rather cultural spaces where musicians and audience members hang out together between sets and before and after performances. For sṭambēlī musicians, it widens their social circle and increases opportunities as audience members may hire the troupe for future events. Audience members commonly take selfies and post them on Facebook, propelling friend requests and invitations to other artistic and social events.

The post-Revolution art and music scene is one that is characterized, in part, by youthful experimentation that looks inward to elements of Tunisian culture that were stigmatized or, at the very least, not granted recognition or support from cultural brokers such as the state or private venues. Musicians, young audiences, and managers of cultural spaces are eager to contribute to the diversification of cultural production. This entails a shift in discourse stemming from a change in the conceptualization of sṭambēlī: in these spaces, sṭambēlī is treated less as a part of the landscape of traditional healing practices and more as part of an ecology of musical practice and entertainment. More specifically, sṭambēlī is redefined as a musical genre that is conceptualized and discussed alongside other global African diasporic genres such as blues, jazz, and rap, thus opening it up to collaborative musical endeavors. While the recontextualization of ritual music to the concert stage is nothing new in Tunisia (see Jankowsky 2017), the adaptation of sṭambēlī as a musical genre relies on a distinctive relationship between ritual and the stage. On the one hand, sṭambēlī stage performance is presented as, and in practice experienced as, being in an either/or relationship with ritual. Healing work at private homes, which provided musicians with most of their (meager) income before the turn of the twenty-first century, is "dead," is "no more," according to both Salah and Belhassen. The annual ziyāra (group pilgrimage) to the shrine of Sīdī Frej, which was a three-day affair bringing together members of the sṭambēlī community from across the country every July, has all but ceased since Baba Majid's death in 2008. In 2014 Belhassen briefly restarted the tradition, but it was limited to a single day and was long and stressful enough for Belhassen, who has extensive ritual knowledge and is fully capable of leading healing ceremonies, to announce to the entire gathering that he was done with ritual work and would only do stage performances.[15] On the other hand, for all its either/or-ness, café sṭambēlī nevertheless relies heavily on its ritual pedigree, both in utilizing selected ritual material and in its cultural-spiritual capital emanating from its association with ritual as a music that has the power to invoke unseen beings and heal. If ritual sṭambēlī is, in part, a form of collective memory, then café sṭambēlī activates a chain of value (see chap. 6) in which stage performances evade but nevertheless rely on the concept of ritual, which in turn evokes a vast, if fading, field of cultural and historical action.

15. Toward the end of the ceremony, he yelled *mā'aditsh khidma 'arbī, khidma sūrī bark!* (lit. "no more 'Arab' work, only 'French' work!"). In Tunisian vernacular, the adjective "Arab" is used to refer to things that are "traditional" and understood to be connected to the Arab heritage, such as the city's medina. In contrast, the portions of the city with wide boulevards, traffic lights, symmetrical urban planning, and tall buildings are called *sūrī,* a term that means "French" (the literal term, *fransāwī,* is not used as such). See Jankowsky (2010: 214 n. 1) for more on this distinction.

5
RITUAL REMNANTS
Legacies of Jewish-Muslim Ritual Musical Convergences

In 1726 Tunisian Jewish authorities drafted regulations prohibiting the performance of rebaybiyya—a trance healing ritual music—in Jewish homes. The prohibition was part of a nineteen-part religious edict concerning the "dangers" facing Tunisian Jews from behavior that could provoke envy or criticism. Several proscriptions concern personal appearance, such as avoiding wearing certain kinds of clothing or jewelry in public. The ninth stated: "No one shall bring into their home the *erbabia* [rebaybiyya], either on a holiday or a non-holiday" (cited in Lévy 1999: 343).[1] Lionel Lévy argues that "without a doubt, this prohibition attempts to counter the appeal of traditional Arab superstition." There is evidence from roughly the same period, however, that one North African rabbi also considered rebaybiyya scandalous because it brought Muslim musicians into the houses of Tunisian Jews for performances where men and women mixed freely. Rabbi Ibn Musa (b. ca. 1680, Tetuán; d. Tunis, 1733) criticized rebaybiyya in all but

1. Such edicts were common in the Sephardic diaspora, where great care was taken by religious leaders to regulate not only the religious lives of Jews but also their social and economic well-being by maintaining good relations with their Christian and Muslim neighbors. The Jewish community in question consisted of Tunisian Jews of Portuguese origin who had settled in Livorno prior to coming to Tunis. Referred to in Tunis as *grāna*, they lived in the European quarters of Tunis, spoke Italian and Spanish, and became an economic and social elite that separated itself from the already established Jews of Tunis (*twānsa*), many of whom lived in the Jewish quarter of the medina (*ḥara*) and spoke Arabic; the two communities had separate synagogues, schools, cemeteries, butcher shops, and religious authorities (Chouraqui 2001; Sebag 1991). The schism lasted until the 1899 decree by the French colonial authorities uniting the two communities. It is unclear whether this schism played a role in the 1726 prohibition against rebaybiyya.

name: "I witnessed a scandal . . . [Jews from Tunis] bring to their houses in holidays, and sometimes on weekdays, gentiles who play kinnor [Arab. *kamanja*] and nevel [Arab. *ʿūd*] and tof [drum, probably ṭār] and *halil* [wind instrument, perhaps the *ghayṭa*] . . . and men intermingle with women" (cited in Seroussi 2015: 434). Well over a century later, Israel J. Benjamin noted that Jewish authorities in Tunis often attempted to put an end to the practice, but "all their efforts have hitherto been in vain" (1863: 258). There is evidence that in 1923 rebaybiyya performances were continuing to traverse religious boundaries by bringing together Muslim and Jewish musicians and participants. Benattar's (1923) account of rebaybiyya in the home of a Muslim patient describes an ensemble of Jewish and Muslim men, four blind and the fifth blindfolded,[2] accompanied by two women playing the large bendīr and darbūka. The men played two lutes, two violins, and a rebāb. A 1904 report on the customs of Tunisian Jews describes rebaybiyya as a women's spirit-possession ceremony, where men are excluded except for musicians who are blind or blindfolded and play the mizwid, large tambourine, and darbūka, but sometimes also other wind instruments (most likely a *zukra*; Vassel 1904).[3] Lumbroso (1860) and Vassel (1904) further specify that rebaybiyya possession ceremonies were called *sṭambēlī* when led by black musicians, signaling not only the trance healing nature of the event but also the close relationship between the Jewish and black Muslim ritual communities (elaborated below).

These accounts, mostly in the form of passing references scattered over more than two centuries, provide limited insights into rebaybiyya. However, they do suggest that rebaybiyya was defined in part by the traversing of religious and gender boundaries, bringing together Jews and Muslims, as well as men and women, in music-driven trance rituals. In this chapter I show how an examination of the silsila of rebaybiyya reveals specific musical mechanics produced by and reflective of this boundary crossing. My analysis of the rebaybiyya silsila of the late twentieth century, in turn, illustrates the trans-Mediterranean movements of rebaybiyya that kept it alive in France after it disappeared from Tunis, and how this extinct tradition left ritual remnants that are hidden in plain sight (or, more accurately, in plain sound) in some of the most widely broadcast recordings of Tunisian popular music.

2. For reasons of propriety in a mixed-gender gathering.

3. The zukra (similar to the ghayṭa), which is made of wood, was preferred on religious grounds by some Jews over the mizwid, which has a goatskin body (Hedi Doniya, pers. comm., 2014).

SITUATING REBAYBIYYA

Jewish contributions to the field of Tunisian music have not suffered from the almost complete, official, and willful forgetting that Shannon (2015) reports for Syria. Early twentieth-century Tunisian Jewish singers such as Cheikh el-'Afrit and Habiba Msika remain some of the most celebrated popular-music figures in the country. Their recordings are widely available, continue to be broadcast on radio and television, and, in the form of YouTube and other internet uploads, often elicit nostalgic reactions for what is considered a golden age of Tunisian song. Their lives are relatively well documented in written works, and they are still considered a standard of excellence in their execution of Tunisian musical modes. Jewish music on the Tunisian island of Djerba has received scholarly attention from prominent musicologists in Germany, Israel, and the United Kingdom (e.g., Lachmann 1940, Seroussi 2015, and Davis 1986, respectively). The island's annual Jewish pilgrimage to the Ghrība synagogue (which involves the celebration of the saint Lilla Ghrība) receives international media attention and is promoted by the state as a symbol of Tunisia as a multicultural space (Carpenter-Latiri 2015). In contrast, rebaybiyya, the trance ritual music cultivated by Jews on the Tunisian mainland, has not only disappeared in practice but is also virtually absent from scholarship and the national collective memory.

The term "rebaybiyya" has been used to refer to two distinct but related ritual healing practices, both based on the silsila ritual musical form: that of mainland Tunisian Jews and that of (Muslim) women. While both are associated with women's trance dance healing rituals, the former was typically performed by men for women and mainly, though not exclusively, in domestic settings, while the latter was, and is, performed by women for women, and mainly, though not exclusively, at saint shrines. References to rebaybiyya in the historical literature and in contemporary discourse tend to mention one or the other but rarely both, creating an impression of mutual exclusivity belied by their common terminology, similar silsila structure, and shared saints. While the two practices have had separate existences, they also intersect, revealing certain overlaps in the social ecology of devotional musics, not to mention the paucity of historical documentation and the ambiguities and fickleness surrounding genre naming in ritual contexts.

The name "rebaybiyya" is often assumed to derive from the name of the rebāb, an instrument that is featured in the ancestry of both the Jewish and the women's traditions but fell out of favor in both cases. More specifically, *rebaybī* signifies a rebāb player, and thus *rebaybiyya* can refer collectively to a group of rebāb players.[4] An alternative etymology was proffered by several of my field consultants, including the mizwid player Hichem Lékhdiri and the local Jewish community leader Jacob Lellouche,[5] who suggested that the term "rebaybiyya" derives from the term "rabbī," not only the term for religious leaders in the Jewish community but also a ubiquitous phrase among Muslim Tunisians meaning "my God"; in both cases the term expresses the general concept of divine authority and reinforces the ritual practices and contexts of rebaybiyya. Rebaybiyya provides yet another example of the common duality and striking etymological ambiguity associated with names of North African ritual genres, including also *zār* (Morsy 1991), gnāwa (Kapchan 2007), and sṭambēlī (Jankowsky 2010).

As a women's practice, rebaybiyya typically refers to devotional music at a zāwiya. Indeed, Fatima, the Mannūbiyya lead musician introduced in chapter 3, told me that the Mannūbiyya could accurately be classified as rebaybiyya, and in the 1960s Salah el-Mahdi referred to the shrines of Sayyda Mannūbiyya and Sīdī Bū Sa'īd as sites of rebaybiyya ceremonies led by women's ensembles playing the rebāb, kamanja, and four bendīrs (Mahdi n.d.a).[6] Writing in the early 1920s, Ṣādiq al-Rizqī (1989 [1968]: 92) presents rebaybiyya as synonymous with *meddāḥāt*, women devotional singers, noting condescendingly that these women's groups are barely worth mentioning (1989 [1968]: 64). Sami Lajmi reports that "rebaybiyya" is still used to refer to similar women's devotional ensembles in the town of Bizerte but points out that in Sousse the name has been replaced by *ḥaḍra al-nisā'* (women's ḥaḍra), which features large tambourines, darbūka, and kamanja and which he believes was first performed by Jewish women (pers. comm., 2015).

The earliest accounts of rebaybiyya, however, describe it in the context of domestic settings, not the zāwiya. The home as a site for healing attracted commentary from male writers interested in the mechanism of ritual therapeutics, such as Lumbroso's *Lettres médico-statistiques sur la régence de Tunis* (1860). This account, like many others, provides little information about

4. According to Taoufiq Ben Amor (pers. comm., June 2018); see also Lévy (1999: 343 n. 19). This term is also used as such in Morocco (Philip Schuyler, pers. comm., June 2018). In Sudan, *rabāba* is the name of the six-string lyre used in *ṭumburah* spirit possession rituals performed by Sudanis descended from black slaves owned by Arabs (Makris 1996).

5. Lellouche is also the curator of Dār Dhikra (House of Memory) museum of Jewish culture.

6. The article is available at http://www.salahelmahdi.com/uploads/document/C027.pdf. Mahdi is a paramount figure in Tunisian musicology. The website linked here is a repository of his papers, compositions, and interviews.

music and is primarily concerned with describing the event as a healing practice:

> When a Tunisian woman wishes to resort to the Rebabia to cure her diabolical illness, she sends an invitation to her relatives and friends, as well as other women who suffer from the same affliction, taking care to prepare in advance a good meal. All men must leave the house, or at least the room where the sick individual resides. Then the women instrumentalists [playing ʿūd, rebāb, bendīr, ṭār, and darbūka], under the authority of an odd old woman, a sorcerer for diabolical illnesses, arrange themselves in a circle, sitting on cushions, around the patient and guests, who are in festive clothing and covered in jewels. The session is opened by spreading that mysterious incense, which I discussed earlier, on burning coals, while the music according to its various tones, provokes a frenetic and truly diabolical dance in sometimes one, sometimes another of the possessed, until, exhausted by their contortions, completely enervated, they fall to the floor. . . . At this moment the relatives of the sick person beg the old woman to ask the evil demon what is needed for it to stop tormenting the patient. . . . The demands of the demon, beyond the offering of the dance, are often limited to imposing upon the possessed the acquisition of new clothing in attractive colors, a stay in some pleasant garden, or in a place near the sea. (1860: 120)

While many such accounts share a condescension toward women's "superstitions" and "excesses," they also reveal that these ceremonies involve both therapeutic work and a festive atmosphere simultaneously. While the space of the zāwiya provides women with a "center of sociability" (Melliti 1993) involving the sharing of food, drink, and talk, as well as music and dance, all in the service of healing, ceremonies in patients' homes further magnify the sense of festivity, with a great deal of attention paid to the preparation of large amounts of food and drink and hosts and attendees wearing some of their finest clothing, often newly purchased. This highly energetic mixture of music, dance, and sociability, through the invocation of religious figures and spirits, is illustrative of many traditions discussed in this book in which entertainment, pleasure, and the religious experience are mutually constitutive. Rebaybiyya, as a concept capturing domestic Jewish ceremonies and Muslim women's rituals at shrines, is a historical pillar of ambient Sufism, drawing attention to the porous social boundaries of ritual practice and the widespread circulation of sounds, spiritual figures, and practices associated with trance and Muslim saints.

Convergences, Spiritual and Musical

Jews and Muslims living in Tunis were mutually dependent in many ways and lived in close physical proximity for centuries. Their lives were so enmeshed economically, politically, socially, and culturally that even the distinctive internal religious and life-cycle needs of each community intersected. The realm of music was a particular point of convergence in these domains, as it brought Jews and Muslims together not only in the public spheres of professional music, but also into saint shrines and one another's homes for devotional and healing ceremonies such as rebaybiyya. Rather than thinking in terms of parallel, separate domains of musical and cultural practice, it is more productive to conceptualize a shared Jewish-Muslim "musical commons" (Glasser 2016b) from which Jewish and Muslim musical practices drew, and which they in turn shaped. Such a perspective avoids the "conceptual pitfalls" of drawing discrete boundaries between the two and instead identifies music, following Edwin Seroussi, as a site of "convergence" characterized by the "sharing of cultural capital . . . that results from extended and close physical contact" as well as the "network of mutual interests deriving both from the diversity of social and aesthetic attitudes to and needs for music and from the system of supply and demand of musical performance emerging from such attitudes and needs" (Seroussi 2010: 498).

The domain of late nineteenth- and early twentieth-century popular music in Tunis confirms patterns of Jewish prevalence and Jewish-Muslim convergences suggested by the historical record and links directly to rebaybiyya. An 1847 account found that fifty-three of the sixty coffeehouse musicians in Tunis were Jewish (Seroussi 2016: 433). Jewish musicians played a central role in shaping the emerging mass-mediated popular-music scene in the early twentieth century. Singing in Arabic, figures such as Cheikh el-'Afrit, Raoul Journo, Louisa Tounsia, and Habiba Msika created a gold standard for Tunisian song. Their careers dovetailed with the establishment of the recording industry and broadcast capabilities, enabling not only the dissemination of their music on a previously unimagined scale but also an enduring place in Tunisian musical memory. 'Ali Louati maintains that the Tunisian musical scene between the two World Wars was "without a doubt . . . dominated" by Cheikh el-'Afrit (1890–1939), whose "powerful voice, rich in nuance, combined Jewish intonation, Bedouin declamation, and the melancholy of the soul of ordinary people, and exudes a deep nostalgia that affects Tunisians even nowadays" (Louati 2012: 149). Indeed, well into the twenty-first century it was still considered a compliment in musicians' circles in Tunis to say that someone performs like a Jew (*yiṭba' kima yuhūd*).[7]

Habiba Msika (1893–1933) is perhaps the most celebrated and storied singer of that era.[8] She recorded for the French Pathé and German Baïdaphone labels and performed with an ensemble that often included Cheikh el-'Afrīt on ṭār, Khailou Esseghir on violin, Bice Slama on *qānūn* (plucked zither), and Messaoud Habib on harmonium (Chelbi 1985: 128). Like many singers of the time, her repertoire included a wide diversity of musical styles, from "light popular" songs and Tunisian Andalusī pieces to Egyptian, Libyan, Algerian, and Syrian folk songs, as well as praise songs for local Muslim saints. Msika, like many of her contemporaries,[9] was strongly influenced by the distinctive "Bedouin-like" musical style of Jewish Tunisians of Libyan origin, such as Abraminu and Rahmin Bard'a, and Dido and Muni Jbali (Louati 2012: 146). Her life and career, cut short by her murder at the hands of a former lover, only obliquely connect to rebaybiyya: Habiba's father Didou Msika was a well-known kamanja player but also played mizwid for rebaybiyya ceremonies,[10] and her uncle, Khailou Esseghir, was a rebaybiyya master who played kamanja (Ben Romdhane, in Chamkhi 2010), although their rebaybiyya activities remain almost entirely absent from the historical record.[11] From the same family comes the most widely recorded vocalist of rebaybiyya, Youssef Esseghir. Louisa Tounsia (1905–1966) recorded the song "'Alā Bāb Dārik" (At Your Door), a nūba in praise of the female (Muslim) saint Umm al-Zīn that is part of the rebaybiyya silsila ana-

7. Literally, the expression means "performs the *ṭubū'* [modes] like a Jew," a phrase that emphasizes the value of musical mastery of the Tunisian modal system (Hamza Tebai, pers. comm., 2014).

8. There are conflicting reports of the year of her birth. Here I rely on Hamrouni (2007) and Louati (2012), although nonacademic accounts commonly state 1903 as the year of her birth. For Msika's equivocal standing in the Tunisian Jewish community, including how laments composed in Judeo-Arabic memorializing her tragic death contributed to her mythic status, see Tobi and Tobi (2014).

9. Particularly the Jewish composers and singers Gaston Bsiri, 'Achir Mizrahi, and Maurice Attun, as well as the women singers Badi'a al-Sghira and Ratiba al-Tunsiyya (Louati 2012: 146).

10. In his musings on the history of rebaybiyya, Mustapha Ben Romdhane refers to Didou Msika as Habiba's brother (Chamkhi 2010). Didou Msika (Daydü Misqa) is listed as the Tunisian bagpiper for the troupe recorded by Paul Traeger in Berlin in 1904. Hornbostel (1975 [1906]) described and analyzed Traeger's recording in his *Phonographierte tunesische Melodien.*

11. Khailou Esseghir is best known for his participation in the Rashidiyya Institute, founded in 1934 to preserve and promote Tunisian mālūf by adhering to what were considered the highest musical standards. For more on the Rashidiyya, see Davis (2004) and Mustaysir (2014).

lyzed below. The song, about a suffering woman visiting the shrine of Umm al-Zīn, includes the line "the drums beat and the rebāb calls me" (*ṭabbāl yuḍrub wal-rebāb yanājī*), lyrics that confirm the connection between the rebāb and devotional practices at the zāwiya.

Devotional activities at saint shrines also constituted a site of Muslim-Jewish convergence. Across North Africa, Jewish communities developed practices involving the veneration of religious figures, who were memorialized with shrines and celebrated with visits and pilgrimages that differed little from those of their Muslim counterparts. On the Tunisian island of Djerba, the shrine of Lilla Ghrība, a Jewish female saint recognized by Jews and Muslims, is hailed as the oldest synagogue in Africa as well as the site of the saint's demonstration of miraculous powers.[12] On the mainland, there are examples of Jewish saints venerated by Muslims, such as Sīdī Frāj Shawwāṭ in Testour,[13] a town populated by large numbers of Muslims and Jews who fled the Christian Reconquista of al-Andalus (Larguèche 1999: 364; M'Halla 1996). Far more widespread, however, are the Muslim saints who were treated with equal respect by Jews and their Muslim counterparts.

One of the most prominent of such saints was Sīdī Meḥrez (951–1022), who is praised in the rebaybiyya repertoire (in the nūba "ʿAddālā ʿAddāla") and is widely regarded as a patron saint of the city of Tunis. Considered a champion of Sunni Islam, Sīdī Meḥrez is credited with leading the military defeat of the Shi'ites of Tunis (Ben Achour 2004: 13). He is also considered a protector of Jews. According to legend, Sīdī Meḥrez felt compassion for the Jews of Tunis, who were required to live outside the walls of the medina, and intervened to establish the *ḥara* or Jewish quarter of the medina (Larguèche 1999: 349).[14] Several Sufis I know in Tunis spoke of a past in which Jews not only visited the shrines of Muslim saints but also participated in rituals, particularly those that involved music. Shaykh Jaied of the Ḥaṭṭābiyya Sufi order told me: "There were Jews in the zāwiyas and some of the ṭarīqas. Why? Because a portion—not all—of Tunisian Jews came from al-Andalus. They came with the Muslims. And this group [of Jews] was preserving the mālūf. They brought their instruments and songs to the ṭarīqas and they

12. The Jewish community of Djerba traces its origins to the year 586 BCE, the year of the destruction of the Second Temple. See Carpenter-Latiri (2010) on Lilla Ghrība's multiple myths of origin, as well as the efforts of the Tunisian state to assert religious tolerance by overstating the extent of shared Jewish-Muslim traditions surrounding Lilla Ghrība in the twenty-first century.

13. Sīdī Frāj Shawwāṭ was a sixteenth-century rabbi known for establishing the genre of Judeo-Arabic poetry in Tunisia (Tobi and Tobi 2014).

14. A branch of the Shādhuliyya ṭarīqa performs their liturgy at Sīdī Meḥrez's shrine each Wednesday, further evidencing the saint's reach across ritually adjacent niches.

also had their own groups that played that music for parties for Muslims" (pers. comm., 2012). This statement corroborates the claim that Andalusī instruments and other musical elements entered into Sufi ritual following the influx of Andalusī exiles, particularly the Sulāmiyya, ʿAwāmriyya, and ʿĪsāwiyya (Jones 1977:16). It also demonstrates how remembrance of Jewish activity in the world of Sufism remains in the oral histories of the ṭarīqas. With regard to the ʿĪsāwiyya, Walid Mennai, shaykh al-ḥaḍra of the ʿĪsāwiyya (chap. 2), told me that Jews were active in Sufi ritual but simply omitted praises to the Prophet Muḥammad because, while they acknowledged the power of holy figures to intercede in human lives, they did not recognize Muḥammad as a legitimate prophet. Indeed, as discussed below, the rebaybiyya silsila, in contrast to the silsila of the Mannūbiyya and sṭambēlī, does not begin with—or even include—a nūba praising the Prophet. As with the other silsila traditions, the beginning of the rebaybiyya silsila does the important symbolic work of announcing the tradition's devotional identity and priorities, in this case through exclusion rather than inclusion.

Iconicity of Musical Texture and Timbre

During the course of the twentieth century, the rebāb all but disappeared from the Tunisian musical landscape and was no longer a defining element of rebaybiyya or of Tunisian Andalusī music. The mizwid bagpipes became rebaybiyya's iconic instrument. The mizwid is a double-reed goatskin bagpipe that produces a continuous sound enabled by the unending stream of air produced by the player's intermittent blowing to fill up the airbag.[15] It has a range of a sixth, with a natural scale of G-A-B𝄳C-D-E𝄳 (corresponding to the melodic mode called *mḥayr ʿirāq*). Playing techniques such as forcefully pushing extra air out of the bag or partially covering a fingerhole enable mizwid players to flatten or sharpen pitches to realize additional modes. Mizwid players consider the instrument to be feminine, which they say explains why it is usually partially covered by a cloth banner tied around its body.

The mizwid is accompanied by several drummers playing bendīrs, in this case the kind featuring gut snares across the inside of the drum but no cymbals. This type of bendīr, it should be emphasized, is the same variety used by Sufi orders such as the ʿĪsāwiyya, and *not* the larger, heavier variety

15. The horns of the instrument are traditionally made from gazelle horns, the dual bell of the instrument is carved from the horns of a bull, and the airbag is made of goatskin (Abdelmajid Zarga, pers. comm., 2018). Zarga also proffered that the instrument, made from a goatskin bag for holding water, is found wherever people had a need to carry water.

used in the popular-music genre called mizwid, discussed below. Use of the Sufi bendīr in rebaybiyya unequivocally announces its ritual trance function. In addition to the use of the Sufi bendīr, two performance techniques of the mizwid and bendīr differentiate the rebaybiyya ritual aesthetic from that of the popular-music genre called mizwid that uses the same instrumentation. First, in rebaybiyya, the mizwid plays unceasingly, never stopping to alternate with vocalists. This contrasts with the mizwid genre, in which the mizwid instrument pauses to provide sonic room for vocalists singing verses, as is common in other popular musics. In rebaybiyya, the continuous sound of the mizwid is a necessity and points to the virtue of textural constancy shared by other silsila-based ritual musics. Second, in rebaybiyya, bendīr players hold the instrument up in front of them, with the left hand supporting the drum from below in a manner that indexes the bendīr playing technique of Sufi ritual. This contrasts with the holding position of the bendīr in popular music, where the drum rests on top of the seated drummer's thigh and the left hand strikes the drum from above. For drummers, this seemingly subtle distinction in fact marks a profound differentiation between ritual and nonritual musics. In situations where both kinds of music are being performed, drummers with experience in both domains may simply ask the leading musician, "Down or up?"—referring to the playing position of the drum—to determine whether the song is from the ritual or nonritual repertoire, and, therefore, which position they should choose for holding the drum.

The mizwid-and-bendīr combination is iconic of rebaybiyya ritual in the same way that the buzzing bass-register sounds of the gumbrī and metallic pulses of the shqāshiq are representative of sṭambēlī and the shimmering jingles of the large tambourines are of the Mannūbiyya. In all three cases, the constancy of these timbres and textures is a central, necessary feature of their respective soundworlds, and as a rule the instruments never stop, even to make room for vocals, creating a continuity of sound that in part defines ritual trance-music aesthetics locally. So while all three share these principles of constancy and continuity, they realize them in distinctive ways that differentiate them from each other. The same is true of the silsila musical form: all three organize their rituals according to this cumulative musical form, but how they do so reveals the specific identity of each. The rebaybiyya silsila, however, makes explicit connections to both the sṭambēlī and Mannūbiyya ritual communities, while doing so in a way that announces its own distinctiveness.

THE REBAYBIYYA SILSILA: INCORPORATION AND EXCLUSION

The most comprehensive audio documentation of a rebaybiyya silsila comes from two recordings of the troupe led by Mustapha Ben Romdhane (Muṣṭafā Ben Ramḍān, a.k.a. Gaṭṭal al-Ṣīd, lit. "Lion Slayer" in Tunisian Arabic, 1941–2011) in 2004 and 2007 at the Center for Mediterranean and Arab Musics (CMAM) in Sīdī Bū Sa'īd, Tunisia. The 2004 recordings were from rehearsals that were part of the documentation and preservation efforts at CMAM, with the live performance staged on September 28, 2007 (table 5.1), as part of their annual Mūsīqāt concert series. Both recordings were acts of historical reconstruction of musical sound. Ben Romdhane was the main authority on rebaybiyya and effectively taught the repertoire to the younger members of the ensemble, sometimes fielding their questions about the tradition during breaks in rehearsals. The silsila presented by Ben Romdhane has a structure and content in common with the few EP and LP recordings of rebaybiyya from the 1960s, as well as with the reports of Hedi Doniya, whose rebaybiyya work is detailed further below. A 1962 EP by Ben Romdhane and Youssef Esseghir presents a condensed silsila that closely resembles the CMAM silsila (table 5.2).[16]

Strategies of sequential intensification (SI) are evident throughout the rebaybiyya silsila. In both the 1962 EP and the 2007 live performance, a progression through the sequence of the first four rhythms reveals this systematic increase in sonic density. Perhaps obscured at first glance by the shifts in time signature (used to best account for local understandings of the rhythms), musical example 5.1 illustrates how this example of SI comes into focus when accounting for tempo in a manner that measures how many times each full rhythmic pattern (referred to as "cells" in the musical example) is repeated per minute. The opening rhythm (*steftūḥ*) is played at a pace of forty cells per minute, followed by a fast 12/8 sa'dāwī rhythm at forty-eight cells per minute. The third rhythm in the sequence is also called *sa'dāwī* (but a different rhythm, one adopted from sṭambēlī) and is a shorter pattern that results in a speed of sixty cells per minute, while the 'ajmī rhythm has the highest density of rhythmic events, at ninety-two cells per minute, and closes the sequence. Episodes of discrete intensifi-

16. The EP lists only three song titles: "Jitaak Chaaki," "Manoubiya," and "Aadela." In such recordings, in which the silsila is performed as a continuous medley with no breaks between songs, there is often a discrepancy between the nūbas performed and the printed list on the record jacket, with the latter typically representing either the first piece on each side of the record or the first nūba of the silsila.

TABLE 5.1 Rebaybiyya silsila of Mustapha Ben Romdhane's 2007 performance, from concert program

Nūba	Melodic mode	Rhythmic mode
"Steftūḥ" / "Jītak Shākī" / "Mā Sabā 'Aqlī"	ḥsīn[a]	steftūḥ
"Ra'is al-Abḥār" (Sīdī Bū Sa'īd)	ḥsīn	Fast sa'dāwī
"Lilla 'Arbiyya"	ḥsīn	Fast sa'dāwī
"Yā 'Arīfa"	ḥsīn	sa'dāwī (with shqāshiq)
"Bū Sa'diyya"	ḥsīn	'ajmī (with shqāshiq)
"Sīdī 'Alī Ḥaṭṭāb"	ḥsīn	bū nawwāra
"Umm al-Zīn"	ḥsīn	bū nawwāra
"'Addāla 'Addāla" (Sīdī 'Amr Bū Khatwa)	ḥsīn	bū ḥilla
"Sayyda Mannūbiyya"	nwā	mannūbiyya (sha'bī)
"Sīdī Bū Yaḥya"	mḥayr 'irāq	bū ḥilla
"Wāfiyat al-Khaṣlāt" (Sayyda Mannūbiyya)	sīka	ḥilla

[a] The mizwid instrument plays the mode ḥsīn on A, rendering the mode by using the pitches A-B𝄳-C-D-E𝄳 (although occasionally utilizing the G below A.)

TABLE 5.2 Silsilas of 2004/2007 recording compared to those of 1962 EP

2004/2007 live recording	1962 EP
"Steftūḥ" / "Jītak Shākī" / "Mā Sabā 'Aqlī"	"Steftūḥ" / "Jītak Shākī" / "Mā Sabā 'Aqlī"
"Ra'is al-Abḥār" (Sīdī Bū Sa'īd)	"Ra'is al-Abḥār" (Sīdī Bū Sa'īd)
"Lilla 'Arbiyya"	"Lilla 'Arbiyya"
"Yā 'Arīfa"	"Yā 'Arīfa"
"Bū Sa'diyya"	"Bū Sa'diyya"
"Sīdī 'Alī Ḥaṭṭāb"	
"Umm al-Zīn"	
"'Addāla 'Addāla" (several saints)	
"Sayyda Mannūbiyya"	"Sayyda Mannūbiyya"
	"'Addāla 'Addāla" (several saints)
"Sīdī Bū Yaḥya"	"Sīdī Bū Yaḥya"
"Wāfiyat al-Khaṣlāt" (Sayyda Mannūbiyya)	

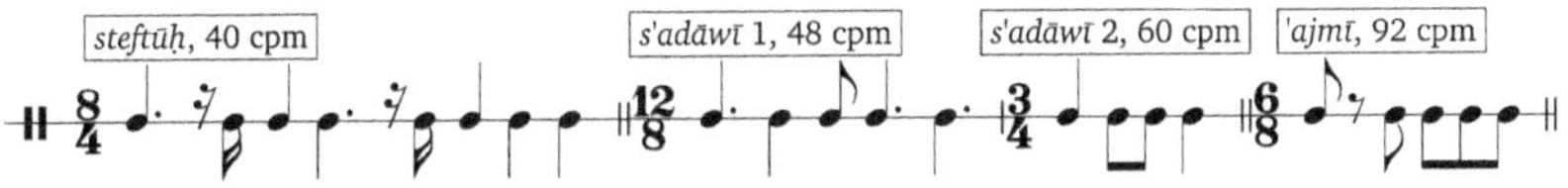

MUSICAL EXAMPLE 5.1. Sequential intensification through rhythmic modulation in rebaybiyya, evidenced by the first four rhythms of the silsila. Cpm refers to rhythmic cells per minute. Note that sa'dāwī 1 is a very fast 12/8, while sa'dāwī 2 is a different pattern, based on the sṭambēlī rhythm of the same name, with a hemiola feel.

cation (DI) also occur, particularly at the end of sequences, when the mizwid and bendīr cycle through a short, repeated phrase while increasing the tempo.

Just like its adjacent ritual communities examined in previous chapters, rebaybiyya's strategies of intensification draw on ritual aesthetic principles that circulate throughout the sonic landscape of ambient Sufism, yet the vehicle for realizing those strategies—namely, the specific rhythms and their order—is distinctive to this ritual community. Timbre does similar signifying work, relying on shared principles of constancy and saturation that are realized through the specific instrumentation of mizwid and bendīr that index this community. This aesthetic rendering of social adjacency is particularly pronounced in the unfolding of ritual musical form examined below, where aesthetic assemblages of commonality and difference abound.

Steftūḥ: Assertions through Inclusion and Exclusion

In contrast to the Mannūbiyya and sṭambēlī silsilas, which begin with a nūba for the Prophet, the rebaybiyya silsila avoids all mention of the Prophet. Instead, and strikingly, the rebaybiyya silsila commences with a nūba whose main lyrical and modal content derives from the Libyan mālūf song "Mā Sabā 'Aqlī," the refrain of which is *mā sabā 'aqlī siwā saḥr al-jufūn* (nothing enchants my mind like the charm of [your] eyelids). This nūba, sometimes referred to as steftūḥ ("opening"), is most commonly called "Jītak Shākī" (I Came to You Complaining), in reference to lyrics that rebaybiyya musicians added to the Libyan ma'luf song.

The coexistence of three names for this one nūba reveals three overlapping performative assertions. The first, "steftūḥ," announces that this nūba is the first of the silsila, cementing it structurally within ritual as the nūba with the privileged place of preceding all others, and therefore particularly weighted with the ritual community's identity. The second, "Jītak Shākī," situates the nūba firmly within the thematic material of other elements of this and other silsilas with its emphasis on the act of looking to saints for help in situations of pain and injustice. The full text of this line is:

jītak shākī min awjāʿ galbī yā sīd al-mellāḥ
I came to you complaining of my heart's pain, O wonderful sir

This line reveals the interpersonal dynamic between saint and supplicant that is at the heart of trance healing practices in Tunisia. The first half of the line announces that the narrator is suffering and seeking the intercession of the saint. The second half calls on the saint through an honorific that emphasizes his virtuous character; in Tunisian Arabic, *mellāḥ* (sing. *mlīḥ*) is an adjective meaning "good" or "accommodating" when it is applied to persons.[17] The state of suffering of the supplicant sets the conditions for the relationship of reciprocity that undergirds the saint-supplicant relationship in the Maghreb, while the act of visiting and praising the saint activates that relationship of exchange.

The third name for this nūba, "Mā Sabā ʿAqlī," reveals another angle on the rebaybiyya's relationship to the wider ecology of Sufism and music. After a few repetitions and variations of the "jītak shākī" line, the musicians sing a stanza that stands out from other nūbas described thus far with its overt romantic sentiments:

mā sabā ʿaqlī	Nothing enchants my mind
siwā saḥr al-jufūn	like the charm of your eyelids
mā sabā ʿaqlī allah allah	Nothing enchants my mind, Allah Allah
ḥillū qutillī bi-ramshāt al-ʿayūn	Open them and kill me with your eyelashes
yā salām allah allah	Yā salām, Allah Allah

While such expressions of worldly love are not uncommon in the lyrical ecology of Sufism—it is well established that Sufi poetry about the beloved may be interpreted as reflecting divine love—these are relatively rare in the silsila, and it is quite a statement to begin a silsila with such a song, particularly when the most common way to do so is with a nūba for the Prophet. The provenance of the song also invites speculation about the ritual activities and geohistorical movements of the Jewish community, as well as their convergences with those of their Muslim neighbors. *Mā sabā ʿaqlī* is a line of poetry found in the text collection (*sfīna*, pp. 167 and 198) of the ʿĪsāwiyya Sufi order and is occasionally sung in their ceremonies. ʿĪsāwis

17. While the term "mellāḥ" refers to the Jewish quarter of cities in Morocco, this is not the case in Tunisia, where *ḥāra* is used. "Mellāḥ" is commonly used in Andalusī poetry to denote someone extremely beautiful or wonderful (Ben Amor, pers. comm., June 2018).

consider it part of the mālūf tradition that they have preserved and believe that all pieces of this "serious" mālūf (mālūf al-jidd) repertoire have sacred meanings, even when they appear to express worldly desires (Mennai, pers. comm., 2017). Well into the twentieth century many of the most successful popular-music artists in Tunisia belonged to Sufi ṭarīqas—particularly the ʿĪsāwiyya, because of its reputation for musical excellence—and as noted above, Jews also took part in these ritual activities. At the beginning of that century, the worlds of sacred and secular—not to mention Muslim and Jew—overlapped in ways that belie the more rigid (yet never unambiguous) conceptual binaries between the two that would solidify later in the century.

But there is perhaps more to "Mā Sabā ʿAqlī" as an iconic song announcing the opening of the rebaybiyya silsila, for it also evokes the historical movement of Jews from neighboring Libya. "Mā Sabā ʿAqlī" never became part of the official Tunisian mālūf repertoire and is instead widely associated with the Libyan mālūf (see Guettat 1980: 338). The northwestern Libyan city of Tripoli was considered a center of Libyan mālūf owing to the influx of Muslim and Jewish exiles from al-Andalus (Ciantar 2012). Because Tunis had become an attractive destination for Jewish immigrants from the region of present-day Libya since at least the eighteenth century, many Tunisian Jews were of Tripolitanian origin (Taieb 1992). The large number of Jews of Libyan origin living in Tunis led Ali Saïdane (2014) to describe the entire Jewish quarter (ḥara) of Tunis as "tripolitaine," and ʿAli Louati provides an impressive list of Jewish musicians of Libyan origin who helped shape the early twentieth-century Tunisian popular-music scene with their "Tripolitanian melodies," whose "Bedouin . . . languor" resonated with Tunisians (2012: 144–145). In addition to their influence on art and popular musics in Tunisia, Libyan Jews were also associated with Muslim saint shrines and spirit possession rituals. Pâques (1964) notes that Jews in Tripolitania, like Libyans of sub-Saharan descent in the southwestern region of Fezzan, were associated particularly with the blacksmithing trade and were considered masters of music and the treatment of spirit afflictions. Jewish Libyan immigrants in in the Tunisian countryside were often caretakers of Muslim saint shrines, becoming the only sedentary families in the context of semi-nomadic Jewish groups of the Tunisian interior during the mid-nineteenth century (Valensi 1977). The mizwid instrument is also widely believed to have come to Tunis from Libya (Saïdane 2014; Stapley 2006), and Jews are credited with mastering the instrument and establishing its place in the urban Tunisian landscape. In addition to these geocultural movements and encounters, Mahmoud Guettat (1980: 230) notes that the opening movement now known as *istiftāḥ* in Libyan mālūf was once called *istiftūḥ*,[18] the term used in rebaybiyya for this opening nūba, thus providing another piece of circumstantial evidence connecting the rebaybiyya tradition of Tunisia's Jewish community to a Libyan past.

The steftūḥ is performed in an eight-beat rhythm of the same name. The 2007 Mustapha Ben Romdhane performance begins with the mizwid playing a free-rhythm introduction establishing the melodic mode ḥsīn, with the drums entering as the mizwid begins to cycle the melody. It continues this cycle, with variations, throughout the nūba with no pauses. The vocals enter with the line "jītak shākī" as the drums and mizwid continue unabated. The text continues with the "mā sabā 'aqlī" verse (see above), set to the same melody (audio ex. 5.1, 0:00–3:02). The Libyan mālūf version of "Mā Sabā 'Aqlī," it should be noted, is also in the ḥsīn melodic mode and in an eight-beat (or slow four-beat) rhythm called *mṣaddar*, although its melody differs considerably.[19] The ḥsīn mode dominates the rebaybiyya silsila (see again table 5.1).[20] It is achieved on the mizwid by using the notes A–B𝄳–C–D–E𝄳 (low to high), establishing A as the mode's low reference pitch. The melodic cycle's closing phrase, however, modulates to aṣba'īn, whose A–B𝄳–C♯–D tetrachord is described by some mizwid players as one of the most difficult to generate on the mizwid instrument and its realization the sign of musical mastery (see musical ex. 5.2), owing mainly to the challenge of raising the C to a C♯. A resounding extended B𝄳 on the mizwid announces the transition to the next nūba, "Ra'is al-Abḥār" (Captain of the Seas; see also chap. 1), which continues the social work of the silsila but in a rather different way.

18. The istiftāḥ is also the name of the introductory movement of the Tunisian mālūf. According to Ben Amor (2010), its history is one of desacralization once it became the subject of nationalist cultural policy. While the istiftāḥ was once a semi-improvised vocal piece on a religious theme in religious mālūf (mālūf al-jidd) of the zāwiya, in the twentieth century nationalist transformations (including the creation of large orchestras and the standardization of repertoire) led to the loss of lyrics, vocals, and improvisation as it was replaced by a purely instrumental introductory piece devoid of any religious referents.

19. When compared to the notation provided by Guettat (1980: 338).

20. The mode ḥsīn is associated with highly charged but mixed emotions owing to its popularity in the repertoire of weddings (often characterized as a combination of happiness and loss for the bride and her family; Hamza Tebai, pers. comm., 2014). The question of whether such an association between mode and emotion obtains in trance rituals (which have their own mixed emotional atmospheres) and is decoded or felt by listeners is an intriguing one but beyond the reach of this study.

MUSICAL EXAMPLE 5.2. "Jītak Shākī" / "Mā Sabā 'Aqlī" main melody. Note the steftūḥ rhythm, continuity of the mizwid, and singing of shrine visitation themes (*jītak shākī*, "I came to you complaining") with amorous ones (*mā sabā ʿaqlī*, "nothing enchants my mind [like the charm of your eyelids]") set to the same melody.

"Ra'is al-Abḥār": Shared Saints, Musical Difference

If the first nūba of the rebaybiyya silsila raises questions of otherness and announces the distinctiveness of rebaybiyya, the following nūba, "Ra'is al-Abḥār," brings the rebaybiyya squarely into the heart of the shared spiritual landscape of Tunisian saints by invoking Sīdī Bū Saʿīd al-Bājī, one of the most well-recognized saints in the region, where the praise song is one of the most widely recorded and performed. The song is a household word in the Tunis area and is featured in the Mannūbiyya silsila, the widely circulated recordings of Hedi Doniya in the mizwid genre (see below), the recordings and staged performances of spectacles such as *el-Hadhra* (see chap. 6), and the standard repertoire of wedding-music troupes, not to mention the demonstrations following the attacks on the shrine of Sīdī Bū Saʿīd (see chap. 1). Ben Romdhane's 2007 concert reconstruction of ritual form features a distinctive version of "Ra'is al-Abḥār," one that is proprietary to rebaybiyya (audio ex. 5.1, 3:02–6:01). The rebaybiyya version differs significantly from the better-known version: although some lyrics are shared (particularly the first quatrain), the melodic and rhythmic modes, as well as the melodic contour, differ significantly. The rebaybiyya lyrics differ from the nūba performed in the context of the Mannūbiyya, as well as in the well-documented versions of the song in the Tunisian turāth (cultural heritage), as evidenced in lyrics published in al-Rizqī (1989 [1968]) and Būdhīna (1997), as well as the classic version by Hedi Habbouba, a superstar of Tunisian popular music. In all of these cases, the first six lines (or variations thereof), reproduced below, are shared, but the rebaybiyya nūba features an additional stanza of lyrics about the baḥriyya (water spirits), revealing its ritual trance healing function:

ra'is al-abḥār yā rafīqī	Captain of the seas, O my companion
nabrā yā bājī ʿalā allah	I am healed O Bājī, by God
fakāk al-muṣāb yā ṭabīb	liberator of the afflicted, O healer
illī ʿaẓmū wājī ʿalā allah	of the weary, by God
madha biyya ʿalā ziyāra	I want to make the pilgrimage
l-bū saʿīdī al-bājī ʿalā allah . . .	To Sīdī Bū Saʿīd, by God . . .
. . . aya anā baḥrī	. . . Yes, I am baḥrī [i.e., possessed by sea spirits]
mā nḥib ilā al-baḥrīyya	I want nothing more than the baḥriyya
baḥrī yughrī yā ilahī nūb ʿaliyyā	The baḥrī entices me, O God, help me
bābā sharīf ʿalājī	Baba Sharīf, heal me
bābā sharīf wal-ʿarbiyya	Baba Sharīf and ʿArbiyya

This nūba is analyzed in more detail further below, where I consider the traces of rebaybiyya that remain in the musical repertoire of the mizwid genre. For the present purpose of analyzing the silsila as a site of managing social, spiritual, and musical proximities, it will suffice for now to note that rebaybiyya here connects to the Mannūbiyya, where Sīdī Bū Saʿīd is a prominent figure in the silsila, and to sṭambēlī, which features an entire section of the black silsila dedicated to the baḥriyya spirits. Neither sṭambēlī nor the Mannūbiyya includes this stanza of lyrics about the baḥriyya, and therefore neither ritual tradition makes as explicit a connection between

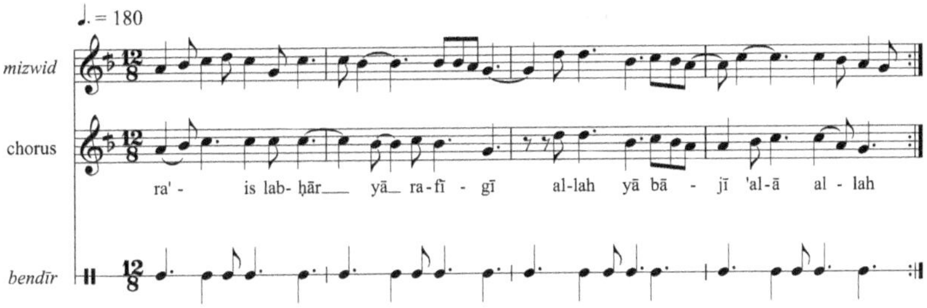

MUSICAL EXAMPLE 5.3. Rebaybiyya version of "Ra'is al-Abḥār" (Captain of the Seas), audio ex. 5.1, 3:02–end). Its rhythm, melodic mode, and melodic motion are proprietary to rebaybiyya and differ from the widely circulating "standard" version made famous by stars such as Hedi Doniya (audio ex. 5.3).

Sīdī Bū Sa'īd and the baḥriyya spirits. Instead, it is in the rebaybiyya that this connection is announced unambiguously—and unsurprisingly, considering the relationship between this saint, the baḥriyya, and the mizwid instrument discussed further below.

The final line of lyrics segues into the nūba for Lilla 'Arbiyya, the female saint discussed in the previous chapter. Her nūba is in the same melodic and rhythmic mode as "Ra'īs al-Abḥār," and there is no pause between songs. The lyrics to this nūba are nearly identical to those of its counterpart in sṭambēlī, in which the nūba is situated in the silsila not as a saint but as a spirit, one of the child spirits (Sghār). In the rebaybiyya silsila, then, Lilla 'Arbiyya occupies a transitional and ambiguous space between the saints and spirits: as a spiritual figure understood to be a saint by some and a spirit by others, Lilla 'Arbiyya appears at the end of a song for a saint (Sīdī Bū Sa'īd) that transitions seamlessly to a song evoking the spirit-possession practices of sṭambēlī.

The 'Ajmī Nūbas: Incorporating the Sounds and Figures of Sṭambēlī

The following two nūbas, sometimes referred to as 'ajmī ("non-Arabic"),[21] invoke figures and sounds associated with the sṭambēlī spirit-possession tradition. Yet they are not borrowed from sṭambēlī. Rather, these rebaybiyya nūbas are *about* sṭambēlī and emulate certain aspects of it, including the rhythms and timbre of its signature iron clappers (shqāshiq) and its quick

21. The term "'ajmī" is a designation of otherness. It is used mainly to refer to any non-Arabic-speaking others, but it can also connote "incorrect" or "barbarous." In Tunisia it is strongly associated with the foreignness of sub-Saharan Africa.

call-and-response vocal formulae. These two nūbas announce a deep familiarity with, and ritual proximity to, sṭambēlī while also indicating an outsiderness that reveals the distance between the two traditions.

The subject of the first ʿajmī nūba is the ʿarīfa, that is, the sṭambēlī healer who diagnoses the patient, determines which spirit is afflicting her, and looks after the patient during and after her trance dance. This nūba is also called "Ḥalwāniyya" (Halouania) because of the line of lyrics referring to the ʿarīfa as the one who also prepares the ḥalwa, a sesame-based sweet that is made on special occasions such as a sṭambēlī ritual. Sṭambēlī does not have a similar nūba describing the ʿarīfa of its own rituals; this nūba is distinctive to rebaybiyya and reveals a kind of outsider's perspective, albeit one that is familiar with sṭambēlī through the Jewish community's well-documented history of hiring sṭambēlī musicians.[22] The lyrics also reveal a racialized understanding of sṭambēlī: the ʿarīfa's brown skin is a recurring theme, referenced through a number of descriptors and metaphors common in Tunisian parlance, such as "red" (*ḥamra*), "brown" (*samra*), and "sub-Saharan" (*sūdāniyya*); euphemistic or ironically positive adjectives such as "fortunate" (*yāmna*) are also commonly applied to black Tunisians:

yā ʿarīfa yāmna	O ʿarīfa the fortunate
hāy hāy hāy hāy	Hey hey hey hey
yā ʿarīfa ḥalwaniyya	O ʿarīfa maker of ḥalwa
hāy hāy hāy hāy	Hey hey hey hey
yā ʿarīfa sūdāniyya	O ʿarīfa the sub-Saharan
ḥanā ḥamra alaʿb yā shūshāna	Brown one, play, O servant
yā shūshāna samra	O brown servant

Musically, the sonic world of sṭambēlī ritual is invoked explicitly through the addition of the shqāshiq, the iron clappers whose sounds dominate sṭambēlī trance ceremonies. While the mizwid and bendīr continue, the shqāshiq perform the ʿajmī rhythm. Naming the rhythm ʿajmī is an act of othering that maintains the arm's-length distance between the rebaybiyya and sṭambēlī ritual communities, since the rhythm has its own name (saʿdāwī) in the sṭambēlī context (see chap. 4). The bendīr players perform a rhythm that aligns with the shqāshiq, creating a strong sense of downbeat by placing the low (dumm) stroke on the longest attack of the four-stroke pattern. By layering this low-high (dumm-takk) percussive paradigm of the bendīr over the monophonic shqāshiq, the rhythmic ambiguities that feature in sṭam-

22. Several accounts, such Lumbroso (1860), Vassel (1905), and Cohen (1964), indicate the coexistence of rebaybiyya and sṭambēlī in the ritual lives of Jewish households.

TABLE 5.3 Comparison of lyrics of the *nūba* for Bū Saʿdiyya in rebaybiyya and sṭambēlī

Rebaybiyya lyrics		**Sṭambēlī lyrics**	
Yā Bū Saʿdiyya	O Bū Saʿdiyya	Baraka Bū Saʿdiyya	blessing of Bū Saʿdiyya
(hāy hāy hāy hāy)		(baraka bū saʿdiyya)	
Sīdī Gnāwa	Sīdī Gnāwa	wild al-gnāwa	son of the gnawa
(hāy hāy hāy hāy)		(baraka bū saʿdiyya)	
Frej ʿalīk frej ʿaliyya	comfort you,	w-allah yarḥmū	God bless him
(hāy hāy hāy hāy)	comfort me[a]	(baraka bū saʿdiyya)	
		ʿalā mā khallālī	for what he left me
		(baraka bū saʿdiyya)	
		w-awlād burnū	people of Bornu
		(baraka bū saʿdiyya)	
		w-awlād hawsa	and the Hausa people
		(baraka bū saʿdiyya)	
		w-awlād bambara	and the Bambara people
		(baraka bū saʿdiyya) . . .	

[a] Frej is also the name of an important sṭambēlī saint (Sīdī Frej) whose shrine outside Tunis was a main site of pilgrimage, giving this line additional semantic density.

bēlī are neutralized. The timing of strokes, however, does maintain a lilting feel that is a defining feature of the rhythmic elasticity distinguishing sṭambēlī rhythmic temporality from other Tunisian musics (Jankowsky 2013), and therefore indexes sṭambēlī in rhythmic feel in addition to timbre and lyrical content.

The second ʿajmī nūba is "Bū Saʿdiyya," named after the masked dancer in sṭambēlī ritual; the dancer represents the first sṭambēlī musician, who, according to legend, came to Tunis from sub-Saharan Africa by following the slave caravan routes across the Sahara (see chap. 4). In this nūba, the shqāshiq play the five-stroke rhythm called *bū saʿdiyya* (sometimes also called ʿajmī). While the instrumentation and melody of the rebaybiyya version of this nūba differ drastically from that of bū saʿdiyya's "home" tradition of sṭambēlī, the rebaybiyya approach does preserve a lyrical structure characterized by a succession of short phrases consisting of phrases associated with Bū Saʿdiyya interspersed with an unchanging choral refrain.

A comparison of lyrics (table 5.3) shows the sṭambēlī version's higher degree of specificity in terms of the identities of the sub-Saharan communities (Bornu, Hausa, Bambara) brought together by the figure of Bū Saʿdiyya, as well as the pride in the traditions that have been left to the musicians (e.g., the line "God bless him for what he left me"). That rebaybiyya lyrics would not express those sentiments is unsurprising, as the rebaybiyya nūba for Bū Saʿdiyya functions as a means of accessing sṭambēlī's healing and spiritual interventions from the outside, through adoption and adaptation encouraged by the silsila form. Tunisian Jews on the mainland were well acquainted with sṭambēlī, as accounts from over a century ago cited above attest. My sṭambēlī teacher, the late Baba Majid, had many experiences playing for the Jewish community in his youth. He remembered large ceremonies that included both sṭambēlī and rebaybiyya troupes, but the sṭambēlī component in these contexts differed from a typical sṭambēlī ceremony. When performed for Jewish patrons, only drums and shqāshiq were played; the gumbrī was not present (on rare occasions when the gumbrī was requested, Baba Majid reported that the sṭambēlī troupe would play the small gumbrī [gnaybra] and not the large gumbrī of spirit-possession rituals). The Jewish Arabic lexicon had its own set of words for sṭambēlī material, such as *shwara'* (for the spirit named Kūrī), *shasharaya* (another name for Bū Sa'diyya), *sarra'* ('arīfa), *gnaybra* (small gumbrī), *'andinā nawb* (we're holding a sṭambēlī ceremony), and, particularly pleasing to Baba Majid, *al-assiyyāt* (the gentlemen, referring to sṭambēlī musicians). Among Tunisian Jewish migrants in Israel, rebaybiyya ceremonies were called sṭambēlī, even though they used the bagpipes (see Somer and Saadon 2000).

The two 'ajmī nūbas, then, testify to this historical relationship between the Jewish and black Tunisian ritual communities. They illustrate vividly the integrative capacity of the silsila, that is, its tendency to incorporate musical and spiritual material from the wider ecology of ritually adjacent practices. Like the silsilas of adjacent ritual communities, the rebaybiyya silsila is characterized by an overriding continuity of sound and constancy of musical timbre and texture. The addition of shqāshiq for the two 'ajmī nūbas is, in a way, an exception that proves the rule. It is an exception that does not challenge that continuity and constancy, for it adds an additional layer of sound, one that signifies in the clearest imaginable way the appropriation of another ritual music while remaining based firmly in the continuous sounds of the mizwid and bendīr.

Sufi Saints and the Mannūbiyya

After the brief 'ajmī section, the performance turns to emphasizing rebaybiyya's connection to the Mannūbiyya. After the shqāshiq are put away, the silsila turns to saints shared with the Mannūbiyya silsila, with "'Addāla 'Addāla," a nūba for Sīdī 'Alī Ḥaṭṭāb, and two nūbās each for Umm al-Zīn and Sayyda Mannūbiyya. These nūbās are illustrative of what could be construed as rebaybiyya's tapered relationship of familiarity with adjacent traditions such as Mannūbiyya and sṭambēlī: beginning with saints that are shared with those adjacent traditions, rebaybiyya lyrics are often similar and sometimes shared, while the melodic and rhythmic treatments, as well as instrumental texture, are, for the most part, distinctive to rebaybiyya.

While there is evidence of rebaybiyya's historical connection to sṭambēlī in accounts dating back over 150 years, the Jewish trance ritual's relationship to the Mannūbiyya is at once more oblique but potentially even closer and more foundational. The attention paid to women saints, in four nūbas—two of which are dedicated to Sayyda Mannūbiyya—as well as two other shared nūbas ("Irfaʿ Ra'sik" [for Sīdī ʿAlī Ḥaṭṭāb] and "ʿAddāla ʿAddāla") is, of course, highly suggestive of a social and ritual overlap between the two practices.[23] And because "rebaybiyya" is a term that has also been applied to ritual trance musics by and for women, there is no reason to doubt that ritual boundaries were just as fluid between Jewish rebaybiyya and women's ritual practices that once carried the same name as they were with sṭambēlī. What is clear is that the Jewish community recognized, and depended on, the spiritual power of Muslim saints in their trance healing practices. Most of these Muslim saints did not have any particular or explicit relationship with the Jewish population; they were simply the same saints that all Tunisians involved in the local therapeutic landscape looked to for intercession in their lives, suggesting that, in North Africa, these "Islamic" practices have been defined in part by an inclusivity that allows the full participation of their non-Muslim neighbors.

That history and those connections are in danger of fading into obscurity. But whatever the overlaps with Muslim women's practices, it is clear that Jewish rebaybiyya developed into something distinctive, with its own identity reflecting its community of patrons and practitioners, and in doing so relied on the adoption and adaptation of ritually adjacent practices. This distinctive rebaybiyya tradition disappeared as the Jewish population of mainland Tunisia dwindled in the middle and late twentieth century, maintaining its last gasps in trans-Mediterranean movements as the growing Tunisian Jewish immigrant community in Paris continued to demand rebaybiyya ceremonies. That demand meant calling on Muslim musicians in Tunis.

Relocating to Paris

The concerts and recordings from 2004 and 2007 showcased the rebaybiyya expertise that Mustapha Ben Romdhane cultivated between Paris and Tunis in the 1960s and 1970s. Ben Romdhane came of age during a time when increasing numbers of Tunisian Jews left the country for Israel or France. The early twentieth-century anticolonial movement that eventually led to

23. The Sīdī ʿAlī Ḥaṭṭāb nūba "Irfaʿ Ra'sik" (Hold Your Head Up) is a particularly important one for mizwid players. According to Mustapha Ben Romdhane (in Chamkhi 2010), the best mizwid players (those who did not "distort" tradition) visited the shrine of Sīdī ʿAlī Ḥaṭṭāb for fifteen days each year to lead trance ceremonies.

Tunisia's independence from France in 1956 was based on a nationalist platform that asserted Islam as a defining aspect of Tunisian identity and therefore alienated the country's Jews (see Tessler 1978). The establishment of the state of Israel in 1948, uncertainty over the treatment of Jews after Tunisia's independence in 1956, and anti-Jewish sentiment during the 1967 Arab-Israeli war each led to waves of Jewish emigration. The aftermath of the 1967 war left the Tunisian Jewish population at under 30,000, down from 85,000 in 1948 (Perkins 2004: 144–145), and that number would continue to decline. In 2017 there were roughly 1400 Jews remaining in Tunisia, with roughly 1000 on the island of Djerba and the remainder in the greater Tunis area (Lellouche, pers. comm., 2015).

A large proportion of the Tunisian Jewish immigrant population to France settled in the Belleville area of Paris (19th arrondissement). There the continued demand for rebaybiyya in the twentieth century led to Paris's becoming the new home for the Tunisian trance ritual as well as a site for continued Muslim-Jewish musical convergence. According to Ben Romdhane, he learned the rebaybiyya tradition from the legendary mizwid player Chedly Hammas (a.k.a. Chedli el-Medellal) and from Khatoui and Khamous Bou Oukez, Jewish brothers whom he describes as famous in the Jewish community and "guardians of the silsila." They in turn had learned from Gagou Ouled Chnichen, Khailou Esseghir, and Didou Msika (Ben Romdhane, in Chamkhi 2010). Ben Romdhane said that after Khatoui and his fellow musicians died, he had nobody in Tunis left to perform with, so in 1968 he moved to Paris, where he stayed for six years. There he was able to maintain his rebaybiyya livelihood after entering the musical community led by such influential Tunisian Jewish immigrants as Joseph Berrebi, Maurice Mimoun, and Lalou Kahlaoui. Kahlaoui (born Elie Touitou in 1932), a singer and percussionist, bought and ran two music venues, the Palais Bergère and the Bataclan theater. He also purchased and led the Dounia record label, one of the most important producers of musics of the Arab world and Jewish North African immigrants to France.[24] Ben Romdhane recorded at least one rebaybiyya album on the Dounia label, *Rebayebiya*, with Youssef Esseghir. The EP names three nūbas: "Jītak Shākī," "'Addāla," and "Mannūbiyya," but in fact it represents a silsila, and several more nūbas are embedded within those titles (see again table 5.2).[25] Youssef Esseghir,

24. There are competing accounts of whether he established or later bought Dounia; see http://www.npr.org/2015/11/26/457490606/from-retirement-in-israel-bataclan-ex-owner-recalls-better-times and https://www.afrik.com/musik/el-kahlaoui-tounsi/artiste/1489.

25. Dounia 1268, recorded in Paris. The nūbas are transliterated as Jitek Chaâki, Aâdala, and Manoubiya on the album.

who was a vocalist and percussionist, also recorded rebaybiyya albums with other mizwid players, including Khlifa el-Mzaoudi and Youssef el-Karoui.

Rebaybiyya continued to be performed in Paris well into the 1990s. At that time, rebaybiyya ceremonies were held monthly in restaurants that had rented out a room for the event, charging a small fee for admission. The attendees were mostly Jewish women of Tunisian descent, many of whom had arrived in Paris in 1957 during a wave of emigration immediately following Tunisian independence (Conord 2011). In many respects the description of the event provided by Sylvaine Conord is similar to that of other observers throughout the centuries: she describes an all-female gathering where only the musicians are male; women falling into trance at the behest of spirits; the air of sociability and celebration; the billowing smoke of Tunisian incense (*bkhūr*), a necessity when dealing with the jinn; and an orchestra consisting of a vocalist, bendīr, darbūka, ṭār, "kralet" ("iron shakers," probably shqāshiq), and ghayṭa (a synonym for zukra, an instrument that sometimes replaced the mizwid). Conord notes, however, that these events were disappearing toward the close of the twentieth century as venues such as the Dar Djerba restaurant closed and the participants, whom she described as in their sixties, seventies, and eighties as of 1994, entered nursing homes or died (2011; pers. comm., 2015).

While rebaybiyya has ceased to exist as such in Tunis and Paris, where it is fading from collective memory, traces of its legacy endure, in a somewhat oblique way, through the music of Hedi Doniya, one of the most successful artists in the popular-music genre called mizwid, named after the bagpipe that provides its signature sound. Specializing in nūbas for saints, Doniya also learned the rebaybiyya repertoire in Paris.

RITUAL REMNANTS: THE MIZWID NŪBA AND ITS TRACES OF REBAYBIYYA

The mizwid instrument provides the signature sound for a mass-mediated popular music, also called mizwid, that has dominated the music market since the late 1960s. Mizwid, as a genre of music, features a repertoire of songs (*aghānī*; sing. *ghnāya*) that are nonritual and focus on themes such as love, relationships, poverty, and exile. Alongside this repertoire, however, is a large number of nūbas, songs in praise of saints that originate in, but have been extracted from, the ritual world of the silsila. Hedi Doniya's name is virtually synonymous with this repertoire of nūbas in the mizwid genre. To fully grasp his interventions, it is necessary to understand the development of this genre, as well as the associations and cultural location of the mizwid instrument. These, in turn, circle back to shed further light on rebaybiyya, its location within a shared ecology of devotional musics, and the traces it has left on what would become the most dominant mass-mediated music of Tunis.

Mizwid, as a popular-music genre, has a contentious place within the Tunisian musical landscape, both despite and because of its unrivalled popularity from the late 1960s to the early twenty-first century. It is a mass-mediated music that thoroughly dominated the commercial recordings market during that time yet in live performance has also been a staple of mainly male social gatherings at weddings or drinking parties called *rbūkh*. Mizwid musicians have a reputation for drinking alcohol and being targeted by the law. During mizwid's heyday of the 1970s and 1980s, time spent in prison came to be a marker of authenticity among mizwid artists with the incarceration of emerging stars such as Salah Farzit and Hedi Habbouba. The association of mizwid with prison is concretized in *zindālī*, a subgenre of mizwid. Zindālī (from Zindāla, the name of the largest prison in Tunis) songs speak from the viewpoint of prisoners and features a lamentlike tone that is considered more plaintive than those of other mizwid songs.[26] These associations with outlaws, migrants, and Tunis's poorer neighborhoods bestowed on mizwid a widespread social stigma magnified by its association with drinking, use of colloquial dialect, and themes of illegal immigration to Europe, family tensions, alcohol, sex, injustice, and other aspects of everyday life that resonate with the urban working class. This stigma put it on a collision course with the cultural elite. Excluded from educational institutions and Tunisian broadcast media, mizwid was first broadcast on Tunisian national media in 1988, prompting the dismissal of the director of the Tunisian national broadcasting company for transgressing moral standards (see Stapley 2006). In the following decades, mizwid dominated the live and recorded music markets and made inroads into national radio broadcasts, although its stigma remained. At the turn of the twenty-first century, rap

26. Zindālī is a polysemic musical signifier in North Africa. In addition to mizwid songs associated with prison (zindāla), it also refers to a 6/8 rhythm used in mizwid for certain nūbas, such as "Bābā Baḥrī" (for the saint Sīdī Manṣūr) and others associated with sṭambēlī (Hichem Lékhdiri, pers. comm. 2014). Mustapha Chelbi defines zindālī as Bedouin songs from the Fezzan region of Libya widespread in Tunisia (Chelbi 1985: 47), while Hans Stumme also considers it a Bedouin song type from Libya (1894). Wolfgang Laade, in his Folkways recording of Tunisian music, describes it as a song type consisting of eleven-syllable verses (1962). In Algeria, zindālī (or zandālī) is the most widespread rhythm in eastern Algerian folk music, where it also refers to instrumental pieces in the 6/8 or 12/8 rhythm of the same name. The rhythm has three variants associated with the cities of Constantine and Annaba, as well as the Tunisian island of Djerba (Saidani 2006).

music began to challenge mizwid's dominance as the music of the streets. The heavily politicized lyrics of Tunisian rap contributed to the spread of revolutionary sentiment as well as a critique of mizwid as insufficiently political (e.g., Gana 2011). The Revolution, however, also prompted a reassessment of previously stigmatized musical practices such as mizwid, leading to a modest resurgence of mizwid in new social spaces, crossing socioeconomic class lines. It is no longer uncommon for middle-class artists, university students, and young musicians to hold mizwid parties in comfortable suburban homes where they dance, drink, and sing along to mizwid nūbas performed live by musicians who previously made their living in lower-income neighborhoods (see video ex. 5.1).

Like the genre that would become its namesake, the mizwid instrument has a history of stigmatization. Its presumed origins are associated with incoming others. In Tunisia, the most widely circulating narrative of the mizwid's origins has it entering the country with sub-Saharan Africans and Jews from the Fezzan region of neighboring Libya via trade routes that extended into sub-Saharan Africa. While nineteenth-century travelers mention bagpipes being played at royal receptions in Ghana in 1817 (Johnson 1995: 259) and the Bornu region of central Africa in 1870 (Nachtigal 1974 [1879]: 101), accounts of bagpipes in Tunisia and Libya as early as 1822 attest to the instrument's being used in both public and domestic settings, often for weddings (Denham, Clapperton, and Oudney 1826; Eyries 1841) and particularly by black or Jewish Tunisians. In Tunisia and Libya,[27] bagpipes reportedly accompanied the urban street performances of black snake charmers (Mayet 1886) as well as black dancers playing drums or shqāshiq and often dressed in the masked costume of Bū Saʿdiyya (see Cowper 1897 and Rae 1877 for Libya; Lallemand 1892 and Lapie 1898 for Tunisia).[28] Jews of Libyan origin, recognizable from their distinctive Libyan clothing, are reported to have

27. In Libya, the bagpipes are called *zukra*. They are larger than their Tunisian counterpart and have a more limited range because they have only four finger holes (see Brandily 1993). The Libyan zukra bagpipes should not be confused with the Tunisian zukra, an instrument called "ghayṭa" in other parts of the Maghreb. The Tunisian zukra has a larger range than the mizwid and, since it does not have an airbag, relies on the technique of circular breathing to achieve the uninterrupted sound. In Tunisia it is mainly associated with rural, outdoor settings but sometimes replaced the mizwid in Jewish rebaybiyya because, as noted above, some Jews did not approve of the goatskin bag of the mizwid and preferred the material of the zukra (Hedi Doniya, pers. comm., 2014).

28. The association of the bagpipes with the black community extends to Algeria, where bagpipes (called *shakwa*) are less widely heard but are used in Biskra to accompany outdoor holiday processions (but not trance rituals) of the communal houses of Dār Bārnū, Dār Hausa, and Dār Baḥrī (Dermenghem 1954). Bagpipes are played more commonly, however, within the music culture of Algerian Kabyles.

also been mendicant mizwid musicians in Tunis and other cities, where, accompanied by drums, they also performed songs and dances of the Fezzan region of Libya (Saïdane 2014: 37).

The mizwid instrument's reputed power to awaken and attract spirits also confers on the instrument a certain amount of "tacit censorship" (Snoussi 1962: 4). Here it is useful to remember that the mechanism of silsila-based trance practices in Tunisia is to attract the presence of spirits, as well as the saints that control them, for offerings of trance and praise, with the goal of appeasing, rather than repelling or exorcising, these unseen beings. Yet, because any mizwid performance is apt to make the immediate physical setting "hot" (*skhūn*) or liable to attract spirits, those who might be vulnerable to spirit possession may seek to avoid being in the presence of the instrument. The instrument established a particularly strong association with the bahriyya ("of the sea"), water spirits, which are among the most widely encountered in Tunisian trance healing practices. This relationship is reinforced through by the role played by Sīdī Bū Sa'īd, the saint known as "Captain of the Seas," as a kind of patron saint protecting mizwid players (Garfi n.d.; Snoussi 1962). During the annual kharja (procession) at the shrine of Sīdī Bū Sa'īd, mizwid players follow the line of 'Īsāwiyya Sufis, playing "Ra'īs al-Abḥār" as well as nubās for other maritime saints such as Sīdī Bū Yaḥya of Radès and Sīdī Ṣālaḥ Bū Gabrīn, who was buried in the seaside town of La Marsa (Garfi n.d.). Although 'Īsāwis in the Tunis area do not play the mizwid, reports from the 1940s indicate that they played the instrument in the coastal city of Sfax to heal women, while in southern Tunisia it is reported that musicians of the Sulāmiyya played mizwid and sang praise songs for the groom during weddings (while the 'Īsāwiyya played the zukra) (Revault 1960: 119).[29] The "mad" female saint Umm al-Zīn al-Būhliyya, who has a prominent place in the silsila of both the Mannūbiyya and rebaybiyya, has been celebrated for at least a century by bagpipe players on the Cap Bon peninsula, to the northeast of Tunis (Marçais and Guiga 1925).

By the middle of the twentieth century, then, the mizwid instrument had established a history of transgressing boundaries: between public and private spaces and between religious and ethnic boundaries, as well as between the human and the spirit worlds. Beginning in the 1950s and 1960s, its role in sounding border-crossing expanded to include rural-to-urban migrants. At that time, with rapid urban development attracting massive numbers

29. Although the mizwid is associated with saints and their shrines, I have found no evidence that the instrument was ever used in the ḥaḍra, the corporate rituals of formal Sufi orders inside their shrines. Hopkins (2018) reports that many families making a pilgrimage (ziyāra) to saint shrines in Testour in the 1970s enlisted the services of mizwid players to lead a trance ceremony.

of migrant workers to the capital city, mizwid became increasingly associated with men's drinking parties called *rbūkh.* These parties became popular after-work occasions for urban migrants and *zūfrīs* (from the French *les ouvriers*) or working-class laborers such as longshoremen, factory workers, and railway workers to socialize, dance, and drink. The mizwid troupe developed a standardized form of a mizwid, several large bendīrs (positioned vertically on the lap, as opposed to held up by the hand, as it is in ritual settings), and one or two small darbūkas, played between the legs (positioned more or less vertically, rather than horizontally, as it is in art music). Members of the troupe began to wear blue dungaree clothing called *dingrī*, indexing their working-class, manual-laborer associations.

Details on rbūkh are scarce in the historical record. In the early twentieth century, the term "rbūkh" referred to often risqué songs played in what al-Rizqī calls "vile cafés" of the "underworld" (*sūqa*), accompanied by mandolin, darbūka, and handclaps (al-Rizqī 1989 [1968]: 98). In the latter half of the twentieth century, the term had become synonymous with mizwid drinking parties of zufrīs, *bandī* ("bandits"), and the urban poor and disenfranchised. Mizwid lyrics are delivered in an urban dialect full of slang and markers of rural origins, such as replacing the "q" sound with "g," as well as the linguistic technique called *gijmī*, which involves adding syllables (particularly "na" and "ni" or "ra" and "ri") in the middle of words. Beyond these performative markers of outsiderness, the act of singing in local dialect itself adds to mizwid's contentious reception. As Marc Schade-Poulsen (1999: 54) notes, potentially risqué or socially critical messages sung in the flowery, metaphorical register of classical Arabic are disarmed through their cultural and historical distance from everyday life, while songs in local dialects are considered to be more threatening to arbiters of culture and social behavior because they relate to real experiences and real possibilities for action. They cover themes of rejection in love and society and the pain of immigration, and while they are sometimes obscene, they often pale in comparison to the highly suggestive sexuality of some songs from the Tunisian turāth songs of the early twentieth century (Stapley 2006). Mizwid songs are revealing of their milieu, but often the themes such as rejection, being looked down upon, backstabbing friends, immigration (something that affects many Tunisians directly or indirectly), and, more specifically, the migrant's sadness at missing his mother are relatable to a wider public. This theme of the difficulties of immigration (*ḥarrāga*) and exile (*ghurba*) speak to the dreams and realities of Tunisian immigration to Europe as much as they evoke the tribulations of internal rural-to-urban migrants of earlier decades. The line "the nights in exile are long" (*līl al-ghurba ṭwīl*), from the iconic mizwid song "Yā Mimtī al-Ghāliyya" (O Precious Mother) by Samir Loussif, is often quoted by listeners to illustrate the lyrical poignancy of mizwid's treatment of such themes, which continues with the following verse:

yā mīmtī al-ghāliyya, yā ʿayn min ʿaynayā	O precious mother, O apple of my eye
mushtāgalik, mushtāg . . .	I miss you, I miss . . .
baʿdik ʿazīza ʿaliyya, liyyām laʿbit biyya	Far from you, dear, and the days you played with me
ū-kwānī l-firāq	I am separated
ṭāl ghiyābī ṭāl, taʿbnī al-tirḥāl	My absence is so long, I'm tired of traveling
ndimt ʿalā hāl-ḥāl, damaʿ skhiyya	I regret this situation, the tears flow
ū-ḥarrāga li-shwāq	Migration [lit. "burning"] brings homesickness

Mizwid's nūbas for saints—and therefore the act of seeking solace from suffering—are, then, quite at home coexisting with songs—however explicit—that speak from the perspective of the disenfranchised and also express pain, misfortune, and injustice. In the mass-mediated world of mizwid that emerged in the late 1960s, the term "nūba" continued to refer to songs for saints, while the term "ghnāya" (song) designated the newly composed pieces from that perspective of the disenfranchised, which became the dominant form of Tunisian popular music. While parallel practices coexisted—ritual musics with the nūba, on the one hand; rbūkh parties and concerts with the ghnāya, on the other—the nūba has developed substantial symbolic importance even in the context of recordings and live performances that are otherwise dedicated entirely to the ghnāya, as the following section reveals.

The Mizwid Nūba

Hedi Habbouba is widely acknowledged as the founder of the modern mass-mediated mizwid genre. He recorded his first 45 rpm record, "Bjāh Allah Yā Ḥubb Asmaʿnī" (By the Glory of God, Listen to Me, My Love), in Paris in 1967 and his first full-length album there in 1974. To the traditional mizwid ensemble he made subtle changes, such as the addition of electric bass guitar, but he maintained the primacy of the signature sounds of mizwid, bendīr, and darbūka, as well as the lyrical themes associated with the working class. His songs are understood to be frank, honest depictions of male life in a poor urban neighborhood. This straightforward approach in lyrics is reinforced by musical aesthetics in recordings (and onstage) that privilege a raw, live sound and avoids slick, highly edited production values. His songs about the pain of exile and immigration contributed to his widespread popularity among Tunisians abroad, particularly in France (Saïdane 2014). The strong, masculine voice of the street he presented was also full of vulnerability and self-awareness, particularly in the many songs about parent-child relationships that became iconic themes of mizwid. Songs about mothers were typically sung from the nostalgic, emotional perspective of an émigré son who missed his mother (e.g., "Yā Lumīma" [O Mother]). Fathers are treated rather differently: the song's narrator typically fears the father and imagines his disapproval and disappointment in the son's bad behavior, such as drinking, which would bring shame to the family (e.g., "Law Kān Irānī Baybay" [If Only My Dad Could See Me]).

Alongside such popular songs (ghnāya), Habbouba recorded many nūbas, often including one or two songs for saints on albums that were otherwise devoted to nonreligious themes. Among the nūbas he recorded are "Nimdaḥ al-Agṭāb" (I Praise the Saints), a song that praises numerous religious figures, providing a kind of who's who of local saints, as well as individual nūbas for Bābā ʿAbd Allah, Sīdī Ṣālaḥ, and Sīdī Brahīm, and two for Sīdī ʿAbd al-Qādir ("Bābā Jallūl" and "Bū Derbāla"). In addition, his repertoire includes at least three nūbas devoted to Sīdī Bū Saʿīd (including "Sīdī Bū Saʿīd al-Bājī," "Bābā al-Bājī," and "Ra'is al-Abḥār"), a further testament to the association between mizwid and this saint. Habbouba credits his knowledge of the mizwid nūba to musicians including Shaykh Abdesalem Bou Okkaz, the mizwid player Chedli Mdallal, and the percussionist Khatoui Bou Okkaz (*al-hādī ḥabbūba* . . . 1999: 13), some of the rebaybiyya masters from whom Mustapha Ben Romdhane also learned. Rebaybiyya and the mizwid genre, then, coexist in an imbricated relationship, such that rebaybiyya musicians and their nūbas factor into the training and standard repertoire of mizwid's most iconic singers, and is never far from the reach of even the most nonreligious performances.

For example, contemporary mizwid musicians may—and according to many, should—begin a party, wedding, or concert performance with one or two nūbas. Hichem Lékhdiri (b. 1974), a successful young *mzāwdī* and the first student at the Institut Supérieur de Musique in Tunis to specialize in mizwid, believes doing so is a sign of authenticity. Lékhdiri, who is known for his superb playing technique, knowledge of melodic modes that are now disappearing from the repertoire, and development of a technique for constructing mizwid reeds so that they do not detune easily, also connected this performative recognition of mizwid's ritual origins to Tunisian Jews:

HL: The origin of the mizwid is the nūba. The nūba is a praise to the saints. It wasn't used in weddings [*afrāḥ*] [like today]. It was played in shrines [*zwī*]. The nūba for Sīdī 'Abd al-Qādir, the nūba for Sīdī 'Abd al-Salām. They played rebaybiyya, as we say. Not with darbūka as we do now. It was just bendīr and the mizwid player [*mzāwdī*]. No darbūka, and no chairs. And the term "rebaybiyya," from "rabbi," is related to the Jews. And we keep returning to the Jews because they were the most active musicians in Tunis.

RJ: If this is the origin of the repertoire, do you still play these nūbas?

HL: A mzāwdī who is a real mzāwdī has preserved this repertoire. A nūba always opens the party [*sahriyya*], before singing a song [*ghnāya*]. At a party the first two will be nūbas.

RJ: And the same at weddings?

HL: Always. The group at a wedding always begins with a nūba. There is a message in it [*fīhā risāla*] that our group knows, that we are professional, that you have the "true" mizwid. (Pers. comm., 2014)

In Lékhdiri's experience, mizwid players' ability to perform nūbas sends a message that the troupe is serious and knowledgeable. Playing them first announces this acknowledgment of mizwid roots. It stakes a claim to an authenticity of continuity with and respect for the past, while also evoking, however obliquely, the sense of ordering inherent in the silsila whereby spiritual hierarchies are created: these first pieces make a statement of values and identity as much as the first two nūbas of the rebaybiyya, Mannūbiyya, and sṭambēlī silsilas declare their sociorituaI identities.

That the nūbas of mass-mediated mizwid are in part the legacy of Jewish mzāwdīs is not lost on Lékhdiri. He, like many musicians in various fields of Tunisian music, recognizes the Jewish contribution to the music he plays. And like many of his generation, that recognition is becoming increasingly vague, lacking in biographical intersections with specific influential musicians. Those specific interactions with Jewish musicians, as well as the conscious adaptation of rebaybiyya to the mizwid nūba repertoire, however, are evident in the profile of Hedi Doniya.

Hedi Doniya: Absorbing Rebaybiyya into the Mizwid Nūba

Unlike his counterparts who specialize in pop songs (ghnāya) and at most sprinkle in a few nūbas in their recordings and concerts, Hedi Doniya (b. 1936) is the only major mizwid artist who has made a career specializing in the nūba repertoire. Doniya's musical biography illustrates the kinds of trajectories that are possible as one navigates a path within an ecology of

Sufism characterized by numerous distinct yet adjacent and available domains of musical experience.

> I fell in love with Sufism when I was young. My brother was always at [the shrine of] Sīdī Belḥassen and loved those things, he was a *dhakkar* [reciter of dhikr] at Sīdī Belḥassen. He used to take me with him so I wouldn't fool around or get into trouble; I was twelve or thirteen. By the third or fourth time I loved it. I listened and learned the songs unconsciously; I loved to listen. When I was eighteen or nineteen I joined a Sulāmiyya troupe and had great times with them. After two years I left and joined people who play mizwid. You know in mizwid there is tuning and work, like the piano, I mean, it needs tuning and work, so I liked it. So I got into this world and learned many things. Then, after 1995, I was free to record. So I recorded a cassette of nūbas. (Pers. comm., 2014)

Doniya saw how popular the nūba repertoire was among his audiences, particularly young people, who, because fewer of them were joining Sufi orders or participating in rituals, had limited access to this repertoire. He continued:

> I didn't record songs [*aghānī*], I recorded nūbas. I said to myself, they enjoy the nūbas. I began to sing for them in Radès and Ariana and other places, because the man I learned from, 'Am 'Azīz, was a great man; they took him to play with the mizwid when he was only seventeen. I chose to record praises to Sīdī 'Abd al-Qādir, Sīdī 'Alī al-Ḥaṭṭāb, and Sayyda Mannūbiyya and Umm al-Zīn al-Jammāliyya and the others because I felt these had been limited to the older generation only. [I sang like] I was in ceremonies, but I changed some things since those songs didn't use the fazzānī rhythm but instead always used *zābī, jdābī,* and *'alwī*. So I had the idea to record the nūbas but change them a bit, making "Sīdī 'Alī 'Azūz" and "Sīdī 'Alī al-Ḥaṭṭāb" in fazzānī. . . . I made "Khdīm al-Jīlānī" [Sīdī 'Abd al-Qādir] in zābī, "Sayyda Mannūbiyya" in ghayṭa, "Sīdī 'Alī 'Azūz" in fazzānī, that was the first record. The second record had "Ra'is al-Abḥār" and "Hadhīlī," as well as "Sīdī 'Alī al-Ḥaṭṭāb" in fazzānī . . . I recorded them in September or October and wanted to release them at a suitable time. By then, 1995, Ramadan would come in February. So I decided to release them. The first copy sold twenty thousand and the next one fifty thousand. The people loved it; it was a language that people were not used to. (Pers. comm., 2014)

Doniya, having been part of the mizwid scene, knew that the fazzānī rhythm was one of the most energetic and popular rhythms—indeed, *the* iconic rhythm—of the mizwid genre. Adding this rhythm, as well as others such as ghayṭa, to the nūba repertoire he developed brought an additional element of excitement and familiarity to a repertoire his young audiences were eager to hear.

Named after the Fezzan region of Libya that borders eastern Tunisia, the fazzānī rhythm carries with it and entrenches mizwid's association with neighboring Libya and, by extension, the Jewish musicians who ostensibly brought it to Tunis. Its iconic status in mizwid ensures that the genre's associations with neighboring others remain enshrined in its sound and nomenclature. Yet there are more direct ways in which his repertoire is indebted to Jewish musicians. Like Mustapha Ben Romdhane, Hedi Doniya learned the rebaybiyya silsila in Paris to perform for ceremonies of the Tunisian Jewish diaspora there.

> Many Jews left for Paris in 1978–1979, after the agricultural cooperatives came to Tunisia. When they settled there, they couldn't find anyone to perform [rebaybiyya] for them. There was one Jewish bendīr player in Paris, but he couldn't perform alone because he needs a good zukra player or mizwid player. So for this reason they sent for 'Am 'Alī, an old man who knows how to sing [this repertoire], and a zukra player. The most important is the singer, because the songs are not written and few people know them. 'Am 'Alī went to Paris and stayed for fifteen days. The next time, though, his sons refused to let him go because he was old and ill, he was in his eighties. So the man that went with him the last time, al-Khaṭwī, came to me and a mizwid player and brought us to Paris for fifteen days so I could memorize the songs. They asked me to stay in Paris, not to return to Tunis. I told them I have a job in Tunis, and they said they would get me a job in Paris and take care of the immigration papers. I told them no, but I continued to go to Paris, each time for fifteen or twenty days, taking leaves from my job. (Pers. comm., 2014)

Much of the remainder of my meeting with Hedi Doniya consisted of a veritable master class in the rebaybiyya silsila as he knew it, listing and describing the nine nūbas he had mastered and providing brief sung examples of most of them. Of particular interest to the present discussion are the traces of rebaybiyya that remain in Hedi Doniya's repertoire, whose recordings and live performances continue to be synonymous with the mizwid nūba repertoire and circulate widely, including high-profile, widely disseminated recordings and broadcasts such as *el-Hadhra* (see chap. 6). Two nūbas in particular carry rebaybiyya into new contexts, although their provenance is undoubtedly obscured for most listeners: the first, "Mā Sabā 'Aqlī," remains relatively obscure in comparison to the second, "Ra'is al-Abḥār," which is now a household name, arguably the most famous nūba in the Tunis region.

"Mā Sabā 'Aqlī" appears on the album *Nūbit Sīdī 'Abd al-Qādir*, one of Hedi Doniya's recordings for Africa Cassette.[30] Although the title refers to the seventh song on the album, the ordering of the album could be read as maintaining a vestige of the spirit of the silsila: after an instrumental introduction, "Mā Sabā 'Aqlī" is the first piece, followed by a variety of nūbas to saints, with nūbas for Sayyda Mannūbiyya, Sīdī 'Abd al-Qādir, and Sīdī Bū Yaḥya closing the album. "Mā Sabā 'Aqlī" is performed in the rebaybiyya style: it utilizes the opening steftūḥ rhythm and includes the iconic rebaybiyya line *jītak shākī min galbī āwjā' yā sīd al-mellāḥ* (discussed above), which is not found in the mālūf version or the version in a mizwid silsila performed by Zied Gharsa.[31] Doniya's recording not only enshrines "Mā Sabā 'Aqlī" as a song in the repertoire of mizwid (albeit rarely performed by other mizwid artists); it also maintains the ritual musical form of the rebaybiyya silsila, including rebaybiyya's use of "Mā Sabā 'Aqlī" in place of a nūba for the Prophet.

In contrast to the relative obscurity of "Mā Sabā 'Aqlī," the melody and chorus of "Ra'is al-Abḥār" enjoy widespread familiarity throughout the Tunis area. And thanks to Hedi Doniya, traces of the rebaybiyya are smuggled into those circulations. According to Doniya, the Muslim version "has limits. Three or four verses and that's it. [The line] *bābā sharīf 'alājī* is not in our [Muslim] lexicon, but in the "Ra'is al-Abḥār" of the Jews, in the silsila of spirit nūbas [*nwib al-jnūn*]; the Jews trance to them." He continued:

> In the ending of their version [*al-qafla mtā'hā*], you see, in the same rhythm, you do what they do. You do their "Ra'is al-Abḥār," which is not like ours. They sing:
>
> | | |
> |---|---|
> | *ra'is al-abḥār yā rafīqī* | Captain of the seas, O my companion |
> | *nabrā yā bājī 'alā allah* | I am healed O Bājī, by God |
> | *madha biyya 'alā ziyāra* | I want to make the *ziyāra* |
> | *l-bū sa'īdī al-bājī 'alā allah* | To Sīdī Bū Sa'īd, by God |
>
> And at the end, they sing:
>
> | | |
> |---|---|
> | *aya anā baḥrī* | Yes, I am baḥrī/of the sea |
> | *mā nḥib ilā al-baḥrīyya* | I want nothing except the baḥriyya |

30. Africa Cassette (CD Pressé) PCP 1006.

31. In Gharsa's performance, this is followed by nūbas for Sīdī Bū Yaḥya ("Māk Sulṭān") and Sīdī Mahrez ("Addāla Addāla"); the video is available at https://www.youtube.com/watch?v=K30w5sSjlco&list=PL-QN3TzDNLCgjg5twJPo4OGrBeANQaXI7.

baḥrī yughrī	The baḥrī/my sea entices me
yā ilahī nūb 'aliyyā	O God, take care of me
aya anā baḥrī	Yes, I am baḥrī/of the sea
mā nḥib ilā al-'awwāma	I want nothing except the swimmer]
bābā sharīf 'alājī	Baba Sharīf, heal me
bābā sharīf wal-'arbiyya	Baba Sharīf and 'Arbiyya

(Pers. comm., 2014)

Given Sīdī Bū Sa'īd's status as captain of the seas, the references to the sea in these last verses might pass without much comment. However, the specific language used in these verses reveals clearly their connection to spirit-possession trance practices. "I want nothing more than the baḥriyya" and "the baḥrī entices me" is the kind of language used by trancers to describe the irresistible urge to dance in ritual, a sense of giving in to the afflicting spirit. "I am baḥrī" is also the kind of statement associated with the perspective of a trancer who is indicating her identification with the baḥriyya spirits that possess her. In his two most widely circulating recordings of "Ra'is al-Abḥār," Doniya also adds the line (shown in square brackets above) "I want nothing except the swimmer." The term "'awwāma" is both the feminine and the plural of "swimmer" in Tunisian Arabic, and in the context of spirit-possession practices, it refers to the dance movements of the trance dance, in which the possessing spirit is understood to make the dancer move in a swimming motion. These lines are followed by lyrics that cement the verses in the Jewish practice of rebaybiyya: first, by imploring Bābā Sharīf—an honorific from the Jewish lexicon for Sīdī Bū Sa'īd—to heal, and second, by ending with the invocation of Lilla 'Arbiyya, indicating a transition to the subsequent nūba in the rebaybiyya silsila.

The musical treatment of these lines in Hedi Doniya's nūba also evokes the rebaybiyya trance context through discrete intensification. When he reaches the line *bābā sharīf 'alājī*, Doniya enters into a call and response with the chorus. In his studio-recording version the chorus sings this line fifteen times as Doniya interjects between each iteration names of other saints, including lesser-known saints such as Sīdī Bū Jlīda and Sīdī Bū Bālba, before turning to the *agṭāb* ("poles," or central, most important or powerful saints) Sīdī 'Alī al-Ḥaṭṭāb, Umm al-Zīn, and Sayyda Mannūbiyya. After this exchange the chorus repeats *bābā sharīf 'alājī* seventeen more times, with an increase in tempo from 148 to 196 bpm and sampled ululations to index, and add to, a heightened sense of musical-ritual excitement. The treatment of these lines takes up almost two minutes and thirty seconds, a full 25 percent of the song (see audio ex. 5.3). The musical treatment of these lines is virtually identical in the version Hedi Doniya sang (and continues to sing) in *el-Hadhra* (see video ex. 5.2), the stage spectacle of Sufi music whose recordings, televised broadcasts (particularly common in cafés during Ramadan), and annual stagings at high-profile events such as the Carthage Festival have made "Ra'is al-Abḥār" a familiar tune all across the country.

In this song, then, the convergence of rebaybiyya, the mizwid instrument, the baḥriyya spirits, and the figure of Sīdī Bū Sa'īd is preserved in what has become the most widely broadcast mizwid nūba. Yet it is an ambiguous and rather frail act of preservation. The reference to the sea in the terms "baḥrī" and "baḥriyya," as mentioned earlier, is normative and intuitive for a nūba for the captain of the seas and does not present any overt indication that it is associated with the Jewish community. The same goes for the names Bābā Sharīf and 'Arbiyya; the former, while commonly used by Jews to refer to Sīdī Bū Sa'īd, nevertheless is entirely compatible with the broader practice of bestowing honorific names on saints, while the latter also fits neatly within the common pattern of mentioning additional names of saints in a nūba. Thus, while a close, contextualized analysis of this song reveals a densely packed record of ritual musical history marked by Jewish-Muslim convergences, that record is all but lost on listeners who do not have access to the historical or ritual knowledge to decode it. These traces of the Jewish contribution to an iconic song for a Muslim saint reveal, in condensed and dissipating form, the end of the life cycle of certain foundational components of ambient Sufism in Tunisia. While the distinctive musical-ritual niche of Jewish rebaybiyya nevertheless relied on its position within a musical and spiritual commons of sounds, saints, and practices, here, in the nūba "Ra'is al-Abḥār," the traces of the Jewish contribution have been swallowed up by its milieu, given a new life and unprecedented dissemination, but only as a faint, spectral sonic image, increasingly failing to signify its specific provenance.

6

RITUAL AS RESOURCE

Set-List Modularity and the Cultural Politics of Staging Sufi Music

Fireworks shot straight upward, in quick succession, around the perimeter of the open-air Carthage Amphitheater, leaving lingering red and white arcs in all directions. The sold-out crowd, gathered for *el-Hadhra*—a staged "mega-spectacle" of Sufi music—cheered and whistled as an additional barrage of colorful explosions, accompanied by a symphony of crackles, booms, and hisses, filled the night sky above the stage. Minutes earlier the crowd had erupted into a standing ovation as then Prime Minister Habib Essid, dressed in a white *jebba* robe, arrived and joined the country's ministers of culture, finance, and civil society in a reserved row just in front of the stage, below an enormous projection of the Tunisian flag. They were welcomed by a cheering crowd chanting patriotic and antiterrorism slogans.[1] *El-Hadhra* was always a big event, but tonight it was not only a feature of the high-profile annual Carthage Festival and a focal point of the festive atmosphere of a midsummer night a week following Ramadan. As "the most anticipated" concert of the summer festival (which featured twenty-two other shows, including concerts by international stars such as Lauryn Hill and Akon, as well as an extravaganza of Tunisian rap featuring Balti and Kafon),[2] *el-Hadhra* also had pride of place in the festival calendar as the event celebrating Republic Day. It was July 25, 2015, more than four tumultuous years after the Tunisian Revolution, and the convergence between the public rep-

1. According to the reporting of Asma Abassi (2015). From my vantage point high up in the amphitheater, behind the sound and lighting controls, the chants were difficult to decipher.

2. The level of anticipation claimed by the official Carthage Festival brochure is evidenced by how quickly the show sold out.

resentation of Sufism and the optics (and acoustics) of the nation was on full display.[3]

Over the course of those four years, the sounds of Sufism had been put on the defensive against the silence imposed by militant Islamists, who had attacked more than forty Sufi shrines since the revolution. The increasing sense of insecurity halted the ritual activities of many Sufi orders for much of 2011 and 2012. In 2013, after the high-profile arsons at the iconic shrines of Sīdī Bū Saʿīd and Sayyda Mannūbiyya, the public demonstrated against these assaults and a government that had done little to prevent them (see chap. 1). Shortly thereafter, the candidate and soon-to-be President Beji Caid Essebsi made a widely publicized visit to the shrine of the saint Sīdī Belḥassen al-Shādhulī, asserted a view of Sufism as representing the tolerance and inclusivity of Tunisian Islam, and received the endorsement of the Shādhuliyya Sufi order.[4] This act made an impression on many of the Sufi ritualists whose performances I had been studying since before the revolution, and several of them had just recently, and rather cautiously, resumed their music-driven ritual activities.

El-Hadhra, however, is not a reproduction of Sufi ritual. Rather, it is a concertlike succession of songs from numerous Sufi orders, with traditional vocals and percussion, that are occasionally combined musically with elements of jazz and rock and roll and visually with complex choreography featuring movements drawn from modern dance, gymnastics, martial arts, and other nonritual performance practices. A rock band of electric guitar, keyboards, bass, and electronic drums, its musicians all dressed in black, is situated within a performance space otherwise dominated by a visually stunning array of nearly fifty white-robed singers and drummers playing the bendīr drums so closely associated with Sufi ritual. A long-haired rock drummer frequently swings his mane around in a manner as evocative of heavy metal head-banging as it is of the typical woman's trance dance at a Sufi shrine, eliciting in the spectacle both cheers and women's ululations, the latter a ritually appropriate (and expected) response to the highly charged moment when a women's hair becomes undone and flails about while she is in trance. Such juxtapositions generate tensions and ambiguities that confront audiences from the opening scene. They happen at multiple levels; they encourage multiple readings and deny definitive interpretive closure; and they raise questions about the relationship between ritual practices and the production values of modern stagecraft, as well as the im-

3. See video 6.1 for a video overview of the event, including behind-the-scenes footage and interviews with performers: https://www.youtube.com/watch?v=Yt4gtQdvfhc.

4. For Beji Caid Essebsi's visit to the Shādhuliyya ṭarīqa, see Young (2015). On the Shādhuliyya in Tunisian society, see McGregor (1997).

plications of valorizing certain aspects of ritual while devaluing others. Because *el-Hadhra* and its performative logic have become the dominant format of Sufism in the Tunisian public sphere, and because public Sufism itself has been the target of competing religious and political interests, an analysis of what *el-Hadhra* accomplishes in Tunisian society is not only timely but also reveals a specific, productive set of ambiguities in staging ritual within the public spiritual economy in the age of the Tunisian mega-spectacle.[5]

In this chapter I assess the cultural work of *el-Hadhra* by focusing on its strategies of both minimizing and maximizing the contextual gap between ritual and spectacle. I am particularly interested in the show's logic of modularity, through which music, dance, trance, and other aspects of ritual are approached as separable, extractable, and available for recombination in a plug-and-play manner. This has particular implications in the context of Tunisian Sufism, where divergent approaches and ideologies of different Sufi orders are, in spectacle, conflated, minimized, or ignored, contributing to new generic understandings of Sufism that bypass local Sufi orders while relying on their aesthetic property. This modular approach to performance, through its selectivity and its valuing and devaluing of certain elements of ritual, also provides the basis for an aesthetically driven, indirect critique of traditional Sufi practice. Through its attention to the aesthetics of performance, this chapter also makes an implicit argument for the utility of a close reading of the performative details and strategies of spectacle. In delving into the poetics of cultural production, the motivating questions revolve not only around the fact that Sufism is on display, but also around how it is displayed, how it is transformed and packaged, how it is received, and how it fits into histories of Sufism in the public sphere. In pursuing a close reading of a staging of Sufi music by and for Tunisians, this chapter departs from and therefore complements other studies of staged Sufi music that focus on international audiences and the allure of cross-cultural spiritual accessibility (Bohlman 1997; Kapchan 2008; Shannon 2003) while building on their shared spirit of acknowledging that such acts of recontextualization and transformation should be analyzed in terms not only of what is lost in the process, but also of what kinds of new meanings and practices are generated.

Despite the apparent newness of such presentational practices and con-

5. *El-Hadhra* followed in the footsteps of *Nouba*, a spectacle devoted to the mizwid genre, also staged by the duo of Samir Agrebi and Fadhel Jaziri. Throughout the 1990s they and other major artists organized similar spectacles, including *Nejma*, *Taht Essour*, *Lamssa*, *el-Zazia*, and *Tunis, chante et danse*, creating an artistic trend and commercial ideal that continues to this day. The phenomenon is most commonly referred to in the local French-language press as *méga-spectacle* and in the Arabic-language press as *'arḍ* (spectacle/show) or *'arḍ farjawī* (visual spectacle).

texts, it is crucial to underscore that Sufism in North Africa had had a very public profile for centuries. Sufisms in the region could be characterized as simultaneously esoteric and exoteric. That is, they harbor hidden forms of knowledge and experience known only to initiates but perform them regularly in rituals that are public or semipublic, making them accessible to a wider audience that partially shares in, and experiences the conditions for, these enhanced devotional practices. Public processions and ceremonies celebrating holidays such as the *mawlid* (the Prophet's birthday), Ramadan, and anniversaries of the death of saints, as well as summer pilgrimage itineraries and performances at weddings and other life-cycle celebrations, bring Sufi sounds and ritual activities to diverse listening publics. This coexistence of private, semipublic, public, and mediatized ritual events challenges binaries such as Sufi/non-Sufi and suggests instead a spectrum of subject positions that Martin Zillinger (2017) refers to as "graduated publics." The already public nature of many Sufi rituals, therefore, complicates analyses of concert stagings that rely on opposing dyads such as spectatorship/participation, loss/renewal, or authenticity/inauthenticity.

ḤAḌRA AND *EL-HADHRA*: FOUNDATIONS OF THE SUFI SPIRITUAL ECONOMY

As chapter 2 established, the term "ḥaḍra" (lit. "presence") refers to the various music-driven rituals associated with Sufism and the healing by saints that take place at a saint's shrine.[6] The term in this context is a multivalent and productively flexible designation; the "presence" it refers to may be that of the collectivity gathered in a sacred space for the ritual, or it may refer to the saint, whose baraka (sacred power) is understood to permeate the ritual space. It can also refer to God, the Prophet Muḥammad, other Muslim saints, and sometimes unseen spirits (jnūn), depending on the ritual tradition. In practice, the ḥaḍra can take on remarkably diverse forms, some of which are considered to be mutually incompatible in terms of ritual objectives, underlying assumptions about the sacred, and aesthetic practice. Indeed, the term "ḥaḍra" usually necessitates a qualifying adjective to clarify which ritual is being referred to. Thus, *al-ḥaḍra al-sulāmiyya* (the ḥaḍra of the Sulāmiyya Sufi order) consists of the relatively reserved, austere chanting of litanies praising God, the Prophet, and Sīdī ʿAbd al-Salām al-Asmar

6. To avoid confusion, I maintain the local Tunisian capitalization and transliteration *el-Hadhra* for the name of the show, even though the standard academic English transliteration would be *al-ḥaḍra*, an identical term differing only in transliteration style; in both cases it refers to the devotional ritual called "ḥaḍra," preceded by the definite article.

(the founder of the order), as well as other Muslim saints. They use no musical instruments aside from frame drums, the songs feature a solo vocalist who is answered by a chorus, and the music of their ḥaḍra elicits very limited physical movement. Indeed, even the high-energy ritual section called *shṭaḥ* (dance) refers to an internal state of excitement rather than the ritual dance or trance the term usually references (Zeghonda, pers. comm., 2012).

The Sulāmiyya are also understood as having close connections to the country's social and political elite; indeed, during the thirty-year presidency of Habib Bourguiba (1957–1987), the Sulāmiyya shaykh and the caretakers of its main shrine were paid government employees (Johnson 1979), and for decades the state-run Tunisian national radio has started its daily broadcasts with Sulāmiyya songs, which, during the Bourguiba era, frequently praised the president. In fact, the Sulāmiyya are such a highly visible and audible part of the spiritual economy of Tunis that Sulāmiyya has also become a generic term referring to musical variety troupes hired to perform sacred music at weddings and other domestic events.

The ritual tradition of the Sulāmiyya is commonly perceived to be more "moderate" and "respectable" (Chelbi 1999; Jones 1977) than the more physically embodied trance rituals of *al-ḥaḍra al-ʿīsāwiyya* (the ḥaḍra of the ʿĪsāwiyya Sufi order), which, as chapter 2 demonstrated, includes dramatic trance episodes involving acts of self-mortification such as the eating of nails, chewing of glass, rolling on cactus pads, and dancing with fire, attracting large crowds to their rituals. In comparison to the Sulāmiyya, the ʿĪsāwiyya have a much broader, mainly working-class, following (which it relies on for the upkeep of its shrines), as well as a history of difficult relations with—including periods of strict suppression by—the state.

The ʿĪsāwiyya also perform their rituals outside the shrine at domestic events such as weddings, as well as on the street in public processions on holidays and commemorative events such as the anniversary of a saint's death. When discussing their different performance contexts, several members of the ʿĪsāwiyya I spoke with proffered the formulation "the shrine is better than the house, and the house is better than the street" (*al-zāwiya khīr mil-dār, wal-dār khīr mil-shārʿ*), giving a sense of a hierarchical spiritual topography of performance whereby each step away from the shrine lessens the control the ʿĪsāwiyya have over their surroundings and further enlarges the interpretive community of potential listeners, thus inviting much more diverse attitudes and subject positions to engage with their ritual. Yet despite this diversity, all audiences gain access to the musical conditions for transcendence that Sufi ritual cultivates, even if they do not partake in the other conditions such as doctrinal and physical training.

Since 1992, however, the term "ḥaḍra" has taken on an additional, more specific meaning. That year the theater director Fadhel Jaziri and musician-composer Samir Agrebi premiered *el-Hadhra*, a musical spectacle of Tunisian Sufi songs and imagery performed before thousands of paying ticket holders. The troupe included an ensemble of nearly a hundred singers and drummers, several solo singers (including Sufi shaykhs as well as famous Tunisian popular singers such as Lotfi Bouchnak and Hedi Doniya), dozens of dancers, and musical arrangements combining the sounds of instruments common to several Sufi orders (frame drums and tambourine) with globally circulating instruments foreign to these ritual contexts (electric bass, keyboards, saxophone, drum set, violin, oboe, and, later, electric guitar), drastically altering the timbre and texture of the ritual musical material. This point will be further elaborated below, but for the moment I will simply provide a reminder that one of the thoroughgoing points made in this book is the importance of constancy of timbre and texture for ritual efficacy, and therefore these changes are not simply aesthetic. While the program consisted of songs from several Sufi ṭarīqas (see table 6.1), the core of the repertoire consisted of songs from the Sulāmiyya and ʿĪsāwiyya traditions, whose ritual and socioreligious differences are discussed further below.

The resounding success of the show resulted in high-profile performances given almost annually; spawned numerous imitators; and led to widely distributed cassette and compact disc recordings, a film version, regular rebroadcasts on Tunisian television, and, more recently, a popular, well-organized Facebook page featuring an abundance of audiovisual material as well as a YouTube channel that has received millions of views for some of its videos. These events and products have been accompanied by a vibrant discourse in the Tunisian media about Sufism, music, and Tunisian society, making *el-Hadhra* not only a household name but also a model for most public stagings of Sufi music in the country.

Unlike Morocco, Tunisia lacks a national music market where recordings of many ritual musics are widely available, and, unlike Egypt, it also lacks an active tradition of *munshidīn* (professional singers who, despite their lack of official status in a ṭarīqa, perform public concerts of Sufi music; see Frishkopf 2001). With few exceptions, consumers in Tunisia seeking to purchase a recording of Sufi music in Tunisia continue to be limited to mp3s, CDs, or Internet streams of *el-Hadhra* (or other similar spectacles), while anyone looking to attend a concert of Sufi music would likely be advised to wait for the next staging of *el-Hadhra*. Given *el-Hadhra*'s prominence in this spiritual musical economy, an account of the shifting role of Sufi music in the Tunisian public sphere is in order before homing in on the spectacle's presentational strategies.

SUFISM, MUSIC, AND THE PUBLIC SPHERE IN TUNISIA

Sufi orders in Tunisia have experienced a tenuous and shifting relationship with the state, and their music is implicated both in their popularity and the state's strategies of managing their role in society. Deeply entrenched in both rural and urban contexts, ṭarīqas were central social institutions that provided essential social services, which were not taken over by the state until the twentieth century (Brown 1964). In the eighteenth and nineteenth centuries, ṭarīqas were a part of everyday life for rulers and ruled alike. Most religious clerics and beys belonged to a ṭarīqa, and the state built many of their zāwiyas (Brown 1964). According to colonial records, 62 percent of adult Tunisian males belonged to a ṭarīqa in 1925, and many more would have watched or participated in their rituals at least occasionally (M'Halla 1996). At the time, it was still common to hear the saying *inna man lā ṭarīqa lahu faṭarīqatuh shayṭāniyya* (he who is without a [Sufi] ṭarīqa is on the path [ṭarīqa] of the Devil; al-Rizqī 1989 [1968]: 101), an adage that highlights the dual meaning of "ṭarīqa" as a path to follow and a Sufi institution.

A general suspicion of Sufi orders grew during the era of the French Protectorate, when some shaykhs and brotherhoods were accused of cooperating with the French and encouraging their followers not to support resistance movements. Many Tunisians pushing for independence from France thus viewed Sufism as politically divisive and a potential breeding ground for opposition to the independence movement (Jones 1977: 40). After independence in 1956, the Bourguiba regime suppressed many ṭarīqas, closing, destroying, or reappropriating many of their shrines (Brown 1985; Ferchiou 1991a). The prohibition on 'Īsāwiyya practices was so severe that many members of the order were convinced that a law had been passed banning their practices (Jones 1977: 38). In contrast, the Sulāmiyya was not only tolerated by the state but was also given a nationwide audience through the Tunisian national radio's broadcast of its chanting each morning. The Sulāmiyya was also the only Sufi order to be included in the first national festivals of Tunisian folklore (Jones 1977: 35).

The government's attitude toward the 'Īsāwiyya shifted over time, especially as Bourguiba, unlike many in his party (see Jones 1977: 40), began to perceive them as keepers of a valuable Tunisian heritage that could be productively integrated into the nascent folklore machinery of the state. Eventually the 'Īsāwiyya were encouraged to perform as musical folklore troupes at state-sponsored festivals, and Sufi singers were required to apply for musician's cards through the Ministry of Culture, which required examinations on musical ability and mastery of the repertoire. It is important to understand this shift toward professionalization and stagecraft not as simply resulting in a loss of meaning; according to Lura JaFran Jones, it also meant that "people who otherwise would have lost interest have been encouraged to cultivate their traditions in a spirit of musical professionalism and with a pride in their guardianship of the national cultural heritage" (Jones 1977: 41).

By the 1980s Tunisia had established a robust calendar of festivals at the local, regional, and national levels that included Sufi music performances. "Bourguiba encouraged this art," Fethi Zeghonda, the former director of music, folk arts, and dance at the Ministry of Culture, told me. He continued:

> When he was in power, he requested from the radio and television broadcast special programs on Sufi music [*inshād al-ṣūfiyya*]. Those who were recorded were paid. And on his birthday, Sufi groups from all regions would come, from many Sufi orders such as the ʿĪsāwiyya, the Sulāmiyya, the ʿAwāmriyya—but they did a bad thing—they would preserve the melodies but change the words to praise Bourguiba instead of the saints. . . . But that is one reason Sufism continued to survive. (Pers. comm., 2012)

When Zeghonda was approached in 1991 by the renowned musician-composer Samir Agrebi and the theater director Fadhel Jaziri with a proposal to create a spectacle of Sufi music, a different set of anxieties over religion was at play. Ben Ali's regime had become more vigilant in its anti-Islamist activities in Tunisia after the 1989 presidential elections showed a surge in support for the Islamist party Ennahda, and he instituted a "severe crackdown" on the party and its sympathizers after a February 1991 bombing of the ruling Rassemblement Constitutionnel Démocratique (RCD) party office in Tunis (Perkins 2004: 193). In neighboring Algeria the Islamic Salvation Front (FIS) won local elections in 1991, prompting government restrictions, strikes, and unrest that would turn into civil war in the wake of the Algerian state's annulment of national elections won by the FIS. Agrebi recalls that he was stunned that he and Jaziri were encouraged by the Ministry of Culture to develop a spectacle devoted to religious music:

> The Ministry of the Interior and the RCD party banned Sufi performances, even in homes, even on the radio. It was banned . . . [so] the Sufi musicians were all out of work. At the time, there was a big conflict with the Nahḍa party; they were being thrown in jail. This was 1991, and the problems in Algeria happened . . . so all religious singing [*ghināʾ dīniyya*] was completely

> forbidden. . . . And here I come, saying let's do a show of religious singing! (Pers. comm., 2014)

Zeghonda, who had just published a book on the music and poetry of the Sulāmiyya (Zeghonda 1991), not only supported the idea but also told me that he would have organized the spectacle himself had his duties at the ministry not taken up so much of his time. Although I could find no evidence of an official ban on Sufi music during those years, it is certainly reasonable to assume that the Ministry of the Interior's suspicion of displays of religious faith would have discouraged the activities of the ṭarīqas and diminished the demand for their musical services at weddings and other domestic events. My conversations with Agrebi and Zeghonda, as well as a review of the Tunisian press coverage of Sufism and *el-Hadhra*, suggest that a Sufi-versus-Islamist narrative had not yet been developed in the early 1990s and that, rather, Sufism operated within a climate of uncertainty in which any display of religiousness could be deemed suspect.

Indeed, the genesis of the idea, and approval, for *el-Hadhra* reveals the contingent and sometimes contradictory nature of cultural policy during the Ben Ali era. Periodic crackdowns on public expressions of religiousness, such as the perceived ban on religious singing that Agrebi recalled or the prohibition against the wearing of the hijab by women in official institutions (Hawkins 2008), often followed periods of time when official attitudes or enforcement were lax. Such diachronic shifts, however, also intersected with synchronic ambiguities whereby seemingly contradictory positions were asserted simultaneously. As Béatrice Hibou (2011) argues, the reason the techniques of creating social order in the Ben Ali regime were so effective was not their fixity or uniformity, but their variability and uncertainty, a condition created in part by the latitude given to individual actors within the state bureaucracy to pursue their own agendas and vision. Thus, it would be reductionist to consider *el-Hadhra* a "top-down" implementation of cultural policy by the state. Rather, as with some other public musical initiatives in North Africa, an initiative by citizens was brought "into the orbit of the state" (Glasser 2016a: 17). Yet both state and citizen shared certain assumptions about the logic of public cultural presentations, coparticipating in an ideological commons that privileged an extractive, modular approach to representing Tunisian culture, a point to which I shall return.

Sufism faced numerous pressures by the turn of the twenty-first century. Decades of nationalist discourse had identified the ṭarīqas as remnants of a backward past, incompatible with the modernizing aspirations of the state except as heritage to be displayed in new contexts. The spread of conservative Islamic views—which many Tunisians blamed on Internet and satellite television broadcasts from the eastern Arab world—also contributed to a discourse of antipathy toward Sufi practices. When Tunisian prisons released all prisoners of conscience, including Islamists, after the 2011 Revolution, the Wahhabi-inspired anti-music and anti-Sufism attitudes that were already gaining some traction at the turn of the twenty-first century were magnified by the postrevolutionary social integration of Islamists emboldened by their newfound freedom. Because of these new pressures, Zeghonda added, "it is impossible to know which traditions will survive and which ones will not. If there are people who say that singing and praising the saints is religiously forbidden [*ḥaram*], then the people will be afraid. . . . Now the danger is that if there is no state support, they will disappear" (pers. comm., 2012). Since the attacks of 2012 and 2013 Tunisian commentators have increasingly deployed the binary of Sufi-versus-extremist in interpreting the socioreligious climate, with Sufism representing tolerance, community, and locality while extremism is associated with violence, division, and foreignness (especially Saudi Wahhabism and the Islamic State; see Omri 2013). Commentators and concertgoers in 2015 presented *el-Hadhra* as a statement challenging religious extremism, at a particularly fragile moment in Tunisian history, through an embrace of the country's Sufi heritage (e.g., Abassi 2015; Barnat 2015).

It is within this context that *el-Hadhra* must be understood, as it (1) occurs in a situation in which Tunisian contact with Sufi sounds in the zāwiya, as part of family celebrations or devotional practice, has greatly diminished and (2) continues the pattern, established by state-sponsored folklore festivals, of extracting Sufi music from its religious institutional context. Thus, the diminishing presence of Sufi music in the Tunisian public sphere suggests that this staging of Sufi sounds in *el-Hadhra* should not be understood as engaging in a process of *de*sacralizing Sufi sounds, in the sense that it extracted the music from its devotional ritual context, as much as a *re*sacralization of public space, in the sense that one of the main goals of *el-Hadhra* was to bring the sonic and visual world of the zāwiya onto the concert stage.

The multiple and shifting layers of tension between *el-Hadhra*'s dynamics of desacralization (of sound) and resacralization (of public space) can be productively analyzed by examining the contextual gap between ritual and spectacle, an idea inspired by the concept of the intertextual gap proposed by the linguistic anthropologists Charles Briggs and Richard Bauman. Like the intertextual gap, which refers to the relative fit or lack thereof between a particular text and the genres of text with which it is associated (Briggs and Bauman 1992; Goodman 2003), the contextual gap draws attention to strategies for either minimizing or maximizing the social and conceptual space between two contexts, in this case ritual and spectacle. The main premise of their argument is that no text (or performance) stands alone; rather, its production and reception are mediated by its relationship to prior texts (or performances) that make up the genre(s) with which it is associated. Therefore, there is always a gap between a performance and its precedents. Some performances attempt to minimize that gap, locating authority in the adherence to established norms and expectations. Others maximize the gap, which builds authority "through claims of individual creativity and innovation" (Briggs and Bauman 1992: 149). Approaching *el-Hadhra* by focusing on its negotiation of the contextual gap, therefore, is not so much an exercise in assessing artistic decisions as it is about illuminating questions of power, representation, devotional style, and the public sphere. By invoking "a particular genre, producers of discourse assert (tacitly or explicitly) that they possess the authority needed to decontextualize discourse that bears these historical and social connections and to recontextualize it in the current discursive setting" (Briggs and Bauman 1992: 148). *El-Hadhra*, as the following sections illustrate, combines strategies of minimizing and maximizing the contextual gap, resulting in a productive ambiguity that allows Sufi music to connect numerous chains of cultural, spiritual, and political value.

EL-HADHRA AND RITUAL SUFISM: OVERLAPS AND DISJUNCTURES

Agrebi and Jaziri presented *el-Hadhra* throughout the 1990s and early 2000s, at first as a collaborative effort and then separately as each pursued his own vision of the spectacle. An account of their 1998 performances, staged at the sports stadium of El Menzah only one week apart, reveals the contrasting approaches. According to Muhammad Kahlawi (1999), Agrebi (who performed on December 24) focused on the music, keeping musical "innovations" to a minimum and featuring minimal choreography and modest scenography. Jaziri (December 31) was more theatrical and impressionistic, with elaborate scenery evoking details from the space of the shrine to distant deserts while introducing saxophone, guitar, bass, violin, oboe, and keyboards into the musical texture. It is the model promoted by Jaziri, whose name has now become inextricable from *el-Hadhra*, that endured to become a staple of Sufi spectacle in Tunisia, while Agrebi's simpler, less modified approach to Sufi song garnered critical acclaim but began to disappear as he turned his focus to his own musical career (he is a renowned singer, violinist, and composer, famous for his song "Anā 'Ashiq Yā Mulātī" and those he composed for Tunisia's biggest mizwid artists). Jaziri continued to experiment with *el-Hadhra*, creating a "version for export" in 2005 and a rhythm and blues–based version for the Fes Festival of Sacred Music in 2008. The controversial culmination of these ventures, *Hadhra 2010*, is discussed further below. However, demand for the less experimental approaches remained high, and a series of cassette, CD, video, and DVD recordings of the earlier, less adventurous stagings—which continue to garner a great deal of airtime, particularly on holidays and throughout the month of Ramadan—established a set of standard songs that continue to be the reference for discussions and imitations of *el-Hadhra*. Many of these songs have also become hits that listeners expect to hear at weddings and other domestic events, cementing them even in the repertoire of variety bands.

Table 6.1 provides the set list of pieces as they appear in the most widely circulating film and audio versions of the spectacle, as well as the majority of staged performances not only of *el-Hadhra* but of also its numerous imitators. They constitute the core repertoire of songs performed onstage since 1992. The first column provides the title of the song, the second indicates the ṭarīqa it is most strongly associated with, and the third describes the main theme of the lyrics. The fourth column characterizes the song's musical texture, that is, the blend of musical instruments and voices, to give a sense of the degree to which each song adheres to or moves beyond the musical aesthetics of ritual practice. The fifth column indicates the main choreographic and scenographic features accompanying each song to give a sense of the overall visual aesthetic as it intersects with the auditory. In the fourth and fifth columns, boldface entries represent actions that explicitly index ritual, while italicized ones indicate strategies of maximizing the gap between ritual and spectacle, such as the addition of electric instruments and modern choreography (regular roman type is used to show ambiguous actions). The following analysis, although based on just one version of *el-Hadhra*, reveals logics of organization and performance that underpin what has become something of an industry of staging Sufi music in Tunisia. Regional variants have proliferated, such as *Hadhra Sfaxienne*, *Hadhra Monastir*, and *Hadhra Rjel Tounes*, as well as the rival spectacle *Ziara*.

Much of the source material for *el-Hadhra* hails from the repertoire of two ṭarīqas: the 'Īsāwiyya and the Sulāmiyya. The relationship between the two ṭarīqas—and among most ṭarīqas more generally—is often framed in terms of competition and rivalry. There are two main reasons for this. First, because ṭarīqas are paid for their domestic performances and family celebrations have traditionally required such performances, there has been a

TABLE 6.1 Standard set list of *el-Hadhra* (based on film and audio versions from 1992 and 2000, respectively)

	Title	Ritual community	Lyrical Themes	Musical texture	Choreography and scenography
1	"al-Du'ā'" (Invocation)	*n/a*	**Supplication to God, praise of the prophets**	**A cappella communal recitation**; *drone strings and brief, quiet saxophone interjections*	Candles lit, **rows of men sitting and chanting, palms facing up**
2	"Wird al-Qudūm: Yā Khūtī" (Arrival Liturgy: O Brothers)	*'Īsāwiyya*	**Praise for Sīdī Ben 'Īsā (founder of the 'Īsāwiyya)**	**Unison and antiphonal singing**; *electric bass follows vocals closely, brief, quiet, oboe interjections*	**Rows of seated men singing; drums thrown to singers (as may be done in 'Īsāwiyya ḥaḍra)**
3	"Meḥrez"	*Sulāmiyya*	**Praise for Sīdī Meḥrez (patron saint of Tunis)**	**Call and response vocals; bendīr-based percussion**; *some electric bass*	Behind seated singers are flag-bearers swinging flags gently while walking; incense walked around
4	"al-Āshwāq" (Yearning)	*Ṭaybiyya*	**Praise for the Prophet**	**Unison rhythmic breathing with solo vocals**; *electric bass; saxophone and nāy interjections*	*Men in back alternate looking to their right and left*; later they intensify movements approximating trance
5	"al-Du'ā'" (Invocation): "Yā Laṭīf" (O Benevolent One)	*Shādhuliyya*	**Praise for God**	**Recitation based on *dhikr***; *electric bass, keyboards, and saxophone increase in prominence as the recitation intensifies*	Children kiss shaykhs on forehead; men carry body in shroud above their heads across stage (evoking Akasha) as chant increases in tempo
6	"al-Layl al-Zāhī" (Magnificent Night)	*Sulāmiyya*	**Praise for Sīdī 'Abd al-Salām (founder of the Sulāmiyya); his presence at the *ḥaḍra***	**Solo vocals with choral response; bendīr-based percussion**; *electric bass; flute and saxophone introduce melody*	*Women sitting in a row, each wearing southern hat; boys walk through the aisles tossing jasmine petals; oboe in B/W and nāy player in color*

TABLE 6.1 Continued

	Title	Ritual community	Lyrical Themes	Musical texture	Choreography and scenography
7	"Khammar Yā Khammār" (Serve the Wine, O Cupbearer)	*'Īsāwiyya*	**Divine intoxication; praise for Sīdī Ben 'Īsā and Sīdī Belḥassen (founder of the Shādhuliyya)**	**Slow bendīr-based percussion; call and response vocals;** *keyboard drone; nāy interjections*	*Nāy player approaches bendīr player*; men standing play bendīr or dance with modified (extra slow) trance movements
8	"Yā Shādhlī" (O Shādhlī)	*Sulāmiyya / Mannūbiyya*	**Praise for Sīdī Belḥassen; saint aiding the faithful and the faithful visiting the shrine**	**Call and response vocals; bendīr-based percussion;** *Western drum set increases in prominence*	*Focus on drum set; all those seated rise*; modified synchronized trance dance (from side to side); flag-waving continues
9	"Hayyā Nzūrū Shaykhnā" (Let's Visit Our Shaykh)	*'Azūziyya / Qādiriyya*	**Praise for Sīdī 'Alī 'Azūz (founder of the 'Azūziyya); visiting his shrine; *ḥaḍra* as healing**	**Call and response vocals, clapping;** *electric bass*	Return to seated position; focus on solo singing of shaykh and choral response
10	"Ibn Miryām" (Son of Mary)	*Sulāmiyya*	**Praise for Jesus and Mary**	**Call and response vocals; bendīr-based percussion;** *electric bass, Arab nāy flute*	*All remain seated except men carrying a woman on their shoulders*; darkness envelops stage, candles lit again; children distribute bread
11	"El-Béji" (al-Bājī) / "Ra'is al-Abḥār"	*Mizwid / 'Alāwiyya / Mannūbiyya*	**Praise for Sīdī Bū Sa'īd al-Bājī and other saints including Sīdī Sharīf, Sīdī 'Alī Ḥattab, Umm al-Zīn, Sīdī Būlbāba, Sayyda Mannūbiyya; saints' capacity to heal**	**Call and response vocals; bendīr-based percussion;** *electric bass, drum set, violin sometimes follows melody*	Standing men hold hands and bend right and left in front of row of seated women; *solo dancer performs tai-chi-like moves*; Akasha, in front, bounces like a boxer, collapses. and is covered with a flag at the end of the song . . .
12	"'Alā Allah Dalālī" (Coaxed by God)	*Sulāmiyya*	**Praise of God**	**Call-and-response vocals; bendīr-based percussion;** *bass*	**. . . only to be picked up by group of men and carried off stage (imitating end of 'Īsāwiyya ḥaḍra)**

13	"Fāres Baghdād" (Horseman of Baghdad)	*Qādiriyya*	**Praise for Sīdī ʻAbd al-Qādir (founder of Qādiriyya); power of music**	**Call and response vocals; bendīr-based percussion;** *bass, nāy, saxophone, oboe*	*Slow procession of veiled women contrasts with jumping moves of male dancers*; women drop veils and mimic trance, on knees, waving head from side to side, with hair flailing
14	"Lawlā al-Luṭf" (Without the Grace [of God])	*Sulāmiyya*	**Praise for Sīdī ʻAbd al-Salām**	**Call and response vocals** *taken over by jazz instrumentation and arrangement*	Darkness, solo singer, all on stage still, quiet, sitting reverently cross-legged with heads bowed; heads raise to sing response; *slow whirling begins with jazz groove*
15	"Jadd al-Ḥassanayn; El-Khatm" (Grandfather of the Two Hassans; The Seal)	*Sulāmiyya*	**Praise for the Prophet Muḥammad and Sīdī Ben ʻArūs (founder of the ʻArūsiyya); the *ḥaḍra***	**Call-and-response vocals; bendīr-based percussion;** *electric bass*	Singers all seated; dancers pseudo-trance in rear; as song intensifies, women trance, held from behind by men
16	"al-Ṣāna'" (The Creator)	*Sulāmiyya*	**Praise for God**	**Unison vocals;** traditional percussion; nāy and saxophone duet in middle	All seated; dancers bow heads forward and back; de-tuned drums replaced by newly-heated ones
17	"Inzād al-Nabī" (Birth of the Prophet)	*Turāth/ Sulāmiyya/ ʻĪsāwiyya (at mawlid)*	**Celebrates the Prophet's birth; calls for Sufis (*fuqāra*) to play the frame drums in his honor**	**Antiphonal vocals and bendīr-based percussion;** *funk-rock drums and bass, with occasional piano*	All rise, hold candles, surround solo singer; *woman on pedestal wearing **all** white* (presumably Aminah, the Prophet's mother)
18	"al-Shaykh al-Kāmal" (The Perfect Master)	*ʻĪsāwiyya*	**Praise for Sīdī Ben ʻĪsā; healing; presence at the ḥaḍra; divine intoxication**	**Clapping and unison vocals; "Huwa" added by subgroup of singers; accelerando**	All standing, holding candles; swaying side to side
19	"al-Taḥiyya"	*n/a*	**n/a**	**Bendīr-based percussion**	

In the "Musical texture" and "Choreography and scenography" columns, entries in boldface indicate strategies of minimizing the contextual gap, while those in italics indicate strategies of maximizing the gap; entries in regular roman type indicate the most ambiguous actions.

competitive market for providing them. Indeed, in early twentieth-century Banī Khiyyār, the rivalry between the ʿĪsāwiyya (with which about three-fourths of the town was affiliated) and the Qādiriyya (which found support in the remaining quarter of the population) was so intense that it led to accusations of murder and resulted in a decree by local authorities forbidding one ṭarīqa from performing at domestic ceremonies without the other (Sassi 2014). When a branch of the Sulāmiyya ṭarīqa was established in the town, the pact between the ʿĪsāwiyya and the Qādiriyya started to fracture, along with the previous balance of sociopolitical control. By the 1930s the ʿĪsāwiyya and a weakening Qādiriyya had agreed to perform separately, but only because the Sulāmiyya was now competing for a share of the market. Eventually, the town's market for domestic Sufi performances was reduced to an ʿĪsāwiyya-Sulāmiyya rivalry that was magnified by nationalist anti-Sufi policies of the 1960s, which suppressed zāwiya activities but encouraged the performance of Sufi music outside the shrine (Sassi 2014).

Second, while the distinctive ritual activities of the ʿĪsāwiyya continued to attract local patrons, the Sulāmiyya underwent a transformation in which it eventually ceased its ritual ceremonies at the zāwiya and established itself as a sacred musical troupe. Significantly, they expanded their repertoire to include (and therefore potentially substitute for) other ṭarīqas, notably the ʿĪsāwiyya, Qādiriyya, and Ṭaybiyya; indeed, one section of the Sulāmiyya repertoire is called "Sulāmiyya," alongside these other repertoires, illustrating the evolution of the ṭarīqa into a professional musical troupe with a broad repertoire extending to adjacent ritual niches.[7] Thus, while table 6.1 identifies pieces from a variety of ṭarīqas, many of those songs are known in Tunisia primarily through their filtration through the Sulāmiyya repertoire rather than from the ṭarīqa of origin. Indeed, Sulāmiyya has become a generic term for a musical troupe that performs Sufi music and therefore provides a cultural precedent for the kind of admixture that occurs in *el-Hadhra.*

An additional, standard, and now classic moment in *el-Hadhra* is the live performance of the nūba "Ra'is al-Abḥār" by Hedi Doniya (see chap. 5), who participates in *el-Hadhra* only as a guest vocalist to sing this one work, which is also the only one in the spectacle to include mizwid. This is the only standard piece in *el-Hadhra* that comes from silsila-based ritual practices, yet it fits in seamlessly thanks in part to the modular nature of the spectacle's aesthetic approach. Its inclusion is a testament to the condition of ambient

7. *La Sulâmiyya: Chants soufis de Tunis* (CD 321025), issued by the Institut du Monde Arabe in Paris and distributed internationally by Harmonia Mundi, illustrates this clearly: more time on the recording is devoted to the group singing the repertoire of the Qādiriyya, Ṭaybiyya, and ʿĪsāwiyya than that of the Sulāmiyya.

Sufism, where references to shared saints reveal a spiritual commons while specific sonic strategies differentiate each ritual niche.

Structure and Choreography: Implications of Modularity

Each Sufi ṭarīqa in Tunisia has its own musicopoetic repertoire as well as its own ritual structure that organizes that content, highlighting the specificities of the ṭarīqa's history, doctrine, and practice. These different ritual structures nevertheless follow a logic of progression and intensification typically based on musical or sonic principles. As previous chapters illustrated, these may take the form of increases in tempo, rises in pitch, transitions from recitation to song, and the introduction of additional layers of percussion instruments and rhythms, as well as shifts from classical to dialectical Arabic and intensification of physical movement. The ritual experience is one of multiple layers of progression, as each piece or section undergoes elements of these transformations while playing a clearly defined part in contributing to the macro-level progression that structures the entire ritual. In other words, in ritual Sufism, the musical pieces are codependent; each song only makes musical and devotional sense in relation to those that precede and follow it. The ritual structure of the Sulāmiyya, for instance, adheres to the following sequence (Zeghonda 1991: 83–100), which includes musical-ritual trajectories from classical Arabic (parts 1–3) to dialectical Arabic (parts 4–8), from a cappella recitation in free rhythm (parts 1–4) to metered songs accompanied by percussion (parts 5–7), and, in its conclusion (part 8), a rise in pitch, tempo, and rhythmic density:

1. Recitation of the Qur'an and ḥizbs
2. *silsila al-dhahabiyya*: Sung poems written by Sīdī ʿAbd al-Salām
3. *silsila al-fuzūʿ*: Sung poems written by Sīdī ʿAbd al-Salām
4. Improvised sung poetry
5. *buḥūr* ("seas"): Call-and-response sung verses with percussion
6. *shaṭḥa* ("dance"): Like *buḥūr* but livelier
7. *khitm* ("finale"): Even faster rhythms
8. *tahlīla*: Chanting of the phrase *lā ilāha illā allāh* (there is no god but God), increasing in pitch and tempo

ʿĪsāwiyya rituals, as chapter 2 illustrates, also proceed through a succession of stages, but according to a different logic and additional goals. Each ritual stage adds a distinctive rhythmic layer and builds to a climax during the trance (takhmīr, "intoxication") section, when individuals are free to move out of the line of dancers to perform individual acts of trance:

1. Recitation of the ḥizb (a cappella, free rhythm)
2. shishtrī: Andalusī songs, including poems by Andalusī poet Abū Ḥasan al-Shushtarī, accompanied by ṭār (tambourine) and kettledrums (naqqārāt)
3. ḥaḍra, consisting of:
    1. wird al-qudūm (arrival liturgy): A cappella songs with regular pulse
    2. mjarred: Songs accompanied by handclaps in the five-beat mjarred rhythm
    3. brāwil (also called *takhmīr*): Drums enter, and trance, sometimes involving acts of self-mortification, ensues; songs in this section must adhere to the same melodic mode (ṭab')
        1. bṭāyḥī: Songs in the eight-beat rhythm of the same name
        2. dkhūl brāwil: Songs in the four-beat rhythm of the same name
        3. hrūbī: Songs in the two-beat rhythm of the same name[8]

The structure of *el-Hadhra*, in contrast, is a concertlike succession of independent songs. As such, it does not adhere to the idiomatic ritual trajectories of Tunisian Sufi ḥaḍras, with one exception: *el-Hadhra* begins with a chanted a cappella invocation (as do most Sufi rituals), which is followed immediately by "Yā Khūtī" (O Brothers), a song that is part of the wird al-qudūm (arrival liturgy) of the 'Īsāwiyya. The remaining pieces in *el-Hadhra* do not correspond to any ritual succession of songs. Instead, "Yā Khūtī" is followed by one song each from the Sulāmiyya, Ṭaybiyya, and Shādhuliyya, followed by seven additional Sulāmiyya songs (mixed freely from the ḅhūr, shaṭḥa, and khitm ritual sections), two more 'Īsāwiyya songs, and one song each from the 'Azūziyya, 'Alāwiyya, and Qādiriyya (see again table 6.1). The 'Īsāwiyya songs are situated in reverse order to which they appear in ritual: "Khammar Yā Khammār" (Serve the Wine, O Cupbearer), which is part of the final, energetic section of the ritual, appears early (song 7) in *el-Hadhra*, while "al-Shaykh al-Kāmal" (The Perfect Master), from the quieter, early mjarred section of the 'Īsāwiyya ritual, is the culminating song of the spectacle. The organization of musical material of *el-Hadhra*, then, maximizes the contextual gap between ritual and spectacle: it is not based on the ritual dictates of devotional Sufism, but rather is arranged according to aesthetic criteria, such as the juxtaposition of sonic textures and intensities, associated with concert and theater production values.

This strategy for appropriating and organizing musical material can be

8. This succession of rhythmic stages is repeated, with each sequence in a different melodic mode. Once the sequences are complete, the ceremony ends with songs in the eight-beat khammārī rhythm, accompanying a dancer named 'Akāsha who is wearing, and attempting to break, heavy chains attached to his wrists (see chap. 2).

considered modular in both form and function. In form, "modularity" refers to an ordering concept in which smaller parts or modules (here, both Sufi orders and their songs) are standardized and made interchangeable in order to fit flexibly within a larger architecture (here, the spectacle). In function, modularity is a powerful means for "confronting and managing complexity": each module "should encapsulate (or 'black box') its messy internal details, thus masking technical, organizational, cultural, and political conflicts to display only a consistent interface" (Russell 2012: 257–258). Tunisian Sufi orders are diverse not only in their ritual structures, but also in their socioeconomic positions, their roles in their communities, and their ideologies of devotion, including different understandings of the role of music in ritual and the nature or even permissibility of trance. *El-Hadhra* obscures the specificity of the Sufi orders; audience members are not told which song comes from which ṭarīqa. Indeed, a common theme in reviews of the spectacle is that *el-Hadhra* triumphed in overcoming the "curiosities" and "aggressive rituals" of the ṭarīqas, as well as their "conflicts" and "rivalries" (Ben Youssef 1993; Kahlawi 1999; Radhouane 1994), a process encapsulated in Jaziri's oft-repeated assertion that *el-Hadhra* transforms the religious into the mystical and "should not be confused with religion" (Ben Youssef 1993). The modular logic of extraction and reassembly transforms the Sufi orders into content providers and in effect creates a genre of Tunisian "Sufi music" by reorienting listeners away from the ṭarīqas and toward the reproductions' new lives as originals in their right.

Does this set-list form of modularity differ from that of the silsila, which could also be considered a modular form? While both are flexible and inclusive and present a survey of the local landscape of ambient Sufism, there are important differences between them. The silsila does not import other pieces wholesale from adjacent ritual practices and present them as exhibits of their ritual community of origin; rather, it embraces the spiritual figure associated with that adjacent practice, creates its own nūba for that figure, and thereby absorbs him or her into the soundworld of the adopting community. A crucial part of this process is ensuring that those pieces adhere to the constancy of timbre and texture that define the ritual tradition in question, in order to create a sequence of timbral, textural, and formal "sames" (that is, a series of nūbas) that serve to domesticate the adjacent tradition within the destination ritual community. What the silsila incorporates is spiritual figures; sounds, texts, and physical movements (trance dance) are entirely "of" the destination tradition. Only then are its *own* nūbas treated in modular fashion. In contrast, *el-Hadhra* re-presents and reconfigures the sounds of ritual material from numerous ritual niches, like islands of sound dropped into a new context. In other words, the silsila, as additive, transformative, and generative of new sonic material, emphasizes the *incorporative* potential of modularity, while *el-Hadhra*, which recontextualizes and reorders preexisting ritual material, highlights the *extractive* aspects of modularity.

This plug-and-play organizational approach also denies performers the possibility of experiencing the progression of states of consciousness that ritual is designed to carry participants through. *El-Hadhra* is not a staging of any actual ritual and does not attempt to represent the experiential journeys of ritual participants. Its choreography invents and standardizes new, impressionistic associations of music with movement by collectivizing individual movements that might be found in ritual, such as a dancer turning his head to the side, or by magnifying collective movements such as *el-Hadhra*'s lengthy extension of a slow, solemn, procession that both opens and closes the spectacle. Other aspects of choreography, such as slow whirling in flowing white robes, are not part of Tunisian Sufism but rather are appropriations of non-Tunisian Sufi traditions (in this case the Turkish Mevlevi, the so-called whirling dervishes). Some scenes provide impressionistic representations of lyrical content (e.g., several men carrying a woman on their shoulders to the song "Ibn Miryām," a Sulāmiyya song about Jesus and Mary), while others involve dramatic tumbling and acrobatic movements reminiscent of gymnastic and martial-arts practices. While such choreographed movements distance *el-Hadhra* from Sufi ritual, they are also interspersed with several instances of staged trance dances, in which a long-haired dancer kneels in the center of stage, rocking her head from side to side, which causes her hair to swing dramatically, that index trance movements at the heart of silsila-based healing traditions as well as at the peripheries of ḥaḍra ceremonies.[9]

These latter dances index familiar trance moves called *jedba* (lit. "attraction"), a common corporeal reaction to songs for saints that involves repeated bending forward and backward from the waist or the vigorous swinging of the head from side to side. Here participation and spectatorship blur as some of the women in the *el-Hadhra* audience perform these typical jedba movements. When attendees at *el-Hadhra* react in such a manner, there is little doubt that they are or have been involved in ritual forms of devotion and healing, demonstrating that cultural presentations retain the potential for audience "reception" (of spiritual entities and trance states) de-

9. As I described in chaps. 2 and 3, women often engage in such trance dances at 'Īsāwiyya, Shādhuliyya, and Tījāniyya ḥaḍras, where they are confined to an adjacent room, out of sight (but not earshot) of the men.

spite their formality as "presentation" (Spadola 2015). I often observed other attendees engaging with the music by performing traditional Arab dance moves typical of wedding receptions, while occasionally teenagers began to break-dance right in front of the stage. This variety of bodily reactions to the music encapsulates the ambiguity of staging Sufi music: for some the musical indexing of ritual context is inescapable, while for others the entertainment value of the concert setting gains primacy. Yet both are available simultaneously.

Intertextuality Begets Self-Referentiality

While *el-Hadhra* dismantles the ritual progressions of the specific ṭarīqas from which it draws its materials, it also reveals and capitalizes on certain shared elements of ambient Sufism, including a musical aesthetic of antiphonal singing and bendīr-based percussion, as well as shared lyrical themes. All of the pieces praise God, the Prophet Muhammad, other prophets, and one or more saints. Taken together, they evoke a spiritual topography of the urban landscape of shrines and, by extension, the rituals held at those shrines. *El-Hadhra*, in its plug-and-play plurality, evokes this vast landscape and reveals a lyrical intertextuality of shared themes and phrases that permeate Sufi repertoires in Tunisia. These themes include the healing capacity of saints, narrations of the act of visiting the saint's shrine, the power of music in transforming consciousness, metaphors of trance as divine intoxication, and themes from the history of Islam, such as the birth of the Prophet and his grandsons Hassan and Husayn. Many songs reference the ḥaḍra ritual itself, drawing attention to the power of these music-driven devotional rituals. In "al-Layl al-Zāhī" (Magnificent Night), from the Sulāmiyya repertoire, the dual meaning of ḥaḍra as ceremony and as the "presence" of the saint is evoked:

yā nās ānā min awlāduh	O people, I am one of his children
bābā asmār ḥaḍratuh mursūma	Baba Asmar's ḥaḍra is established
al-layl al-zāhī	The night is magnificent
bil-qamr w-ājnāduh	from the full moon and his soldiers
w-ānā zāhī	And I am magnificent
bi-qdurtī w-awrāduh	from my strength and his sung liturgies

The main theme of "Hayya Nzūrū" (Let's Go Visit), from the 'Azūziyya repertoire, is making the visit to the saint's shrine for the ḥaḍra, which has the power to heal:

hayyā nzūrū shaykhnā bil-'āda	Let's go visit our shaykh, as is our custom
sīdī 'alī 'azūz muḥammī awlāduh	Sīdī 'Alī 'Azūz protects his children
mā aḥlā al-ḥaḍra	There is nothing sweeter than the ḥaḍra
wal-shama' waqqāda	And its illuminating candles
ahiyya al-nasrī illī yudhūqhā yibrā	Those who taste its water will be healed

The arrival of the saint at the ḥaḍra ceremony and his healing effect on participants is the theme of "al-Shaykh al-Kāmal" (The Perfect Master) from the 'Īsāwiyya:

dāwīlī qalbī	He heals my heart
yibrā min sharr al-'ayūb	and cures the evil of my faults
al-shaykh jā' lil-ḥaḍra	the shaykh came to the ḥaḍra
w-asqānī mashrūbī	and poured me my drink
w-asqānī min kisānū	From his cup he served me
khamra rabbāniyya	divine wine
bihā nilt masarra	which delighted me
w-nilt marghūbī	and satisfied my desires

The concept of the Sufi ḥaḍra carries with it the assumption that the musical experience is central to the ceremony. Some songs make explicit reference to the power of music. "Fāres Baghdād" (Horseman of Baghdad; from the Qādiriyya repertoire) invokes the power of music to effect devotional passion and to broadcast the power of the saint (in this case, Sīdī 'Abd al-Qādir al-Jilānī) across nations:

'ashqī jā' fi-ṭṭār wa-funūn qwiyya	My passion comes from the tambourine and the powerful arts
nasma' al-inshād tuṭfā nīrānī	Listening to the songs puts out my fire
yabdā ṭablī yufazza' kull bilād	My drum wakes all the countries
min fās li-baghdād barrā wa-bḥūrī	From Fez to Baghdad, by land and by sea

The lyrical self-referentiality of songs of the ritual ḥaḍra takes on an additional layer of meaning when those songs are recruited for the stage of *el-Hadhra*. The use of the same term to refer to ritual (ḥaḍra) and the staged spectacle (*el-Hadhra*) creates a semantic slippage that elides the two contexts, allowing the spectacle, with all its acoustic and visual references to ritual, to become the object to which the term "ḥaḍra" refers. Such a productive ambiguity, I should clarify, is not about blurring the lines between the spectacle and ritual—attendees are well aware that *el-Hadhra* is not a bona fide substitute for the ritual practices of Sufis. Rather, it is about asserting the validity of *el-Hadhra* as a means of *accessing* the power of ritual, namely, through its music. The lyrics to songs such as "Fāres Baghdād," which reference the power of music, are equally productive for *el-Hadhra*, for they reinforce the message that the music itself has devotional and social power and is therefore extractable from ritual and available for recontextualization in spectacle, where its main aesthetics remain, for the most part, intact. It is to this last point that I now turn.

Musical Texture: The Enduring Appeal of Ritual Aesthetics

Musically, the dominant aesthetic of *el-Hadhra* consists of antiphony between a solo vocalist and a large chorus of singers, accompanied by a large percussion section of more than twenty drummers playing the bendīr, an instrument whose buzzing timbre immediately indexes local trance-ritual music. This musical texture is common to all the Sufi orders represented in the spectacle (with the exception of the Shādhuliyya, which does not use percussion instruments) and is present in all selections of *el-Hadhra*. Atop this foundation of traditional vocals and percussion, most pieces in *el-Hadhra* also adopt musical instruments, such as electric bass, electric guitar, keyboards, drum set, saxophone, violin, and *nāy*, that are not part of ritual practice. They are deployed in a variety of ways, resulting in different musical textures that could be placed on a spectrum ranging from songs that closely imitate ritual performance, with virtually no nonritual instrumentation (e.g., "al-Shaykh al-Kāmal"), to songs dominated by nonritual instruments playing in an arrangement distinctly inspired by jazz or funk (e.g., "Lawlā al-Luṭf").

The majority of songs fall somewhere between these two extremes. In several pieces the nonritual instruments are mainly relegated to a secondary role in relation to the dominant vocals and percussion. For example, in songs 3, 9, 12, and 15, the only additional instrument is an electric bass that follows the vocal melody closely and is mixed at low volume, making it relatively unobtrusive. In several other songs, keyboards, saxophone, violin, and/or nāy are featured, but only in interjections between song sections, so that they do not overtake the traditional vocal and percussion.

In "Lawlā al-Luṭf," however, the keyboards, electric bass, and drum set take over the sound and impose a jazz arrangement over the vocals and percussion, adding a new layer of listener associations and expectations based on the musical norms, such as swung rhythms and bluesy chord progressions, of jazz (video ex. 6.2).[10] Such cosmopolitan fusions have become a flash point of debate surrounding *el-Hadhra*. For Fadhel Jaziri they are necessary improvements, for "without development, tradition is a dead weight" (Medded 2000). Some commentators who are highly supportive of the concept of *el-Hadhra*, such as Muhammad Kahlawi, nevertheless find these additions "unnecessary" and even "foolish" transformations of an already beautiful and expressive Tunisian Sufi heritage (1999: n.p.). Indeed, it seems that *el-Hadhra* continued to attract large audiences despite of, not because of, Jaziri's musical "updates." *Hadhra 2010* is a case in point.

Hadhra 2010 was a product of Jaziri's concern that, like the Sufi traditions his spectacle drew on, *el-Hadhra* itself was becoming "fossilized." By most accounts, *Hadhra 2010* had more in common with the MTV Arabia and Rotana pop-music-video channels than with the sounds of devotional rituals. While the white-robed singers and drummers continued to fill the stage, in front of them rock and pop-music aesthetics were more prominent, with an electric guitarist playing flashy solos and singing in front of a microphone positioned at the front and center of the stage. Flamenco costumes, blasts of shimmering glitter, and dance numbers choreographed in the style of pop-music videos dashed the expectations of the audience (see web figs. 6.1w and 6.2w). Gone were the now-standard songs, such as "Yā Belḥassen Yā Shādhlī" and "al-Layl al-Zāhī," that had been reliable crowd pleasers and made household names by *el-Hadhra*. Instead of the loud cheers characteristic of audience reactions to previous versions of *el-Hadhra*, boos and hisses emanated from parts of a crowd so overwhelmingly disappointed that they also chanted "*Hadhra! Hadhra!*" (a demand for the old *Hadhra* they expected to witness). Postperformance interviews with audience members, aired later on Hannibal TV, revealed two main reactions, the spirits of which could be seen in the ensuing heated media commentary and criticism. Positive reactions tended to describe Jaziri as first and foremost an artist, and therefore expected to push boundaries to realize his vision. *El-Hadhra* was described by many as a product of Jaziri's artistry, a modernized spectacle, adhering not to the cultural expectations of Sufism but rather to those of the artistic "cocktail" or *shakshuka* (lit. "mixture," referring to a breakfast

10. Video ex. 6.2 is available (starting at 3:12) at https://www.youtube.com/watch?v=36oysXWSNJs.

stew), the cut-and-paste theatrical approach that commonly animates institutionalized musical performances in Tunisia. More critical reactions called it something "foreign" or bemoaned the continued absence of Samir Agrebi, while many simply replied that it was "not the real *el-Hadhra*." Jaziri defended his artistic decisions, explained that *Hadhra 2010* was designed to appeal to the youth, and in radio interviews on Mosaïque FM later admitted that, because of the entrenched audience expectations he had established with his prior versions, the spectacle had become very difficult to update. In the following years he toned down his adoption of pop music sounds and stagecraft, and by 2015 *el-Hadhra* had returned to its former approach—based on a foundation of Sufi songs and sounds, choreography that evoked ritual dance and trance but sometimes stretched into the realms of martial arts and acrobatics, and more judicious use of rock aesthetics by showcasing them in a few select pieces (see video ex. 6.1). Most members of the audience within my line of sight used those rock-inspired selections—that is, the pieces with the greatest contextual gap—as opportunities to sit down (often checking or posting to social media) after expending energy on their feet dancing, cheering, and singing along to songs that demonstrated minimal contextual gap.

SPECTACLE, RITUAL, AND CHAINS OF VALUE

These reactions to differences in musical texture and instrumentation, whether in the audience reaction to the 2015 version of *el-Hadhra* or the controversy generated by *Hadhra 2010*, reveal the high value the listening public placed on the musical sounds that most closely indexed those of Sufi ritual. Can spectacle substitute for ritual? Are the two cultural forms mutually exclusive? Is it even useful to maintain the categories of spectacle and ritual as analytical units?

Don Handelman (1997) argues that ritual and spectacle are mutually incompatible because they adhere to different "metalogics." The metalogic of ritual, for Handelman, is one of transformation: ritual has a stated outcome, enacting some kind of change (in participants or society). It is self-regulated and based on uncertainty; that is, some parts may need to be repeated or changed in the moment, and failure is a potential outcome. Spectacle, on the other hand, is presentational, mirroring the vision of its designers, and is associated with the social logics of bureaucratic statecraft and its practices of classification. Spectacles invent and imagine nationhood and the civic collectivity through the act of displaying culture in such an open and totalizing manner that analyses must ask what is being excluded, transformed, or disguised. In other words, it creates order out of the perceived disorder of lived reality, while ritual (despite doing its own ordering work) is treated as part of that disorder.

Yet, as forms of performance, both spectacle and ritual share certain features that suggest they should not always be treated as categorically opposed and mutually exclusive. Richard Schechner (1985), for example, argues that all performance moves between the two poles of ritual efficacy and theatrical entertainment. Just as rituals are also entertaining, with great care taken in preparing musical and physical aspects, so too can spectacles take on aspects of ritual in their interventions in social and individual lives. The ambiguous relationship between spectacle and ritual is further complicated when, as in the case of *el-Hadhra*, the concept of the spectacle explicitly relies on ritual content. In this case it might be useful to consider spectacle as a conduit or node in a series of "chains of value" that extend into the world of ritual.[11]

First, *el-Hadhra* is a node in the chain of value between audiences and the ritual practices of the Sufi orders. Despite its obfuscation of many elements of those rituals, *el-Hadhra* nevertheless provides a means of access to ritual experience for audiences, albeit one that is highly mediated and filtered. It is not a reproduction of ritual but rather an evocation of it, prompting work of the listeners' imagination; the spectacle references shrines, saints, and traditions that factor into the lived environment and histories of many Tunisians, often connecting to familial memories. Yet it does so without requiring the effort or investment in making one's way to the zāwiya, a commitment that typically involves the immediacy and responsibility of entering into new social and spiritual relationships. While *el-Hadhra* may allow audiences to bypass such efforts, this is not to say it is devoid of religious meaning; rather, the spectacle sharpens audience awareness of Tunisia's Sufi landscapes and practices. Indeed, in the wake of the attacks on Sufi shrines, the heightened security—including metal detectors, bag searches, and public and private security guards—surrounding *el-Hadhra* and similar events, as well as the national news coverage of Essebsi's visit to the Shādhuliyya Sufi order, the effect was magnified. The chain of value between audiences and ritual experiences also extends to the state's concern to demonstrate Sufism—in the zāwiya and onstage—as acceptable forms of religious citizenship emblematic of the nation at large.

On a broader level, *el-Hadhra* and ritual Sufism share in demonstrating

11. I am indebted to Martin Zillinger and Dorothea Schulz for this formulation, which is the title of their conference Making and Breaking Chains of Value: Rethinking Cultural Commodities (January 24–25, 2017, Cologne, Germany), where portions of this chapter were presented.

that aesthetic pleasure is paramount to the religious experience. The enduring popularity of *el-Hadhra*, as well as the controversy surrounding *Hadhra 2010*, shows that audiences expect and value an entertainment experience that clearly indexes Sufi ritual, with the dominant musical aesthetics of the zāwiya intact. Indeed, *el-Hadhra*'s prominence in the public spiritual economy is based on music. While the act of turning complex local traditions into aesthetic presentations introduces tensions and loss, it can also produce new things and possibilities (see Guss 2000; Kirshenblatt-Gimblett 1998). The idea of a globally valid genre of "Sufi music" may be untenable musically, but it is attractive to world-music marketers (Bohlman 1997; Shannon 2003), and *el-Hadhra* has succeeded in genrifying local Sufi music. Its process of extraction, recombination, and presentation flattens out difference, highlights similarities, and distills this diverse material through the singular sonic aesthetics of the *el-Hadhra* ensemble.

A second chain of value mediated by *el-Hadhra* is the one connecting to the idea of a Tunisian music and the anxiety over a supposed lack of a living national musical tradition. For *el-Hadhra*'s producers and many commentators, Tunisian music lost its identity because it moved away from Sufism, and to Sufism it must return if it is to establish a "viable national music promoted globally" (Kahlawi 1999). The influential Tunisian author and music critic Mustapha Chelbi argues that "if Arab music is suffering from a loss of memory and identity, it is because it has lost its connection to the art of *tajwid* [melodic Qur'anic recitation] and the music of Sufism" (Chelbi 1999), a sentiment echoed by many commentators on *el-Hadhra*. Although Tunisian musical nationalism is generally associated with cultural-policy makers and public institutions involving Andalusī music in the mid-twentieth century, the idea of individual artists such as Agrebi and Jaziri creating something new out of Sufi music seemed to assuage some nationalist anxieties over the supposed absence of a representative Tunisian musical tradition at the turn of the twenty-first century. Sufi music, framed as a cultural resource to be discovered, extracted, and researched, was construed as a living but comatose tradition, with the Sufi ṭarīqas barely preserving a tradition that lay "lethargic for five centuries" (Ben Youssef 1993) or came from a "time we forgot" (Catzaras 1993). From this perspective, the ṭarīqas are viewed not as the rightful owners of Sufi tradition, but rather as inept caretakers who have failed to make their music up to date and relevant for a broader swath of Tunisian society. This ambiguity between a lost yet available musical repertoire allows projects such as *el-Hadhra* to claim rediscovery while relying on the knowledge and expertise of living Sufi shaykhs, whose melodies, rhythms, and lyrics are highly valued but whose musical contexts, forms, functions, and techniques (not to mention politics) are considered expendable.[12] Thus, through its processes of selective and simultaneous valorization and devaluation, spectacle not only perpetuates nationalism's logics of cultural extraction and presentation, but also masks the things it displays, providing an indirect critique of the very traditions it purports to re-present.

That *el-Hadhra* acts as an implicit critique of Sufi ritual while providing audiences with an alternative means of accessing Sufi ritual content is a fundamental ambiguity of the spectacle. This ambiguity is perhaps more productively conceptualized as a set of specific ambiguities, made legible in this chapter through attention to the spectacle's methods for both maximizing and minimizing the contextual gap between ritual and the concert stage in the domains of organization, choreography, lyrical intertextuality, and musical texture. And this set of ambiguities in turn enables multiple and sometimes contradictory chains of value to be activated simultaneously, including access to ritual aesthetics, an anti-Islamist posture, a recovery of heritage, a critique of traditional Sufism, the promise of a national music, and a modern individualistic artistic accomplishment.

In this spiritual economy, music is the currency that activates those chains of value; it is a resource treated as separable from the social and religious practices that created it. Yet because music encourages work of the imagination, the spectacle nevertheless provides a means of access to ritual. What makes music so effective in this regard is its ability to *be* the experience, not just a representation of it, even in recontextualized situations. In semiotic terms, it is music's role as an index, rather than as a symbol, that provides satisfaction in listeners (see Turino 1999). That *el-Hadhra* and its kindred spectacles maintain so many ritual musical elements suggests it is the specificity of its referents—that is, its indexical associations with socially meaningful landmarks, institutions, histories, and spiritual personalities and practices—that have made its transition to the concert stage largely successful for audience members, who, in their insistence on access to ritual aesthetics, remind us that entertainment, pleasure, and the religious experience are not mutually exclusive.

12. Rehearsals for *el-Hadhra* often included professional singers training the Sufi shaykhs in "proper" (that is, Western conservatory) vocal techniques (Haythem Hadhiri, pers. comm., 2015).

7
CONCLUSION
Ritual Niches and the Social Work of Musical Form

The chapters of this book have charted several interwoven paths through a densely populated topography of ambient Sufism where, even within the limited geographical confines of urban Tunis, over seventy saints and spirits receive targeted musical treatment in the form of praise songs. That number jumps to well over a hundred if we take into consideration spiritual figures who are simply mentioned in these songs and other recitations. While the origins of those spiritual figures range from the local to distant—across North Africa, sub-Saharan Africa, and the Middle East—they are active and activated locally. The ritual musical forms of the communities examined in these pages act in selective and centripetal fashion to draw inward and include those spiritual figures that factor into each community's social identity.

Throughout this terrain of ambient Sufism, ritual authority is widely distributed, located in the voices of women, "intoxicated" Sufis, black Tunisians, Jews, singers at drinking parties, and even musical instruments that "speak to" and summon unseen beings. The case studies of this book, then, contribute to an emerging literature that challenges prevailing assumptions about authority in Islamic practice. Shahab Ahmed (2016) argues that academic and popular discourse about Islam has disproportionately focused on prescriptive authority, with an overriding emphasis on the regulation of behavior determined by legalistic interpretations of revelatory text. This emphasis on the regulatory, for Ahmed, has resulted in an overdetermined sense of contradiction when considering, for example, the historically and geoculturally widespread practices of music, figurative art, erotic poetry, wine drinking, and Sufism throughout the Islamic world. Such deeply entrenched social and artistic practices, Ahmed argues, are more productively analyzed by taking into account what he calls "explorative authority," the formation of moral selves involving the "urge to *explore and expand the dimensions of the meaningful*" (2016: 286; emphasis in original). Explorative authority, in contrast to the orthodoxizing impulse of prescriptive authority, allows for and celebrates ambiguity, ambivalence, and a multiplicity of truths and "constitutes the historical *bulk* of the normative discursive tradition of Muslims" (2016: 285–286; emphasis in original).

The case of rebaybiyya (chap. 5) demonstrates how non-Muslims historically have had access to such authority and were active in the social and musical practices of ambient Sufism as coparticipants with their Muslim neighbors. That these practices are distributed across all social fields in Tunisian society, across boundaries of religion, gender, ethnicity, and class, also reveals how such explorative authority inheres in the prevailing belief in the Islamic world that all members of society have direct access to the "revelatory potential of the invisible realm" (Taneja 2018: 6). Studies on revelatory dreams in Egypt (Mittermaier 2011), saintly visions at a shrine in India (Taneja 2018), and dancers inhabited by possessing spirits in Morocco (Kapchan 2007), to name a few, reveal the continuing normative nature of such expectations of direct access to the otherwise unseen.

The abundance of ritual niches associated with specific religious, gender, ethnic, and class backgrounds complicates this radically inclusive nature of exploratory authority. If each ritual niche of ambient Sufism intercedes with the unseen world of saints and spirits in its own distinctive way and there is mutual recognition and a high degree of interdependence between them, a sense of hierarchy is also evident. The case of the Shādhuliyya is illustrative. The Shādhuliyya is unequivocally the most highly esteemed Sufi order in the region and is looked upon as a paragon of social respectability and Sufi propriety. As the "mother of all Sufi orders" (*umm al-ṭuruq*) in Tunis, the Shādhuliyya has a structural supremacy owing to its founder Sīdī Belḥassen's location at the apex of the local Sufi genealogy. The hierarchy, however, is not absolute. The Shādhuliyya cements its place in society in part through its own recognition of adjacent ritual communities that, in turn, recognize its authority. Yet the Shādhuliyya do not have a monopoly on the spiritual intercession of its founding saint Sīdī Belḥassen, whose spiritual presence is routinely summoned and deployed by musicians of the Mannūbiyya, sṭambēlī, rebaybiyya, and mizwid communities. The Shādhuliyya host ritually adjacent communities whose "excessive" or "superstitious" practices their members sometimes criticize. They visit the shrine of Sayyda Mannūbiyya weekly (and dedicate a room to her) and acknowledge the healing premises of these adjacent communities by welcoming patients from them to be healed at their own ceremonies (albeit in a separate room). There is, then, a structural condition in which the authority of the Shādhuliyya relies in part on the circumvention of its own place atop the hierarchy. Such "coherent contradictions" are defining features of Ahmed's (2016: 405) explorative authority in Islam and illustrate that, while the fluid relationships that obtain in the context of ambient Sufism do boundary-crossing work, they do not efface—on the contrary, they often reinforce—those boundaries.

The boundaries between the ritual niches of ambient Sufism are rendered through each community's cultivation of specific musical practices, but these practices are based on shared underlying sonic and social principles that also transcend those boundaries. In what follows, I pull the analytical threads of the previous chapters together to offer a perspective on music and trance that asserts that the underacknowledged yet substantial social and cultural work of trance musics is thoroughly intertwined with, and just as important as, the trance states they elicit.[1] This approach is founded on the dynamic between two thoroughly interrelated aspects of the sonic-temporal experience: first, the large-scale structuring of ritual through sound; and second, specific sonic processes that balance constancy and continuity, on the one hand, with transformation, on the other.

TIMBRAL CONSTANCY AND SONIC CONTINUITY

When considering the entirety of the ritual musical experience from start to finish, certain sonic principles may be so foundational that they may at first elude analytical attention. The importance of the continuity of sound and constancy of timbre and texture is a case in point. These elements provide participants a steady sonic experience of reliable layers of sound, devoid of situations that demand shifts of attention or introduce jarring changes. This steadiness, however, does not preclude excitement and interest from development and transformation, which are produced by specific strategies of intensification that do not violate the foundational principles of constancy and continuity.

Each ritual niche in ambient Sufism is strictly defined by its instrumentation and accompanying timbres and texture. Every song of a silsila is a product of the proprietary, reliably predictable soundworld of its troupe, and ritual efficacy relies on the distinctive timbral aspects of each ritual community's sonic aesthetics. The metallic tones of the shqāshiq and the subtle buzz and percussive sound of the gumbrī define every song of the sṭambēlī silsila

1. Because of my overriding concern for the musical conditions for trance rather than the mechanisms of trance consciousness, my analysis here is not incompatible with, but rather should be construed as complementing, theoretical approaches to the psychology of trance such as Becker (2004).

and announce sub-Saharan connections that situate sṭambēlī musicians as specialists in dealing with the spiritual unseen. Sīdī Aḥmed al-Tījānī won't descend into a trance ritual that involves the jangling cymbals of the Mannūbiyya tambourines, while Sayyda Mannūbiyya demands that thick timbral spectrum in order to be summoned in ritual and cannot tolerate the clear tones of the drum of the women's Tījāniyya. The piercing, reedy sound of the mizwid and the understated buzz of the snares of the bendīr are definitive of rebaybiyya, whose traces remain in the sacred repertoire of the mizwid genre. Crucially, these instruments never stop playing in the course of a nūba, creating a continuous and overwhelming timbral saturation of the sonic atmosphere.

The few exceptions prove the rule. When the Mannūbiyya switch out their tambourines for drums with no cymbals or snares for the song of Sīdī Aḥmed, they are acknowledging the central role of timbre—in this case the clarity of tone—for the women of the Tījāniyya, who are treated as guests. When the gumbrī is replaced by the ṭabla for pre-sunset sṭambēlī ceremonies, the ṭabla takes on the same principles of timbral constancy and continuity of sound as the gumbrī. And when the rebaybiyya troupe adopts the shqāshiq from sṭambēlī, it does so in order to index sṭambēlī's own timbral saturation, all without losing its own timbral emphasis on bagpipes and bendīr. In the ʿĪsāwiyya ḥaḍra, each ritual section is defined by its own consistent timbre; when there is a change in timbre through the addition of a layer of texture (e.g., the handclaps in the mjarred or the drum ensemble in the shishtrī or ḥaḍra sections), these are major transitions, highlighted by emphatic signaling, that mark the close of one ritual section and the beginning of another, each with its own defining, and unceasing, timbral essence. An individual's trance never straddles these sections; trance episodes occur within the confines of a single ritual section defined by a singular timbral spectrum.[2]

Vocals also contribute to this timbral condition. The timbre of sṭambēlī vocals index a "non-Arabic" (ʿajmī) and sub-Saharan (sūdānī) aesthetic. These vocals are distinctive for *not* producing the expected clarity and diction of Arabic song but instead using a nasal, understated timbre and manner of delivery that elides words drawn from sub-Saharan and Arabic languages. When the Mannūbiyya sing about suffering, unjust accusations of shame, and the pride of motherhood, these messages are inextricably entwined with the timbral quality of the women's higher-register call-and-response

2. Walid's assertion that, for him, takhmīr begins in the ḥizb section (chap. 2) does not contradict this statement. Trance states can be interrupted and the flow of trance restarted in a new section. Indeed, between major ritual sections Walid, like other participants, leaves the ritual area to socialize and rehydrate.

singing. In silsila-based practices, when the vocals cease it is often at a point of heightened ritual affect to highlight the lead instrument, whether it is to refocus on the jangly tambourines Sayyda Mannūbiyya prefers or to underscore the gumbrī's or mizwid's communications with the world of saints and spirits. When vocals are the primary vehicle of performance, as is the case with the ḥizb of the ʿĪsāwiyya, timbral constancy is also a virtue. The antiphonal structure of the vocals, in which half the group sings while the other half catches their breath, ensures the maintenance of unceasing waves of vocal recitations in which the timbre of forceful, emphatic communal male recitation and singing continues unabated.

Like this structure of antiphonal singing, the playing techniques and morphology of the musical instruments encourage this continuity of sound. The mizwid bagpipes are designed with the express purpose of producing continuous sound, and the gumbri's resonating metallic plate and playing technique ensure that each articulation of the instrument overlaps in time with subsequent attacks to create a large acoustic envelope with a long (and never fully realized) decay. When these ritual musics are recontextualized to concert stages or popular-music realms, it is common for musicians to do away with this continuity of sound, a transformation that further illustrates the ritual importance of this constancy. In mass-mediated mizwid music, for example, the mizwid alternates with lead vocals, pausing to shift attention to the lyrics and solo voice. In fusion sṭambēlī, the gumbrī alternates with other instruments and is often played without the resonating metallic plate that extends and thickens the sound of the instrument. These changes to the music when recontextualized outside of ritual demonstrate (by breaking the rule) that the ritual functions of these musics demand a continuity of sound. From the perspective of the patient who dances for healing purposes, this constancy and continuity provide the comfort of predictable, uninterrupted sound to support trance. On a broader level, adhering to the general virtues of constancy of timbre and continuity of sound does the connective work of establishing each ritual niche as fully "of" the world of ambient Sufism, while the specifics of each niche's timbre and texture do the boundary work of distinguishing them from each other.

INTENSIFICATION AND TRANSFORMATION

This insistent continuity of sound and constancy of timbre should not be taken to suggest that ritual is about a series of unchanging musical events. Indeed, these continuities and constancies are necessary conditions for the sonic and musical transformations that are normative, defining features of ambient Sufism. The most prominent of these is intensification. The analyses of ritual musical form in the preceding chapters produced a perspective on intensification encapsulated in a tripartite model consisting of discrete, sequential, and global intensification (DI, SI, and GI) processes. All three involve an increase in sonic density; that is, they generate intensity through an increase in the number of sound events per time unit.

DI occurs when a single cyclic pattern systematically increases in tempo and/or pitch level. Tempo increase is the standard means of intensification in the nūba form of silsila-based musics and is closely associated with trance. The acceleration increases the frequency of beat onsets, corresponding to an increase in the speed, sonic density, and intensity of the movement of dancers. The dance associated with DI may be individual, as in the healing trance associated with the silsila, or communal, as in the line dance of the ʿĪsāwiyya ḥaḍra. The process of DI also commonly involves increasingly compressed rhythmic and melodic units, frequently with shorter call-and-response volleys or unison phrases. Sṭambēlī is distinctive in that its process of DI also commonly involves rhythmic elasticity, a state in which acceleration produces a subtle and gradual compression of the rhythmic pattern that leads to metric transformation. Dhikr formulas of Sufi orders such as the ʿĪsāwiyya, Tījāniyya, and Shādhuliyya may also transform metric perception through compression, for example in the contraction of the *al-lah* dhikr phrase from a pattern of four beats (1 + 3) to three beats (1 + 2) or the *lā ilaha illā allah* that gradually reshapes its rhythmic pattern to approximate the fazzānī drum pattern. These examples constitute transformations in temporality not only by accelerating musical time and increasing sonic density, but also by transforming the organization of time units metrically. These discrete temporal intensifications (DTIs) may be distinguished from intensification through systematic rises in pitch or discrete pitch intensifications (DPIs); passages such as the dhikr formulas that use both simultaneously can be further categorized as discrete temporal and pitch intensifications (DTPIs). All forms of DI, then, are internally transformative: they cycle through a discrete musical phrase, transforming it gradually.

With SI, in contrast, that transformation is external; that is, it proceeds by switching to an entirely different pattern that structurally exhibits more sonic density than the one preceding it. This sense of increased intensity in SI is realized by proceeding through a prescribed series of rhythmic patterns such that each rhythmic modulation leads to shorter rhythmic cycles, a sense of fewer "beats," and faster subdivisions. Both the shishtrī and takhmīr sections of the ʿĪsāwiyya ḥaḍra feature these sequential intensifications. The shishtrī follows a rhythmic sequence from bṭāyḥī to dkhūl brāwil to brāwil to khatm, each rhythm shorter and faster, with the closing khatm rhythm featuring the fast short-long pattern it shares with mjarred handclaps and the most common dhikr pattern (*al-lah*), while the takhmīr section follows a similar rhythmic sequence from bṭāyḥī ʿīsāwī to dkhul brāwil to hrūbī. In this context, a group of songs performed in order to realize such prescribed sequences is called a "nūba," a use of the term that is aligned with the broader definition used in Andalusī music across North Africa.

SI is an important feature of the silsila, although there it is less systematic and may be interrupted. In the silsila, SI takes the form of a short sequence of nūbas considered linked together that modulate rhythmically. The Mannūbiyya silsila, for example, sometimes features such groupings, particularly pairings that move from a nūba in the four-beat fazzānī rhythm to one in the shorter three-beat khatm rhythm, which increases sonic density through a rise in tempo along with faster subdivisions and beat onsets. This shift from four-beat to three-beat rhythms shares general principles of contraction and reduction with the DI of sṭambēlī's sūdānī rhythm and the ʿĪsāwiyya dhikr, both of which compress to three pulses in the culmination of their processes of intensification.[3] The rebaybiyya silsila begins with the stately 8/4 steftūḥ rhythm, followed by a fast 12/8 rhythm for the saints Sīdī Bū Saʿīd and Lilla ʿArbiyya, before adding further intensification through adopting four-pulse sṭambēlī rhythms, all without stopping between pieces. The increase in sonic density is striking and quantifiable: in this rebaybiyya example, the number of rhythmic cells played per minute more than doubles from forty to ninety-two. SI is an especially clear example of how principles that are shared in the musical commons of ambient Sufism are nevertheless realized in different ways that reveal the distinctiveness of each ritual niche within it.

GI involves a larger-scale increase in sonic density throughout a section or entire ritual. Here, GI relates to changes in texture involving an increase in timbral density through adding layers of instruments, as is most apparent in the third and final section of the ḥaḍra, in which the musicians progress from a cappella singing to accompanying themselves with handclaps and, finally, adding drums. Generally speaking, GI is more prevalent in ḥaḍra ritual forms than in their more steady-state silsila counterparts. In most ṭarīqas, a cappella recitation precedes more frankly musical activities, which take a different form for each ṭarīqa but generally adhere to strategies of development (e.g., moving from classical to dialectical Arabic) and forms of

3. SI can also take the form of upward modulations of melodic mode, though this is less common in the Maghreb than in the eastern Arab world. Such modulations move up the scale of a mode stepwise, performing pieces in the new mode established on each new pitch plateau. In Egypt, Marcus (2012: 52–53) describes the stepwise upward modulations through a series of melodic modes (*rāst* on C, *bayyātī* on D, *sīkah* on E𝄳, *jahārkāh* on F), while Shannon (2006: 216–217 n. 31) describes three such patterns in Syria, where the process is called *tarqiyya* (elevation), a term that connects elevation in pitch with elevation of the spirit.

intensification. Nested intensifications, which involve the overlap of two or more layers of intensification, generate considerable ritual affect. The dramatic clap of the shaykh al-ḥaḍra in the ʿĪsāwiyya ḥaḍra marks a climactic moment of arrival as it signals the end of one episode of DI, the beginning of a sequence of SI, and the establishment of a new plateau of GI. It is my conviction that the reason this moment is such a profound climactic point is largely due to its location at the intersection of several trajectories of intensification, which combines the culminatory power of DI with the confirmatory power of GI and the anticipatory power of SI (and its inherent episodes of additional DI).

In all their forms, individual components of GI and SI also typically undergo DI before switching to the next pattern in the sequence. The result is a situation of nested intensifications, each becoming increasingly faster, denser, more compressed, and/or higher, thus situating listeners within multiple temporal frames, along with their respective teleologies, simultaneously. Expressed as such, this tripartite model is about the *scale* of intensification. DI concerns the internal transformation of a single phrase or musical unit of the same rhythmic pattern, SI involves a sequence of multiple units with differing rhythmic patterns, and GI occurs over a large scale and can transcend or subsume DI and GI. The *method* of intensification, however, can be extracted from these designations for a more fine-grained analysis. DI, as illustrated above, is internally *transformational*, undergoing gradual changes in temporality and pitch. SI is *modulatory*, in that it takes the form of a sequence of pieces whereby each successive piece intensifies through rhythmic (or pitch plateau) modulations. GI, in the examples in this book, is about *layered* methods of intensification, whereby layers of sound are gradually added to the sonic texture to increase sonic density. So, whereas DI, SI, and GI are primarily about scale, their respective processes of internal transformation, modulation, and textural accretion indicate methods of intensification.

This model of three forms of intensification is a way to locate, give a name to, and encourage analytical attention to processes of transformation that are central to the musical "journey" (riḥla) of the ritual experience. Yet this model, the transformations it emphasizes, and the larger sense of journey all rely on the virtues of continuity of sound and constancy of timbre and texture. Transformation, in the musical potencies of ambient Sufism (table 7.1), is thoroughly contingent upon a foundation of constancy.

Attention to intensification also sheds light on other nonritual musics in Tunisia. In some cases, the relationship is clear: as chapter 5 illustrates, DI is also a common feature of local mass-mediated popular music, namely mizwid, a genre that emerged in the late twentieth century but that has a ritual genealogy reaching back to rebaybiyya; musicians performing nonritual mizwid music not only recognize the ritual origins of the genre, but also point to specific aspects of intensification—such as increases in tempo toward the end of a song and shorter, cyclic melodic phrases—as indexing the ritual function of music related to trance. In other cases, a less linear and more intertwined, synergetic relationship between ritual and nonritual contexts is suggested, because SI is also a defining feature of art music (mālūf) and the ʿĪsāwiyya's cultivation of mālūf was central to its preservation and development. Mālūf repertoire, conceptually and in performance, revolves around the movement through a prescribed sequence of sections, defined mainly by rhythmic patterns. Like the ʿĪsāwiyya nūba, mālūf performances close with a bṭāyḥī-brāwil-khatm sequence, although a full mālūf performance has additional sections.[4] The relationship to GI is less evident outside ritual. While mālūf commences with a progression from instrumental pieces without percussion to instrumental pieces with percussion and then adds vocals to those layers, there are instrumental interludes that interrupt that progression, and resumption does not lead to additional timbral intensification. It thus appears that GI is largely proprietary to ritual contexts, particularly the Sufi ḥaḍra. The hadra and silsila, as cumulative ritual musical forms, provide an architecture within which these intensifications occur. But those forms, to which I now turn, do much more.

CUMULATIVE RITUAL MUSICAL FORMS: THE SILSILA AND ḤAḌRA

As a flexible series of independent nūbas, each dedicated to and named after a saint or spirit, the silsila provides connective tissue conjoining disparate spiritual figures to descend into the same ritual space, one at a time. In the broader context of Sufism and religious authority throughout the Islamic world, the term "silsila" is commonly associated with a spiritual filiation in the form of a genealogy of Sufi masters (disciples who become teachers) traced back to the Prophet. The silsila as a ritual musical form maintains the general sense of performing connections among spiritual figures, although it is not meant to present a chronological history of those relationships. Indeed, part of the work of the silsila is to bring all of these spiritual figures

4. Such as draj (6/4) and khfīf (6/8). Mālūf also features instrumental sections that are absent from the ʿĪsāwiyya of Tunis, with the istiftāḥ and mṣaddar opening the suite and the *tūshiya* and mshadd inserted in the middle. Notably, the istiftāḥ, which is now an instrumental introduction, was previously a sung poem on a religious theme, indexing a time when religious and nonreligious material coexisted in nonritual mālūf performances (see Ben Amor 2010; Louati 2012: 247).

together in the time and space of ritual. While there is a loose sense of hierarchy (typically beginning with the Prophet and then prioritizing saints particularly important to the ritual community), the hospitality of the ritual musical form must ensure that everyone in attendance who needs to trance gets her or his turn. Musicians think about the progression of the silsila in terms of the needs of those in attendance; the nūba for someone who has been waiting for two hours is as important, ritually and socially, as a nūba at the beginning of the ceremony.

Thus, and crucially, the silsila is, in a sense, a series of "sames." While the melody, lyrics, and choice of rhythmic mode differentiate the nūbas from each other, the musical form and aesthetics of timbre, texture, and transformation are, generally speaking, the same. This is one reason the silsila is so closely associated with DI, which correlates directly with the nature of trance healing. In silsila-based healing practices, each nūba is performed for a single trancer who dances for the entirety of the nūba, then faints or collapses onto the floor, indicating a successful culmination to the trance. The whole process is repeated throughout the ritual, with each subsequent nūba attracting a different trancer.[5] The ritual hospitality of these healing practices demands that each dancer (and saint or spirit) gets his or her due time and attention.

The cultural work of the silsila, as I have emphasized, goes beyond the individual trancer. As the silsila unfolds, nūba by nūba, it progressively discloses knowledge about the ritual community's values and histories. The first and second nūbas of a silsila are profoundly symbolic in establishing unequivocally the distinctive identity of the ritual community. The Mannūbiyya silsila begins with a nūba for the Prophet that emphasizes his birth and the figure of his mother, followed by a nūba for Sayyda Mannūbiyya that narrates unjust accusations of shame and presents Sayyda as a maternal figure providing spiritual kinship for women seeking ritual therapy. Sṭambēlī commences with nūbas for the Prophet and his companion Bilāl, situating black Muslims centrally within a genealogical line that extends back to the historical origins of Islam, yet does so through the Songhay figure of Jerma, who, in turn, embodies the trans-Saharan movements that gave rise to sṭambēlī. The Jewish rebaybiyya silsila reveals its Jewish Libyan roots by avoiding the figure of the Prophet Muḥammad, beginning instead with a modified version of the love poem "Mā Sabā 'Aqlī" (Nothing Enchants My Mind), from the Libyan mālūf repertoire, which segues into a unique and proprietary version of the most widely known nūba in the realm of ambient

5. Some of the more popular nūbas attract two or more dancers simultaneously, but it is also common for the musicians to repeat nūbas if several attendees trance to the same nūba.

Sufism, namely "Ra'is al-Abḥār" (Captain of the Seas). With every additional nūba, each of these three silsila traditions reveal additional facets of their histories and identities as the roster of spiritual figures—along with their cultural associations—expands. This accumulation of nūbas also reveals implicit and explicit connections among adjacent practices in the shared ritual ecology. The Mannūbiyya ritual proceeds to Sīdī Belḥassen, Sayyda Mannūbiyya's spiritual mentor, but in a manner that directly indexes the Shādhuliyya dhikr. Sṭambēlī includes an entire section for baḥriyya spirits, which are addressed in the lyrics of the rebaybiyya silsila's "Ra'is al-Abḥār" and evoked via Sīdī Manṣūr (a.k.a. Bābā Baḥrī) in the Mannūbiyya. The rebaybiyya silsila includes numerous nūbas for Sayyda Mannūbiyya and a distinctive set of nūbas that are about sṭambēlī, evoking a history of Jewish-Muslim ritual musical convergences.

While the silsila structure embodies the potential for archiving and activating collective memory, its flexibility and malleability underscore its capacity for ritual hospitality. The silsila structure encourages adaptations and additions that fulfill the needs of new participants, particularly from adjacent ritual practices. Sṭambēlī's "on-demand" nūbas, appended to the end of the silsila, are gestures of hospitality to women in attendance from adjacent trance practices invoking Sayyda Mannūbiyya and Lilla 'Arbiyya, while the Mannūbiyya's adaptation to include Sīdī Aḥmed (and his timbral musical preferences) accommodates the needs of women left without a reliable trance outlet after the death of musicians from a neighboring ritual niche. Outside ritual, the sṭambēlī silsila has been adapted onstage to emphasize the familiar over the alter in order to connect to new audiences. The silsila structure, then, creates the conditions for—and expectations of—inclusivity and hospitality. Yet it also does double duty in terms of communicating the ritual community's identity and social location: it embodies the collective memory of that specific ritual community while simultaneously offering a window into the shared landscape of ambient Sufism it shares with other ritual niches.

Like the silsila, the ḥaḍra is also a ritual form that is organized sonically and with a sequential logic.[6] Its structure is more loosely defined than that of the silsila. Rather than a series of "sames" (that is, a succession of nūbas), the ḥaḍra proceeds through a sequence of mutually exclusive performance formats, with a sense of trajectory from recitation to song, from a cappella

6. As mentioned in chap. 2, "ḥaḍra" may refer specifically to the music and trance portion of a Sufi ceremony, or it may be used synonymously with *al-'aml* (the work) or *al-'āda* (the custom), which convey the entirety of the ceremony. It is in this latter sense that I use the term here. It should be noted that the terms "al-'aml" and "al-'āda" are also used to refer to specific sections of a ceremony, particularly in the Shādhuliyya tradition.

to accompanied singing, from classical to dialectical Arabic, from long to short phrases, from slow to fast tempos, and from less to greater sonic density. The ḥaḍra, as a result, tends to involve all three types of intensification (discrete, sequential, and global). Yet ḥaḍras are not all cut from the same cloth: the content and performance style of the ḥaḍra is the most prominent element that distinguishes one ṭarīqa form another (it is germane to reiterate here that "ṭarīqa" also means "method"). The ḥaḍras of the 'Īsāwiyya, the Sulāmiyya, the Tījāniyya, and the Shādhuliyya have important sonic, textual, physical, and ideological differences. Some, such as the latter two, prohibit musical instruments, recite instead of sing, and discourage trance states, while others, such as the former two, prioritize music but have different interpretations of trance manifestations (e.g., internal vs. external). While each ṭarīqa's ḥaḍra has different sections with different names, there is a sense of trajectory through different modalities of performance. As in the silsila, this progression works reflexively to convey knowledge about the ṭarīqa's history and values, like the 'Īsāwiyya's progression from "Sufi" recitation to the singing of Andalusī songs to its distinctive trance music demonstrates.

The silsila and ḥaḍra, then, are both cumulative ritual musical forms in the sense that they reveal more and more information about the ritual community as they proceed through time. They contain and are shaped by the constancy-intensification dynamic so essential to the ritual experience. But they also encourage reflexive participatory stances and convey histories, geocultural movements, and shared values of ambient Sufism in their creation of welcoming spaces for alleviating suffering through trance healing.

REMNANTS AND RECONTEXTUALIZATION OF RITUAL MUSIC

Chapters 4, 5, and 6 form their own subset of case studies that deal with three ways in which ritual music has been repurposed for nonritual contexts. Studies on heritage and cultural presentations have evolved to a point where it is untenable to rely uncritically on a priori cynical stances that view such stagings as feeble attempts to reproduce something else that is more "real." Yúdice (2003) reminds readers of the dangers of engaging in moralism that assumes there is a stance on right and wrong that exists above the fray of the play of interests of complex networks of actors. He proposes a "performative understanding" of the uses of culture that focuses on "strategies implied in any invocation of culture, any invention of tradition, in relation to some purpose or goal" (2003: 38). In the preceding chapters, I have proceeded in like spirit: rather than fixate only on loss, I find it more pro-

TABLE 7.1 Ritual musical potencies: A summary

Much more than musical elements or sonic features, the trio of timbre, intensification, and form creates musical potencies that signify and act, providing ritualists with aesthetic tools and processes to make their spiritual and social interventions. Each is based on shared underlying principles across ambient Sufism's ritual niches but is realized in a distinctive way that reinforces the specific identity of each niche.

Timbre: Quality of sound associated with specific instruments or voices; inseparable from **texture**, the layering of timbres resulting from totality of instrumentation

Shared principles in ambient Sufism: Constancy, saturation, standardization, indexicality, buzzing quality

Different types, specific to each ritual niche:

Mannūbiyya: Jangly, thick timbre of large tambourines; also features darbūka (goblet drum) and female antiphonal singing

sṭambēlī: Metallic and buzzing timbre of iron clappers (shqāshiq) and resonating metallic plate of gumbrī (bass-register lute); also features male antiphonal singing

rebaybiyya: Shrill, constancy of sound from bagpipes (mizwid), and buzzing of snares on frame drums (bendīr); also features male antiphonal singing

ʿĪsāwiyya: Percussion; changing timbre from unaccompanied vocals to handclaps culminating in buzzy timbre of frame drums (bendīr); also features ṭār (small tambourine) and naqqārāt (small kettledrums) in Andalusī section and male unison and antiphonal singing throughout

Intensification: Systematic increases in sonic density, made possible through baseline temporal conditions created by **cyclicity**

Shared principles in ambient Sufism: Sense of goal-oriented trajectory, recognized as yielding excitement and ritual transformations

Different types, depending on ritual musical form and ritual niche:

Discrete intensification (DI): Silsila and ḥaḍra (throughout both)

Sequential intensification (SI): Silsila (select combinations of pieces) and ḥaḍra (shishtrī and ḥaḍra sections)

Global intensification (GI): Ḥaḍra only

Ritual musical form: Large-scale architecture of ritual based on ordering of sonic and musical material principles

Shared principles in ambient Sufism: Emphasizes salient social-spiritual connections with adjacent niches; sequential logic progressively discloses each ritual community's history, connections, and priorities

Two main types, specific to each ritual niche:

silsila: Series of "sames" in being a sequence of nūbas, each summoning a specific saint or spirit

ḥaḍra: Progression of mutually exclusive sections, with sense of global trajectory (e.g., increase in layers of texture; move from classical to dialectical Arabic and from recitation to song) ductive to also assess what is accomplished. Close readings of nonritual performances reveal a number of ways that performers manage the contextual gap between ritual and stage. In other words, to get at Yúdice's performative strategies, I have analyzed strategies of performance.

In the twentieth and twenty-first centuries, the contextual drift of ritual musics to the stage has contributed to the public life of ambient Sufism, particularly as ritual participation has diminished. These movements to the stage and studio extend the life of ritual musics temporally and their reach contextually, whether they are recreated, disappeared and then hidden in plain earshot, or collected, displayed, and transformed. Café sṭambēlī, in the example analyzed in chapter 3, is *self-presentational*. The sṭambēlī musical troupe, with its ritual instrumentation and characteristic timbres and textures, remains intact in its recontextualization onto the café stage. The performers are representatives of their own ritual heritage, selecting which aspects of that heritage to share with a college-aged, mixed-gender, and relatively privileged audience understood to have little in-group knowledge. Against the sonic assertion of otherness of sṭambēlī's sounds Belḥassen has opted to adapt the silsila to emphasize the familiar over the alter. Sṭambēlī remains other, yet within reach. It is identifiable as a distinctive if threatened part of Tunisian culture, one that intersects with more widely recognizable saints. In other words, the ritual niche of sṭambēlī, in this performance, embraced and magnified its connections to other parts of the shared ecology of ambient Sufism.

Rebaybiyya's relationship to nonritual settings in postrevolutionary Tunisia is rather different. It is *absorptive*, in a manner that leaves rebaybiyya unnamed. Although Hedi Doniya's early motivation was to liven up the ritual repertoire to share with younger, wider audiences, his performances and recordings of rebaybiyya nūbas are not announced or advertised as rebaybiyya. Doniya freely shared information about the Jewish ritual pedigree of his most well-known nūbas, but I have yet to encounter reviews, biographical sketches, or other discourses of reception surrounding his musical work that imply the preservation or influence of an extinct ritual tradition associated with Tunisian Jews. Instead, even though rebaybiyya nūbas are defining features of the larger mizwid nūba repertoire in which Doniya specializes, they are thoroughly subsumed by that sacred mizwid repertoire, leaving only subtle clues about their provenance.

If café sṭambēlī tends toward the self-presentational and mizwid the absorptive, *el-Hadhra* is *curatorial*. It is based on the act of collection and the visual and sonic principles of the theater and concert stage, with the goal of updating and improving Sufi music for consumption by a broader audience. The spectacle is plural and diverse, providing an aesthetic taste and sampling of the landscape of ambient Sufism. The practices of local ṭarīqas are simultaneously valorized and devalued, one of the many paradoxes of such stagings that rely on living traditions. The spectacle obviates the need for ritual attendance to experience Sufi music, instead providing audiences an alternative to ritual while relying on ritual's social and spiritual capital.

Although these three examples illustrate contrasting outcomes and strategies of (re)presentation, they could also be situated on a continuum, with each one representing a further disintegration of the cumulative ritual musical form. In café sṭambēlī, the silsila structure remains intact, yet partial, in the service of providing the audience familiarity. In mizwid, the silsila structure of the rebaybiyya material is for the most part gone, with the exception of knowledgeable mizwid artists who begin concerts and parties with two nūbas, in the service of recognizing the ritual and sacred roots of the genre. In *el-Hadhra*, the teleology and reflexivity of the hadra sonic ritual form is entirely absent, replaced by set-list modularity.

In set-list modularity, ritual progressions and teleologies disappear and are replaced by exhibitional variety that samples from the landscape of ambient Sufism. New opportunities arise in the set-list approach, such as mixing nūbas from silsila-based practices with pieces from ḥaḍra ceremonies.[7] This modularity and sense of collection and display have precedents in local histories. The Sulāmiyya Sufi order, whose priorities have shifted away from devotional rituals and toward dominating the market for Sufi musical troupes hired for domestic ceremonies, are a case in point. The nationalist cultural policy of suppressing zāwiya activities while encouraging the staging of Sufi music in festivals during the 1960s also created new audience expectations for variety while encouraging Sufis to focus on their musical art. That the ḥaḍra and silsila forms are not adhered to in concert-stage performances is highly suggestive of just how important they are to the work of ritual. Yet while such performances may be infused with an implicit critique of ritual itself, they achieve their power and popularity largely from their capacity to index the power of ritual.

. . .

And the rituals continue. The fourteen-week summer ritual season has regained its vibrancy as Tunisia approaches its tenth anniversary of the 2011

7. Sami Lajmi's *Ziara* is a spectacle in the same vein as *el-Hadhra* but features more nūbas—particularly from the Mannūbiyya—and pieces from the ʿĪsāwiyya.

Revolution, and the group pilgrimage to the shrine of Sīdī ʿAlī Ḥaṭṭāb that begins that period of heightened ritual activity continues to be a showcase for the remarkable variety of practices that inhabit the landscape of ambient Sufism. Fatima Lwelbani, the leader of the Mannūbiyya troupe introduced in chapter 3, describes the scene with a sense of awe that conveys the continued vitality of ritual performance, the diversity of ritual communities represented at the pilgrimage, and the affective power of their copresence in one ritual space:

> It's something amazing [*shay' min ʿajib*] . . . each group has a specialty. [The] Sīdī Belḥassen [group makes] its entrance [*dakhla*] at midnight, with candles and incense, the incense holder with chains. And there are the Sīdī ʿAmor ʿAjmī people, who are from Raoued, they enter with sṭambēlī, Sīdī Manṣūr [and] Sīdī ʿAbd al-Salām also with sṭambēlī, then Sīdī ʿAlī Ḥaṭṭāb. At the end of the procession, the Sīdī Ben ʿĪsā group dances with broken glass, needles, knives, and nails, they have a huge wooden board, all with nails and fire . . . the fire grows while the coal is red in the brazier, they put a sword into it and then the dancer licks it as if he is eating sweets, and then Sīdī Belḥassen, they dance with the Berber wool coat [*burnūs*]. . . .
>
> . . . They all meet there [at the shrine of Sīdī ʿAlī Ḥaṭṭāb], because it's vast, like the desert. The troupes of Sīdī Ben ʿĪsā, Sīdī Meḥrez, Sīdī ʿAbd al-Salām, Sayyda Mannūbiyya, Sīdī Bashīr, and Sīdī Belḥassen, the troupe of Sīdī Bū Saʿīd, like Belḥassen, make their entrance in recitation [*bil-qrāya*], the troupe of Sīdī Bū ʿAlī Nafṭī, Sīdī ʿAbīd, or the people of Umm al-Zīn al-Sahliyya . . . do you know how many bands are there? Twenty-five troupes, Sīdī ʿAbd al-Qādir's troupe enters in green, with flags and they chant, they do not drum, you have the Belḥassen group, they do not drum, and you have Sīdī ʿAbd al-Qādir too, they also enter [only reciting] the word of God, and you have Sīdī Bū Saʿīd, these three bands do not drum, they only have "Allah" and hit the ground [reciting] "Allah, Huwa, Allah, Huwa Allah," you see, and the light goes out and the place is dark, you see more people falling to the ground than are left standing, when I remember it I get goosebumps.
>
> From midnight to three in the morning they restlessly beat the ground and recite the name of Allah. After that the place is lit up again [to the sound of] ululations and candles are lit and people put out sweets, baklava, olives, bread, and pastries of all sorts . . . [The troupes of] Rjāl Ṣabrā and Sīdī Ṣaḥbī also gather in Ḥaṭṭāb. . . . And Sīdī Bū Saʿīd, what do they do? They start with someone putting down big brass bowls filled with saltwater from the sea and candles will be lit inside, you understand? I will demonstrate that for you. . . . They light these candles inside the water and start [reciting]

> "Huwa, Huwa," and the candles will be fine inside the water without dying out, from 1:00 a.m. to 3:00 a.m. The last remaining ones [come with] drums and horsemen, the Sīdī Bū ʿAlī group with horsemen and drums, and the Sīdī Meḥrez group with the Qur'an, too, only God's words, because he is a religious scholar [*ālim*], he and Belḥassan are scholars.

Fatima's evocative observations are a fitting summary of how the landscape of ambient Sufism accommodates a remarkable diversity of ritual niches, each with its own specialty, and allows ritual communities with marked philosophical and differences to share ritual and social space. She finishes with a description of how that vast diversity is absorbed into her own troupe's silsila, which she describes as a "journey" (riḥla) through this landscape:

> We are Mannūbiyya, we enter by [playing the nūba of Sayyda] Mannūbiyya, we dress in our cloaks and we enter with flags, and later they set carpets for us, so we sit on floor and work [perform]. . . . We start with the Prophet first, *istighfār allah*, after that Belḥassen, and then Sīdī Meḥrez, then Sīdī ʿAbd al-Qādir, and then Sīdī Ben ʿĪsā, then Sīdī Bū Saʿīd, then Sīdī ʿAlī Ḥaṭṭāb, then Sayyda Mannūbiyya, as Ḥaṭṭāb is close to Mannūbiyya, and thus we follow the *riḥla* [journey]. And after that, Sayyda Mannūbiyya at around 6:30 or 7:30, as some people need us to repeat [a nūba], as one may faint [i.e., finish her trance] and [another needs] us to repeat. (Pers. comm., 2014).

Musical sound, as the case studies of ambient Sufism demonstrate, provides a particularly reliable and widely recognized means of accessing the unseen realm. Yet thinking about the relations between music and trance only in terms of music's "tranceability" is to ignore music's other affordances, particularly as the sonic materiality of music also carries sensory knowledge that goes beyond the immediacy of healing and into the realm of each ritual community's history, social and spiritual connections, and ritual priorities. So whereas, for example, timbral saturation and the trajectory of ritual musical form are necessary conditions in the local context for supporting trance at the level of the individual, the specific timbral dimensions and particular strategy for the unfolding of ritual musical form are proprietary to, and therefore index, each ritual community's identity in toto.

All of these sonic, spiritual, and social experiences and forms of knowledge converge in what Fatima describes as the journey of ritual performance. While the Arabic term "riḥla" is used colloquially to refer to any kind of journey, it also remains infused with its historical sense in the Islamic world of travel to seek knowledge, particularly religious knowledge.[8] Such a riḥla is based on the premise that valuable knowledge results from encounters with other places and other people. The experience of ritual as riḥla brings participants into contact not only with the powers of unseen beings, but also with the people and practices that animate adjacent ritual niches. Just as music socializes trance (Rouget 1986), trance rituals also musicalize the social: women, "intoxicated" Sufis, Jews, black Tunisians, and popular musicians have shaped the shared spiritual and musical commons of ambient Sufism. They have cultivated musical potencies that not only support the immediacy of trance and the ritual work of reflexivity, memory, hospitality and alterity, but also convey commonality and difference by distilling and revealing the histories, values, and social networks of their respective communities. Trance ritual as riḥla, then, is similarly founded on insight gained through encounters with others, both social and spiritual, yet the journey is shaped by and realized through the sonic sensory experience. The sensory experience of the ritual journey, as the chapters of this book have argued, is most pronounced in the musical potencies of timbral saturation, sonic intensification, and, especially, the unfolding of ritual musical form.

8. As such, the riḥla was considered a prized intellectual pursuit by Muslim scholars from the influential Sufi al-Ghazali to the great Tunisian historian Ibn Khaldun (see Eickelman and Piscatori 1990; Touati 2010).

Glossary

al-arba'tāsh	Fourteen-week summer season of heightened ritual activities at Tunisian shrines; lit. "the fourteen"
baḥriyya	General term for water spirits; also a specific family of spirits in sṭambēlī (Baḥriyya)
Banū Kūrī	Group of spirits in sṭambēlī named after the spirit Kūrī; lit. "Kūrī's tribe" or "Kūrī's people"
baraka	Positive spiritual force associated with Muslim saints; lit. "blessing"
barwal (pl. *brāwil*)	1. A rhythm of the 'Īsāwiyya ḥaḍra, also present in mālūf. It appears as the third rhythm in the shishtrī section. 2. Plural (brāwil) refers to the third section of the 'Īsāwiyya ḥaḍra named after the rhythm
bendīr (pl. *bnādir*)	Circular frame drum, typically with a goatskin head and two or three gut snares. Large varieties that have cymbals may also be called daff (pl. dufūf)
bey	Head of the Tunisian state during the Husaynid era (1705–1957)
Bēyāt	Royalty spirits of sṭambēlī; lit. "the beys"
bṭāyḥī (pl. *bṭayḥiyyāt*)	First rhythm of the shishtrī section of the 'Īsāwiyya ḥaḍra; the same rhythm is also a rhythmic mode in mālūf
bṭāyḥī 'īsāwī	First rhythm of the brāwil section of the 'Īsāwiyya ḥaḍra, when trance begins
bū sa'diyya	Sṭambēlī rhythm named after the mythic first sṭambēlī musician, Bū Sa'diyya
darbūka (pl. *drābik*)	Goblet-shaped drum

dhikr (pl. *adhkār*)	Recitation of a name of God; lit. "remembrance"
fātiḥa	Opening chapter of the Qur'an, often recited to commence a ceremony.
ghnāya (pl. *aghānī*)	Song, used in mizwid to distinguish from sacred nūba song form
gijmī	Musicolinguistic technique used by mizwid vocalists involving the insertion of syllables such as "na," "ni," "ra," and "ri" into a word
gnaybra	Small gumbrī, used by sṭambēlī practitioners outside trance ceremonies but occasionally used when sṭambēlī musicians performed ceremonies for Jews
gumbrī	A three-stringed lute with a cylindrical body; the main instrument of sṭambēlī
ḥaḍra	1. Sufi ceremony, typically organized according to principles of sonic-spiritual progression. 2. Name of the third and final section of the 'Īsāwiyya ḥaḍra, featuring music, dance, and trance
hallāla	circle of singers in the 'Īsāwiyya ḥaḍra, organized into two halves: qawwāla ("callers") and raddāda ("responders")
ḥizb (pl. *aḥzāb*)	Recited liturgies, typically attributed to the founder of the Sufi order and performed a cappella
ḥzāba	Name given to the group of 'Īsāwī Sufis reciting the ḥizb
hrūbī	Third, final, and fastest rhythm in the rhythmic sequence of the brāwil section of the 'Īsāwiyya ḥaḍra
jedba	State of trance associated with ritual music; lit. "attraction"; called *jadhba* in standard Arabic
jinn	Class of often malevolent spirits in the Islamic world (also jnūn; m. sing. jinnī, f. sing. jinniyya)
kharja	Street procession commencing a ziyāra and some other Sufi ceremonies; lit. "departure"
khatm/khitm	Three-beat rhythm often concluding a sequence of songs; lit. "sealing"
mālūf (ma'lūf)	Andalusī art music of Tunisia
mizwid	1. Tunisian bagpipes, with a bag made of goatskin. 2. Mass-mediated genre of music featuring this instrument
mjarred	Iconic five-beat handclap pattern of the 'Īsāwiyya
nūba (pl. *nwib* or *nūbāt*)	1. Praise song to a spiritual figure in the context of silsila-based rituals and the mizwid music genre. 2. Sequence of songs in the same or related melodic mode but in a prescribed series of different rhythmic modes, associated especially with mālūf and 'Īsāwiyya performance

qawwāla	"Callers," one half of the ʿĪsāwiyya singers who sing antiphonally with the other half, called *raddāda* ("responders")
raddāda	"Responders," one half of the ʿĪsāwiyya singers who sing antiphonally with the other half, called *qawwāla* ("callers")
rbūkh	Social gatherings primarily associated with urban manual laborers and featuring mizwid music, dancing, and drinking
rebāb	Two-stringed, upright bowed fiddle
rebaybiyya	Music-driven trance rituals associated with 1. domestic ceremonies of Tunisian Jews, featuring the rebāb or mizwid, and 2. zāwiya ceremonies of Tunisian women playing percussion instruments
riḥla	Journey to seek new knowledge and experience
saʿdāwī	1. 12/8 rhythmic pattern in mizwid and other Tunisian popular-music contexts. 2. Four-stroke hemiola rhythm in sṭambēlī
ṣalḥīn	General term for sṭambēlī spirits
Sghār	Group of child spirits in sṭambēlī
shaykh al-ʿaml	Shaykh who leads the group of singers (ḥallāla) during the shishtrī and ḥaḍra sections of the ʿĪsāwiyya ḥaḍra
shaykh al-ḥaḍra	Shaykh who leads the group of dancers (ṣaff) in the ʿĪsāwiyya ḥaḍra
shaykh al-ḥizb	Shaykh who leads the reciters (ḥzāba) of the ḥizb in the ʿĪsāwiyya ḥaḍra
shishtrī	Section of the ʿĪsāwiyya ḥaḍra involving the performance of Andalusī song and named after Andalusī Sufi poet Abū Ḥasan al-Shushtarī
shqāshiq	Handheld iron clappers used in sṭambēlī
sifsārī	Large white cloth used in Tījāniyya ceremonies
silsila	"Chain" of nūbas that creates the large-scale ritual musical form of trance ceremonies
ṣaff	Line of dancers in the ʿĪsāwiyya ḥaḍra
sṭambēlī	Trance healing music and ritual associated with historical movements of sub-Saharans to Tunisia
sunjuq	Colorful cloth banners, often representing specific saints or spirits and draped over the bodies of trancers
ṭabʿ (pl. *ṭubūʿ*)	Melodic mode; consists of (a) a discrete, named set of pitches, (b) conventions for how those pitches are used, and (c) their extramusical associations such as emotional states
ṭabla tījāniyya	Large, bowl-shaped drum played by the women's Tījāniyya
tahlīla	Cyclic recitation of the phrase *lā ilaha illā allah* (there is no god but God)

takhmīr(a)	Ritual trance associated with musical invocations of saints and spirits; lit. "intoxication."
ṭār	Tambourine
ṭarīqa (pl. *ṭuruq*)	Refers to both a Sufi order and its methods; lit. "path"
turāth	Heritage, in the sense of cultural inheritance or tradition
walī (pl. *āwliyā'*)	Muslim saint; lit. "close [to God]"
waẓīfa	Recited prayers and invocations (especially of the Shādhuliyya and Tījāniyya) or the weekly office of performing such recitations
wird	Liturgy or group of recited prayers and invocations
wird al-qudūm	Opening section of the dance and trance section of the 'Īsāwiyya ḥaḍra when the dancers arrive to the unaccompanied singing of the hallāla; lit. "arrival liturgy"
zāwiya (pl. *zwī* or *zwāya*)	Shrine of a Muslim saint, often housing the saint's tomb and featuring a courtyard for ritual ceremonies
ziyāra	Individual or communal pilgrimage to a saint's shrine; lit. "visit"
zūfrī	Working-class laborers associated with after-work drinking parties (rbūkh) featuring mizwid music; from the French *les ouvriers*
zukra	1. Tunisian reed instrument similar to the ghayṭa whose playing technique involves circular breathing to create a continuous sound; 2. Libyan bagpipes

Bibliography

al-hādī ḥabbūba w-al-mūsīqā al-sha'biyya bi-tūnis/Hedi Habbouba and the Pop Music/Hedi Habbouba: Le folklore et le Pop tunisiens. 1999. Tunis: Sotepa.

'Abīd, Hishām. 2009. *Tūnis wa-awliyāwuhā al-ṣālihūn fī madawwana al-munāqib al-ṣūfiyya* [*Tunisia and Its Holy Saints in the Literature on Sufi Virtues*]. Tunis: Markiz al-Nashr al-Jāma'ī.

Abassi, Asma. 2015. "El Hadhra 2015 au festival international de Carthage: Sacré Jaziri!" *La Presse*, July 28. http://fr.allafrica.com/stories/201507282091.html.

Abu-Nasr, Jamil M. 1965. *The Tijaniyya: A Sufi Order in the Modern World.* London: Oxford University Press.

Ahmed, Shahab. 2016. *What Is Islam? The Importance of Being Islamic.* Princeton, NJ: Princeton University Press.

Alvarez, Lourdes María. 2009. *Abū al-Ḥasan al-Shushtarī: Songs of Love and Devotion.* New York: Paulist Press.

Amri, Nelly. 2008. *La sainte de Tunis: Présentation et traduction de l'hagiographie de 'Āisha al-Mannūbiyya* (m. 665/1267). Paris: Sindbad.

———. 2009. "Le *Samā'* dans les milieux soufis du Maghreb (VIIe-X^{e}/XIIIe-XVIe siècles: Pratiques, tensions, et codification." *Al-Qantara* 30 (2): 491–528.

———. 2015. *Sīdī Abū Sa'īd al-Bājī (1156–1231).* Sousse: Contraste Éditions.

Anderson, Benedict. 1990. *Language and Power: Exploring Political Cultures in Indonesia.* Ithaca, NY: Cornell University Press.

Andézian, Sossie. 1986. "La *ḥaḍra* des *'Isâwa*: Cérémonie religieuse ou spectacle?" In *Nouveaux enjeux culturels au Maghreb*, 373–381. Paris: Éditions du Centre National de la Recherche Scientifique.

———. 1996. "L'Algérie, le Maroc, la Tunisie." In *Les voies d'Allah: Les ordres mystiques dans l'islam des origines à aujourd'hui*, edited by Alexandre Popovic and Gilles Veinstein, 389–408. Paris: Fayard.

Austin, John L. 1975. *How to Do Things with Words*. Oxford: Oxford University Press.

Barnat, Rachid. 2015. "El-Hadhra à Carthage: Le soufisme dans l'âme des Tunisiens." *Kapitalis*, July 26. http://kapitalis.com/tunisie/2015/07/26/el-hadhra-a-carthage-le-soufisme-dans-lame-des-tunisiens/.

Bateson, Gregory. 1972 [1955]. *Steps to an Ecology of Mind: Collected Essays in Anthropology, Psychiatry, Evolution, and Epistemology*. San Francisco: Chandler.

Becker, Judith. 2004. *Deep Listeners: Music, Emotion, and Trancing*. Bloomington: University of Indiana Press.

Bell, Catherine. 1997. *Ritual: Perspectives and Dimensions*. New York and Oxford: Oxford University Press.

Bellamy, Carla. 2011. *The Powerful Ephemeral: Everyday Healing in an Ambiguously Islamic Place*. Berkeley and Los Angeles: University of California Press.

Ben 'Amor, Hishām. 2008. *'Īsāwiyya Banī Khiyyār: Tārīkhhā wa-Inshādha* [*The 'Īsāwiyya of Banī Khiyyār: Their History and Songs*]. Tunis: Turath.

Ben Achour, Mohamed El Aziz. 2004. *Zaouïas et confréries: Aspects de l'Islam mystique dans l'histoire tunisienne*. Tunis: Sagittaire Éditions.

Ben Amor, Taoufik. 2010. "The Making of Tradition: Standardisation of the Lyrics of the Tunisian Andalusian Mālūf Repertoire." In *Reflections on Knowledge and Language in Middle Eastern Societies*, edited by Bruno De Nicola, Yonatan Mendel, and Husain Qutbuddin, 193–214. Newcastle upon Tyne: Cambridge Scholars.

Ben Youssef, Amira. 1993. "Fadhel Jaziri met en scene 'Hadhra': L'appel à la vie." *Le Renouveau*, n.d.

Benattar, S. C. 1923. *Le bled en lumière: Folklore tunisien*. Paris: J. Tallandier.

Benjamin, Israel Joseph. 1863. *Eight Years in Asia and Africa from 1846 to 1855*. Hanover, Germany: The author.

Besmer, Fremont. 1983. *Horses, Musicians, and Gods: The Hausa Cult of Possession-Trance*. South Hadley, MA: Bergin and Garvey.

Boddy, Janice. 1989. *Wombs and Alien Spirits: Women, Men, and the Zār Cult in Northern Sudan*. Madison: University of Wisconsin Press.

Bohlman, Philip V. 1997. "World Musics and World Religions: Whose World?" In *Enchanting Powers: Music in the World's Religions*, edited by Lawrence E. Sullivan, 61–90. Cambridge, MA: Harvard University Press.

Boissevain, Katia. 2006. *Sainte parmi les saints: Sayyda Mannūbiya ou les recompositions cultuelles dans la Tunisie contemporaine*. Paris: IRMC and Maisonneuve & Larose.

Brandily, Monique. 1993. "La pratique musicale traditionnelle en Libye et ses instruments." *Maghreb Review* 18 (1–2): 116–134.

Briggs, Charles L., and Richard Bauman. 1992. "Genre, Intertextuality, and Social Power." *Journal of Linguistic Anthropology* 2 (2): 131–172.

Brown, Kenneth. 1985. "The Discrediting of a Sufi Movement in Tunisia." In *Islamic Dilemmas: Reformers, Nationalists, and Industrialization*, edited by Ernest Gellner, 146–168. Berlin: Mouton.

Brown, L. Carl. 1964. "The Islamic Reformist Movement in North Africa." *Journal of Modern African Studies* 2 (1): 55–63.

———. 1974. *The Tunisia of Ahmad Bey, 1837–1855*. Princeton, NJ: Princeton University Press.

Būdhīna, Muḥammad. 1992. *Dīwān al-Ma'lūf [Ma'lūf Anthology]*. Tunis: Dār Sīrās L-il-Nashr (CERES).

———. 1995. *Mūsīqā al-Ma'lūf [Ma'lūf Music]*. Tunis: Dār Sīrās L-il-Nashr (CERES).

———. 1997. *Ughniyyāt min al-Turāth [Songs from the Cultural Heritage]*. Hammamet, Tunisia: Manshūrāt Muḥammad Būdhīna.

Carpenter-Latiri, Dora. 2010. "The Ghriba Pilgrimage in the Island of Jerba: The Semantics of Otherness." *Scripta Instituti Donneriani Aboensis* 22: 38–55.

Catzaras, Marianne. 1993. "'El Hadhra' ou la danse des étoiles." *Le Temps*, March 2.

Centre des Musiques Arabes et Méditerranéennes. 2013. *Al-'Ādah: Min Anāshīd al-Ṭarīqa al-Shādhuliyya bi-Tūnis/Al-'Ādah: Chants soufis de la confrérie Chādhuliyah à Tunis*. Tunis: Éditions Ennejma Ezzahra.

Chamkhi, Sonia. 2010. *L'art du mezoued*. Documentary film. Tunisia: Moustaches.

Chelbi, Mustapha. 1985. *Musique et société en Tunisie*. Tunis: Salambo.

———. 1999. "Eloge de la soulemiya." *La Presse*, December 30.

———. 2002. *La musique en Tunisie*. Tunis: Finzi.

Chlyeh, Abdelhafid. 1999. *Les Gnaoua du Maroc: Itinéraires initiatiques, transe et possession*. Paris: Pensée Sauvage.

Chouraqui, Andre N. 2001. *Between East and West: A History of the Jews of North Africa*. Translated by Michael M. Bernet. Skokie, IL: Varda.

Ciantar, Philip. 2012. *The Ma'lūf in Contemporary Libya: An Arab Andalusian Tradition*. Farnham, Surrey: Ashgate.

Cohen, David. 1964. *Le parler arabe des juifs de Tunis: Textes et documents linguistiques et ethnographiques*. Vol. 1, *Étude linguistique*. Paris: Mouton.

Colla, Elliott. 2012. "The People Want." *Middle East Report* 263: 8–13.

Comaroff, John L., and Jean Comaroff. 2009. *Ethnicity, Inc.* Chicago: University of Chicago Press.

Conord, Sylvaine. 2011. "Sociabilités de femmes juives tunisiennes: Approche photo-ethnographique." In *Belleville, Quartier Populaire?*, edited by Roselyne de Villanova and Agnès Deboulet, 173–183. Paris: Créaphis.

Cowper, Henry S. 1897. *The Hill of Graces: A Record of Investigation among the Trilithons and Megalithic Sites of Tripoli.* London: Methuen.

Csikszentmihalyi, Mihaly. 1990. *Flow: The Psychology of Optimal Experience.* New York: Harper & Row.

Davila, Carl. 2015. "The Andalusi Turn: The Nūba in Mediterranean History." *Mediterranean Studies* 23 (2): 149–169.

Davis, Ruth F. 1986. "Some Relations between Three Piyyutim from Djerba and Three Arabic Songs." *Maghreb Review* 11 (5–6): 134–144.

———. 2004. *Ma'lūf: Reflections on the Arab-Andalusian Music of Tunisia.* Lanham, MD: Scarecrow Press.

Denham, Dixon, Hugh Clapperton, and Walter Oudney. 1826. *Voyage et découvertes dans le nord et les parties centrales de l'Afrique (1822–1824).* Vol. 1. Paris: Arthus Bertrand.

Dermenghem, Émile. 1954. *Le culte des saints dans l'islam maghrébin.* Paris: Gamillard.

During, Jean. 1992. "The Organization of Rhythm in Baluchi Trance Music." In *European Studies in Ethnomusicology: Historical Developments and Recent Trends*, edited by Max Peter Baumann, Artur Simon, and Ulrich Wegner, 282–302. Wilhelmshaven: F. Noetzel.

———. 1997. "Rythmes ovoïdes et quadrature du cycle." *Cahiers d'ethnomusicologie* 10: 17–36.

Échard, Nicole. 1989. *Bori: Aspects d'un culte de possession hausa dans l'Ader et le Kurfey (Niger).* Paris: École des Hautes Études en Sciences Sociales.

Eickelman, Dale F., and James Piscatori. 1990. *Muslim Travellers: Pilgrimage, Migration, and the Religious Imagination.* Berkeley and Los Angeles: University of California Press.

Emoff, Ron. 2003. *Recollecting from the Past: Musical Practice and Spirit Possession on the East Coast of Madagascar.* Middletown, CT: Wesleyan University Press.

Engelhardt, Jeffers. 2014. "Music, Mediation, and Post-Secular Religion: Perspectives from Estonia and Greece." Department of Music Colloquium, Tufts University, October 6.

Engelke, Matthew. 2012. "Angels in Swindon: Public Religion and Ambient Faith in England." *American Ethnologist* 39 (1): 155–170.

Ernst, Carl W. 1997. *The Shambhala Guide to Sufism.* Boston: Shambhala.

Errington, Shelly. 1989. *Meaning and Power in a Southeast Asian Realm.* Princeton, NJ: Princeton University Press.

Eyries, J. B. 1841. *Voyage pittoresque en Asie et en Afrique: Résumé général des voyages anciens et modernes.* Paris: Furne & Cie.

Ferchiou, Sophie. 1972. "Survivances mystiques et culte de possession dans le maraboutisme tunisien." *L'Homme* (July–September): 47–69.

———. 1991a. "La Possession: Forme de Marginalité Féminine." *Annuaire de l'Afrique du Nord* 30: 191–200.

———. 1991b. "The Possession Cults of Tunisia: A Religious System Functioning as a System of Reference and a Social Field for Performing Actions." In *Women's Medicine: The Zar-bori Cult in Africa and Beyond*, edited by I. M. Lewis, Ahmed Al-Safi and Sayyid Hurreiz, 209–218. Edinburgh: Edinburgh University Press for the International African Institute.

Feuchtwang, Stephan. 2010. "Ritual and Memory." In *Memory: Histories, Theories, Debates*, edited by Susannah Radstone and Bill Schwarz, 281–298. New York: Fordham University Press.

Friedson, Steven M. 1996. *Dancing Prophets: Musical Experience in Tumbuka Healing*. Chicago: University of Chicago Press.

Frishkopf, Michael. 2001. "Tarab in the Mystic Sufi Chant of Egypt." In *Colors of Enchantment: Theater, Dance, Music and the Visual Arts of the Middle East*, edited by Sherifa Zuhur, 233–269. Cairo: American University in Cairo Press.

———. 2009. "Globalizing the Soundworld: Islam and Sufi Music in the West." In *Sufis in Western Society: Global Networking and Locality*, edited by Markus Dressler, Ron Geaves, and Gritt Klinkhammer, 56–86. London and New York: Routledge.

———. 2013. "Against Ethnomusicology: Language Performance and the Social Impact of Ritual Performance in Islam." *Performing Islam* 2 (1): 11–43.

———. 2014. "Social Forces Shaping the Heterodoxy of Sufi Performance in Contemporary Egypt." In *Music, Culture and Identity in the Muslim World: Performance, Politics, and Piety*, edited by Kamal Salhi, 35–56. London and New York: Routledge.

Gana, Nouri. 2011. "Rap Rage Revolt." *Jadaliyya*, http://www.jadaliyya.com/pages/index/2320/rap-rage-revolt.

Garfi, Mohamed. N.d. "L'apologie du mizwid, pourquoi?" *Le Quotidien*.

Geoffroy, Éric. 1996. "La Chādhiliyya." In *Les voies d'Allah: Les ordres mystiques dans l'islam des origines à aujourd'hui*, edited by Alexandre Popovic and Gilles Veinstein, 509–518. Paris: Fayard.

Gidal, Marc. 2016. *Spirit Song: Afro-Brazilian Religious Music and Boundaries*. Oxford and New York: Oxford University Press.

Glasser, Jonathan. 2016a. *The Lost Paradise: Andalusi Music in Urban North Africa*. Chicago: University of Chicago Press.

———. 2016b. "Muslim-Jewish Musical Interaction at Algeria's Spanish-Ottoman Frontier." Society for Ethnomusicology Annual Conference, Washington, DC, November 13.

Gobin, Emma, and Maxime Vanhoenacker. 2016. "Innovation rituelle et réflexivité. Retours aux rituels: une introduction." *Ethnographiques* 33. https://www.ethnographiques.org/2016/Gobin-Vanhoenacker.

Goodman, Jane. 2003. "From Village to Vinyl: Genealogies of New Kabyle Song." *Emergences* 13 (1–2): 75–93.

Guettat, Mahmoud. 1980. *La musique classique du Maghreb*. Paris: Sindbad.

Guss, David M. 2000. *The Festive State: Race, Ethnicity, and Nationalism as Cultural Performance*. Berkeley and Los Angeles: University of California Press.

Hagene, Matthieu. 2011. *Le spleen du yenna*. Documentary film. France: Par les Chemins.

Hamrouni, Ahmed [Aḥmad Ḥamrūnī]. 2007. *Ḥabība Msīka: Ḥayā wa-Fann [Ḥabība Msīka: Life and Art]/Habiba Messika: Artiste accomplie*. Tunis: ʿĀlam al-Kitāb/L'univers du livre.

Handelman, Don. 1997. "Rituals/Spectacles." *International Social Science Journal* 49 (153): 387–399.

Hassnaoui, Amira. 2017. "Stambeli Awakening: Cultural Revival and Musical Amalgam in Post Revolution Tunisia." Master's thesis, Bowling Green State University.

Hawkins, Simon. 2008. "Hijab: Feminine Allure and Charm to Men in Tunis." *Ethnology* 47 (1): 1–21.

Hibou, Béatrice. 2011. *The Force of Obedience: The Political Economy of Repression in Tunisia*. Translated by Andrew Brown. Cambridge: Polity Press.

Hobart, Angela, and Bruce Kapferer, eds. 2005. *Aesthetics in Performance: Formations of Symbolic Construction and Experience*. New York: Berghahn.

Hopkins, Nicholas. 2018. "Family Rites in Testour, Tunisia, in the 1970s." *Journal of North African Studies* 23 (4): 694–715.

Hornbostel, E. M. von. 1975 [1906]. "Phonographierte tunesische Melodien." *Opera Omnia* 1: 323–380.

Ihde, Don. 2007. *Listening and Voice: Phenomenologies of Sound*. 2nd ed. Albany: State University of New York Press.

Jankowsky, Richard. C. 2007. "Music, Spirit Possession, and the In-Between: Ethnomusicological Inquiry and the Challenge of Trance." *Ethnomusicology Forum* 16 (2): 195–218.

———. 2010. *Stambeli: Music, Trance, and Alterity in Tunisia*. Chicago: University of Chicago Press.

———. 2013. "Rhythmic Elasticity and Metric Transformation in Tunisian Stambeli." *Analytical Approaches to World Music* 3 (1): 34–61.

———. 2017. "Absence and 'Presence': El-Hadhra and the Cultural Politics of Staging Sufi Music in Tunisia." *Journal of North African Studies* 22 (5): 860–887.

Johnson, James Weldon. 1995. *The Selected Writings of James Weldon Johnson: Social, Political, and Literary Essays*. Oxford: Oxford University Press.

Johnson, Pamela. 1979. "A Sufi Shrine in Modern Tunisia." Ph.D. diss., University of California, Berkeley.

Jones, Lura JaFran. 1977. "The ʿĪsāwīya of Tunisia and their Music." Ph.D. diss., University of Washington.

Kahlawi, Muhammad. 1999. "Bayna Ḥaḍra al-Agrebī wa-Ḥaḍra al-Jazīrī [Between Agrebi's Ḥaḍra and Jaziri's Ḥaḍra]." *Al-Ṣaḥāfa*, January 3, n.p.

Kapchan, Deborah. 2007. *Traveling Spirit Masters: Moroccan Gnawa Trance and Music in the Global Marketplace*. Middletown, CT: Wesleyan University Press.

Kapchan, Deborah A. 2008. "The Promise of Sonic Translation: Performing the Festive Sacred in Morocco." *American Anthropologist* 110 (4): 467–483.

Kapferer, Bruce. 1984. "The Ritual Process and the Problem of Reflexivity in Sinhalese Demon Exorcisms." In *Rite, Drama, Festival, Spectacle: Rehearsals Toward a Theory of Cultural Performances*, edited by J. Macaloon, 179–207. Philadelphia: Institute for the Study of Human Issues.

———. 2005. "Ritual Dynamics and Virtual Practice: Beyond Representation and Meaning." In *Ritual in Its Own Right: Exploring the Dynamics of Transformation*, edited by Don Handelman and Galina Lindquist, 35–54. New York and Oxford: Berghahn.

Kirshenblatt-Gimblett, Barbara. 1998. *Destination Culture: Tourism, Museums, and Heritage*. Berkeley and Los Angeles: University of California Press.

Kramer, Fritz. 1993. *The Red Fez: Art and Spirit Possession in Africa*. Translated by Malcolm R. Green. London and New York: Verso.

Laade, Wolfgang. 1962. Liner notes to *Tunisia, Volume 3: Folk Music*. Folkways Records FW 8863. New York: Folkways Records.

Lachmann, Robert. 1940. *Jewish Cantillation and Song in the Isle of Djerba*. Jerusalem: Hebrew University.

Lallemand, Charles. 1892. *Tunis et ses environs: Texte et dessins d'après nature*. Paris: Librairies-imprimeries réunies.

Lambek, Michael. 1993. *Knowledge and Practice in Mayotte: Local Discourses of Islam, Sorcery, and Spirit Possession*. Toronto: University of Toronto Press.

Lapie, Paul. 1898. *Les civilisations tunisiennes (musulmans, israélites, européens): Étude de psychologie sociale*. Paris: Félix Alcan.

Larguèche, Abdelhamid. 1999. *Les ombres de la ville: Pauvres, marginaux et minoritaires à Tunis (XVIIIème et XIXème siècles)*. Tunis: Centre de Publication Universitaire, Faculté des Lettres de Manouba.

Lauzière, Henri. 2016. *The Making of Salafism: Islamic Reform in the Twentieth Century*. New York: Columbia University Press.

Lévy, Lionel. 1999. *La nation juive portugaise: Livourne, Amsterdam, Tunis, 1591–1951*. Paris and Montreal: L'Harmattan.

Lewisohn, Leonard. 1997. "The Sacred Music of Islam: Samāʿ in the Persian Sufi Tradition." *British Journal of Ethnomusicology* 6: 1–33.

London, Justin. 2012. *Hearing In Time: Psychological Aspects of Musical Meter*. Oxford and New York: Oxford University Press.

Louati, Ali. 2012. *Musiques de Tunisie*. Tunis: Simpact.

Lumbroso, Abraham. 1860. *Lettres médico-statistiques sur la Régence de Tunis*. Marseille: Typographie Roux.

M'Halla, Moncef. 1996. "Le confrérisme, religion diffuse: Les zaouias en Tunisie au XIXe siècle." *Cahiers des arts et traditions populaires* 11: 119–160.

Mahdi, Salah el-. N.d.a. *al-Mūsīqā al-Ṣūfiyya fī Tūnis* [*Sufi Music in Tunisia*]. Tunis.

———. N.d.b. *Patrimoine musical tunisien 8: Étude comparative des modes tunisiens/al-Maqāmāt al-Tūnisiyya al-Muqārana*. Tunis: Ministry of Cultural Affairs.

Makris, G. P. 1996. "Slavery, Possession, and History: The Construction of Self among Slave Descendants in the Sudan." *Journal of African History* 66 (2): 159–182.

———. 2000. *Changing Masters: Spirit Possession and Identity Construction among Slave Descendants and Other Subordinates in the Sudan*. Evanston, IL: Northwestern University Press.

Marçais, William, and Abderrahman Guiga. 1925. *Textes arabes de Takroûna*. Paris: Ernest Leroux.

Marcus, Scott. 2012. *Music in Egypt: Experiencing Music, Expressing Culture*. Oxford and New York: Oxford University Press.

Margulis, Elizabeth. 2013. *On Repeat: How Music Plays the Mind*. New York: Oxford University Press.

Mayet, Valéry. 1886. *Voyage dans le sud de la Tunisie*. Montpellier: Boehm & Fils.

McGregor, Richard J. A. 1997. "A Sufi Legacy in Tunis: Prayer and the Shadhiliyya." *International Journal of Middle East Studies* 29 (2): 255–277.

Medded, Abdelwahab. 2000. Liner notes to *El-Hadhra de Fadhel Jaziri* (2 CDs). Philips/Universal.

Melliti, Imed. 1993. "La zawiya en tant que foyer de socialité: Le cas des Tijaniyya de Tunis." Ph.D. diss., Université Paris V, René Descartes.

Mernissi, Fatima. 1977. "Women, Saints, and Sanctuaries." *Signs* 3 (1): 101–112.

Middleton, Richard. 1983. "'Play It Again Sam': Some Notes on the Productivity of Repetition in Popular Music." *Popular Music* 3: 235–270.

Mittermaier, Amira. 2011. *Dreams That Matter: Egyptian Landscapes of the Imagination*. Berkeley and Los Angeles: University of California Press.

———. 2014. "Bread, Freedom, Social Justice: The Egyptian Uprising and Sufi Khidma." *Cultural Anthropology* 29 (1): 54–79.

Mizouri, Laroussi. 1996. "La Hadra en Tunisie." *IBLA* 59 (177): 33–42.

Montana, Ismael Musah. 2004. "Enslavable Infidels: Sūdān-Tūnis as a Classificatory Categorization for New Wave of Enslaved Africans in the Regency of Tunis." *The Maghreb Review* 29 (1–4): 78–98.

———. 2013. *The Abolition of Slavery in Ottoman Tunisia.* Gainesville: University Press of Florida.

Morsy, Soheir A. 1991. "Spirit Possession in Egyptian Ethnomedicine: Origins, Comparison, and Historical Specificity." In *Women's Medicine: The Zar-Bori Cult in Africa and Beyond,* edited by I. M. Lewis, Ahmed Al-Safi, and Sayyid Hurreiz, 189–208. Edinburgh: Edinburgh University Press.

Mustaysir, Mukhtār. 2014. *Nashāt al-Rashīdiyya: al-Mu'lan wal-Makhfī* [The Establishment of the Rashīdiyya: The Told and Untold]. Tunis: Jamī' al-Ḥaqūq Maḥfūẓa lil-Mu'llaf.

Nabti, Mehdi. 2010. *Les Aïssawa: Soufisme, musique et rituels de transe au Maroc.* Paris: L'Harmattan.

Nachtigal, Gustav. 1974 [1879]. *Sahara and Sudan.* Translated by Allen B. Fisher and Humphrey J. Fisher. London: C. Hurst.

Nasr, Seyyed Hossein, ed. 2015. *The Study Quran: A New Translation and Commentary.* New York: HarperOne.

Omri, Mohamed-Salah. 2013. "The Perils of Identity Politics in Tunisia." *Al-Jazeera,* January 27, 2013. http://www.aljazeera.com/indepth/opinion/2013/01/2013127142856170386.html.

Pâques, Viviana. 1964. *L'arbre cosmique dans la pensée populaire et dans la vie quotidienne du Nord-Ouest Africain.* Paris: Institut d'Ethnologie.

Perkins, Kenneth J. 2004. *A History of Modern Tunisia.* Cambridge: Cambridge University Press.

Racy, Ali Jihad. 1983. "The Waṣlah: A Compound-Form Principle in Egyptian Music." *Arab Studies Quarterly* 5 (4): 396–403.

Radhouane, Nébil. 1994. "Al Hadhra de Jaziri et Agrebi: Erotique de la transe." *Le Temps,* August 23, 1994, n.p.

Rae, Edward. 1877. *The Country of the Moors: A Journey from Tripoli in Barbary to the City of Kairwan.* London: John Murray.

Revault, Jacques. 1960. "Notes sur les instruments traditionnels de musique populaire dans le sud tunisien." In *Actes du sixième Congrès international des sciences anthropologiques et ethnologiques.* Paris.

Rice, Timothy. 2014. "Ethnomusicology in Times of Trouble." *Yearbook for Traditional Music* 46: 191–209.

Rizqī, al-Ṣādiq al-. 1989 [1968]. *al-Aghānī al-Tūnisiyya.* Reprint, 2nd ed. Tunis: Dār al-Tūnisiyya lil-Nashr.

Rouget, Gilbert. 1986. *Music and Trance: A Theory of the Relations between Music and Possession.* Translated by Brunhilde Biebuyck. Chicago: University of Chicago Press.

Russell, Andrew L. 2012. "Modularity: An Interdisciplinary History of an Ordering Concept." *Information and Culture* 47 (3): 257–287.

Saïdane, Ali. 2014. *La saga du mezoued en Tunisie*. Tunis: Sindbad.

Saidani, Maya. 2006. *La musique du constantinois: Contexte, nature, transmission et définition*. Alger: Casbah Éditions.

Sassi, Asma. 2014. "Histoire nationale ou histoire locale? Concerts liturgiques et confréries dans les fêtes familales en Tunisie." *Ethnographiques* 28. https://www.ethnographiques.org/2014/Sassi.

Schade-Poulsen, Marc. 1999. *Men and Popular Music in Algeria: The Social Significance of Raï*. Austin: University of Texas Press.

Schechner, Richard. 1985. *Between Theater and Anthropology*. Philadelphia: University of Pennsylvania Press.

Schmalfeldt, Janet. 2011. *In the Process of Becoming: Analytic and Philosophical Perspectives on Form in Early Nineteenth-Century Music*. Oxford and New York: Oxford University Press.

Sebag, Paul. 1991. *Histoire de Juifs de Tunisie: Des origines à nos jours*. Paris: L'Harmattan.

Seddik, Youssef. 2013. "Incendie du mausolée de Sidi Bou Saïd: 'Des Coran précieux sont partis en fumée.'" *France 24*, January 14. http://observers.france24.com/fr/20130114-incendie-mausolee-sidi-bou-said-corans-calligraphies-plus-proches-disciples-saint-tunisie. Accessed October 11, 2017.

Seroussi, Edwin. 2010. "Music." In *Encyclopedia of Jews in the Islamic World*, edited by Norman A. Stillman and Phillip I. Ackerman-Lieberman, 498–519. Leiden and Boston: Brill.

———. 2015. "Islands of Musical Memory: Performing *Selihot* according to the Codex *Siftei Renanot* in al-Andalus, Djerba, Tripoli, and Israel from the Eleventh to the Twenty-first Centuries." In *Musical Exodus: Al-Andalus and Its Jewish Diasporas*, edited by Ruth F. Davis, 181–198. Lanham, MD: Rowman & Littlefield.

———. 2016. "Music: Muslim-Jewish Sonic Encounters." In *The Routledge Handbook of Muslim-Jewish Relations*, edited by Josef Meri, 429–448. New York: Routledge.

Shannon, Jonathan. 2003. "Sultans of Spin: Syrian Sacred Music on the World Stage." *American Anthropologist* 105 (3): 266–277.

———. 2004. "The Aesthetics of Spiritual Practice and the Creation of Moral and Musical Subjectivities in Aleppo, Syria." *Ethnology* 43 (4): 381–391.

———. 2006. *Among the Jasmine Trees: Music and Modernity in Contemporary Syria*. Middletown, CT: Wesleyan University Press.

———. 2015. *Performing al-Andalus: Music and Nostalgia across the Mediterranean*. Bloomington: Indiana University Press.

Shaw, Rosalind. 2002. *Memories of the Slave Trade: Ritual and the Historical Imagination in Sierra Leone*. Chicago: University of Chicago Press.

Snoussi, Manoubi. 1962. "Initiation à la musique tunisienne: Folklore tunisienne

III—Le mizwid ou cornemuse tunisienne." Collection Manoubi Snoussi Archives Ennejma Ezzahra, Centre du musiques arabes et méditerranéennes, Sidi Bou Saïd, Tunisia.

Somer, Eli, and Meir Saadon. 2000. "Stambali: Dissociative Possession and Trance in a Tunisian Healing Dance." *Transcultural Psychiatry* 37 (4): 580–600.

Spadola, Emilio. 2015. "Rites of Reception: Mass-Mediated Trance and Public Order in Morocco." In *Trance Mediums and New Media: Spirit Possession in the Age of Technical Reproduction*, edited by Heike Behrend, Anja Dreschke, and Martin Zillinger, 137–155. New York: Fordham University Press.

Stapley, Kathryn. 2006. "Mizwid: An Urban Music with Rural Roots." *Journal of Ethnic and Migration Studies* 32 (2): 243–256.

Stokes, Martin. 1994. "Introduction." In *Ethnicity, Identity, and Music: The Musical Construction of Place*, edited by Martin Stokes, 1–27. Oxford: Berg.

Stoller, Paul. 1989. *Fusion of the Worlds: An Ethnography of Possession among the Songhay of Niger*. Chicago: University of Chicago Press.

———. 1995. *Embodying Colonial Memories: Spirit Possession, Power, and the Hauka in West Africa*. New York: Routledge.

———. 1997. *Sensuous Scholarship*. Philadelphia: University of Pennsylvania Press.

Stumme, Hans. 1894. *Chants des Bédouins de Tripoli et de la Tunisie*. Translated by Adrien Wagnon. Paris: Ernest Leroux.

Taieb, Jacques. 1992. "Les Juifs du Maghreb au XIXe siècle: Aperçus de démographie historique et répartition géographique." *Population* 47 (1): 85–103.

Taneja, Anand Vivek. 2018. *Jinnealogy: Time, Islam, and Ecological Thought in the Medieval Ruins of Delhi*. Stanford, CA: Stanford University Press.

Tessler, Mark. 1978. "The Identity of Religious Minorities in Non-Secular States: Jews in Tunisia and Morocco and Arabs in Israel." *Comparative Studies in Society and History* 20: 359–373.

Touati, Houari. 2010. *Islam and Travel in the Middle Ages*. Chicago: University of Chicago Press.

Tobi, Yosef, and Tsivia Tobi. 2014. *Judeo-Arabic Literature in Tunisia, 1850–1950*. Detroit, MI: Wayne State University Press.

Tremearne, Arthur John Newman. 1968 [1914]. *The Ban of the Bori: Demons and Demon-Dancing in West and North Africa*. London: Frank Cass.

Trimingham, J. Spencer. 1998. *The Sufi Orders in Islam*. New York: Oxford University Press.

Turino, Thomas. 1999. "Signs of Imagination, Identity, and Experience: A Peircian Semiotic Theory for Music." *Ethnomusicology* 43 (2): 221–255.

———. 2008. *Music as Social Life: The Politics of Participation*. Chicago: University of Chicago Press.

Turner, Tamara Dee. 2017. "Algerian Dīwān of Sīdī Bilāl: Music, Trance, and Affect in Popular Islam." Ph.D. diss., King's College London.

Turner, Victor. 2016 [1983]. "A Review of 'Ethnopoetics'." In *Symposium of the Whole: A Range of Discourse Toward an Ethnopoetics*, edited by Jerome Rothenberg and Diane Rothenberg, 337–342. Berkeley and Los Angeles: University of California Press.

Valensi, Lucette. 1977. *Fellahs tunisiens: L'économie rurale et la vie des campagnes aux 18e et 19e siècles*. Paris: Mouton.

Vassel, Eusèbe. 1904. *La littérature populaire des Israélites tunisiens*. Paris: E. Leroux.

Witulski, Christopher. 2018. *The Gnawa Lions: Authenticity and Opportunity in Moroccan Ritual Music*. Bloomington: University of Indiana Press.

Wolf, Anne. 2013. "An Islamist 'Renaissance'? Religion and Politics in Post-Revolutionary Tunisia." *Journal of North African Studies* 18 (4): 560–573.

Young, Elizabeth L. 2015. "Islam and Islamists in the 2014 Tunisian Elections." In *Rethinking Nation and Nationalism*, Project on Middle East Political Science Studies 14 (June 2): 52–55.

Yúdice, George. 2003. *The Expediency of Culture: Uses of Culture in the Global Era*. Durham, NC: Duke University Press.

Zarcone, Thierry. 1996. "La Qādiriyya." In *Les voies d'Allah: Les ordres mystiques dans l'islam des origines à aujourd'hui*, edited by Alexandre Popovic and Gilles Veinstein, 399–407. Paris: Fayard.

Zeghonda, Fethi. 1991. *Al-Ṭarīqa al-Sulāmiyya fī Tūnis: Ashʿārha wa-Alḥānha* [The Sulāmiyya Sufi Order in Tunis: Its Poetry and Music]. Carthage: Dār al-Ḥikma.

Zillinger, Martin. 2017. "Graduated Publics: Mediating Trance in the Age of Technical Reproduction." *Current Anthropology* 58 (15): 41–55.

Index

Page numbers in italics refer to figures, tables, or musical examples

Abassi, Asma, 173n1, 182
'Abīd, Hishām, 6n6
Abū Muḥammad, 44
Abu-Nasr, Jamil, 95
Abū Ya'za, 44
"'Addālā 'Addālā," *79*, 142, 145n16, *146*, 156, 157, 158, 169n31
'Afrit, Cheikh el-, 137, 140, 141
Agrebi, Samir, 175n5, 178, 180–81, 183, 196, 199
Ahmad, Shahab, 201–2, 203
Aḥmad Bey, 19
'ajmī
  language and aesthetic in ṣtambēlī, 132, 153n21, 204–5
  rhythm (*see under* rhythmic modes)
  sequence of nūbas in rebaybiyya, 153–56
'Akāsha, 64, *185*, *186*, 190n8
"'Alā Allah Dalālī," *186*
"'Alā Bāb Dārik," 141–42
"'Alā Umm al-Zīn," *79*
'Alāwiyya Sufi order
  concert staging of, *186*, 190
"Allah Allah Yā Bābā," *79*
"Allah Dā'im Ḥayy," 55
"Allah Yā Mulānā," *57*
Alvarez, Lourdes María, 47, 48n24
ambient Sufism
  as connecting and differentiating ritual niches, 13–14, 25, 58, 103–4, 117–18, 123, 188–89, 202–3, 205, 207, 211, 213, 217–18
  overview of, 2, 7–12
  scope of ritual authority within, 201–3
  See also ritual niches
Amri, Nelly, 5, 72, 76, 87n15
"Anā Bdayt Bismillah al-Ḥayy al-'Aẓīm," *57*
Andalusī music, 32, 46, 47, 48, 51, 142–43, 149, 199, 207. *See also* mālūf; shishtrī
Anderson, Benedict, 13
Andézian, Sossie, 30, 88
'Arbiyya. *See* Lilla 'Arbiyya
"'Ārī al-Mannūbiyya," 74, *79*, 82–87, *86*
'arīfa, 106, 111, 128, 129, 154
'Arūsiyya Sufi order, 2
"Ashwāq, al-," *185*
Attun, Maurice, 141n9
Austin, John L., 82
'Awāmriyya Sufi order, 48, 143, 180
'Aziz, 'Am, 167
'Azūziyya Sufi order
  concert staging of, *186*, 190, 193–94
"Aẓẓam Aẓẓam b-illah Lā Yanām," 54–55

"Bābā 'Abd Allah," 165
"Bābā Baḥrī," *79*, *128*, 160n26
"Bābā Jallūl," *79*, 165
Bard'a, Abraminu, 141
Bard'a, Rahmin, 141
Barnat, Rachid, 182
Barnawi, Baba Majid, 105, 108, 111, 116, 134, 156
Baṣrī, Ḥasan, 44

Bateson, Gregory, 45
Bauman, Richard, 182, 183
Becker, Judith, 123, 203n1
"Béji, el-." *See* "Ra'is al-Abḥār"
Bell, Catherine, 32
Bellamy, Carla, 18, 75
Ben Achour, Mohamed, 142
Ben Ali, Zine El Abidine, 3, 19
 ambiguities of religious policy of, 181
 and Sufism, 180
Ben 'Amor, Hishām, 31n6, 61n38
Ben Amor, Taoufiq, 138n4, 148n17, 150n18, 209n4
Benattar, S. C., 136
bendīr. *See under* musical instruments
Benjamin, Israel J., 136
Ben Romdhane, Mustapha, 141, 145, 150, 152, 157–59, 165, 168
Ben Youssef, Amira, 191, 199
Berrebi, Joseph, 158
Besmer, Fremont, 108
Bilāl. *See* Jerma
"Bisma al-Karīm Bdayna," *57*
Boddy, Janice, 108
Bohlman, Philip V., 8, 175, 199
Boissevain, Katia, 11, 19, 72, 73, 76, 83n11, 87n15, 90, 94n21, 99n24, 131
Bouchnak, Lotfi, 178
Bou Oukkez, Abdesalem, 165
Bou Oukkez, Khamous, 158
Bou Oukkez, Khatoui, 158, 165
Bourguiba, Habib, 20
 and Sufism, 177, 179, 180
Brandily, Monique, 161n27
brāwil
 rhythm (*see under* rhythmic modes)
 trance section of 'Īsāwiyya ceremony, 53, 190
Briggs, Charles, 182, 183
Brown, Kenneth, 179
Brown, L. Carl, 19, 179
Bsiri, Gaston, 141n9
Būdhīnā, Muḥammad, 52, 83n11, 152
Bū Sa'diyya
 itinerant masked dancer, 161
 legendary figure of, 129–30, 131, 155
 nūba for, *128*, 129, 130, *146*, 155
 rhythm (*see under* rhythmic modes)

Carpenter-Latiri, Dora, 137, 142n12
Carthage Festival, 173
Catzaras, Marianne, 199
Centre des Musiques Arabes et Méditerranéennes, 145
Chamkhi, Sonia, 141, 157n23
Chelbi, Mustapha, 49n27, 141, 160n26, 177, 199
Chlyeh, Abdelhafid, 126n13
Chouraqui, Andre, 135n1
Ciantar, Philip, 149
Clapperton, Hugh, 161
Cohen, David, 154n22
Colla, Elliot, 4n3
Comaroff, Jean, 125
Comaroff, John, 125
Conord, Sylvaine, 159
constancy of sound, 17, 40, 78–80, 86, 118, 119, 144, 156, 191
 as hospitality, 87, 117
 and ritual efficacy, 178, 203–5, 208
Cowper, Henry, 161
Csikszentmihalyi, Mihaly, 86–87
cyclicity, 17, 80, 93
 vs. repetition, 38n17, 56
 and transformation, 17, 119

Dakākī (a spirit), 114
dance, 117n5, 123, 161, 162, 206, 210
 'Īsāwiyya, 6, 14, 29, 35, 53, 54–55, 56, 59, 62, 63, 66, 67
 Mannūbiyya, 85, 87, 89
 rebaybiyya, 139, 170
 in stagings of ritual, 174, 192, 193
 sṭambēlī, 107, *109*, 111, 114, 117, 128–29, 131
 Sulāmiyya, 177
 See also trance
Dār Bārnū, 108, 111
Darwish, 'Ali, 60n37
Davila, Carl, 14
Davis, Ruth, 5, 15, 47, 49n27, 53n32, 76n7, 137, 141n11
Dendri (musical group), 132n14
Denham, Dixon, 161
d'Erlanger, Rodolphe, 5, 49n27
Dermenghem, Émile, 9, 28n3, 30, 161n27
dhikr
 'Īsāwiyya, 35, 40–42, *42*, 56, 207, 216
 in relation to the Mannūbiyya silsila, 99–102, 102–4
 Shādhuliyya, 88, 89–90, 97, 99–102, *100*, *101*
 and temporal transformation, 41, 42, 51, 89, 99–100, 206, 207
 Tījāniyya, 93

discrete intensification (DI). *See under* intensification
Doniya, Hedi, 7, 24, 128, 130, 131, 136n3, 145, 151, 159, 161n27, 166–71, 178, 188
Dounia record label, 158
During, Jean, 123

Échard, Nicole, 108
Eickelman, Dale, 218n8
Emoff, Ron, 108
Engelhardt, Jeffers, 11n9
Engelke, Matthew, 11n9
Ennahda (al-Nahḍa) Party, 5, 180
Ernst, Carl, 8
Errington, Shelly, 13
Essebsi, Beji Caid, 5, 174, 198
Esseghir, Khailou, 141, 158
Esseghir, Youssef, 141, 145, 158
Essid, Habib, 173
Eyries, J. B., 161

"Fāres Baghdād," *187*, 194, 195
Farzit, Salah, 160
fātiḥa, 36–40, *39*, 63, 77
Ferchiou, Sophie, 85, 102, 179
festivals
  Carthage Festival, 171, 173
  Fes Festival of Sacred Music, 184
  of Sufi music, state-sponsored, 20, 24, 179–80, 215
Feuchtwang, Stephan, 108
Friedson, Steven, 123
Frishkopf, Michael, 4n2, 8, 35n13, 68, 178

Gana, Nouri, 161
Garfi, Mohamed, 162
Gaṭṭal al-Ṣīd. *See* Ben Romdhane, Mustapha
Geoffroy, Éric, 34n9, 88
Ghannouchi, Rachid, 5
Gharsa, Zied, 169
ghayṭa
  musical instrument (*see under* musical instruments)
  rhythm (*see under* rhythmic modes)
Ghazālī, Abū Ḥāmid al-, 44
Gidal, Marc, 13, 71
Glasser, Jonathan, 47, 140, 181
global intensification (GI). *See under* intensification
gnāwa, 126, 138
Gobin, Emma, 29

Goodman, Jane, 182
Gouja, Zouheir, 130
Guettat, Mahmoud, 49, 53n32, 76n7, 149, 150n19
Guiga, Abderrahman, 162
Guss, David, 199

Habbouba, Hedi, 152, 160, 164–65
Habib, Messaoud, 141
Haddad, Hafez, 130
"Hadhīlī," 167
Hadhiri, Haythem, 200n12
Hadhra, el-, 7, 10, 24, 152, 168, 171, 173–200
  and contextual gap with ritual, 175, 182–83, 190, 195–97, 200, 214
  controversy over 2010 version of, 184, 196–97
  as implicit critique of Sufism, 199–200, 215
  rock and jazz components of, 174, 195, 196, 197
  See also ritual: staging of
ḥaḍra
  as ritual musical form, 7, 13, 14, 24, 27, 29, 189–90, 207, 211–12
  self-referential lyrics of, 44–45, 54, 59, 82, 193–95
  sense of trajectory of, 14, 189–90, 211–12
  as term for Sufi ceremony, 13–14n10, 176–77, 211n6
  as third section of ʿĪsāwiyya ceremony, 28, 29, 32, 53–68
Hagene, Matthieu, 106
Hamami, Lotfi el-, *109*
Hammas, Chedly, 158
Hamrouni, Ahmed, 141n8
Handelman, Don, 197
Hassnaoui, Amira, 125, 126
Ḥaṭṭābiyya Sufi order, 78, *79*, 91, 99n22, 142
Hawkins, Simon, 181
"Hayyā Nzūrū Shaykhnā," *186*, 193–94
Hibou, Béatrice, 181
ḥizb
  ʿĪsāwiyya, 27–28, 32, 33–46, *41*, 43, 51, 190, 205
  Shādhuliyya, 33, 88, 98, 99
  Sulāmiyya, 189
Hobart, Angela, 16, 32
Hopkins, Nicholas, 162n29
Hornbostel, E. M. von, 141n10
Hosni, Sallouha, 69, *70*
Hosni, Zahra, 107

"Ibn Miryām," *186*, 192
Ibn Musa, Rabbi, 135–36
Ihde, Don, 38n18
Institut Supérieur de Musique, 130, 165
intensification, 6, 12, 16–17, *62*, 116, 189, 205–9, 212, 213
  discrete, 16, 38–41, *43*, 45–46, 53, 55, 56, 57, *58*, 60, 61, *62*, 81, 87, 89–90, 99, 100, 118, *120*, 147, 170, 206, 208, 210, 212
  global, 16–17, 61, *62*, 206, 207–8, 212
  and ritual vs. non-ritual musics, 208–9
  scale vs. method of, 208
  sequential, 16, 51–53, *52*, 60, *61*, *62*, 81, 100, 118, 145, *147*, 206–7, 208, 212
"Inzād al-Nabī," *79*, 82, *187*
"Irfa' Ra'sik," *79*, 157
'Īsāwiyya Sufi order, 5, 6, 14, 18, 20n12, 22, 24, 27–68, 78, *79*, 90, 93, 100, 118, 119, 130, 143, 148, 149, 162, 177, 180, 188, 206, 207
  of Banī Khiyyār, 31n6, 188
  concert staging of, 184, *185*, *186*, *187*, 190, 194
  ḥaḍra of, 27–68, 177, 190, 204, 206, 211
  of Morocco, 31n6
  state suppression of, 177, 179
Islamic Salvation Front (Algeria), 180
Islamists, 21–22, 107
  attacks on shrines by, 3–5, 19, 21, 67, 69–70, 174, 198

"Jadd al-Ḥassanayn," *187*
Jaied, Zouheir, 99n22, 142
Jaziri, Fadhel, 175n5, 178, 180, 183, 191, 196, 199
Jazūlī, Muḥammad al-. *See* Sīdī Ḥmīd Jazūlī
Jbali, Dido, 141
Jbali, Muni, 141
Jerma, 112–13
  nūba for, *109*, 112, 119–22, 127, 210
Jewish Tunisians, 18, 22, 24, 135
  convergences with Muslim Tunisians, 140, 149
  in Djerba, 137, 142
  geohistorical connection to Libya, 149–50, 168
  immigration to France, 157–58, 168
  prominent role in Tunisian music, 137, 140, 149, 166
  See also rebaybiyya
"Jītak Shākī." *See* "Mā Sabā 'Aqlī"
Johnson, James Weldon, 161
Johnson, Pamela, 44, 45, 94n21, 131, 177
Jones, Lura JaFran, 20, 30n5, 31n6, 48, 49n27, 143, 177, 179, 180
Journo, Raoul, 140
Junayd, 44

Kahlaoui, Lalou, 158
Kahlawi, Muhammad, 183, 191, 196, 199
Kapchan, Deborah, 126 n13, 138, 175, 202
Kapferer, Bruce, 16, 32, 51, 123
Karaoui, Youssef el-, 159
"Kās Ydūr, al-," 56–59
"Khammar Yā Khammār," *186*, 190
Kirshemblatt-Gimblett, Barbara, 125, 199
Kramer, Fritz, 108
Kūrī (a spirit), 114

Laabidi, Houcine, 21
Laade, Wolfgang, 160n26
Lachmann, Robert, 137
Lajmi, Sami, 138
Lallemand, Charles, 161
Lambek, Michael, 103
Lapie, Paul, 161
Larguèche, Abdelhamid, 18, 142
Lauzière, Henri, 22
"Lawlā al-Luṭf," *187*, 195, 196
"Layl al-Zāhī, al-," *185*, 193, 196
Lékhdiri, Hichem, 138, 160n26, 165
Lellouche, Jacob, 22, 138, 158
Lévy, Lionel, 135, 138n4
Lewisohn, Leonard, 65
Lilla 'Arbiyya, 131, 211
  nūba for, *128*, 130, *146*, 153, 170, 207
Lilla Ghrība, 137, 142
Lilla Malīka, 115
Lilla Shrifa, 94
London, Justin, 122n8
Louati, Ali, 49, 53n32, 140, 141, 149, 209n4
Loussif, Samir, 163
Lumbroso, Abraham, 136, 138, 139, 154n22
Lwelbani, Fatima, 22, 24, 69–70, *70*, 138, 216–17
lyrics
  and historical memory, 43–46
  as indexing ritual adjacency, 155–56
  intertextuality of, 81–82, 193–95
  power of in local dialect, 163
  and reflexivity, 57–59, 82, 193–95
  romantic themes in, 148–49
  themes of in ambient Sufism, 11, 82, 83, 148, 164, 193

traces of sub-Saharan African languages in, 108, 112, 124
and trance, 66

Mahdi, Salah el-, 138
Mahmoud Bey, 76
Makris, G. P., 108, 112n2, 138n4
"Māk Sulṭān," *79*
Ma'llem Sofū (a spirit), 115
mālūf, 5, 21, 30, 46–47, 48, 52, 56, 100, 142, 149, 150n18, 169, 209
Libyan, 147, 149, 150, 210
Mannūbiyya Sufi order, 6, 13, 14, 22, 24, 69–104, 105, 118, 119, 202, 217
concert staging of, *186*
and motherhood, 82, 210
and rebaybiyya, 144, 152, 156–57, 210
and shame, 74, 83, 87
silsila of, 71, 76–92, *79*, 90–92, 97, 111, 115, 151, 207, 210, 211
soundworld of, 78–80, 89, 91, 97
See also Sayyda Mannūbiyya
Marçais, William, 162
Marcus, Scott, 14, 207n3
Margulis, Elizabeth, 85
Marzouki, Moncef, 5
"Mā Sabā 'Aqlī," 145n16, *146*, 147–50, *151*, 158, 168–69, 210
Mayet, Valéry, 161
McGregor, Richard, 99, 174n4
Mdallal, Chedli, 165
Medded, Abdelwahab, 196
Melliti, Imed, 94, 95
melodic modes
aṣba'īn, 56, *57*, *79*, 150
dhīl, *79*
ḥsīn, 50n28, 56, *57*, *79*, *146*, 150
ḥsīn ṣabā, 56, *57*, *79*
'irāq, 50
mazmūm, 54n33, *80*
mḥayr 'irāq, *79*, 143, *146*
mḥayr sīka, *79*, 81
nwā, *79*, *80*, *146*
rahāwī, 49
raṣd dhīl, 54n33
sīka, *79*, *146*
"Men Ghā'ib Sirr Allah," 55
Mennai, Walid, 22, 24, 27–28, 33, 34, 35, 37, 42–43, 47, 64, 65–66, 67, 68, 107, 143, 149
Mernissi, Fatima, 75
Meski, Hatem, 64
Meski, Marouene, 34, 60, 66
Mevlevi Sufi order, 192
M'halla, Moncef, 142, 179
Middleton, Richard, 86
Migzū (a spirit), 114
Mihoub, Belhassen, 24, 105, *109*, 111, 125, 126, 127, 131, 132n14, 134, 214
Mimoun, Maurice, 158
Mittermaier, Amira, 75, 202
Mizouri, Laroussi, 20n12
Mizrahi, 'Achir, 141n9
mizwid
musical genre, 7, 11, 24, 93n19, 101, 130, 131, 144, 151, 159, 160–61, 202, 208, 209; association with prison and drinking, 160; concert staging of, *186*, 188; and rap, 161; social stigma, 160–61
musical instrument (*see under* musical instruments)
Morsy, Soheir, 138
Msika, Didou, 141, 158
Msika, Habiba, 137, 140, 141
Montana, Ismael Musah, 18, 19
Mulay Brahīm (a spirit), 131
nūba for, 127, *128*, 130
musical form, 12, 13–16, 17, 29, 32, 32n7, 213
as cumulative ritual forms, 15, 25, 144, 209–12
nawba, 15, 49
waṣla, 14–15
See also ḥaḍra; set-list modularity; silsila
musical instruments
bagpipes (*see* mizwid; shakwa; zukra, Libyan)
bass, electric, 174, 183, 195
bendīr, 59–60, 80, 96, 130, 136, 138, 139, 143, 154, 159, 163, 164, 166, 193, 204; indexical associations with trance, 60, 93, 144, 195
clarinet, 31n6
darbūka, 78, 80, 96, 130, 136, 138, 139, 154, 163, 164, 166
drum set, 174, 195
gambara, 132n14
ghayṭa, 136, 159, 161n27
gnaybra, 156
gugāy, 129
guitar, electric, 174, 183, 195, 196
gumbrī, 13, 108, 114, 116–17, 126, 130, 132, 144, 156, 203, 204, 205
halil, 136
harmonium, 141

musical instruments (*continued*)
kamanja, 136, 138, 141
keyboards, electronic, 174, 183, 195
kinnor, 136
mandolin, 163
mizwid, 5, 7, 13, 130, 136, 141, 143, 144, 146, 149, 150, 153, 154, 159, 161–63, 164, 165, 166, 168, 204, 205; association with Jewish Tunisians, 165–66; association with spirits, 162; connections to Libya and sub-Saharan Africa, 161–62; as transgressing boundaries, 162–63
naqqārāt, 48, 50, 59
nāy, 195
nevel, 136
oboe, 183
qānūn, 141
rabābā, 138n4
rebāb, 7, 48, 136, 137–38, 139, 143
saxophone, 183, 195
shakwa, 161n28
shqāshiq, 108, 117, 119, 126, 129, 130, 132n14, 144, 153, 154, 156, 159, 203, 204
ṭabla, 129, 204
ṭabla tījāniyya, 92, 94, 204
ṭār, 48, 50, 59, 92, 96, 136, 139, 141, 159
tof, 136
ʿūd, 136, 139
violin, 136, 141, 183, 195
zukra, 31, 136, 159, 161n27, 162, 168; Libyan, 161n27
musical potencies, 12–13, 17, 97, 104, 115, 213, 218. *See also* intensification; musical form; timbre
Mustaysir, Mukhtār, 88, 141n11
Mzaoudi, Khlifa, 159

Nabti, Mehdi, 31n6
Nachtigal, Gustav, 161
"Nādīt Rahum Jūnī," *79*
"Nādūlī Nādūlī," *79*
"Naghghāra Yā Sayyda," 74, *79*
"Nibtadā Bismillah ʿAlim fī Kul Makān," 62
"Nimdaḥ al-Agṭāb," 165
nūba (praise song), 14, 76–77
vs. ghnāya, 159, 164, 165, 167
ʿĪsāwiyya, 60, 77, 207, 209
as large-scale art-music form (also nawba), 15, 49, 50, 76n7, 77
as marker of authenticity in mizwid, 166
See also individual names of songs, saints, and spirits

Omri, Mohamed-Salah, 19, 182
Oudney, Walter, 161
Ouergli, Salah el-, 24, 105, 106, *109*, 111, 125, 132n14, 134
Ouled Chnichen, Gagou, 158

Pâques, Viviana, 149
Perkins, Kenneth, 20, 158, 180
pilgrimage (ziyāra), 19n11, 27, 30n4, 78, 90, 91, 105, 134, 137, 142, 162n29, 176, 216–17
Piscatori, James, 218n8
Prophet Muḥammad, 27, 35, 51, 77, 82, 94, 95, 98, 143, 176, *185*, 193, 209
nūbas for, 77, *79*, 82, *109*, 111, 112, 119, 120, 127, 143, 147, 148, 209, 217 (*see also* "Ṣlāt al-Nabī")
protests, 3–6, 7, 8, 152, 174

Qādiriyya Sufi order, 18, 34, 44, 63, 78, *79*, 90, 188
of Banī Khiyyār, 188
concert staging of, *187*, 190, 194
"Qaṣdī Anẓur Ilīk," 49–51, *50*

Racy, Ali Jihad, 14
Radhouane, Nébil, 191
Rae, Edward, 161
"Ra'is al-Abḥār," 6–7, *79*, *146*, 151–53, 162, 167, 169–71, *186*, 188, 210
Rashidiyya Institute, 141n11
rbūkh parties, 160, 163–64
rebaybiyya, 7, 13, 14, 24, 71n4, 80n9, 101, 135–71, 202
absence from collective memory, 137
attempts to prohibit, 135–36
domestic vs. shrine contexts of, 137–38, 139
etymological ambiguity of, 137–38
in France, 157–59
in Israel, 156
and Jewish emigration from Libya, 147–50, 210
Jewish-Muslim convergences in, 136, 140–43, 148–9, 151–52, 156–57, 158, 171
and the Mannūbiyya, 152, 156–57
mixing of genders in, 136
as Muslim women's practice also, 137, 138
remnants of in the mizwid genre, 165–66, 171, 214
silsila of, 145–59, 169, 207, 211
soundworld of, 143–44, 153–5
and sṭambēlī, 152, 153–56

recitation. *See* dhikr; ḥizb
repetition, 38–40, 85–86, 99, 101. *See also* cyclicity
Revault, Jacques, 162
Revolution of 2011, Tunisian, 3, 4, 5, 8, 12, 19, 22, 67, 69n3, 70, 105, 106, 107, 161, 173, 216
rhythmic elasticity, 118–24, 155, 206
rhythmic modes
  ʿajmī, 145, *146*, *147*, 154
  brāwil, 51, *52*, 206, 209
  bṭāyḥī, 50, 51, 52, 206, 209
  bṭāyḥī ʿīsāwī, 60, *61*, 63, 190, 207
  bū ḥilla, *146*
  bū nawwāra, *146*
  bū saʿdiyya, *110*, 118n6, 124n11
  dkhūl brāwil, 51, 52, 60, *61*, 63, 190, 206, 207
  fazzānī, *79*, *80*, 81, 89, 130, 167, 207; as implicit in Shādhuliyya dhikr, 101, 206
  fazzānī lībī, *79*
  ghayṭa, 168
  ḥilla, *146*
  hrūbī, 60, *61*, 63, 190, 207
  khammārī, 190n8
  khatm, 51, 52, *79*, *80*, 81, 86, 206, 207, 209; as implicit in Shādhuliyya dhikr, 100
  mdawr gharbī, 100
  mdawr ḥawzī, *79*
  mjarred, 53, 55–59, 118, 130, 190, 206
  mrabbaʿ, *79*
  mṣaddar, 150
  muthallith, *109*, *110*, 118, 124n11
  saʿdāwī, *109*, *110*, 118n6, 124n11, 145, *146*, *147*
  ṣteftūḥ, 145, *146*, *147*, 150, *151*, 169, 207
  sūdānī, *109*, *110*, 117, 118, 119, 120, 121, 122, 124n11, 207
  sūga, *79*
  zindālī, 160n26
Rice, Timothy, 3
ritual
  and chains of value, 198–200
  decline of, 24, 124, 134, 171
  as highlighting the power of music, 17
  and historical memory, 43–45, 108, 124
  hospitality, 24, 71, 87, 111, 115, 117, 129, 211
  as journey, 28–29, 42, 71, 78, 91, 208, 217–18
  and pleasure, 2, 12, 139, 199, 200
  reflexivity, 24, 31–32, 45–46, 54–55, 67, 68
  and social intimacy, 132–34
  vs. spectacle, 197–98
  staging of, 24, 125–26, 127–32, 133, 134, 173–200, 214–15
  traces in popular music, 141–42, 165, 166–71
ritual communities. *See* ritual niches
ritual niches, 2, 7, 14, 25, 103, 115, 116, 118, 123, 171, 188, 191, 202, 203, 205, 207, 211, 213, 217–18. *See also individual names of genres and Sufi orders*
Rizqī, Ṣādiq al-, 138, 152, 163, 179
Rjāl Ṣabrā, 216
Rouget, Gilbert, 65, 102, 123, 218
Russell, Andrew, 191

Saadon, Meir, 156
Ṣāghī, Khāled, 93
Saïdane, Ali, 149, 162, 164
Saidani, Maya, 48, 160n26
saints, 8–11, 17–18, 77–78, 148, 176
  intrinsic vs. adjacent, 115
  in relation to spirits, 5, 7, 10, 64, 72, 77, 85, 96, 113, 115–16, 153
  See also specific names of saints
Salafism, 21–22. *See also* Islamists
"Ṣalū Yā Khwānī," *57*
"Ṣānaʿ, al-," *187*
Sayyda Mannūbiyya, 1, 6–7, 18, 19, 69, 70, 72–76, 92, 94, 97, 132, 170, 203, 205, 211, 216
  legend of, 74
  nūbas for, 77, *79*, 82–87, 145n16, *146*, 156, 157, 158, 167, 169, 210, 217 (*see also* "ʿĀrī al-Mannūbiyya"; "Naghghāra Yā Sayyda")
  and the Shādhuliyya, 73, 87–88, 98, 103, 202
  and shame, 74, 78, 87, 210
  shrine of, 70, 72, 75, 92, 95, 98–99, 103, 105, 138, 174
  and Sīdī ʿAbd al-Qādir, 90
  and the Tījāniyya, 92, 93, 94
Schade-Poulsen, Marc, 163
Schechner, Richard, 198
Schmalfeldt, Janet, 32–33n7
Schultz, Dorothea, 198n11
Schuyler, Philip, 138n4
Sebag, Paul, 135n1
sequential intensification (SI). *See under* intensification
Seroussi, Edwin, 136, 137, 140
set-list modularity, 15–16, 175, 181, 188, 190–92, 215
Sghira, Badiʿa al-, 141n9

Shabbi, Abul Qassim al-, 4
Shādhuliyya Sufi order, 1, 19, 29, 33–35, 44, 62, 71, 73, *80*, 87, 88, 90, 97, 174, 195, 198, 206, 212
  and ambiguities of authority surrounding, 202–3
  and coffee, 88n16
  concert staging of, *185*, 190
  rituals at the shrine of Sayyda Mannūbiyya, 98–104
  rituals at the shrine of Sīdī Meḥrez, 142n14
Shannon, Jonathan, 17, 32, 34–35n12, 38n19, 47, 137, 175, 199, 207n3
Shaw, Rosalind, 108
"Shaykh al-Kāmal, al-," *128*, 130, *187*, 190, 194, 195
shishtrī, 27, 32, 46–53, 190, 206
shrines, 8, 17–20
  Islamist attacks on, 3–5, 19, 21, 67, 69–70, 174, 198
  as sites of healing, 71, 85, 89–90, 176
  as sites of Jewish-Muslim convergence, 142–43, 149
  as symbols of community, 4, 91
  and women, 9n8, 75, 103, 138, 192n9 (*see also* Mannūbiyya Sufi order)
  See also individual names of saints
Shushtarī, 'Abū al-Ḥasan al-, 27, 47–48
Sīdī 'Abd al-Qādir, 18, 194, 216
  nūbas for, 77, *79*, 81, 90, *109*, 111, 127, 128, 165, 166, 167, 169, 217
Sīdī 'Abd al-Salām, 48, 64, 176, *185*, 216
  nūba for, *79*, *109*, 111, 166
Sīdī 'Abīd, 216
Sīdī Aḥmad al-Tījānī, 78, 84, 92, 94, 95, 96, 97, 115, 204
  nūba for, *79*, 92, 96, 97, 204, 211
Sīdī 'Alī 'Azūz, 167
Sīdī 'Alī Ḥaṭṭāb, 19, 84, 91, 170, 216
  nūba for, 77, *79*, 91, *146*, 156, 157, 167, 217
  shrine of, 27, 62, 70, 90, 91, 99n22, 157n23, 216
Sīdī 'Āmār, 48
  nūba for, *109*
Sīdī 'Amor, 216
  shrine of, 69
Sīdī 'Amr
  nūba for, *109*, *128*
Sīdī 'Amr Bū Khatwa
  nūba for, *79*, *109*, 111, 128, *146* (*see also* "'Addālā 'Addālā")
Sīdī Bashīr, 18, 88, 216
Sīdī Belḥassen al-Shādhulī, 1, 19, 33, 34, 73, 87, 94, 97, 98, 202, 216
  nūbas for, 77, *80*, 88–90, 91, 98, 103, 115, 211, 217 (*see also* "Yā Belḥassen")
  shrine of, 62, 73, 92, 100, 102, 167, 174
Sīdī Ben 'Arūs, 1, 9n7, 78
Sīdī Ben 'Īsā, 6, 18, 30, 34, 45, 54–55, 63, 64, 130, 132, *185*, 216
  legend of, 65
  nūba for, 77, *79*, 90, 217
Sīdī Brahīm
  nūba for, 165
Sīdī Bū 'Alī, 114, 216, 217
Sīdī Bū Bālba, 170
Sīdī Bū Jlīda, 170
Sīdī Bū Ra's al-'Ajmī
  nūba for, *109*, *128*
Sīdī Bū Sa'īd, 1, 5–7, 18, *80*, 91n18, 115, 151, 162, 170, 216
  nūbas for, 6, 77, *79*, 81, *146*, 162, 165, 167, 169–71, 207, 210, 211, 217 (*see also* "Ra'is al-Abḥār")
  shrine of, 3, 5, 8, 30n4, 49n27, 70, 80n9, 138, 152
  town of, 3, 5, 8
Sīdī Bū Yaḥya
  nuba for, *146*, 162, 169
Sīdī Bū Zīd (Sidi Bouzid), 8
Sīdī Frej, 18, 111
  nūba for, *109*, 127
  shrine of, 105, 111, 134
Sīdī Frej Shawwāṭ, 142
Sīdī Ḥammūda
  nūba for, 128
Sīdī al-Ḥārī, 30n4
Sīdī Ḥmīd Jazūlī, 34, 44
Sīdī Ibrāhīm al-Riyāḥī, 95, 96
Sīdī Manṣūr, 216
  nūba for, *79*, 81, *109*, 111, *128*, 160n26, 210 (*see also* "Bābā Baḥrī")
Sīdī Marzūg
  nūba for, *109*, 127, *128*
Sīdī Meḥrez, 2, 18, 142, *185*, 216
  nūba for, 77, *79*, 142, 169n31, *185*, 217 (*see also* "'Addālā 'Addālā")
Sīdī Qashshāsh, 48
Sīdī Sa'd, 18, 111
  nūba for, *109*, 127, *128*
  shrine of, 111
Sīdī Ṣaḥbī, 216
Sīdī Ṣālaḥ Bū Gabrīn, 162, 165
Sīdī Ṣālaḥ Bū Ḥijba, 120n7
  nūba for, *109*, 119, 120, 127

silsila, 7, 13–14, 24, 71, 143, 203, 209–21
vs. chronological spiritual genealogy, 44n23, 209
hospitality of, 76, 87, 104, 117, 118, 129, 210, 211
importance of first pieces of, 82, 112, 143, 147–48, 149–50, 166, 210–11
sociospiritual inclusivity of, 78, 90–91, 97, 103, 155, 156, 209–10, 211
See also under Mannūbiyya Sufi order; rebaybiyya; sṭambēlī
singing
a cappella, 53, 55, 189, 190, 207
ʿajmi style of delivery, 204–5
antiphony, 54, 117, 132, 170, 195, 205
and constancy of sound, 144, 205
dhikr patterns in songs, 56, 89–90
gijmī style of delivery, 163
primacy of on stage, 132
at protests, 6
vs. recitation, 49–50, 101
responsorial and dhikr style of the ʿĪsāwiyya, 56
round style of Ḥaṭṭābiyya, 78
tempo in relation to texture of, 36, 37
Slama, Bice, 141
"Ṣlat al-Nabī," *109*, 120, 127, *128*
Snoussi, Manoubi, 5, 162
Somer, Eli, 156
Soudani, Noureddine, *109*, *127*
Spadola, Emilio, 193
spirit possession
diminishing familiarity with, 107
and the ʿĪsāwiyya, 64
and the Mannūbiyya, 72, 77, 85, 90–91, 96, 98, 102, 103
mizwid instrument's association with, 162
and rebaybiyya, 136, 149, 153, 162, 170
as sociopolitical encounter, 108
and sṭambēlī, 105, 107, 112, 114–15
and the Tījāniyya, 96
spirits, 108, 113–16, 169, 176
baḥriyya, 6, *79*, *80*, 81, 152, 162, 169–70, 171, 210; in sṭambēlī (Baḥriyya), *110*, 113–14, 118, 127, 210
Banū Kūrī, *110*, 113
Bēyāt, *110*, 113, 114, 115
ruḥāniyyāt, 96, 114–15
See also saints: in relation to spirits; spirit possession; *and individual names of spirits*
sṭambēlī, 7, 13, 14, 19n11, 24, 64, 77, 91, 105–34, 202, 204, 206, 207, 210
and Jewish Tunisians, 136
as managing the familiar and alter, 127–32
perceived decline of, 105–6
and rebaybiyya, 144, 152, 153–56
ritual vs. stage performance of, 107, 125–34, 214
silsila of, 108–11, 114–15, 117, 124, 127, 131, 203, 211
soundworld of, 108, 116–17, 118
and sub-Saharan Africanness, 106, 108, 116, 124
Stapley, Kathryn, 149, 160, 163
ṣteftūḥ
as first piece in rebaybiyya silsila (*see* "Mā Sabā ʿAqlī")
rhythm (*see under* rhythmic modes)
Stokes, Martin, 13
Stoller, Paul, 108, 112, 124
Stumme, Hans, 160n26
Sufi orders
antipathy toward, 179–80, 181–82
discord between, 78, 184, 188, 191
as esoteric and exoteric, 176
role in society, 18–20, 47, 71, 76, 85, 87–88, 179, 180
See also individual names of Sufi orders
Sufism, 8–10
vs. Islamism narrative, 173–74, 181, 182
See also ambient Sufism; Sufi orders
Sulāmiyya, Sufi order, 34, 44, 64, *79*, 143, 162, 180, 181, 184
of Banī Khiyyār, 188
concert staging of, 184, *185*, *186*, *187*, 190, 192, 193
ḥaḍra of, 176–77, 189, 211
state support of, 177, 179
transformation into professional sacred music troupe, 167, 177, 188, 215

Taieb, Jacques, 149
takhmīr, 27, 28, 29, 62–67
and lyrics, 66
Taneja, Anand Vivek, 202
ṭarīqa. *See* Sufi orders
Tarnane, Khmaïs, 49n27, 60n37
Ṭaybiyya Sufi order, 34, 188
concert staging of, *185*
Tebai, Hamza, 69n2, 141n7, 150n20
Tessler, Mark, 158
texture, musical, 195–97, 203–5, 207–8. *See also* intensification: global; timbre
Tījānī, Aḥmad al-. *See* Sīdī Aḥmad al-Tījānī

Tījāniyya Sufi order, 78, *79*, 92, 95, 102, 206, 211
men's, 71, 92, 93, 97
women's, 71, 77, 91, 92–97, 114–15, 204
timbre, 12, 13, 17, 60, 61, 80, 93, 94, 116, 131, 132n14, 195, 203–5, 213
and ritual efficacy, 92, 96, 178, 203–5
as signifying difference, 13, 80, 93, 94, 108, 118, 144, 147, 155, 156, 191, 203–5, 217
Tobi, Tsivia, 141, 142n13
Tobi, Yosef, 141, 142n13
Touati, Houari, 218n8
Tounsia, Louisa, 140, 141
Trabelsi, Leila, 19
Traeger, Paul, 141n10
trance, 62–67, 73, 78, 98, 102, 103, 124, 162, 191, 204
and bendīr, 60
and constancy of sound, 80, 85, 86–87, 117, 205
and metric ambiguities, 123–4
and nested temporalities, 85–87
social and cultural work of, 203, 217–18
and staging of Sufism, 192–93
swinging of hair as indexing, 174, 192
as test of limits of the self, 65–66
of women at men's rituals, 9n8, 98, 102, 103, 192n9, 202
See also spirit possession; takhmīr
translocality, 30–31
Tremearne, A. J. N., 115
Trimingham, J. Spencer, 34n10
Tunsiyya, Ratiba al-, 141n9
Turino, Thomas, 102n26, 200
Turner, Tamara, 11–12
Turner, Victor, 31–32

Umm al-Zīn, 18, 162, 170, 216
nūba for, 77, *79*, 141, *146*, 156, 157, 167
Ummī Yenna (a spirit), 91n18, 115
nūba for, 77, *79*, 81, 114n3, 115

Valensi, Lucette 149
Vanhoenacker, Maxime, 29
Vassel, Eusèbe, 136, 154n22
vocals. *See* lyrics; singing

Wafi, Ahmad al-, 49n27
"Wāfiyat al-Khaṣlāt," *146*
Wahhabism, 21
wajd. *See* takhmīr
walī. *See* saints
"Wallah Salām 'Alaykum," *128*, 130
waṣla. *See under* musical form
wird al-qudūm, 53, 54–55, *185*, 190
Witulski, Christopher, 106n1, 126n13
Wolf, Anne, 22

"Yā 'Arīfa," *146*, 154
"Yā 'Ashiqīn," 52
"Yā Bābā Tījānī," *79*
"Yā Belḥassen" ("Yā Shādhlī"), *80*, *186*, 196
"Yā Khūtī," *185*, 190
"Yā Laṭīf," *185*
"Yā Mimtī al-Ghāliyya," 163
Young, Elizabeth, 174n4
Yúdice, George, 125, 212

"Zambala," *128*
zār, 138
Zarcone, Thierry, 63
Zarga, Abdelmajid, 143n15
zāwiya. *See* shrines
Zaytouna Mosque, 21
Zaytouna University, 19
Zeghonda, Fethi, 177, 180, 181, 182, 189
Ziara (Sufi spectacle), 22, 184, 215
Zillinger, Martin, 176, 198n11
zindālī
rhythm (*see under* rhythmic modes)
subgenre of mizwid associated with prison, 160

www.ingramcontent.com/pod-product-compliance
Lightning Source LLC
Chambersburg PA
CBHW051353290426
44108CB00015B/1998
* 9 7 8 0 2 2 6 7 2 3 4 7 1 *